"The wild is a space that is not accounted for by the ideological trappings that regulate and organize societies by white supremacy. The wild does not give a pass to brutality because it doesn't fit into the tightly drawn script of non-negotiable offenses that organize too much of white Christianity. In the wild, murdering black people remains murder, patriarchy is a problem, and social justice is not an optional category after the core matters of personal salvation are addressed. With *Homeland Insecurity*, Professor Hodge offers an important reframing of the work of evangelism and missions, aimed at youth in a post-soul generation, to allow for an understanding of the presence of the body of Christ, church, in the wild."

Reggie L. Williams, associate professor of Christian ethics,
McCormick Theological Seminary

"Weaving biblical studies, pop culture antidotes, and historical narrative, Hodge seamlessly engages the social justice issues of our day, such as systematic racism. *Homeland Insecurity* is an imperative work that will prove to be an asset not only to college students as required reading but also to anyone wrestling with how to address missions in a relevant and practical manner."

Gabe Veas, associate professor of mentoring and community development,
Ashland Theological Seminary

"In the complex and challenging context of ministry in North America in the twenty-first century, we can escape to the same old, tired approaches that privilege the narrative and worldview of the dominant culture. But those approaches will only result in disappointment or worse, prostitution with the American empire and the desire to Make America Great Again. Dr. Daniel White Hodge is asking the right questions about twenty-first-century missiology and ecclesiology. These questions will not yield simple, easy answers. Instead, we are introduced to a complex missiology that provides a necessary engagement with and a needed corrective from an emerging culture."

Soong-Chan Rah, Milton B. Engebretson Professor of Church Growth and
Evangelism, North Park Theological Seminary, author of *The Next Evangelicalism*

"Daniel White Hodge is a dynamic voice who has found the intersection of black liberation, Hip Hop, and reconciliation theology. He bridges the profane and prophetic for purposes of holistic transformation. Once again, he delivers a powerful resource."

Efrem Smith, copastor, Bayside Church Midtown, author of *The Post-Black and Post-White Church*

D1567880

"Daniel White Hodge is the preeminent Hip Hop theologian of our generation. *Homeland Insecurity* only adds to his legacy as he speaks directly to contemporary missiology through the political lenses of rap, racism, and white privilege. He also critically addresses the complexities of reconciliation in a power structure, even in the church, where there has only ever been one racial winner and one racial loser. Hodge has lived a theological reality of the sacred, secular, and profane from inside and outside the academy and is able to construct this theology of mission with unmatched authority. *Homeland Insecurity* is a text I will be using in my courses for years to come."

Andrew Marin, research associate, Centre for the Study of Religion and Politics, University of St. Andrews

"This book has been desperately needed. While there have been questions raised about a Euro American–centric theology of mission for some time, Hodge gives a treatment with fresh eyes that aim to reconstrue missiology through the lens of Hip Hop in Trump's America. His call for a new theology of mission is clear, and it is imperative that Christians hear it."

Mary Veeneman, associate professor of biblical and theological studies, North Park University, author of *Introducing Methods of Theology*

"Hodge introduces us to the prophets and poets who have discovered God at the margins and invites us to take a seat and learn from them. This is not a manual for church renewal. This is an invitation to resurrection, to join the Spirit, to discover new life on the other side of death, and to find a firmer foundation, one that moths cannot eat and rust cannot destroy. The Hip Hop church is good news for us all."

JR. Forasteros, author of *Empathy for the Devil*, teaching pastor, Catalyst Community Church

"Christians have as their mission and vocation the saving of souls. But who or what will save Christians from themselves? In this deeply moving, personal, political, and richly sociological study, Daniel White Hodge proposes Hip Hop as a soteriology for US churches. Hodge offers an unflinching diagnosis of the idol worship of whiteness that has permeated mission efforts abroad and blinded US Christians to the kinds of suffering that now mark home as the last mission field, a wild country filled with those who have rejected the idolatry inside of the church."

Christopher M. Driscoll, author of *White Lies*

HOMELAND INSECURITY

DANIEL WHITE HODGE

A HIP HOP MISSIOLOGY
FOR THE POST-CIVIL RIGHTS CONTEXT

IVP Academic

An imprint of InterVarsity Press
Downers Grove, Illinois

InterVarsity Press
P.O. Box 1400, Downers Grove, IL 60515-1426
ivpress.com
email@ivpress.com

InterVarsity Press® is the book-publishing division of InterVarsity Christian Fellowship/USA®, a movement of
students and faculty active on campus at hundreds of universities, colleges, and schools of nursing in the United
States of America, and a member movement of the International Fellowship of Evangelical Students. For
information about local and regional activities, visit intervarsity.org.

All Scripture quotations, unless otherwise indicated, are taken from The Holy Bible, New International Version®,
NIV®. Copyright © 1973, 1978, 1984, 2011 by Biblica, Inc.™ Used by permission of Zondervan. All rights reserved
worldwide. www.zondervan.com The "NIV" and "New International Version" are trademarks registered in the
United States Patent and Trademark Office by Biblica, Inc.™

While any stories in this book are true, some names and identifying information may have been changed to protect
the privacy of individuals.

Note: This book contains occasional language and profanity that some readers may find offensive.

Cover design: David Fassett
Images: relief of hand and microphone: © Henrik Sorensen / Getty Images
       amplifier knobs: © GiorgioMagini / iStock / Getty Images Plus
       American flag: © sigurcamp / iStockphoto / Getty Images Plus

ISBN 978-0-8308-5181-2 (print)
ISBN 978-0-8308-9087-3 (digital)

Printed in the United States of America ♾

Library of Congress Cataloging-in-Publication Data
Names: Hodge, Daniel White, 1974- author.
Title: Homeland insecurity : a hip hop missiology for the post-Civil Rights
   context / Daniel White Hodge.
Description: Downers Grove : InterVarsity Press, 2018. | Includes
   bibliographical references and index.
Identifiers: LCCN 2018012254 (print) | LCCN 2018019988 (ebook) | ISBN
   9780830890873 (eBook) | ISBN 9780830851812 (pbk. : alk. paper)
Subjects: LCSH: Christianity and culture—United States. | Hip-hop—Religious
   aspects—Christianity. | African Americans—Religion. | Missions.
Classification: LCC BR517 (ebook) | LCC BR517 .H525 2018 (print) | DDC
   261—dc23
LC record available at https://lccn.loc.gov/2018012254

P	23	22	21	20	19	18	17	16	15	14	13	12	11	10	9	8	7	6	5	4	3	2	1
Y	37	36	35	34	33	32	31	30	29	28	27	26	25	24	23	22	21	20	19	18			

I'd like to dedicate this to my G-moms, Beki Virgen.

Without you and your fire/passion, I would have

never gotten out of that racist town in Texas;

I would have never survived the tumultuous racism;

I would have never been able to stand on

the ground I'm standing on now.

Thank you! I love you!

CONTENTS

FOREWORD

Jude Tiersma Watson

THIRTY YEARS AGO a struggling immigrant neighborhood in Los Angeles beckoned me to come and see. I had just graduated with an MA in missiology, with plans to go back to Asia, and found myself in central L.A. before gentrification was even imagined. The Mexican ballads and Cumbia music were expected. The sound of rap music in the air and graffiti art on the walls were the surprise. Immigrant youth were acculturating to life in Los Angeles, listening to Power 106, where Hip Hop lives. Once I began to listen, the voice of Tupac was everywhere.

Ray Bakke, Roger Greenway, Harvie Conn, and Manny Ortiz had been calling attention to mission in ever-growing megacities. At the time, raising awareness was an important role, but the time has long come for new voices in urban missiology—postcolonial voices valuing mutual transformation, rooted deep within our cities and communities. Dan White Hodge is such a voice. Dan carries within himself multiple consciousnesses, having traversed various urban cultures. He listens to voices many of us can't hear, asks questions we don't know to ask, and pays attention to the rage that society fears.

When Dan came to Fuller Seminary's School of Intercultural Studies to go deep into the missiology of Tupac Shakur, I knew this would take urban missiology to places the discipline needed to go. Tupac was the prophet youth were attuned to, yet I listened as an outsider. Dan was a prophetic missiologist who heard things I could not. He dared to ask, "What is a missiology that arises as a response to the New Jim Crow and Doctrine of Discovery, that arises from the conflicted spaces in our own land? What is a missiology demanding not only missional action but a prophetic stand against cultures of injustice, a missiology that sees pain and embraces lament as an integral part of mission, that moves beyond a culture of 'niceness' as we navigate very complex and difficult social realities?" These are core to the work of urban missiology.

Dan embodies this new urban missiology on the wild edges of society. The ancient Celts used the term *wild goose* for the Holy Spirit, reminding us that the Holy Spirit cannot be tamed or domesticated but may lead us to places outside our comfort zone. Creative mission has always happened on the periphery of society. With Dan as our guide, we can allow the Wild Goose to lead us to uncomfortable places, outside the gate, where our Lord was crucified.

ACKNOWLEDGMENTS

BOOKS ARE NOT WRITTEN IN A VACUUM. While this is a monograph text, if the publisher would allow it, I would name numerous other "authors" who have helped out in thought, moral support, and just plain holy goodness! I'd like to start off by thanking my ongoing mentor and former dissertation chair Dr. Roberta King. Without the research and critical thinking seeds she planted in me, this book would not have been possible. The structure she gave me to write and critically think through writing is and was invaluable. Thank you. I'd also like to thank Dr. Jude Tiersma Watson for her continued support not just of me but also of ethnic-minority postindustrial people groups. Her unwavering love for people of color has been renowned, and her continued input into my life has helped in forming my own framework for not just this text but also for future ones to come. These two women have helped shape my theological and ideological structure and have worked with me face to face; my thank you to them will be never ending and their continued insight into my life is priceless.

I have to send much love to my humanist community from AAR (American Academy of Religion), Monica Miller and Anthony Pinn. Dr. Miller is a brilliant mind who has constantly challenged me to think outside of evangelicalism and "evangelically" language. Thank you. I really do owe you! Dr. Miller is a genius when it comes to religion and people groups. Her frameworks are echoed throughout this book. Dr. Pinn, what can I say. I realize he has been a mentor to many, and while I was never a student of his, he has influenced me through his talks, research, and critical inquiry. I have admired his hard-ass approach to Black theology. Doc, your work is powerful and is helping shape a new era of critical thought! I cannot leave out

Dr. Christopher Driscoll, who has given me a new framework for Whiteness in the age of Trump. Dr. Driscoll's work is also peppered throughout this book; our countless late-night conversations on race, religion, politics, and Whiteness have been invaluable—thanks, man!

To my thinking group of colleagues at North Park, Drs. Liza Ann Acosta, Joel Willitts, Mary Veeneman, Marcus Simmons (soon to be Dr.), Soong-Chan Rah, Rachelle Ankney, Rich Kohng, Nancy Arnesen, Greg Clark, Michelle Clifton-Soderstrom, Katrina Washington (soon to be Dr.), Chris Hubbard, Mary Hendrickson, Peter St. Jean, Gregor Thuswaldner (one bad-ass dean), and Elizabeth Pierre—you have been a light for me in many dark days dealing with racism, sexism, the Trump election, and just all the crap that happens to people of color in higher education; seriously, thank you. I cannot express my continued admiration of you all and the support you bring to me dealing with the difficulties of life. I cannot leave out my provost, Dr. Michael Emerson, who has broken down walls in a manner only a White-cis-male can do! Thanks, Doc! It's part of why I'm still at North Park!

To the realist homies a brutha could have, Dr. Gabe Veas, Travis Harris (soon to be Dr.), Pablo Otaola (soon to be Dr.), Dr. Andre Johnson, Dr. Earle Fisher, Mark Skiles, Joseph Boston, and Dr. Jon Gill. You all have kept me sane as man in these crazy sociopolitical days. Your friendship is invaluable and has provided me with a stronger sense of who I am. Thank you. You really have no idea the help and friendship you provide. I wish we all lived in the same city!

To the younger and strong voices that have helped guide the shape of this book: Brandi Miller, Josiah Daniels, Rediet Mulugeta, Daniel Camacho, Kenji Kuramitsu, Daniel Michel, Tamisha Tyler (soon to be Dr.), Latina Harris, Jeanelle Austin, Julie Tai, Austin Brown, Naomi Chisman, Kate Sanchez, Melina Pagliuzza, Ericka Husby, Audrey Velez, Ra Mendoza, David Jamies, Teresa Mateus, and Katrina Washington—thank you. Keep that fire and disruption going. Hope this book makes you proud of the work we are all doing.

To the O.G. women holding it down day after day, Kathy Khang, Irene Cho, Mayra Nolan, Dr. Mary Trujillo, Dr. Velda Love, Reesheda Graham-Washington, Alison Burkhardt, Laura Truax, Lenora Rand, and Dr. Cynthia Stewart. Keep hope alive and the fight going!

To my LGBTQ family in the fight, who have provided me with much insight and wisdom, Dr. Robyn Henderson-Espinoza, Darren Calhoun, and Joseph Mole. Thanks for your patience and fight that I will never completely know. You are all superheroes to me!

I saved the best for last: my wife, Emily White Hodge, who has stood with me during the toughest storms (depression, anxiety, PTSD, rage). You are my rock. I wouldn't be at this point in my life if it had not been for your constant Enneagram-One self! I know I don't always appreciate the "push," but I need it. Thank you for your continued love and telling me, "Yes you can, in fact, hell yes you can!" I'm very lucky to have a life partner like you. And of course, my little kiddo, Mahalia, I've loved all our talks on race and gender that we have each Friday on our weekly dates. Part of this book has come out of those conversations, so keep up that critical mind my love!

A MISSIOLOGY IN AN ERA OF CIVIL DISRUPTION

AS I SIT WRITING THIS BOOK, the current time, context, climate, and culture in the United States is fraught with racial, gender, and cultural strain the likes of which have not been seen since the Jim Crow era. It is a time unlike any other. While the period prior to the 1970s was marked by direct and intense racism, in the present context, social media, passive-aggressive behavior, and microaggressions sustain hegemonies and create a culture of hate. I am a Black male living in the United States and trying to live out a faith rooted in Christianity. But I struggle with the objectionable history of North American Christianity, which is antithetical to not only the color of my skin but also my narrative, body, and life.[1]

For me personally, the events started to erupt during the Troy Davis murder trial. Here, a young Black male, who was convicted of shooting and killing a White police officer, sat on death row. When I began to research the issue and Davis's case, I discovered that little physical evidence to incriminate him was actually found, and the "eyewitness" later recanted the story of seeing Davis murder the police officer.[2] Despite a strong social media

---

[1]One must consider the use of Christianity as both a racist and violent tool of oppression toward many Africans and African Americans—not to mention other ethnic-minority groups such as Mexicans, Chinese, Japanese, and Native Americans. This will be engaged more later in this text as it relates to missions and colonialization.

[2]I realize this is a controversial case; in fact, most Black-and-White cases typically are. From my research, Troy Davis should have had another trial, and the new evidence should have been admitted into that trial. I am fully aware that many White evangelicals took issue with the Davis

campaign in support of him, and even phone calls to elected officials, Troy Davis was executed on September 21, 2011. Then came Trayvon Martin and later Michael Brown, both the Ferguson and Baltimore uprisings, and the terrorist acts of Dylann Roof in Charleston, South Carolina.[3] Roof mercilessly murdered nine Black church members of the historic Emmanuel AME Church. Then came Tamir Rice, Dante Parker, John Crawford III, Sandra Bland, and Laquan McDonald. This list could go on; it seems the killing of Black persons has become a sport in the United States.

In all of these tragedies Christian discourse such as "forgive," "love your enemies," and "bless those that curse you" is used to continue the subjugation of Black bodies. And while in theory, at least, those platitudes are hoped for and desired, the reality is that when white America feels threatened or is attacked (e.g., 9/11), the opposite of those platitudes is taken. A type of "holy violence" often commences.[4] And while I see white evangelical youth dancing to Lecrae at one of his concerts, the irony is revealed when those same youth tell me things like "Michael Brown wasn't innocent and probably deserved to die." Or "These 'thugs' were asking for it." Or the classic "This was part of God's plan."[5] They say such things as they enjoy and embrace Black culture.

Further, the election of Donald J. Trump as the forty-fifth president of the United States on November 8, 2016, shook many of us in the ethnic-minority community.[6] This sent a direct message to ethnic-minority communities:

trial and sided with the courts. This is part of the ongoing tension in the United States and especially in Christian evangelical circles.

[3]This is in no way minimizing the women and other Black youth who have been murdered or killed at the hands of either police officers or vigilante White citizens. What I suggest here are the capstone events that have shaped both our nation and where I personally stand as a Black Christian male.

[4]The use of violence and the construct of a "just God" is a matter we will engage briefly in this text. For a greater examination see Daniel White Hodge, *Hip Hop's Hostile Gospel: A Post-Soul Theological Exploration*, ed. Warren Goldstein, Studies on Critical Research in Religion (Boston: Brill Academic, 2017), 6:122-47.

[5]These are all direct quotes taken from two summer youth events in 2014 and 2015. The latter quote came from George Zimmerman's interview with Sean Hannity (2012) in which he stated that the killing of Trayvon was part of "God's plan" and that he "pray[s] for them [Martin's family] daily." This type of discourse is common and is part of the ideological structure that many post–civil rights millennials refuse to engage with or adopt. This has ramifications for evangelicalism as many in the post–civil rights millennial generation view evangelicals as outdated, racist, sexist, and having a very skewed reality of who "God" is.

[6]While the goal here is not to condemn those who favor a conservative perspective, it is however important to note that Trump's rhetoric, policies, and many of his appointed cabinet members are aligned with an alt-right worldview, which is in direct contradiction to social justice and

your voice does not matter.[7] Our hope for the Obama legacy was shown to be mythological in nature, and our optimism about the coming "demographical changes," in which minorities were finally to triumph and use their power for justice, was just another neo-liberal delusion.[8] It also shook those of us who have dedicated our lives to intercultural and racial justice work that 81 percent of white evangelicals voted for a person like Trump and continue to support his policies.[9] That was an awakening for me, and it made me question the work I do. Had it mattered? Did any of it sink in? How could all the speeches and all the material published be ignored?

All these questions developed while I was writing this book. My heart is heavy, and my mind full.

What does faith look like in this context? What does a missiological response look like when the bodies of Black youth are celebrated and adored on one platform yet hated and seen as of little worth on the other? What does all of this mean for those doing short-term missions in domestic urban contexts—especially if those doing ministry favored Trump in the election?

---

intercultural work. Therefore, it is difficult to entertain the notion of Trump being "for all Americans" when it is clear, by his actions and cabinet, that he is only for the continuation of Whiteness as equivalent to "American." I would challenge anyone who voted for Trump to defend someone such as Steven Bannon, for example, who has spewed a rhetoric of hate over the years toward Jews, Blacks, Palestinians, and even women. His perspective does not fit a "Christian worldview." It is imperative that we wrestle with these matters critically because they are of utmost importance for anyone who regards Christianity as their faith.

[7]It is also noted in emerging research that the presence and notion of "growing diversity" creates fear in many Whites who concern themselves with the changing electorate. This also illustrates the fear that has existed in many White churches for decades regarding growing ethnic-minority populations. See Brenda Major, Alison Blodorn, and Gregory Major Blascovich, "The Threat of Increasing Diversity: Why Many White Americans Support Trump in the 2016 Presidential Election," *Group Processes & Intergroup Relations*, October 20, 2016. A type of warning, if you will, was issued by Michael O. Emerson and Christian Smith in their classic text *Divided by Faith: Evangelical Religion and the Problem of Race in America* (Oxford: Oxford University Press, 2001), which, even then, outlined the growing gap within evangelical churches.

[8]Those that are rooted in the notion that somehow the rise of ethnic-minority population in the United States will somehow skew voting to reflect a more diverse country, one with an emphasis on social justice. While no one can accurately predict the future, I would argue that possibly in two or three generations we may well be in such a space within the United States. From the history of South Africa we have learned that those in power do not have to have the majority in ethnic numbers.

[9]See Gregory A. Smith and Jessica Martínez, "How the Faithful Voted: A Preliminary 2016 Analysis," in *Fact Tank: News in the Numbers* (Washington, DC: Pew Research Center, 2016); Myriam Renaud, "Myths Debunked: Why Did White Evangelical Christians Vote for Trump?," The Martin Marty Center for the Advanced Study of Religion, January 19, 2017, https://divinity.uchicago .edu/sightings/myths-debunked-why-did-white-evangelical-christians-vote-trump.

How is it possible for the multiethnic dissonance of our culture to manifest itself in the popularity of an artist such as Lecrae? Do we as mission-minded people take race, gender, and class into account when we evangelize? How do we contend with someone such as Darren Wilson, who spoke of Michael Brown as a "demon" coming after him? Does the Christian faith, as the mystic and Black Christian theologian Howard Thurman asks, "make room" for concerns such as racism and the disinherited?[10] Some still argue that the only ministry or mission worth doing is preaching the "gospel" to the "lost," and that is where mission ends.

I take issue with *ministry* and *mission* defined so narrowly. Woven into those definitions is a faulty understanding of mission and *who* mission extends to, who *does* mission, and *why* it is conducted. With Richard Kyle, I contend that "reflecting the old Puritan heritage and American individualism, evangelicals focus on abortion and sexual immorality while downplaying the issues of poverty, racism, and social injustice. And when they address such problems, they believe that the problems can be solved primarily through individual, church, or local efforts."[11] Race, gender, and class are lost within that narrow definition. Given the current state of American Christianity, race, gender, and class can no longer be avoided.

One of the reasons Christianity is viewed as irrelevant, useless, sexist, racist, and exclusive is because of the narrowly defined concepts of ministry and mission. The simplicity this depicts is much too utopian for a world that has rejected almost every form of utopianism and given creed to complexity, mystery, ambiguity, and a disruptivist worldview.[12] The *gospel* means nothing to someone who lives in a constant state of terror from institutional racism

---

[10]Howard Thurman, *Jesus and the Disinherited* (Boston: Beacon Press, 1976).

[11]Richard G. Kyle, *Evangelicalism: An Americanized Christianity* (New Brunswick, NJ: Transaction, 2006), 314.

[12]In fact, most post-soul theorists resist simplicity and utopianism as a form of thinking and life. See Dick Hebdige, "Postmodernism and 'the Other Side,'" in *Cultural Theory and Popular Culture: A Reader*, ed. John Storey (London: Pearson Prentice Hall, 1998). See also Garth Alper, "Making Sense Out of Postmodern Music?," *Popular Music and Society* 24, no. 4 (2000); Nelson George, *Post-Soul Nation: The Explosive, Contradictory, Triumphant, and Tragic 1980s as Experienced by African Americans (Previously Known as Blacks and Before That Negroes)* (New York: Viking, 2004); Mark Anthony Neal, *Soul Babies: Black Popular Culture and the Post-Soul Aesthetic* (New York: Routledge, 2002); Paul C. Taylor, "Post-Black, Old Black," *African American Review* 41, no. 4 (2007); and Joseph Winters, "Unstrange Bedfellows: Hip Hop and Religion," *Religion Compass* 5, no. 6 (2011).

personified in a police uniform. "Jesus' good news" is empty discourse to those whose lives are disrupted by short-term missionaries who pose for selfies, write cute newsletters, and seek narcissistic emotions while taking advantage of others' misery and despair. Therefore, at this point in Christian history, we find ourselves in a moral quandary. Whose narrative will win, we wonder—conservative or liberal?

I suggest that the issues we face as Christians and missiologists alike are much more multifaceted and broader than binary constructs such as left versus right; they are much broader than simply saying ministry and mission end when a person accepts Jesus into their life. I assert that the issues we face in terms of racism, sexism, fascism, and classism are worsened by a myriad of media outlets claiming to be "truth tellers" or "fact checkers"; they drive people deeper into their binary corners and thereby ignore the complexity of the middle.

We need a church in the wild: a church that embraces a mission of complexity, mystery, ambiguity, and high concentrations of doubt—the same mindset that makes up large portions of this generation's ethos. A church bold enough to disrupt the complacency of American evangelicalism and create a much more contextual approach to Jesus. A church creative enough to use Hip Hop and its theological core as a missiological premise.[13] A church confrontational enough to interrupt white supremacy in American Christianity.

We need a church in the wild that does not yet exist.

THERE IS NO CHURCH IN THE WILD

Jay-Z and Kanye West's song "No Church in the Wild," from their 2012 album *Watch the Throne*, lays out the genesis of this book:

> Human beings in a mob
> What's a mob to a king?
> What's a king to a god?
> What's a god to a nonbeliever?
> Who don't believe in anything?[14]

---

[13]Hip Hop is a theology of suffering, a theology of community, a theology of the Hip Hop Jesuz, a theology of social action and justice, and a theology of the profane. See Daniel White Hodge, *The Soul of Hip Hop: Rims, Timbs and a Cultural Theology* (Downers Grove, IL: InterVarsity Press, 2010).

[14]Jay-Z and Kanye West featuring Frank Ocean, "No Church in the Wild," *Watch the Throne*, Roc-A-Fella, Roc Nation, Def Jam, 2012.

Note the progression of the chorus. It follows a linear hierarchy of reasoning. Human beings can organize as a group, a community, or a specific
locality, but what does that matter to someone like a *king* or highly established official? In other words, with all the issues and problems someone has
on a moment-by-moment basis, why would a king—or queen—care one bit
about those issues? How might something like the Laquan McDonald
murder by a police officer affect a high city official like the mayor? How
might something as trivial as a parking ticket—which could financially dev-
astate a family on a tight budget—distress someone like the president of the
United States? But the chorus continues: what is a king to a *god*? This type
of analogy and symbolism repeats itself throughout the Bible. Matthew 6:33
urges us to seek first the kingdom of God. In John 18:36 Jesus says his
kingdom is not of this world. Daniel 2:44 tells of God setting up a kingdom
that will never be destroyed. And Zechariah 14:9 reminds us that one day
God will be king over all of the earth. Throughout the Bible, there are references that give credence to God not caring much about kingdoms that
humans create; God's kingdom is much more important and much more
tangible. So, what's an earthly king to a God? Yet the song comes back,
almost to a singularized point, in asking, "What's a god to a nonbeliever?";
what does all that even matter if you do not believe in anything?

This, then, is where Christianity finds itself in the present era: post–civil
rights and post-soul, trying to *prove* itself relevant, desiring to argue the
"truth," engaging in an us-versus-them debate.[15] It is in this era that Christianity, in all its complexity, beauty, force, intricacy, and faith, is reduced
to binary options: good and bad, moral and immoral, conservative and
liberal (or progressive). But what does this matter to someone who (1) has
lost faith in God altogether, (2) has been oppressed and disenfranchised
by Christians, (3) has read, and possibly lived, the destructive history of
Christian faith being weaponized for violence and death, (4) has been
psychologically affected by fundamentalism, and (5) simply does not
believe there is a god? Given the current age of information and interplanetary

---

[15]While *post–civil rights* and *post-soul* will be defined later in the introduction, I am using these to
name (1) the current generation of young people between the ages of fourteen and twenty-nine,
and (2) the era of the past thirty-five years, which questions metanarrative, meta-ideology, and
agency defined from hegemonic positions.

exploration, God may not be a literal figure but rather one created in the minds of humans, right?

It does not matter to someone who does not believe in anything! The debate on abortion does not matter. Prayer in public schools does not matter. Creation versus evolution does not matter. Whether or not your church has an American flag displayed in the sanctuary does not matter. Is the rapture prior to or after the tribulation? It does not matter. It does not even matter whether being LGBT is a sin or not. These side issues are merely noise to someone who does not believe in anything. As Christians and missiologists, this should be of great concern.

Christian theologians, pastors, and priests—Protestant, Catholic, evangelical, and Orthodox—seem to want to convince nonbelievers that those things, and other issues, are important. Somehow if the articulation of the Christian faith is done in just the right manner, nonbelievers will believe. Jay-Z and Kanye, however, got it right. They ask the pertinent question. They force us to wrestle with those five little lines, and they identify the problem for anyone wanting to "preach the gospel" or carry out mission in the United States. Simply put, there is no church in the wild. A church that can sit with questions and doubt rather than answers and solutions. A church that disrupts its own thinking on race, gender, and class. A church that is able to transcend tradition, dogma, and rigid theological stances and push for relationships, community, and the mysterious enlightenment of who God is in this present age. Is there a church that can do that? Is there a church that pushes past the age-old arguments for the sake of a conversation with a person? Is there a church inside the Hip Hop generations? Is there a church for the thugs, the pimps, and the drug pushers? Jay-Z and Kanye are wrestling with this! They ask us to grapple with it as well.

The Christian church has been tamed for quite some time. The 1960s (the decade that ushered in the post-soul era) was the last stage for binary Christian thought.[16] It is argued that WWII was the last "just war," one in

---

[16]While an exact date and time is not clear, most scholars suggest that the decade of the 1960s gave rise to a deconstruction we are still wrestling with. In many regards this was labeled as "postmodernism" and is said to have restructured the way church and state relate and began the "culture wars." For the purpose of this book, I will use this decade as ground zero for the post-soul era. See Zygmunt Bauman, "Postmodern Religion?," in *Religion, Modernity and Postmodernity*, ed. Paul Heelas (Malden, MA: Blackwell, 1998); Daniel Bell, *The Coming of a Post-Industrial*

which the enemy and the hero were clearly defined—one of the many reasons almost every year there is a new film dealing with some facet of that era. The era prior to the 1960s was a heyday for missionaries, a time when a white heterosexual male was the model for Christian missions and the "sending forth" to missions came from the United States to "them, out there."[17] That era was a time when society "made sense," an era when many had a traditionalist ideology.[18] It was time when men were men, children listened, and people—particularly ethnic minorities—knew "their place." It was an era that created America as the powerhouse-sending agent of missionaries,[19] the authority for missions and "truth" for those "out there" on foreign soil.[20]

Yet today the decline of Christianity, as noted by scholars such as Christian Smith, Robert Putman, and David Kinnaman, situates the United States as a "lost" and "pagan" ground. The United States looks more like the godless

---

Society: A Venture in Social Forecasting (New York: Basic Books, 1973); David J. Bosch, *Transforming Mission: Paradigm Shifts in Theology of Mission*, American Society of Missiology Series (Maryknoll, NY: Orbis Books, 1991); Don Cupitt, "Post-Christianity," in Heelas, *Religion, Modernity and Postmodernity*; Norman K. Denzin, *Images of Postmodern Society: Social Theory and Contemporary Cinema* (Thousand Oaks, CA: Sage, 1991); David A. Escobar, "Amos & Postmodernity: A Contemporary Critical & Reflective Perspective on the Interdependency of Ethics & Spirituality in the Latino-Hispanic American Reality," *Journal of Business Ethics* 103, no. 1 (2011); Jean-François Lyotard, *The Postmodern Condition: A Report on Knowledge* (Minneapolis: University of Minnesota Press, 1984); Anthony B. Pinn, *The Black Church in the Post–Civil Rights Era* (Maryknoll, NY: Orbis Books, 2002).

[17]Soong-Chan Rah, *The Next Evangelicalism: Freeing the Church from Western Cultural Captivity* (Downers Grove, IL: InterVarsity Press, 2009), 127-31. Also see William R. Jones, *Is God a White Racist? A Preamble to Black Theology* (Garden City, NY: Anchor, 1973); John D. Wilsey, *American Exceptionalism and Civil Religion: Reassessing the History of an Idea* (Downers Grove, IL: IVP Academic, 2015); Richard Twiss, *Rescuing the Gospel from the Cowboys: A Native American Expression of the Jesus Way* (Downers Grove, IL: InterVarsity Press, 2015); Trevor B. McCrisken, "Exceptionalism," in *Encyclopedia of American Foreign Policy*, ed. Richard Dean Burns, Alexander DeConde, and Fredrik Logevall (New York: Charles Scribner's, 2002). Note that the majority of missions material between 1950 and 1961 was written by men, most of whom were White.

[18]In particular, for those in the boomer, builder, and civil rights generations.

[19]In Robert Glover's text *The Progress of World-Wide Missions*, he notes the missionary's motives, and while those motives are, in some regard, rooted in a biblical manner, the "sending agents" were primarily from North America, and the United States to be precise. To further this, a majority of these missionaries were White males coming from a strict evangelical perspective. As I will note later, those perspectives do not come without bias, prejudices, racial constructs, and racist presuppositions, and thereby create a settler-colonialist missiological space. This practice, continued over decades, is debilitating and does not allow for a full view of the breadth of Christianity.

[20]This is noted throughout the PBS documentary *God in America: How Religious Liberty Shaped America* (2010) and also by William Ernest Hocking, who noted the "error" and "mistaken" approaches of many missionaries abroad. See William Ernest Hocking, *Re-thinking Missions: A Layman's Inquiry After One Hundred Years* (New York: Harper, 1932), 29-32.

societies of the 1950s and 1960s. It could then be argued that the United States is a missiological ground. This shift, in fact, led Ray Bakke to make the case for urban missions and a theology for the city. Domestic missions were not something taken seriously, and not until the last decade has it become an area of study for missionaries.[21] But what do we do with the shifting of Christianity in the twentieth and twenty-first centuries? How might we contend with a generation of ethnic-minority Millennial Gen Ys? This group calls out the white hegemonic structures of inequality but also seeks to disrupt those hegemonic structures of older ethnic minorities as well. When a god does not mean a thing to a nonbeliever, it is time to see the United States as a mission field.

This book arrives amid the tension of these questions and insights and recognizes that many Christians are scurrying to keep some remnant of what they have understood as traditional Christianity. This book enters at a time when racial unrest is at, or in some cases beyond, the levels it was in 1969.[22]

PREMISE AND STRUCTURE OF THIS BOOK

The white homogeneity of missions in North America is problematic not solely because of white homogeneity (white people) but because many whites are ignorant of the issues surrounding racism, white supremacy, and systemic racism. They have therefore continued a legacy of colonialism, microaggression, and passive discrimination. Those issues are conflated under the premise of "Christian mission" and do not have the cultural

---

[21]When I first attended Fuller Theological Seminary's School of Intercultural Studies (formerly School of World Missions), I was required to have at least five years of crosscultural work in a mission's field. While I thought about using the fact that I had been a Black man working in predominantly White Christian settings as my qualification, I decided to use my more than ten years domestic missions work as my entry point. I was denied entry and had to appeal, because "local missions" was not considered missions work. This will be taken up later, but often, especially for White missionaries, only overseas missions work is worthwhile. Overseas work, however, ignores the brutality and severity of White supremacy and White racism. So, in turn, it is much easier to deal with a genocide your ethnic heritage had nothing to do with than to engage the issues we face currently in the United States.

[22]Many scholars argue 1969 is a time when "we almost lost our civility" in society due to the racial, cultural, sexual, and political unrest and violence in the United States. For examples of this see George Ritzer, *The McDonaldization of Society* (Thousand Oaks, CA: Pine Forge Press, 2004); Robin D. G. Kelley, *Race Rebels: Culture, Politics, and the Black Working Class* (New York: Free Press, 1994); Gordon Lynch, *Understanding Theology and Popular Culture* (Malden, MA: Blackwell, 2005); and Mark Anthony Neal, "Sold Out on Soul: The Corporate Annexation of Black Popular Music," *Popular Music and Society* 21, no. 3 (1997).

relevancy or competencies to enact a contextualized, culturally proper missiology. Therefore, the thesis of this book can be broken down into two parts: (1) current missiological approaches are impaired, and missiological methods need a difficult yet necessary transformation that allows for ethnic-minority leadership, vision, and theology; and (2) Hip Hop theology is a missiological framework that will help create community, church context, and a stronger relationship to the Trinity in a wild context.[23]

This book explores missiological engagement within post–civil rights contexts in the United States and focuses on Hip Hop theology as a missiological tool for radical engagement of emerging adult populations in the wild.[24] I argue that Hip Hop provides a space for youth and emerging adults to (1) find God in a contextual manner, (2) have room for lament, ambiguity, doubt, and the profane, and (3) find diversity within Christianity and remain true to their own cultural heritage. This book will suggest new conceptual models for domestic missions within an ever-growing multiethnic demographic. My argument speaks to and from three disciplines simultaneously—missiology, Hip Hop studies, and youth ministry—in an attempt to bring them together around the themes of my thesis and a hybridity of *lived missiology* grounded in the subject of Hip Hop studies.[25]

I must note that while many Christian authors conclude with a course of action or methodological solution—which I have done in other works—this book will not. The goal here is to sound the alarm and present the issues,

---

[23]The use of *wild* here does not imply that people who are non-Christian or those who are Christian but do not fit the traditional evangelical Christian image are "less than" or actually wild. The use of this word continues the conversation raised in the song "No Church in the Wild" and is more of a symbolic term I use to describe things outside of tradition or even a stereotypical missiological lens rooted in Western Christianity. The current shift occurring in the United States is creating a healthy deconstruction of what it means to be Christian and how a "Christian" looks, talks, believes, and loves; this would be an example of what I mean by *wild*, not the literal definition of the word.

[24]The post-soul/post–civil rights context is made up of a matrix of people, cultures, subcultures, groups, ideologies, theologies, and events. I do not desire to take anything away from these important areas. However, a book, as vast as it can be, has limitations. This book will focus primarily on urban/city culture with a strong emphasis on Hip Hop, Black, Latinx, and US contexts. Many works deal with areas outside of these contexts, yet few deal specifically with "our" (meaning ethnic minorities) areas. Thus, this book will have a specific focus on this part of the canon.

[25]That is, the notion that missions, rather than a sending forth to some foreign land, is lived, breathed, and carried out on a day-to-day basis in the sacred, secular, and profane—an everyday lifestyle and engagement within a community.

arguments, and areas of need. You have a part in this; you can help create solutions and practical approaches to the issues I am raising in this book. I assume that you are curious about these issues and want to see some type of change. Thus, my goal is to steer away from a step-by-step process of what to do next and being positive for the sake of positivity. We are in a critical state within missiology—at DEFCON 1. The American Society of Missiology (ASM) is composed of older, white, cis-gendered males who struggle to "find diversity" in speakers. We have a problem. The Association of Professors of Mission (APM) can count the number of ethnic minorities in their guild (on one hand?). Things are not right. To single out this text as *the* guide rather than a *developing* guide is both precocious and arrogant. To have an "expert" as the only voice is egotistical. If we are to move forward, we need to do so in community. We need to examine what a church in the wild might look like, possibly in a generation from now. I present research and findings with some brief thoughts on those; you are to begin to formulate what solutions might be within your own context. This is a shift away from having a one-stop shop within a text. Instead I seek to create dialogue and community while working toward a common goal. This book serves as a missiological exploration into an era and time that is relatively unexplored and untamed. Therefore, the conclusion and thoughts about moving forward are suggestions, not solutions. This book is an invitation to move beyond the traditional missiological response of "going out there" to "reach them" for God, and to commune and sit with those who are in the wild. This book *is not* an authoritative guide to the post-soul or post–civil rights era. I come to this work as a participant and learner and ask you to do the same; let us explore *what is* to better see what *may be.*

Moving forward, I will lay out definitions that will be used in this book throughout. I use the word *wild* to symbolize the uncharted, nondomesticated, non–evangelically tamed area of ideological thoughts, theological principles, and generational motifs of those from the Hip Hop and urban multiethnic generation. This generation is asking how Christianity can be of any help during a time of Black death. The wild is the context of Black Lives Matter and the Black Youth Project. The wild is a not a place of methods, standardized curriculum, and oversimplified theologies that do not consider race, gender, and class as central principles. Therefore, the wild is a new space not designed for white supremacy; it is seeking a Jesus outside of evangelicalism and is in continual transformation. The wild is not easily grappled with, even in a book like this. In other words, the wild is just that: an ongoing development and creation of ideas pushing away from Western white evangelicalism and moving toward a more holistic space in which all are truly welcomed and embraced.

The term *sacred* refers to those areas held as hallowed, consecrated, or revered—the areas we tend to hold near us and keep as special. In essence, the sacred can be that space in which God finds us, even if in a tattered state; it also can be the journey of the Christian toward faith while being held in tension with the *secular* (that which is not just devoid of divine presence but also hints at God's manifestation, or God's living and taking up residence in a non-church context and environment). The secular has traditionally been used in Christian discourse as an ungodly or non-Christian place. I will suggest that the secular can also nuance the sacred while seeking a nondeity. In other words, it is in some sense the notion of being "spiritual but not religious." However, I too suggest that those who are secular and want to remain so do not necessarily wish to remove themselves from all socio-spiritual notions and affiliations.[26] This then brings us to the *profane*, the process of deconsecrating that which was once considered consecrated and sacred: the funk and the treacherous, or those areas in a society labeled or given the designation of being outside the given morals, codes, ethics, and values established as "good" or "right."[27] When combined (sacred, secular, profane), we have a rich and complex intersection of a faith holding the three elements in tension. It can be, particularly on first contact, an uncomfortable space to exist in, yet the wild is in constant tension with all three, sometimes one more than the other. This is no different than any human experience. All three of these elements are present in everyone's life. It is unwise to think that one can be sacred all the time or profane at the core.

---

[26]This was a crucial finding in my interviews with Hip Hoppers who insisted that they were not affiliated with a church or denomination yet desired to pursue a relationship with God in a secular space. As one interviewee exclaimed, "I don't need a church to find God; nor do I need a pastor to get wisdom and insight on the Word. I like finding God in the void of everyday life."

[27]In addition to these three definitions, this book will make use of these definitions of the *sacred*, *secular*, and the *profane*: *sacred*: those things that are divine or could be construed as divine; *secular*: that which is devoid of a God or lacks in spirituality; *profane*: that which is nefarious, oblique, and at times, contrary to "good."

Thus, this book will keep the three elements of the sacred, secular, and profane in tension as we explore the wild.

I also think it is important to define what Hip Hop culture and theology means for this book. Hip Hop culture is an urban subculture that seeks to express a *lifestyle, attitude,* and *urban identity.* Hip Hop at its core—not the commercialization and commodity it has become in certain respects—*rejects* dominant forms of culture and society and seeks to increase a social consciousness along with a racial-ethnic pride. Thus, Hip Hop uses rap music, dance, music production, MC-ing, and allegory as vehicles to send and fund its message of social, cultural, and political *resistance* to dominant structures or norms.[28] Therefore, Hip Hop theology is derived from this latter definition and from the bowels of oppression, marginalization, and disenfranchisement. It rejects normative and simplistic responses to such issues. Hip Hop theology is a post–civil rights theology, and therefore this book will argue for its use as a missiological premise and construct as we move into the wild. Hip Hop theology is composed of a theology of suffering, a theology of community, a theology of a Hip Hop Jesuz, a theology of social action and civil disruption, and a theology of the profane.

Thinking about Hip Hop and its culture, I think it is wise to define a word that has become quite coded in missiological contexts: *urban.*[29] For some, everything associated with Black and Latinx is urban—meaning poor, in need of help, and impoverished. For others, it is negative and a place in ministry they want none of because it is loud, aggressive, and unfamiliar to their own worldview and cultural backgrounds. For still others, *urban* means a new space to use wealth, where industry caters to people; the stereotype of the "inner city" is now gone—urban communities have been gentrified. And yet for other people, *urban* is a place of ministry, life, missions, and community within a growing geographical area that has little to do with an actual city. For our purposes, *urban* is defined as the conflation

---

[28]See Hodge, *Soul of Hip Hop*; Hodge, *Hip Hop's Hostile Gospel*, 6; Efrem Smith and Phil Jackson, *The Hip-Hop Church: Connecting with the Movement Shaping Our Culture* (Downers Grove, IL: InterVarsity Press, 2005).

[29]This term was popularized by urban theologians such as Ray Bakke, Roger Greenway, Harvie Conn, and the legendary John Perkins. This does not take anything away from the work that these pioneers have done. It simply means that times have changed and we have entered a new era with emerging definitions. Thus we need to further develop the canon of urban missiology.

of low income, poverty, disenfranchisement, dislocation in society (e.g., anomie), and a sense of deprivation. We will use this term *not* as a geographical location but as a societal and cultural one. In other words, various locations within a city such as Los Angeles or Chicago can be urban; it is not just the "inner city" in many regards.[30]

I also find it necessary, although it is not a central premise of the book, to define an emerging term: *the postindustrial era*. This is the era of electronics, digital narrative, commodification, and co-opting of other cultures by White dominant structures. In a theological sense, this is the era in which knowledge is no longer the private domain of those with pedigree and status; instead, it is the era of transmediated deity. It is an information age encasing industry rooted in the digital age and focusing primarily on the glorification of the self through social media spaces.[31] On the other hand, it is also a time when a rapper such as Chance the Rapper can create a masterpiece without the help of major record label. It is the era in which a social media platform such as Twitter helped in the formation of a powerful movement called Black Lives Matter. It is a time when those suffering oppression in Palestine can connect with those suffering similarly in Ferguson, Missouri, and lend advice on how to resist. These are spaces that people of color reclaim through using current technologies. The postindustrial era is developing, and although it is not a term used in missiological literature, it needs to be researched more so that it can be. We are quickly leaving the era in which categorizations fit nicely in the scientific lab; the postindustrial era reshapes how we view the basic elements of the "how" in life.

In addition, it will be helpful to examine a few other definitions to be used with the previous list. The *post-soul context/era* is typically referred to as the boomer generation (1948–1969) but encompasses a much broader multiethnic variable. It is the era of the civil rights generation. This era is steeped in the church and raised on traditional, primarily Protestant Christian,

---

[30]Scholars of urban studies also agree that this term is rapidly changing; see Edward W. Soja, *Postmetropolis: Critical Studies of Cities and Regions* (New York: Blackwell, 2000); William E. Thompson and Joseph V. Hickey, *Society in Focus*, 7th ed. (New York: Pearson Books, 2011); and William H. Whyte, "The Design of Spaces," in *The City Reader*, ed. Richard T. Le Gates and Frederic Stout (New York: Routledge, 1996).

[31]Craig Detweiler, *iGods: How Technology Shapes Our Spiritual and Social Lives* (Grand Rapids: Brazos, 2014), 199-210.

values. Faith and religious overtones mark its norms, values, and belief system in the Christian church—especially the Black Christian church. This era gave us the likes of Marvin Gaye, Aretha Franklin, and Ray Charles. Culturally speaking, life and society seemed to move in a linear process. During this era many strived to achieve the American Dream.[32] Leadership was top-down and singularized—meaning one voice for the masses. This period helped shape a large part of the African American diaspora. It also situated the Black church as an authority and a sociopolitical space for justice and civil protests. Without this period, there would be no Hip Hop, soul, funk, disco, or Black liberation movement.[33]

Still, even with the optimism of Black middle-class life during the 1950s and great hope for the civil rights movement of the 1960s, the post-soul context/era came at a time when Black values in the public sphere were declining and leaders of Black life, iconic even in their own time, were either killed or sent into exile. The following generation was raised in that void and at a time when media was creating tropes of Black life through shows such as *The Jeffersons* (1975–1985) and *Sanford and Son* (1972–1977). This is the era and context, similar to what is termed the *postmodern period*, following the soul era. The post-soul era lost its leadership, and this emerging generation, those born from 1971 on, was disconnected from earlier ones. The youth born during this time were disconnected and disjointed from society. Moreover, with the rise in the absence of Black fathers during this time, Black youth especially found it difficult to adjust to a world not socially, religiously, and morally logical to them.[34] This era created the first Hip Hop generation.[35] This era is the base on which I will build a missiological premise.

A term that attained some traction after Barack Obama was elected as president in 2008 was *post-racial*. This is a false dichotomy created to insist that American society has somehow moved beyond or past the racial divide;

---

[32]See Hodge, *Hip-Hop's Hostile Gospel*, chap. 1; and Hodge, *Soul of Hip Hop*, chap. 2.

[33]Some content in this section was originally published in Daniel Hodge, "The Post-Soul Context," ConversantLife.com, March 13, 2008, www.conversantlife.com/belief/the-post-soul-context-pt-1.

[34]Angela J. Hattery and Earl Smith, *African American Families* (Thousand Oaks, CA: Sage, 2007), 9-37. There is a host of literature discussing the denigration of Black fathers and the creation of the welfare system during the late 1960s and early 1970s.

[35]These concepts will be explored more in chapters 1-2.

in some regard, it is a wishful hope that suggests we—meaning society—no longer see color or race. In this sense, this would mean we overlook the issues of white privilege, white supremacy, and the legacy of racism this country has endured. This book rejects a post-racial society and maintains that the issues of race are even more pronounced in the twenty-first century.

The post–civil rights context/era will be further clarified in chapters one and two, but for now it is the generation of youth born during the post-soul era/context and raised on a transmediated diet, disconnected from previous generations both locally and ideologically, and currently have nonbinary issues to contend with in a post-9/11 society. This generation of youth does not have the binary issues to contend with that the civil rights generation did (e.g., more Blacks in leadership or the right to vote). While those issues are still present, they manifest themselves in a matrix of problems that involve sexuality, socioeconomics, class, and race.

Another sociogeographic term, *suburban*, also needs to be defined. The movement of resources and people to the outer cities is called *suburbanization*. Suburbs are the smaller cities outside a metropolitan area; they vary in size and distance from a central business district (CBD).[36] Wealth, traditional approaches to the American Dream, legacy prosperity, and the concept that "blessings are from God" are encapsulated in the suburbs. It also includes an ideological framework that situates the suburban locale as a desired place to dwell. This framework carries with it a certain manner of division and separation. Suburban areas are noted for having gates, guards, privatized resources, and allocated locations for the demonstration of power and wealth. Yet, ironically, the geographic location of the suburbs is quickly moving back into the city via gentrification, also known as "urban renewal."

Finally, I will define several racial terms used throughout the text. *Black* and *White* are both racialized terminology that are subjective and debated.[37]

---

[36]William A. Darity Jr., "Suburban Sprawl," in *International Encyclopedia of the Social Sciences*, ed. William A. Darity Jr. (Detroit: Macmillan Reference, 2008), 208-9.

[37]I will discuss this further in section one, but color prejudice is part of a much larger issue of racism and oppression. The White gaze on Blackness stems back into precolonial periods when Europeans first laid eyes on central Africans. It was quickly noted that they were inferior and that "their religion was un-Christian; their manner of living was anything but English." In essence, the "Negro" was a lesser being. Early missionaries saw them "in need of God" and European-style education. Winthrop Jordan notes that prior to the sixteenth century *Black* carried connotations of being soiled, muddied, evil, dark, twisted, and foul (from the *Oxford*

However, for the purposes of this book, I use these terms to categorize ethnic groups in a pan-ethnic sense. Throughout the book, when speaking of a specific ethnic group, I will state that group specifically. I also want to make clear that while there is still discord between how those of African heritage living in the United States wish to be defined, I am in no way belittling those definitions. In other words, there are some who desire to be called *African American*, others like the term *Black*, and still others desire to only be referred to as their ethnic heritage. *African American* is typically preferred in academic settings; however, I will use a pan-ethnic term such as *Black*. Thus, *Black* is the racial term to identify anyone from a Pan-African, Afro-Latino, or multiethnic background that appears Black in race. I contend that race is a socially constructed category rooted in colors (e.g., white, brown, yellow, black, and red). *Ethnicity* is, conversely, a biological and a much older term used to identity people and cultural groups much more accurately. *White* is the racial term to identify anyone from a European, Russian, Norwegian, Swedish, or ethnically fair-skinned background. *White* can therefore be understood as "a position in a racialized social structure; that is, it is a label that is meaningless outside a social system where racial categories influence access to social, political, and economic resources and in the absence of other socially constructed identities such as 'black' or 'Asian.'"[38] I assert that race is always on display, while ethnicity can always be hidden; hence the use of these terms.

Racism, then, is set of ideologies, beliefs, and worldviews regarding the superiority of one race over the other. It is rooted in a system that reinforces that doctrine.[39] Such systems include education, criminal justice, health care, the military, the food industry, politics, and religion. The latter is of most importance for this book as it relates to the way in which White

---

English Dictionary). This engrained worldview stretched well into the creation of North American slavery; it saw the African as less than human. This same worldview has continued and created great divides and tensions all in the name of "mission of God." Winthrop D. Jordan, *White Over Black: American Attitudes Toward the Negro, 1550-1812*, Omohundro Institute of Early American History and Culture (Chapel Hill: University of North Carolina Press, 2012), 4-11.

[38]"Whiteness," in *International Encyclopedia of the Social Sciences*, available at Encyclopedia.com, www.encyclopedia.com/social-sciences/applied-and-social-sciences-magazines/whiteness.

[39]Richard Delgado and Jean Stefancic, "Critical Race Theory," in *New Dictionary of the History of Ideas*, ed. Maryanne Cline Horowitz (Detroit: Charles Scribner's, 2005); and Jonathan Marks, "Racism: Scientific," in *Encyclopedia of Race and Racism*, ed. Patrick L. Mason (Detroit: Macmillan Reference, 2013).

missionaries have for centuries gazed on Black bodies. The systemic approach to missions, including funding, social agency, networks, and access
to seminary education, has privileged Whites and given them the advantage
to "present the Gospel" in a one-dimensional manner.[40] Thus Whites, often
unaware, have created a system in which those who are similar may enter
and "do the work." This will be examined further in the coming chapters,
but it is worthwhile to note the use of *racism* and how it will be applied
through this text.

As a qualitative researcher, I am compelled to *tell the story*; while
numbers and hard data has its place, this book will rely heavily on qualitative interviews and narrative methods.[41] The research for this book is
founded on two primary studies I have done. First is research that began
in 2005 while I was completing my doctoral degree at Fuller Seminary
and working with youth in the northwest sector of Pasadena, California.
At that time, at least a dozen white evangelical churches were bringing
their youth groups to the "'hood" to do "mission work" among the "poor
kids" of our community. I began to document the experience and narratives of those being "ministered to," the "'hood kids," as one short-term
missionary kid would later come to say. The first part of this book's research is based on five urban former students/mentees of mine between
2005 and 2010.[42] The makeup of this group was three females and two
males; their ethnic makeup was Mexican American, African American,
Caribbean, and two Euro-Americans. The interviews were conducted

---

[40]Samuel L. Perry, "Social Capital, Race, and Personal Fundraising in Evangelical Outreach Min-
istries," *Journal for the Scientific Study of Religion* 52, no. 1 (2013); Perry, "Diversity, Donations,
and Disadvantage: The Implications of Personal Fundraising for Racial Diversity in Evangelical
Outreach Ministries," *Review of Religious Research* 53, no. 4 (2012); and Perry, "Racial Habitus,
Moral Conflict, and White Moral Hegemony Within Interracial Evangelical Organizations,"
Qualitative Sociology 35, no. 1 (2012).

[41]Some content in this book was originally published in Daniel White Hodge, "Between Selfies
and Colonialism: The Effect of White Evangelical Outreach on Multi-Ethnic Young Adults
Within the Los Angeles Region," *Open Theology* 2, no. 1 (2016): 1018-23, https://doi.org/10.1515
/opth-2016-0079.

[42]While the term *urban* is becoming vaguer by the year, and there is a growing debate about how
the term is applied and to whom in what context, I will limit the use of the word to those who
live in or engage with the issues of poverty, gang violence, single parenthood, low-income housing, lack of adequate education, systemic dysfunction, and violent contexts within families,
communities, neighboring spaces, educational constructs, or community surroundings. While
this definition too can present its racial, gender, and class challenges, it offers the necessary
framework for this research.

bimonthly from 2005 to 2007 and then five times a year thereafter. The interviews and research began in later summer 2005. Semistructured interviews were utilized from 2005 to 2007. From autumn 2007 to 2010 active interviews were used in group settings because all but one of the students had graduated from high school. All the students were living in a gentrified urban-suburban blend and attending a predominantly white/Euro-American affluent church that had once been located in a primarily white/Euro-American community in Southern California. Each of the students started attending the church in early middle school and continued through their early college years. I chose these students for five reasons: (1) they were the most outspoken on issues of race, class, and gender in the group, (2) they each represented an ethnic-minority group, (3) they were each leaders of their respective peers, (4) each had some type of leadership position in their late high school years, and (5) they represented the feelings of many ethnic minorities who did not have the access each of them did to senior leadership.[43] I also worked and my wife volunteered for this ministry organization, and we had access to detailed information in regard to training and background context.[44]

Second is the research I started with my book *The Soul of Hip Hop*, which investigated not just Hip Hop culture but the Hip Hop generation itself. That research, largely qualitative, has grown and continues to develop along with the current racial issues occurring in the country with police terrorism, police brutality, and the continual disdain for Black life. Thus, in the fall of 2011, I began doing active interviews with those in the age range of seventeen to twenty-nine, targeting specifically urban multiethnic young people and emerging adults.[45] I asked open-ended questions such as the following:

---

[43]The interviews began with the prompt, "Tell me about your experience in X ministry organization" and then led to deeper probing questions as respondents gave their answers.

[44]All of the names have been changed in this book to protect the identity of the participants. Further, any identifying names or attributes to the ministry have been removed as well. What follows is not an exhaustive breadth of their experience; rather, using grounded theory, themes and patterns will be highlighted to connect their experiences to the broader issue of what Soong-Chan Rah describes as "Western Cultural Captivity" among White/Euro-American evangelical churches (Rah, *Next Evangelicalism*, 27-44).

[45]This age group is the emerging adult group most research is based on. Further, age twenty-nine is the age when most psychologists now assert that brain development ends and adulthood begins. Last, this is the largest generation of individuals and the group most Christian churches tend to target.

- Tell me your religious affiliation.
- How do you define *Christianity*? *Evangelicalism*?
- How has Hip Hop informed your worldview, if at all?
- How might Hip Hop culture provide a space to think, love, play, pray, and converse?
- How does God speak to you, specifically?
- How do you define *salvation*? *Sin*? *The devil*?
- Where is God, and how does God speak in this current era/generation?

Demographic data was collected, but the heart of the research allowed the participants to speak and direct the story. From this arose these central themes, which will drive this book:

- God is pluralistic in nature.
- Corporate and institutional sin are much greater than individual sin.
- God loves the marginalized.
- Media speaks of God, and media creates a transmediated experience for those seeking God.
- Hip Hop is a way for peace and religious expression.
- Hip Hop is a space and place, theologically, for all, even those considered sinful by other Christians.
- God will not judge humans.
- Jesus is who you make him to be.
- Christianity needs a reboot.
- Ethnic minorities struggle and tend to not identify with evangelicals and evangelicalism.

These themes might present challenges for some evangelical Christians. Yet, missionally speaking, it is exactly where we need to go and be, and where this book takes up exploration.[46] These two research findings will provide the engine for both the thesis and direction of this book.

---

[46]These central themes will add to the core specialization of missiology, which is to contextualize for a current context. See Glenn Rogers, *A Basic Introduction to Missions and Missiology* (Bedford, TX: Mission and Ministry Resources, 2003), 79-81.

The three sections of this book will guide the discussion. The first section, "Elements of an Impaired Missiology," provides an overview of the how and why of this era and generation. This section will present the construction of a post-soul context and also highlight the continuing significance of race, gender, and class for missiologists.

The second section, "A Cultural Exegesis," explores nontraditional pathways to God, which are crucial for missiologists as they develop a relationship with this generation. This section will present the connections between the sacred, secular, and profane, and assert that all three are needed to develop a missiological approach in the post-soul context.

The third section, "Church in the Wild: Unconventional Missiology in the Twenty-first Century," will unpack what a missiology in the wild could look like and what is currently being implemented. This section lays out exploratory concepts from my research and derives its concepts from the interviews, films, songs, and cultural themes of the post-soul context. A strong push will be made toward issues on race, gender, and class in this section, as these are continuing issues within Christian and missiological circles.

The flow of this book illustrates and explores how Hip Hoppers (artists and the broader community), post-soulists, and urban multiethnics who have grown weary of Christianity and construct and develop a post-soul ideology and post-soul theology, which is formed in the social conditions of the urban and ghetto enclave, create a theology and missiological response that is contextual and relevant for this generation. This is useful for those seeking to find a god outside approved pathways and approved theodicies of suffering and violence. This book will utilize a theomusicological approach to the study of Hip Hop and urban popular culture. As the field of missiology develops, it is imperative new methodological frameworks like theomusicology be engaged and utilized.

Established by Jon Michael Spencer, theomusicology is defined as "a musicological method for theologizing about the sacred, the secular, and the profane, principally incorporating thought and method borrowed from anthropology, sociology, psychology, and philosophy."[47] Theomusicology is, as

---

[47]Jon Michael Spencer, *Theological Music: An Introduction to Theomusicology*, Contributions to the Study of Music and Dance (New York: Greenwood, 1991), 3. Theomusicology is a methodological inquiry that seeks to understand the theological inferences within the studied culture's music. This

Cheryl Kirk-Duggan and Marlon Hall state, "Music as spiritual practice . . . [to] hear the challenges and evils in the church and the world as the music reveals."[48] What distinguishes theomusicology from other methods and disciplines, such as ethnomusicology, is that

> its analysis stands on the presupposition that the religious symbols, myths, and canon of the culture being studied are the theomusicologist's authoritative/ normative sources. For instance, while the Western music therapist would interpret the healing of the biblical patriarch Saul under the assuagement of David's lyre as a psychophysiological phenomena, the theomusicologist would *first* take into account the religious belief of the culture for whom the event had meaning. The theomusicological method is therefore one that allows for scientific analysis, but primarily within the limits of what is normative in the ethics, religion, or mythology of the community of believers being studied.[49]

Therefore, the theomusicologist is concerned with multilevel data within the context of the people studied, and subsequently analyzes the material within the proper time, culture, and context in which it was created. This book will encompass not just the music but art and the artists themselves. This will give us a broader picture of the context and allow room for further development and research. Thus a trinary approach to theomusicology utilizes the sacred, the secular, and the profane. It also discloses what spirituality and theology look like within the Hip Hop community.

---

method has been used by scholars to examine other areas of music and popular culture such as sexuality and promiscuity (see, e.g., Angela McRobbie, "Recent Rhythms of Sex and Race in Popular Music," *Media, Culture & Society* 17, no. 2 [1995]; Heidi Epstein, "Re-Vamping the Cross: Diamanda Galas's Musical Mnemonic of Promiscuity," *Theology and Sexuality* 8, no. 15 [2001]), understanding poetry in context (Sandra L. Faulkner, "Concern with Craft: Using Ars Poetica as Criteria for Reading Research Poetry," *Qualitative Inquiry* 13, no. 2 [2007]), understanding the basic elements of Hip Hop spirituality (Jon Michael Spencer, "Rhapsody in Black: Utopian Aspirations," *Theology Today* 49, no. 2 [1992]), to examine the sacred and profane within Black music (Melva Wilson Costen, review of *Protest & Praise: Sacred Music of Black Religion*, by Jon Michael Spencer, *Theology Today* 48, no. 3 [1991]), and examined as a methodology in practice (Stephen A. Reed, review of *Exodus*, by Terence E. Fretheim, *Theology Today* 48, no. 3 [1991]).

[48]Cheryl Kirk-Duggan and Marlon F. Hall, *Wake Up! Hip-Hop, Christianity, and the Black Church* (Nashville: Abingdon Press, 2011), 77.

[49]Spencer, *Theological Music*, 3-4. There is no universal or singular definition of *ethnomusicology*. As William Darity states, several words come to mind for ethnomusicology such as *sound*, *music*, *performance*, *context*, and *culture*. For some it is the study of music in culture, or, more broadly, the study in context (William Darity, "Ethnomusicology," in *International Encyclopedia of the Social Sciences*, 20-22).

Theomusicology rises above simple lyrical analysis and imagines what the artists might be attempting to say. It goes into the complex arena of where the sacred, secular, and profane intersect. This means songs that express an explicit sexuality might, in fact, be connecting to a spiritual realm. Theomusicology broadens the discussion of missions within a post-soul context and asks, "What is a post-soul community saying in the context in which the music, art, album, and artist were created in?" The following considerations are also used in this study in order to provide a clearer picture of Hip Hop's theological construction:

- cultural context
- political climate
- artist's upbringing and background
- album cover and art
- cultural era
- religious landscape
- geographic location[50]

I find it necessary to describe, albeit not exhaustively, the social, cultural, political, theological, and varying geographic conditions in which this music was created, because as missiologists there is a dearth of knowledge about almost all forms of media in the current era. We must not overlook the various eras and societal shifts that gave rise to Hip Hop and urban popular culture. And we must examine their connections, implications, and contributions to missiology for the twenty-first century.

So, let's begin this exploration and give precedent to a more applicable missiological approach to North American missions. I invite you to be challenged and keep an open heart as we explore a newer expanse for missiology scholarship and practice.

---

[50]In *Protest & Praise*, Spencer asserts that these areas are crucial in the understanding of the theological message at the time the song was created.

PART 1

ELEMENTS OF AN IMPAIRED MISSIOLOGY

The English church is like the pattern on wallpaper. Religion is visible, but its meaning has faded, and no longer invites attention.

DAVID KETTLE, "THE HAZE OF CHRISTENDOM"

How do you feel about the Greek god Zeus? That's how I feel about your God.

AGNOSTIC FRIEND QUOTING A MEME ON THE INTERNET

Faith is believing what you know ain't so.

MARK TWAIN, *FOLLOWING THE EQUATOR*

All thinking men are atheists.

ERNEST HEMINGWAY, *A FAREWELL TO ARMS*

The cause of freedom is not the cause of a race or sect, a party or a class—it is the cause of humankind, the very birthright of humanity.

ANNA JULIA COOPER

Christianity: The belief that some cosmic Jewish Zombie can make you live forever if you symbolically eat his flesh and telepathically tell him you accept him as your master, so he can remove an evil force from your soul that is present in humanity because a rib-woman was convinced by a talking snake to eat from a magical tree. Yup. Makes perfect sense.

INTERNET TROPE REGARDING CHRISTIANITY

I think we have to own the fears that we have of each other, and then, in some practical way, some daily way, figure out how to see people differently than the way we were brought up to.

ALICE WALKER, *THE COLOR PURPLE*

THIS SECTION EXAMINES the *how* and *why* of the wild within a post-soul and post–civil rights era. These factors are important because without knowledge of how things happened or why they occur, the same problems can, and often will, be repeated. As missiologists, we are concerned with culture, people, and God's mission (e.g., the Great Commission), so it is important to figure out the present in order to map a future. This section is meant to create a sense of crisis and tension. It maps where we are missiologically and theologically.

Therefore, the chapters present three central themes that will guide the discussion. Chapter one discusses the shift in Christianity over the last fifty years. We will examine existing tropes that have helped in shaping the shift and created a turn in the attitudes toward Christianity. Chapter two will examine the effects of a popular trend among Christian evangelicals: short-term missions. This chapter will look into the narrative from those who were on the receiving end of that mission experience, and argue for the deconstruction of short-term missions as it creates colonialist and imperialistic imprints that move people further from the gospel in the wild.

1

WHAT HAPPENED?

*Christianity and the Theological Turn
of the Twentieth Century*

W**HEN MY DAUGHTER** has an amazing experience or just a good time doing something, she usually wants to repeat the exact same event, such as doing the same things or eating the same food. I do not fault her. I am the same way. I always remember Christmas as a nostalgic, fun event. In my teen years, my mom and I would travel in a Honda Civic, packed to the brim, from Northern California back to my birth town in Menard, Texas, to visit my grandmother. Along the way, we would stop at the same locations, eat at the same dives, and even fill up at the same gas stations. Upon arriving in Menard, I made sure I ate at one of the best burger joints, which would make a hamburger from In-N-Out or Whataburger beg for mercy! My grandmother baked my favorite pies, and every Christmas Eve we traveled to see lights in the neighboring counties. For a few years it was a joyous reliving of events and memories. Psychologically, it was very comforting. But, after a while, some of the places we stopped at were closed or had changed ownership. The restaurant meals tasted different. Not all of the same houses had their Christmas lights up. Gas prices rose. As I got older, my vacation time was not as long as when I was a teenager. I now had ministry responsibilities at home and eventually got married, which ended the yearly trips to Texas. My grandmother aged, her arthritis worsened, and eventually the inevitable happened. She passed away at ninety-one. Aside from her actual death, one of the most difficult things to deal with was the change in our Christmas tradition.

Change is difficult. And nostalgia is a powerful phenomenon.

Change is inevitable. This reminds me of where North American Christianity finds itself at the onset of the twenty-first century. It's a world of change and out-of-routine events. The once-familiar territory of church and evangelism has changed. Those same rest stops are gone, closed forever. The recipe of the once-familiar meal of the church service has changed, and the taste is sour for many. In the wake of these developments, a generation of hypercritical and informed young people has risen, but what appears as a move toward secularization, atheism, and gnosticism is not what is actually happening. Yet the nostalgia for what was remains, and those who cling to denominationalism and fundamental values are hanging on for dear life. Those who desire the "good ol' days" to return are experiencing a sort of culture shock.

How did things end up this way? In many regards, the twentieth century was an unexpected century for Christianity.[1] It was a century of great change, and with the influx of other ethnicities and cultures, Western evangelicalism faced its greatest challenge to its hegemonic authority. Our new information society has helped to shape a society that does not need church services, sermons, or, in many regards, salvation. All of those things have been rated, commented on, and relegated to 140-character posts. North American Christians are facing a multifaceted conglomerate of change.

Missions carries a bad connotation for many. Take, for example, the response to missions from Jimmy, ethnically African American and Mexican American:

> I think most of them folks coming into our neighborhood is full of sh--. I mean, they only come once and then leave. What the f--- is that? I don't think they have any sense of what's going on in the city. None. And to boot, they'z white and trippin. It's like we a zoo for them. You know? Shoot. Missionaries have always been white.[2]

While Jimmy's belief that all missionaries are White may be a bit skewed, it reveals a deep-seated notion that Christianity is equated with being White. The sense that missions is a colonialist activity is not lost on urban young people. Dane, a Native American living in the Midwest, said,

---

[1]Scott Sunquist argues this in his text, yet the point I am making is that while the sociocultural and sociotheological changes are a factor, race and ethnicity also have a role and are often overlooked by White Christian authors, thereby furthering the problem. See Scott W. Sunquist, *The Unexpected Christian Century: The Reversal and Transformation of Global Christianity, 1900–2000* (Grand Rapids: Baker Academic, 2015), 135-52.

[2]Interview by the author, June 2015.

What most missionaries do not realize is that they have yet to reconcile with themselves on their own racist history. We in the Native American communities see them as trespassers in many regards. So, some group or organization trying to do "God's work" is simply a colonialist who wants to check some mark off their Great Commission task list. I do not welcome those who cannot or will not commune with us as a people. But to do that, one must face their past; acknowledge it, right; and then ask for forgiveness of the land, the people, and of God. I have not seen any of that yet.[3]

Friend and colleague Mark Charles has echoed these sentiments regularly to me in conversations we have had regarding missions. He has told me on countless occasions that it is impossible for Whites to realize their own racist tendencies, because racism is like a mental illness. Jerry, a Mexican American male, observed,

I don't think White people like to acknowledge their history. Like, at all really! [*laughs*] I've seen a lot of good Christian White people come through my community over the years here in L.A., but, not once, not once . . . have any of them ever stopped to ask what happened here—why so many cities have Hispanic names? Not once have any of those good-willed people gone deeper with us in the community, about the history of our family here. . . . They just kept coming and coming, but it was like some sort of assembly line, you know [*smiles, then laughs*]. I can't make sense of it. Why come at all? I think White Christians are misled and misguided. They need to acknowledge their own heritage first before they try and come to someone else's and pretend like they're the expert, you know?[4]

Therefore, in this chapter I will lay out the theological, societal, and missiological points of change that have occurred over the last sixty years, which, as this chapter will assert, prepared the way for some of the greatest and momentous changes that have laid the groundwork for the post-soul context. This chapter will join the conversation that Wilbert Shenk, Philip Jenkins, and David Bosch have begun in regards to postmodern and post-Christendom change, and give a picture of the main reasons the twentieth century was in

---

[3]Email interview by the author, August 2015.
[4]Interview by the author, 2013.

fact the most unexpected for Christianity.[5] I will lay out these major changes in trinary form: (1) the emergence of a post–civil rights and post-soul context, which will give an overview of the dynamics of generational change before moving into specifics of the problems of North American Christianity; (2) a "proofing and chaplaincy" Christianity, which will explore the issues within evangelism models and its inherit problem with multiethnic emerging adults; and (3) religiosity and Western confinement of Christianity, which has made Christianity irrelevant to anyone not from a White and affluent context.

THE WHITE SUPREMACY OF MISSIONS

Christianity is an African religion. Christianity was shaped by people of color and theologically developed by what we would now consider ethnic minorities. The roots of Christianity lay in the hearts of people who are dark-skinned, community oriented, and focused on a relationship with God, the earth, and family.[6] Long before the influence of Western thought, Christianity was familial,

---

[5]Shenk, in *The Changing Frontiers of Mission*, gives us an accurate picture of what the cultural changes in the late twentieth century were having on mission and the Christian church. His work here gives credence to the post-millennial context in the early twenty-first century that the Christian church is struggling to comprehend (Wilbert R. Shenk, *Changing Frontiers of Mission*, American Society of Missiology Series 28 [Maryknoll, NY: Orbis Books, 1999], 118-30). *In The Next Christendom*, Jenkins reviews the ethnic and racial changes within Christianity and that the point of Christian growth in the twentieth century is not located in North America but in Asia, Africa, and Latin America. This work is crucial in understanding part of the racial and ethnic changes happening within the Christian church and the resistance to it from White-dominated Christianity (Philip Jenkins, *The Next Christendom: The Coming of Global Christianity* [New York: Oxford University Press, 2011]). Bosch outlines the "contemporary crisis" within the church and what it points toward, which is what I will assert in this chapter: the coming of a postindustrial/post-soul context. Though his argument was made over twenty years ago, it is still accurate today (David J. Bosch, *Transforming Mission: Paradigm Shifts in Theology of Mission*, American Society of Missiology Series [Maryknoll, NY: Orbis Books, 1991], 1-9).

[6]This is well recorded in history. Darlene Clark Hine, William Hine, and Stanley Harrold document the religious aspects of central, western, and northeast African culture. Here, it is revealed just how intricately Christianity was weaved into African culture long before Western White influence (Darlene Clark Hine, William C. Hine, and Stanley Harrold, *The African-American Odyssey*, 4th ed. [Upper Saddle River, NJ: Prentice Hall, 2010], 1:2-26, 80-130). Hine, Hine, and Harrold also describe the elements of a Christian heritage within African culture (Darlene Clark Hine, William C. Hine, and Stanley Harrold, *African Americans: A Concise History*, 5th ed. [Upper Saddle River, NY: Pearson, 2014], 2-33). This is not to suggest that Christianity was the primary religion, but that it was a part of many civilizations. Andrew Walls discusses elements of this as well in Andrew F. Walls, *The Cross-Cultural Process in Christian History: Studies in the Transmission and Appropriation of Faith* (Maryknoll, NY: Orbis Books, 2002). It should be noted that Christianity throughout Africa was contextual and relevant for each country, clan, and tribe. There was not a singular version or message of Christianity—rather, it was a collective faith deeply rooted in Jesus' message and Old Testament prophets.

communal, and dealt with day-to-day life. It was not centered on a "personal relationship" with Jesus. It was much more intuitive, and its followers respected other faiths. This all changed once the faith was centered in Rome.

With this in mind, why are many North American mission organizations still led by White people—particularly White males?[7] Part of what is problematic with this is that many White evangelicals have difficulty both embracing and envisioning anything they did not (1) create or (2) have a strong influence in or on. Therefore, the civil rights movement, for example, is not seen as a Christian evangelical movement. The missiological influence on Christianity originating from ethnic-minority communities is overlooked and not acknowledged. This is a problem in current missiological approaches that creates a wall between people. Whites are oblivious to the issue of historical and present racism, which is deemed nonessential. Yet it is essential to the people groups these missionaries claim to serve. Though I am not a historian, I will briefly discuss some key historical moments that have reinforced racism, colonialism, and vicious ideologies in Christian missions' practice and theology. For this, I will rely on the work of Winthrop D. Jordan as a guide.[8]

The age of discovery, 1500 to 1600, was flawed with outright violence and extreme racism. While some have heralded this period, I, along with other scholars, assert that it had a horrendous effect on native people groups and Africans. Winthrop Jordan notes that "by the early years of the seventeenth century Englishmen had developed a taste for empire and for tales of adventure and discovery."[9] This taste came with a host of problems rooted in

---

[7]While someone might argue this is merely anecdotal and does not equal causation or correlation, I suggest they read William R. Jones, *Is God a White Racist? A Preamble to Black Theology* (Garden City, NY: Anchor, 1973); Peggy McIntosh, "White Privilege: Unpacking the Invisible Knapsack," *Independent School* 49, no. 2 (1990); bell hooks, *Yearning: Race, Gender, and Cultural Politics* (Boston: South End Press, 1990); Samuel L. Perry, "Diversity, Donations, and Disadvantage: The Implications of Personal Fundraising for Racial Diversity in Evangelical Outreach Ministries," *Review of Religious Research* 53, no. 4 (2012); and Samuel L. Perry, "Racial Habitus, Moral Conflict, and White Moral Hegemony Within Interracial Evangelical Organizations," *Qualitative Sociology* 35, no. 1 (2012). I also suggest that those then be applied to mission context; Perry's work is a direct examination into White-led Christian organizations.

[8]For an even greater examination of this important history, I recommend the following works: J. Kameron Carter, *Race: A Theological Account*, American Council of Learned Societies (Oxford: Oxford University Press, 2008); and Willie James Jennings, *The Christian Imagination: Theology and the Origins of Race* (New Haven, CT: Yale University Press, 2010).

[9]Winthrop D. Jordan, *White Over Black: American Attitudes Toward the Negro, 1550–1812*, Omohundro Institute of Early American, History and Culture (Chapel Hill: University of North Carolina Press, 2012), 3.

a twisted and unexamined knowledge of the Bible. Moreover, the fetish and obsession with the "oddity" of Blackness—as many Europeans noted—was already beginning to head in the wrong direction.[10] Jordan continues, "Englishmen found the natives of Africa very different from themselves. Negroes looked different; their religion was un-Christian; their manner of living was anything but English."[11] The assumption of superiority was clear. The European standard of living was held high, and Africans and those from India were unknowledgeable of the "right way." Exploration continued, but with an intent to master and heal African communities. Jordan adds,

> In England perhaps more than in southern Europe, the concept of blackness was loaded with intense meaning. Long before they found that some men were black, Englishmen found in the idea of blackness a way of expressing some of their most ingrained values. No other color except white conveyed so much emotional impact. As described by the *Oxford English Dictionary*, the meaning of *black* before the sixteenth century included, "Deeply stained with dirt; soiled, dirty, foul. . . . Having dark or deadly purposes, malignant; pertaining to or involving death, deadly; baneful, disastrous, sinister. . . . Foul, iniquitous, atrocious, horrible, wicked. . . . Indicating disgrace, censure, liability to punishment, etc." Black was an emotionally partisan color, the handmaid and symbol of baseness and evil, a sign of danger and repulsion.
>
> Embedded in the concept of blackness was it direct opposite—whiteness.[12]

This attitude of superiority would continue long after the dictionary definition was changed in missions. Those categorized as "black" did not always mean ethnically African. Sometimes it meant South American, Indian, or Native American.[13] Because this placed darker-skinned people in a hierarchy, this ideological construct resulted in the subjugation and eventual enslavement of Blacks. Skin color placed those groups below European Whites.

As missionary movements spread southward and westward from Europe, the entanglement with race and Christianity became even more distinct. The concept of Whiteness became the prime factor in being Christian and moral.

---

[10] Ibid., 4-7.
[11] Ibid., 4.
[12] Ibid., 7.
[13] Winthrop D. Jordan, *The White Man's Burden: Historical Origins of Racism in the United States* (London: Oxford University Press, 1980), Kindle ed., loc. 143-289.

In other words, to be White was to be human and Christian.[14] It was the duty, then, of Whites (Europeans) to evangelize the world and help the "savages" in their lost nature.[15] Jordan states,

> In the long run, of course, the Negro's color attained greatest significance not as a scientific problem but as a social fact. Englishmen found blackness in human beings a peculiar and important point of difference. The African's color set him radically *apart* from Englishmen. But then, distant Africa had been known to Christians for ages as a land of men radically different in religion.[16]

The stage was being set, which would affect worldviews for centuries to come. And the age of discovery created an ethos that held anyone of Black skin as inferior and in need of help. The essence of a Christian hegemony was a sentiment of missions in which ethnic minorities and their cultures were seen as inferior. With this sense of inferiority came the heathenistic Native Americans, who needed to be "won" for God.[17] Willie Jennings, discussing White American attitudes toward property and control in relation to Native Americans, says,

> The grid pattern of sellable squares of land signified the full realization of property ownership. It also displayed the complete remaking of indigenous

---

[14]Jones, *Is God a White Racist?*, chaps. 1-5. This particular concept carries on today. The following quote from Reverend Buchner Payne makes this point: "Now as Adam was white, Abraham white and our Savior white, did he enter heaven when he arose from the dead as a white man or as a negro? If as a white man, then the negro is left out; if as a negro then the white man is left out. As Adam was the Son of God and as God is light (white) and in Him is no darkness (black) at all, how could God then be the father of the negro, as like begets like? And if God could not be the father of the blacks because He was white, how could our Savior, 'being the express image of God's person,' as asserted by St. Paul, carry such a damned color into heaven, where all are white, much less to the throne?" (ibid., 258).

This historical ideological construct has multifaceted implications for domestic missions. One element is how to interpret the gospel. How might domestic missionaries respond to racial profiling, police killings of Blacks, Muslim bans, and White racism? Often these go unnoticed, and the sole goal of missionary work becomes "winning souls." Thus, social ills are often passed over and avoided as not part of "ministry" or part of the mission ethos.

[15]White Europeans saw the African religion as "defective" and of no worth; it was heathenism at its highest and therefore in need of the one "true God." Jordan notes that this was cause for proselytizing of the "Negro" for it then became evident that "his religion was in fact defective" (Jordan, *White Over Black*, 20-22).

[16]Jordan, *White Man's Burden*, loc. 189.

[17]Richard Twiss, *Rescuing the Gospel from the Cowboys: A Native American Expression of the Jesus Way* (Downers Grove, IL: InterVarsity Press, 2015), 61-70.

land. Now, under the grid system, each space of land could be surveyed and designated for purchase by measurement and location. All native peoples, no matter what their claims to land, no matter what designations they had for particular places, no matter their history and identity with specific lands, landscape, and indigenous animals, were now mapped on to the grid system.[18]

In many regards, the notion of America being God's chosen land for Whites was deeply embedded in the White imagination. It created a sense of White rights as they gazed at anyone non-White; it created a sense of ownership of both land and body. It created a sense of calling that, with the mandate of western expansion through Manifest Destiny, gave Whites, as God's chosen, the freedom to missionize the lost and create God's kingdom in the image of Whiteness.[19]

By the 1700s, the economic force of indentured servitude had turned into African slavery, which was reinforced by a twisted interpretation of the Bible.[20] Missionizing was set in the context of regulation. Passages in the Bible that discussed injustice, love of neighbor or stranger, and God's love were placed in the trash can.[21] The eighteenth century was one of brute violence; it was a century that juxtaposed freedom from an "oppressor," England, with the brutality of slavery. And Blacks were not considered worth missionizing as much as Native Americans. Dysfunctional in approach, missions to Native Americans was seen as a help to Whites during this century. To this Jordan says,

> Indeed they went so far as to conclude that converting the natives in America was sufficiently important to demand English settlement there. As it turned out, the well-publicized English program for converting Indians produced very meager results, but the avowed intentions certainly were genuine. It was in marked contrast, therefore, that Englishmen did not avow similar intentions concerning Africans until the late eighteenth century. Fully as much as with skin color, though less consciously, Englishmen distinguished between the heathenisms of Indians and of Negroes.[22]

This distinction is important because its sentiments carried over into the nineteenth-century mission ideology in the form of fear. In some regard, the

---

[18]Jennings, *Christian Imagination*, 225-26.
[19]Hine, Hine, and Harrold, *African-American Odyssey*, 140-60.
[20]Jordan, *White Over Black*, 101-2.
[21]To this Jordan discusses the relevant literature and material published to justify Black enslavement. Titles such as *Anglican Humanitarianism in Colonial New York* or *An Appraisal of the Negro* used biblical prooftexts to support slavery (ibid., 180-81).
[22]Jordan, *White Man's Burden*, loc. 207.

missionizing of Black peoples was regarded as making them "too smart" or "aware."[23] Some were converted and placed as literate ministers (e.g., Nat Turner) who were to keep the form of Christianity that kept Blacks oppressed.[24]

Yet, revolts and uprisings were common, particularly during the early 1800s. But the voice of God spoke not only to White men but to Blacks as well. Nat Turner, after prayer and much consideration, saw it as part of the *missio Dei* to kill his White slavers. It was, he believed, part of God's will that death and violence be used as a means of freedom. (This concept is nothing new and is carried out to this day in our modern warfare against "terrorism.")

David Walker's *Appeal* (see fig. 1.1) was, in one sense, a calling to Blacks to take up arms and fight for freedom and justice. The image depicts a Black Moses receiving divine laws guaranteeing liberty and justice. Therefore, it was missionizing Black slaves to come out of darkness and pursue violence as a means of reaching their freedom and liberty—as mandated by God.[25]

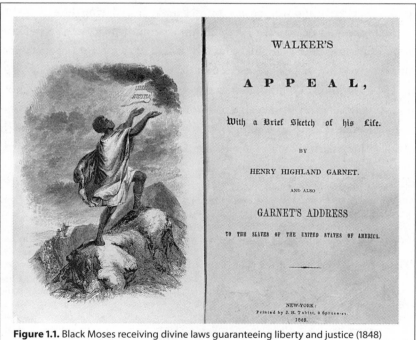

Figure 1.1. Black Moses receiving divine laws guaranteeing liberty and justice (1848)

---

[23]Jordan, *White Over Black*, 181-82.

[24]Today, many ethnic-minority millennials argue that Christianity is the oppressor's religion and not worth inspection because Whites control it and have manipulated it.

[25]Hine, Hine, and Harrold, *African-American Odyssey*, 204-5.

Turner, inspired by Walker's *Appeal* and commissioned to "preach" to Black slaves for better slave production, came to a point where he had a sense of consciousness and enlightenment that led him to do the things he did. This of course created a genuine fear in White slavers, who saw Blacks attaining knowledge and a God that could speak to Blacks.[26] Was slavery therefore justified by the Bible and God?[27] If diplomacy did not work, was the Black now to take up arms and fight for liberty, existence, and freedom?

The notion of freedom through violence has been long debated, yet for many White Christians it was excusable when it was White violence toward an oppressor (e.g., England and the American Revolution). But when Blacks (and Native Americans) used that same construct to pursue their freedom, it was met with fear, blockade, and violence. This created a conundrum for some Christians. A group of Methodists and Quakers in the North began to seriously question the relevance and biblical significance of slavery and violence: "Black men and women also formed auxiliaries during the early 1830s to the Quaker-initiated Free Produce Association, which tried to put economic pressure on slaveholders by boycotting agricultural products produced by slaves."[28] Acts like these combined with denominational splits (e.g., the 1844 Methodist separation over slavery), the ongoing pressure of abolitionists, and slave revolts began a path toward the Civil War. While popular history situates Whites as leading this movement, careful historical research reveals that many Blacks helped shaped the abolitionist movement.[29]

---

[26]Jordan, *White Over Black*, 398-402.

[27]Jordan makes an interesting comment: "What the colonists feared, of course, was the dimly recognized challenge to their distinct status and the mental differentiation upon which it rested. For by Christianizing the Negro, by giving him even the meager crumbs of religious instruction which were prerequisite to baptism, the colonist was making the Negro just so much more like himself. The African's inevitable acquisition of the white settler's language and manners was having precisely this effect. It was virtually inevitable, too, that the colonists should have abhorred the prospect that Negroes might come to resemble them. For if the Negro were like themselves, how could they enslave him? How explain the bid on the block? Slavery could survive *only* if the Negro were a man set apart; he simply had to be different if slavery was to exist at all" (Jordan, *White Man's Burden*, loc. 1121). This tension begin to shift the conversation, but more importantly it created a type of contextualized theology that rooted itself in justice and freedom from a violent oppressor.

[28]Hine, Hine, and Harrold, *African-American Odyssey*, 219.

[29]Numerous Black churches protested slavery in the North (ibid., 214-31). And with the works of Frederick Douglass, Harriet Tubman, Sojourner Truth, Robert Purvis, and even Nat Turner, the movement was far from just White. Yet Whites often see themselves as heroes; thus the supremacy of Whiteness continues (Jordan, *White Man's Burden*; and Jordan, *White Over Black*).

Nevertheless, the narrative posits Whites as saviors and the powerhouse of intellect and virtue—White supremacy knows no bounds.

It is therefore problematic to embrace a perception that missionaries such as John Philip (1175–1851), Donald Fraser (1870–1933), William Carey (1761–1834), and Donald A. McGavran (1897–1990), and even administrators such as Henry Venn (1796–1873) had an untarnished ideology concerning race. Given the power of White supremacy, it was difficult for White men such as these to transcend their own racist views concerning ethnic groups outside of Europe and somehow create a missiology free from racist ideology. And while they might not have been maliciously racist, given the context of how race was developed and the entrenchment of it in the White imagination, the reality is that most of these missionaries carried with them a strong sense of subjective racism toward the other. We have told ourselves that these missionary men and women ministered with great valor, bravery, and courage for the kingdom of God and *missio Dei*. This is true, in some part. Yet given how pervasive attitudes toward ethnic groups were and that there are few writings from those who were not White, male, Western Christians, it is far truer that race had a strong role in missions' engagement with non-Whites. The posthumous view recalls the past in positive light. This is detrimental to Black, Latinx, and other ethnic minorities; it favors Whiteness, glorifies the hope of reconciliation, and overlooks race as a factor in almost everything. The missiological imagination, then, favors White men and excludes ethnic minorities.

Moving forward into the early twentieth century, we see Christian missions moving into the furthest reaches of the world. These mission agencies, however, were controlled by White men. Thus, even though a civil war had "freed the slaves" and created a sense of liberty for not just Blacks but also other ethnic minorities, theology remained solely in control of Whites. Christianity had lost its Afrocentric roots and became one of personal salvation and winning souls. The early 1900s witnessed an explosion of evangelical thought that gave precedence to the European mind and theology. German, French, and English theologians dominated seminary classrooms. This was not accidental. The notion that ethnic minorities were inferior remained; Blacks needed saving, but for them to be theologians was absurd. White Christianity carried on as if it were *the* religion and all others were "contextual." But change was coming—change that would create a new theological continuum and re-create the Christian imagination. The mid-twentieth century was a time of ideological, theological, and epistemological change.

THE EMERGENCE OF A POST-SOUL CONTEXT
AND SHIFTING TIDE FOR THE CHURCH

It is no mystery that a cultural, societal, political, and ideological shift has taken place within the last sixty years. The prefix *post* is affixed to words such as *modernism, millennial,* and *Christian. Post* has found its way into many Christian scholars' work—including my own. Something happened, and ground zero for this shift occurred after WWII.[30] In the 1950s the collective imagination of the dominant culture created archetypal religious themes, such as the following:

- Moral authority and dominion of men (White, heterosexual, and affluent)

- The Christian church as the sending agent to the world[31]

- Morality and values rest with the homogenous family from America

- Father knows best, or at least has the privilege to do so

- America is God's nation

- America is the moral and religious authority for all nations

- America is a model for what is "right" and "just" (e.g., the winning of WWII and salvation of Jewish people from Nazi Germany)

- Christianity is the authoritative religion in the United States and the moral proxy for the country

---

[30]David Sills notes that there was a rapid growth in missionaries post-WWII and leading into the 1960s. This was one of the largest growths for missiology as the discipline was being developed. See David Sills, "Missiology in a Changing World Since World War II," a paper delivered at the Future of the Discipline of Missiology, American Society of Missiology, Chicago, 2012, 1-2. Also see Brian M. Howell, *Short-Term Mission: An Ethnography of Christian Travel Narrative and Experience* (Downers Grove, IL: IVP Academic, 2012), 45-65.

[31]For an overview of how North American Christians felt about being the "sender" society, read Harvie M. Conn, *Reaching the Unreached: The Old-New Challenge* (Phillipsburg, NJ: P&R, 1984); David MacDonald Paton, *Christian Missions and the Judgment of God* (London: SCM Press, 1953); and Donald A. McGavran, *Effective Evangelism: A Theological Mandate* (Phillipsburg, NJ: P&R, 1988). Today, as Jenkins and others contend, that paradigm has and is vastly changing (see Jenkins, *Next Christendom*).

- Faith and family, from a heteronormative perspective, are normative

- White male dominance and chief power structure for religious and missional authority

World War II marks the last "just war" for our country and a time when simplicity, binary ways of life (e.g., right is right, wrong is wrong, sin is clear, and morality is the pathway), Christianity/faith, and a conservative view of life were prevalent.[32] It was a time when mission-sending churches saw themselves as moral managers for "spreading the gospel." The era following WWII created the United States as a popular global police force. Religiously, the growth of the megachurch, the expansion of churches into the suburbs (e.g., White flight), and the development of professionalized ministry led to a commodified Christianity. The United States and its churches experienced tremendous economic growth from 1945 to 1958.[33] It began what has come to be known as the Christian marketplace, in which Christian material wealth created a marketplace for training, methods, and evangelism; some have called this the McDonaldization of the church.[34] For White, heteronormative Christians, and especially those who were middle to upper-middle class, life was good. Life was a foretaste of what the kingdom of God might be. This time period signified a zenith of Christian values for White Christians and provided a way of life that became synonymous with being blessed and having favor with God.

I would be remiss if I did not mention the contributions and social significance of the Black church. As a haven and theological space for Blacks, the Black church provided the framework for civil disruption. It was the

---

[32]It was the last time that the US Congress enacted the war powers and declared war on a country. All other "wars" since have been defined as "operations," "maneuvers," or "missions." WWII also established the United States as the chief police officer of the world. Images and cinematic events reflected these social mores as well and created a paradigm that many, especially those who are White and conservative, desire to return to (see Norman K. Denzin, *Images of Postmodern Society: Social Theory and Contemporary Cinema* [Thousand Oaks, CA: Sage, 1991]).

[33]See Stephen B. Bevans and Roger Schroeder, *Constants in Context: A Theology of Mission for Today* (Maryknoll, NY: Orbis Books, 2004), 239-79, for a detailed look into the sociopolitical, religious, and institutional context of the Christian church between the years of 1919 and 1991.

[34]This argument is made clear in the works of John William Drane, *The McDonaldization of the Church: Spirituality, Creativity, and the Future of the Church* (London: Darton Longman & Todd, 2000), and George Ritzer, *The McDonaldization of Society* (Thousand Oaks, CA: Pine Forge Press, 2000). I believe that the growth of marketplace Christianity—books, Bibles, jewelry, and the like—is a relic of a McDonaldized faith.

locale within most Black communities that served as a moral compass for those communities.[35] These spaces, while not all utopian, were the incubator for protest and praise. The Black church was the backbone of the soul era. It provided the foundation for singers such as Aretha Franklin, Stevie Wonder, and the Temptations. The Black church stood as a civil rights generation icon and still provides a space for those still living from that generation. The time was hardly utopian. The great social ethics professor Peter J. Paris tells us that many of the causes within the White church (e.g., prohibition, temperance, sexual laxity, divorce, revivalism) also became causes in the Black church.[36] This became problematic because the focus of the Black church was to create "law-abiding respectable citizens." However, the soft nationalism of Black churches did nothing for race relations. Many Black ministers hoped that Whites would be convicted of their sin of racism through the gospel of Jesus and thus change. As Paris observes, "Thus, ironically, the long years of commitment to 'racial uplift' on the part of the black churches were destined to nonfulfillment, because their ideal vision contradicted the idea of a separate racial development. Black churches have been guided more by their ideal vision of a racially integrated society than by the idea of racial development."[37] This notion of racial development and integration would create contention decades later in younger generations. But it was a strong hope for the soul-era generation and context. Still, the Black church was a formidable power structure that fought the "last battle of the Civil War."

But the 1960s created a disruption, and the ensuing civil rights movement, which was rooted in evangelical Christianity, began to create a rift in the ideals of American Christians.[38] The 1960s also saw the creation of electronic

---

[35]Peter J. Paris, *The Social Teaching of the Black Churches* (Philadelphia: Fortress Press, 1985), 6-9.
[36]Ibid., 44.
[37]Ibid., 45.
[38]I am not suggesting that major uprisings such as the Farm Workers Rights Movement or the disruption of the Bracero Program, which displaced thousands of legal Mexican immigrant workers, did not create disruptive tones in this era. These were important too, but in many regards the issues behind them remained hidden and isolated rather than systemic societal and structural problems that Christians needed to actively address. For Black Americans, this was a sort of awakening for the Black social church. For an exhaustive look at the contributions of the Black church during this era and how the social and protesting voice of the Black church was developed, see James H. Evans Jr., *We Have Been Believers: An African-American Systematic Theology* (Minneapolis: Fortress Press, 1992); John Hope Franklin and Alfred A. Moss Jr., *From Slavery to Freedom: A History of African Americans*, 8th ed. (New York: McGraw Hill, 2000); E. Franklin Frazier and Nathan Glazer, *The Negro Family in the United States* (Chicago: University

grids that would later make way for the information age and the Internet, the development of marketplace knowledge beyond libraries, and the creation of information in transmediated forms (e.g., news shows). These gave the US population a sort of awakening to the harsh truth of injustice, disinheritance, and social anomie for many of its ethnic-minority citizens.[39] The baby-boomer generation came of age in the 1960s. And their ideals laid the foundation for five points of the main post-soul taxonomy:

1. questioning moral authority

2. disruption of normative ideologies

3. movement away from ideals about faith, religion, and spirituality established after WWII

4. civic and societal intolerance of inequality and racism

5. voices from the marginalized

This post-soul taxonomy is alien to the Christianity of the 1950s. And while ideally we could imagine that progress would dictate change in the Christianity of the 1950s, many of those religious idealistic conservative principles, if not all in some regard, are still present today. They drive a lot of political discourse, clinging to denominationalism, fear of and panic over the loss of morality in society, and how many evangelicals theologize today. To explain further, I will briefly deconstruct the post-soul era and its significance for the turn in Christianity in the twentieth century.

The work of scholars such as Mark Anthony Neal, Michael Eric Dyson, and Nelson George, as well as my own, use a more contextual term for what has come to be known as postmodernism: *post-soul*.[40] Post-soul is a

---

of Chicago Press, 1966); Alphonso Pinkney, *Black Americans*, 5th ed. (Upper Saddle River, NJ: Prentice Hall, 2000); and Anthony B. Pinn, *Terror and Triumph: The Nature of Black Religion* (Minneapolis: Fortress, 2003). I believe this is part of the backbone, both theologically and ideologically, of the post-soul generation.

[39]See Sally Richards, *Futurenet: The Past, Present, and Future of the Internet as Told by Its Creators and Visionaries* (New York: Wiley, 2002).

[40]See Mark Anthony Neal's books: *New Black Man* (New York: Routledge, 2005); *Soul Babies: Black Popular Culture and the Post-Soul Aesthetic* (New York: Routledge, 2002); *What the Music Said: Black Popular Music and Black Public Culture* (New York: Routledge, 1999). See Michael Eric Dyson, *Holler If You Hear Me: Searching for Tupac Shakur* (New York: Basic Civitas, 2001). See also Nelson George's books: *Where Did Our Love Go? The Rise and Fall of the Motown Sound*, 2nd ed., Music in the American Life (Chicago: University of Illinois Press, 2007); and *Buppies, B-Boys, Baps & Bohos: Notes on Post-Soul Black Culture* (New York: HarperCollins, 1992). Finally,

rejection of soul-era values, traditions, metanarratives, theological accounts, and societal structures stemming from hierarchal systems attempting to control various societal areas.[41] Nelson George contends that "documenting the post-soul era is not about chronicling the straight line of a social movement, but collecting disparate fragments that form not a linear story, but a collage."[42] Further, the post-soul vernacular better suits the Black and Brown social structure.[43] Mark Anthony Neal tells us that "the political, social, and cultural expressions of the African-American community since the civil rights and Black Power movements" is essentially the point of birth for the post-soul era.[44] Neal notes that the persons born or raised during this era came of age during the tumultuous 1980s, witnessed Reaganomics and its destructive forces in the 'hood, experienced change from industrialism to deindustrialization, experienced the move from segregation to desegregation, and went from strong notions of Blackness to nostalgic metanarratives of Blackness.[45]

Therefore, the term *post-soul* encompasses the aforementioned issues and also embraces the significance of race, class, and gender. Post-soul is the cradle in which Hip Hop created its theological and spiritual sensibilities and formed its ideological positions.[46]

---

see Daniel White Hodge, "Hip Hop's Prophetic: Exploring Tupac and Lauryn Hill Using Ethnolifehistory," in *Religion in Hip Hop ("the Volume")*, ed. Monica R. Miller, Bernard Freeman, and Anthony B. Pinn (London: Bloomsbury Academic, 2015); Daniel White Hodge, "No Church in the Wild: Hip Hop Theology & Mission," *Missiology: An International Review* 40, no. 4 (2013); and Daniel White Hodge, *The Soul of Hip Hop: Rims, Timbs and a Cultural Theology* (Downers Grove, IL: InterVarsity Press, 2010).

[41]See J. Andrew Kirk, "Following Modernity and Postmodernity: A Missiological Investigation," *Mission Studies* 17, no. 1 (2000); and Cornel West, *Race Matters* (Boston: Beacon Press, 1993).

[42]As argued by Nelson George, *Post-Soul Nation: The Explosive, Contradictory, Triumphant, and Tragic 1980s as Experienced by African Americans (Previously Known as Blacks and Before That Negroes)* (New York: Viking, 2004), ix.

[43]Paul C. Taylor, "Post-Black, Old Black," *African American Review* 41, no. 4 (2007); and George, *Post-Soul Nation*.

[44]Neal, *Soul Babies*, 3.

[45]Neal also contends that the post-soul era could be feasibly documented in its emergence with the rise of the 1980s "Reagan Right." Because of this, Neal argues that Reagan's policies further helped to instigate the advent of Hip Hop music, and culture as Hip Hop became the most visible site of an already hostile and oppositional urban youth culture (ibid., 102-3).

[46]Admittedly, *post-soul* is still under development, and, in the postmodern spirit, we must recognize that a singular term will not do justice to the current era.

Christians to want to prove they were right and on God's side.[73] In turn, a type of crisis was created that was also conflated with the development of an individualized faith that made God personal and individualized—your relationship with God is about you and no one else. While there are aspects about that that are good, historically Christianity grew as a communal faith more focused on the development of people and community; the shift was the result of the rise of enlightenment individualism.[74] This crisis drove evangelism and church growth for over a century and gave way for American exceptionalism,[75] a term used to describe the belief that the United States is an extraordinary nation with a special role to play in human history; a nation not only unique but also superior because of God and his provisions for that nation.[76] Therefore, *missions* to those who are in need, lost, and, for many centuries, non-White, is not only acceptable but expected—even at the expense of colonialism and racism.[77]

So proof is a powerful component of Christian theology. This trope has helped create seminary curriculum, Bible tracts, and countless Christian art forms designed to prove God is real and convince those who do not believe.

---

[73]This is a notion that says, "I am right, and I'm right because I am with God." Knowledge is at the center of this too: the more you know and the more *they* know, the better chance the gospel has to take hold. See Zygmunt Bauman, "Postmodern Religion?," in *Religion, Modernity and Postmodernity*, ed. Paul Heelas (Malden, MA: Blackwell, 1998); Daniel Bell, *The Coming of a Post-Industrial Society: A Venture in Social Forecasting* (New York: Basic Books, 1973); David J. Bosch, *Transforming Mission: Paradigm Shifts in Theology of Mission*, American Society of Missiology Series (Maryknoll, NY: Orbis Books, 1991); Don Cupitt, "Post-Christianity," in Heelas, *Religion, Modernity and Postmodernity*; George, *Post-Soul Nation*; Angela S. Nelson, "Theology in the Hip-Hop of Public Enemy and Kool Moe Dee," in *The Emergency of Black and the Emergence of Rap*, ed. Jon Michael Spencer (Durham, NC: Duke University Press, 1991); and Taylor, "Post-Black, Old Black."

[74]Soong-Chan Rah, *The Next Evangelicalism: Freeing the Church from Western Cultural Captivity* (Downers Grove, IL: InterVarsity Press, 2009), 35-42.

[75]John Wilsey gives an excellent examination on American exceptionalism and provides insight into the development and construct of a "chosen nation" along with the effects of such an ideology (John D. Wilsey, *American Exceptionalism and Civil Religion: Reassessing the History of an Idea* [Downers Grove, IL: IVP Academic, 2015], 92-117). For an overview of the effects of American exceptionalism see Twiss, *Rescuing the Gospel from the Cowboys*, 61-90.

[76]Trevor B. McCrisken, "Exceptionalism," in *Encyclopedia of American Foreign Policy*, ed. Richard Dean Burns, Alexander DeConde, and Fredrik Logevall (New York: Charles Scribner's, 2002). Relics from the Manifest Destiny mantra "God with us" and "God has called us to . . ." gave many Whites agency to do "God's will and work" for the betterment of the kingdom. Thus, the notion that the United States is in fact "God's nation" is merely mythical and part of a colonialist ideology for most ethnic minorities; Hine, Hine, and Harrold, *African-American Odyssey*, 214-27.

[77]Bosch, *Transforming Mission*, 290-91.

Proof that there is a God. Proof that our version of Christianity works. Proof that God will do what he says. Proof that if you do not accept Christ as your Savior, you will go to hell. *Proof.* While proof is a concept from both the Enlightenment and modern eras, it remains a core aspect of Western Christianity because as churches developed in the late 1950s, church growth was predicated on convincing people that God that was real and living. Take, for instance, Donald McGavran's church growth model:

> (1) an emphasis on making disciples over securing decisions; (2) the use of sociological research to analyze data, discern receptivity, set goals, and design strategies; (3) a recognition that context and culture—not ecclesiastical tradition —properly determine the methods employed; (4) an acceptance of the fact that people most naturally trust and converse with others like themselves (the homogeneous unit principle); (5) an appreciation of the indigenous church as God's instrument for evangelizing all peoples; and (6) an optimism based on case studies from around the world.[78]

The model, as it developed, utilized social science to further prove and grow congregations. Yet these are still grounded in proof. Proof suggests that one side must be wrong and the other right; one has the truth while the other is lost. Proof has driven evangelistic curricula. The drive to prove what is "right" and "wrong" created a church that sought to be "right" and not "wrong" at every turn. The foundation, of course, is that because Christianity has truth from God, which is rooted in the Bible, it cannot be wrong. If God is on our side, who can be against us? And the goal is to "win" others *out there*, and to bring them *in here* so they can be saved. Salvation is predicated on the proof that people need to be changed by the truth in order to enter the church and be properly related to God.

Almost all of the ethnic minorities I interviewed and engaged with over the last decade had a negative experience with *proof.* God did not "show up" the way they were told; just praying about something did not solve the crisis. Further, the "proof" that God would protect is questioned by groups such

---

[78]Ronald K. Crandall, "Church Growth Movement," in *Contemporary American Religion*, ed. Wade Clark Roof (New York: Macmillan Reference, 1999). In addition, Soong-Chan Rah suggests that these church-growth-movement principles tend to emphasize the Great Commission over the Greatest Commandment to love your neighbor and love God as yourself. In other words, personal salvation is triumphant over the power of the gospel to transform systemic racism or inequality (Rah, *Next Evangelicalism*, 95).

as Black Lives Matter, Black Youth Project, and Ferguson Action, to name just a few. Their tongue-in-cheek attitude is that God's "hedge of protection" must be for Whites and those God deems worthy. For social action groups such as these, and for many ethnic minorities, proof of God is simply not enough to sustain faith. Perhaps the current disillusionment with Christian faith is because of the concept of proving.

Let's turn now to the chaplaincy model, which has a long legacy in Christendom and views the church-culture relationship from a nonmissional perspective.[79] It tends to see all forms of culture not associated with a Christianity as secular (not of God). Popular culture, including Hip Hop, are worldly and need to be redeemed, or "saved." References "to them" and "out there" combined with a need for "winning souls" arise frequently in the chaplaincy model. Using proof as its thesis, the chaplaincy model engages the world merely to grow, build, or develop the church's flock. I believe it avoids culture and focuses on all things Christian. Anything of the "world" is not of God and therefore should be avoided.

The "lost" are seen as projects to be won for God. Relationships are developed with the goal that the "lost" person will eventually give their life to the Lord. If the person does not respond positively, it is time to cut them off. The following conversation illustrates this. It's an interview with a young church-planting pastor who was doing door-to-door evangelism in his neighborhood.

> **PASTOR:** You have to dust the dirt off your feet sometimes when doing the Lord's work.
>
> **INTERVIEWER:** Can you explain a little more what that means?
>
> **PASTOR:** Yes. I mean that these people I'm out here talking to are stiff-necked and hardhearted when it comes to the Word of God. I've spent the last two weeks going street by street spreading the Word of God, and no one has responded.
>
> **INTERVIEWER:** I see. Have you had any prior contact with this community or neighborhood?
>
> **PASTOR:** No.

---

[79]See Wilbert R. Shenk, ed., *The Transfiguration of Mission: Biblical, Theological and Historical Foundations*, Missionary Studies 12 (Scottdale, PA: Herald Press, 1993); and Shenk, *Changing Frontiers of Mission.*

INTERVIEWER: Okay. Sounds like you just went in cold?

PASTOR: Of course not. I had God on my side and the Holy Spirit. . . . When people don't respond to the truth, that which is the Word of God, then that's on them, the person. You know? I mean, God's Word is the living Word and a word that needs no defense. These people in that neighborhood are lost, and it's now on them.

INTERVIEWER: Have you tried to spend some time in that community? Maybe develop a relationship with a family or person?

PASTOR: Listen, God has called me to spread his Word. I don't have time for relationships or making "friends" [*signals air quotes*]. I'm here to spread the Word of God. Let him who hears, hear the Word![80]

This type of chaplaincy is typical of modern Christian evangelism. While the intent may be fair and good, the impact of merely wanting to convert without ever knowing or having a relationship is not.

The chaplaincy model condones religiosity and the status quo in the church. Adhering to tradition is crucial to maintaining what is perceived as Christian.[81] Events such as public prayer, funerals, weddings, births, and confirmation are a part of chaplaincy too. They offer just enough public engagement for the chaplaincy model to appear to be open to "the other," yet there is no real connection to deeper issues such as police brutality, systemic racism, or the harmful effects of the centrist position.

The "personal" gospel and salvation are at chaplaincy's core, not systemic, structural, and societal problems. This was true of Billy Graham's ministry, which is the archetypal chaplaincy—bring people to the cross and the rest will "solve itself."[82] For Graham, issues such as racism are a

---

[80]Interview with author, November 2010.

[81]This does not mean I am against tradition or that tradition is problematic for multiethnics or for this era. I am suggesting, though, that a strict adherence to tradition without the space for change or vision for forward movement is problematic. Later in the book, I will make the case for respecting tradition in conjunction with intergenerational contexts.

[82]It is not my intention to negate the ministry of Billy Graham or to undermine his place in contemporary church history. Yet his message, theology, and views on society—especially as channeled through his son Franklin—do not embody any of the ideas, morals, principles, and especially theology of the post-soul generation. So Graham stands as more of a symbol for chaplaincy and a representative of what was, not what is or will be, for the future of Christianity. For Graham, "racial intolerance" was part of the "sin" problem, and therefore not something to focus on. As he stated, "racism [and all social injustice] is not a social/structural issue; it is merely a symptom of sin" (quoted in Greg Barker, *God in America: How*

human "sin problem," something that could be resolved if enough people heard the gospel and became Christian. In a 1963 *New York Times* article, Graham was noted as telling Martin Luther King Jr. to "put the brakes on a little" in connection with the civil rights movement.[83] Graham assumed King was much too radical and needed to pull back on his efforts for justice and equality. "What I would like to see now is a period of quietness, in which moderation prevails," Graham said. In response to the continued sit-ins and arrests, he said, "I seriously doubt, from what I have heard from friends, the negro community supports it."[84] When asked in public about segregation, some of which was happening in his own crusades, Graham avoided the questions and continued to "pray" for the "healing of the nation."[85]

Thus, there was no need to protest the segregation of Blacks at his own crusade or to pressure the president for the civil rights of Blacks. There was no need to attend to the economic inequality growing among Black and Latino populations of the 1960s, because God's plans were bigger. Chaplaincy demands a centrist position and a nondisruptive social position; this was Graham's perspective during the nation's most tumultuous civil unrest since the Civil War. In the chaplaincy model, the church is normative and should be seen as a public institution, but it should not speak too often on issues regarding inequality. Hence, Graham's crusades, focused on proving Christianity, did not speak of the treatment of Blacks, the struggle for women's rights, or the death of prominent civil rights leaders. There was no call from Graham's camp for the government to act. Graham's voice and ideology is similar to responses from White evangelicals today toward the protests and uprisings in places such as Ferguson and Baltimore.[86]

Religious Liberty Shaped America, PBS, 2010).

[83]Foster Hailey, "Billy Graham Urges Restraint in Sit-Ins," *New York Times*, April 18, 1963.

[84]Ibid.

[85]Billy Graham, in Barker, *God in America*.

[86]This is misleading in some regard. Social issues such as abortion, gay marriage, prayer in schools, and a perceived "lost voice" of the Christian right are touted as *the* issues of the Christian faith. Voices typically emerging from the right focus on these issues as more important than, say, police brutality. For issues such as these, the Christian "voice" is very loud and seems to have resources to help fund comprehensive campaigns against what is felt as a marginalization of the Christian faith in America.

The chaplaincy model desires a peaceful road and a centrist response to issues such as inequality and disenfranchisement. By referring to Christian "chaplains," I don't mean the actual profession of chaplaincy but rather a form of caretaking of Christianity where a "centrist" position is taken on most issues except for core issues (which I will define momentarily). Those leaders who embrace the chaplaincy model are beholden to their stake-holders (i.e., donors), who, in typical fashion, tend to be older, male, White, and conservative. Current issues that negatively affect multiethnics, such as police brutality, racism, and profiling, are not issues a chaplain is willing to engage. For chaplains, the core issues are the following:

- the authority of the Bible
- sin and salvation
- human sexuality
- abortion
- creation versus evolution
- prayer in schools
- gun rights

All other issues are "sin" related. But phrases such as, "We live in a fallen world," or, "Sin is at the heart of the matter," are not acceptable to our current generation. Thus, the chaplaincy model of Christianity combined with the need to prove it is "right" are the reasons Christianity is losing ground among multiethnics and those in the wild. These two positions have para-lyzed many into thinking Christianity is static and singular, something the current generation neither agrees with nor embraces.

Now we will turn to the third motif that gave Christianity an unexpected turn in the twentieth century: the Western confinement of Christianity.

WESTERN CONFINEMENT OF CHRISTIANITY

Emerging from the post-soul shift and proofing-chaplaincy model is a par-alyzing notion that (1) America is God's favored nation (e.g., exception-alism) and (2) conservative religiosity will somehow "win" souls. Thus, views represented by sayings such as "Make America great again," "Taking back our country," "America has lost its way," and "America is the immoral harlot" are popular among both politicians and Christian leaders who want to prove something about a "lost" or "immoral" generation or culture. These represent an ideological structure, worldview, and social construct, and are often codes for

- making America White again (underlying the theme of Donald Trump's political campaign, "Make American Great Again");

- taking back our country back from immigrants (conservative evangelicals views on immigration and undocumented people groups, especially from Black and Brown countries);

- the belief that America has lost its White roots (the alt-right's view of what is happening to White America);

- the belief that America is much too liberal, and liberalism is akin to sin (many current views regarding a leftist perspective); and

- a desire to return to (fill in the blank of a perceived era of innocence).

Obviously, these do not encompass or include ethnic minorities. These tropes are exclusionary and mean little to most in a post-soul context.[87] Moreover, ethnic-minority theology, ideals, worldviews, and Christianity are foreign to White majority culture and Christianity. A theology rooted, for example, in Black liberation theology or womanism presents an obstruction of Euro-centric ideas, theology, spirituality, culture, and way of living; it disrupts the norm in faith expression, demanding that it be heard and respected.[88] Yet these new movements are precisely what is needed in order to purge ourselves from the Christian religiosity of the

---

[87]In my research, nine out of ten Black and Latino young adults felt that the current "American Dream" idea did not include them. Further, Black millennial youth tend to look very negatively on Christianity and evangelicalism, stating these institutions do not make room for them or their cultural heritage, and that their image of Jesus was not a Jesus they could embrace.

[88]The Pew Research study on American values had similar findings. More than seven in ten White evangelical Protestants (72%), white mainline Protestants (73%), and White Catholics (71%) believe that killings of Black men by police are isolated incidents. Contrast that with eight in ten (82%) Black Protestants who believe those same police killings of Black men are part of a broader pattern of systemic injustice. Robert P. Jones et al., "Anxiety, Nostalgia, and Mistrust: Findings from the 2015 American Values Survey," Public Religion Research Institute, Washington, DC, 2015, 25-28.

twentieth century. However, far too often, religiosity rooted in a Western confinement of Christianity is dominant.[89]

Philip Jenkins gives us an accurate picture of this ethnic and cultural change:

> Over the last century, however, the center of gravity in the Christian world has shifted inexorably away from Europe, southward, to Africa and Latin America, and eastward, toward Asia. Today, the largest Christian communities on the planet are to be found in those regions. If we want to visualize a "typical" contemporary Christian, we should think of a woman living in a village in Nigeria, or in a Brazilian *favela*. In parts of Asia too, churches are growing rapidly, in numbers and self-confidence.[90]

The growth of Christianity and its "center of gravity"—as Jenkins states— is no longer centered in a European, Greek, Western cultural landscape:

> Over the last five centuries, the story of Christianity has been inextricably bound up with that of Europe and European-derived civilizations overseas, above all in North America. Until recently, the overwhelming majority of Christians have lived in white nations, allowing some to speak of "European Christian" civilization.[91]

Christianity has been the narrative of those of European and White ancestry. Male dominated in many respects, Christian knowledge derives itself from a White notion of supremacy and dominance, and regards

---

[89]There is also a strong contention that White Christian America is losing its power and place. Therefore, the feeling of imminent loss causes a shift of cultural mores toward what can be seen as religious, but it is driven by fear of ethnic-minority ascension into power positions once held by Whites. For White Christians, there are symbolic shifts that mark the decline, according to Robert P. Jones: "Training the camera on White Christian America's monuments to its own power reveals similar social transformations. White Christian America's story can be read in the changing uses of three iconic structures: the United Methodist Building in Washington, D.C.; the Interchurch Center on New York City's Upper West Side; and the Crystal Cathedral in Garden Grove, California. These buildings, edifices of the white Protestant Christian hope and power that rose and receded over the course of the twentieth century, represent—respectively—the high-water mark of the first wave of white mainline Protestant denominational optimism in the Roaring Twenties, the second wave of white mainline Protestant ecumenism at midcentury, and the third wave of white evangelical Protestant resurgence in the 1980's." Combined with White fear, White racism, and intercultural ignorance, Jones argues that this trend of power loss can be traced right up to the 2016 election. Robert P. Jones, *The End of White Christian America* (New York: Simon & Schuster, 2016), Kindle edition, loc. 70.
[90]Jenkins, *Next Christendom*, 1-2.
[91]Ibid.

anything outside of "Christian theology" as the other.[92] Therefore, missions from this perspective connotes the White Western confinement of Christianity, which spreads this dominance further. For example, when Kenyan pastors attempted to implement the principles of Rick Warren's *The Purpose Driven Church* in their context,[93] the result was a failure on many levels. The churches in the Kenyan location were not from an affluent suburban location and therefore could not relate to the issues raised in the book. Kenyans are communal, so the book's individualistic view of personal salvation was foreign to them. This is just one example of what does not work.

White evangelicalism has run its course for those in ethnic-minority contexts living in the wild.[94] In the interviews I conducted, ethnic minorities had the following responses when discussing their church experience in Christian settings:

- The music is too White.

- Why is Jesus always White?

- Could it be that people in Africa have something to say about salvation too?

- Is it only dead Germans that make good theologians?

- When can we have a Christianity that keeps up with modern times?

- I think even the Black churches got White theology in them; how could they have avoided not being tainted by that?

---

[92]"Christian theology" here refers to that stemming from a White evangelical perspective. The others are those typically exoticized and assumed to be adjuncts to the "Christian story," such as Black liberation theology, womanism, Asian third-eye theology, and Latin American liberation theology.

[93]It is no surprise that Kenyans, along with many other Africans, view the American Christian marketplace in both high regard and as "gospel." In turn, the commodities that are exported do not always carry over to the Kenyan (or other's) context; many of the philosophies, principles, and theories do not match their setting. This makes yet another reason why those contexts need their own Christian theology and educators to create relevant and appropriate material for that community.

[94]See Richard Twiss's discussion of White evangelicalism's limitations among Native American people groups. He argues that even the terminology of "missions" and "going forth" is racist, pejorative, and demeaning. I would add that this is the case for many Black and Latinx ethnic minorities too, and that an organization such as Black Lives Matter provides more theology in one protest than a whole year's worth of church services that follow a White evangelical motif (*Rescuing the Gospel from the Cowboys*, 158-62).

Jenkins observes, "Europe is demonstrably *not* the Faith. The era of Western Christianity has passed within our lifetimes, and the day of the Southern churches is dawning. The fact of change itself is undeniable: it has happened, and will continue to happen."[95]

Thus, White Western confinement of Christianity is problematic for those in this current generation. It stands to reason why many in the social groups such as the Black Youth Project and Ferguson Action reject the *evangelical* label; those who do hold Christian values do not want to be associated with the term. As one Black emerging adult put it:

> That term does not represent me. It means nothing. In fact, if that is what Christianity is about, then I want nothing to do with it. I'd rather be an atheist. Now, I know that is not the case. Christianity is much more complex and varied than just one definition of it. Anyone who's educated should know that. But White people would have you thinking that their way is the only way to God and that if you don't subscribe in some fashion to their way, you're lost. I don't buy that. Not one bit. It's bullshit.[96]

Soong-Chan Rah contends that "racism divides human community by elevating one race as the standard by which all other races should be judged, thereby placing the dominant race in the position of God. It disrupts the image of God in the fellowship of one human to another."[97] This is where contemporary Christianity finds itself now.

In part, contemporary Christianity has lost its relevance because it has refused to recognize the changing ethnic and cultural landscape. This is particularly evident in the North American church. It has met that change with resistance, rejection, denial, rebuttal, and debate, and it has circled its dogmatic wagons around White Western evangelicalism. For ethnic minorities living in a post-soul era, this is the end of the road for them. They cannot accept a one-sided story of Christianity. Any movement toward a colonized form of missions is vehemently rejected.

Using aggregated data from Jenkins's work, the World Christian Database, and current US census data gathered in 2010, table 1.3 illustrates and estimates the ethnic population projections to 2025. As seen in the table, the

[95]Jenkins, *Next Christendom*, 3.
[96]Interview by the author, 2014.
[97]Rah, *Next Evangelicalism*, 82.

growth of Christian ethnic-minority presence is great and exponential. In the United States, cities such as Los Angeles are a nearing a Latino majority (48.6%).[98] But finding a seminary that focuses primarily on Latin theology and culture is difficult. This is just one example, but White Christianity has insisted on keeping Christianity White. For many post-soul ethnic minorities and some millennial Whites, this is problematic.

Table 1.3. Growth of Christian ethnic-minority presence in the United States

	1900	2005	2025
Africa	2%	19%	35%
Asia	4%	17%	26%
Europe	68%	26%	10%
Latin America	11%	24%	28%
North America	14%	13%	10%
Oceana	1%	1%	1%
	White 83% **Non-White** 16%	**White** 40% **Non-White** 60%	**White** 28% **Non-White** 75%

This cultural shift cannot be ignored, overlooked, or prayed away. The consequence of ignoring these changes over the past years has resulted in

- stricter discriminatory laws on immigration;

- deterioration of the Voting Rights Act;

- White Christian evangelical support of political candidates with racist and extremist views;

- an insistence on exceptionalism;

- expulsion and termination of ethnic-minority faculty; and

- the development of policies that exclude the ethnic-minority experience and narrative (such as a White-dominant worship experience, curricular materials that testify to the existence of Whiteness, or senior leadership teams that are all White or have few ethnic minorities).

---

[98]US Census Bureau, "Los Angeles County Quick Facts," www.census.gov/quickfacts/fact/map /losangelescountycalifornia/IPE120216.

Christianity that emphasizes a "White is right" theme continues to be problematic for a newer, more informed generation tired of a one-sided theological canon. As Jenkins asserts, "This global perspective should make us think carefully before asserting what Christians 'believe' or 'how the church is changing.'"[99] Grasping for "tradition" and "biblically rooted morals," Western Christianity is in a struggle for its values in an ever-changing era. It fails to realize the potential and possibilities in the ethnic-minority change. While evangelical Christianity struggles to return to the 1950s, a growing ethnic-minority population resists and repels most of the ideology from that era.

---

[99]Jenkins, *Next Christendom*, 3.

2

MISSIONS, RACE, AND GOD

*The Impairment of Short-Term Missions
and White-Led Urban Ministries*

A N OUTREACH ORGANIZATION exhibited itself as a "community leader";
it was an organization that was "for youth in the city" and "creating
relationships across cultures." The organization had been in the city for a
decade, had citywide support and major funders, and stated that all their
money went to "urban needs." The youth served by organization came from
underresourced schools, and most were from single-parent families.
Moreover, this organization was located in a "crime zone," according to the
city's "crime tracker." The leaders of this organization operated out of their
home, and one of them was a former educator in the public school system
that still had many connections to high-ranking administrators. It was an
outreach organization that was holistic and connected in the community,
and it had the trust of the community.

However, under this seemingly perfect veil, one needed only to ask a
student who attended this organization about their perceptions of it. The
answers were astoundingly contrary to the public persona of this organization: "I've never really ever felt welcomed here as a Black person," stated
one young woman. "They have plastic all over their furniture so that we
don't get their nice stuff dirty. What's up with that?" exclaimed another
young woman. One young man asserted, "I never feel at home with them,
like there is always a straight arm every time I enter their property."[1] To add

---

[1]In the spirit of full disclosure, I was an employee at this organization at the time, and these
responses were taken from the young people under my care. They motivated me to further

insult to racial injury, the family had added a type of "outhouse" bathroom to their home so that the students would not enter and use their personal bathroom. They had added a meeting room to their house as well, and the students had to stand if they could not fit on the four-person couch. Moreover, the organization's underlying outreach statement could be interpreted as having authority over the students they served.[2]

This type of passive racism, microaggression, and patriarchy toward students is not uncommon among many White evangelical outreach organizations centered in or around urban regions.[3] Thus, these types of issues add to high racial tensions in the United States.[4] The rise of White evangelical outreach organizations in urban and city areas has increased significantly in the twenty-first century.[5] While the notion of outreach and evangelism is central to a Christian evangelical theology, the issues of race and ethnicity continue to be unheeded. Moreover, the issue of systemic racism is typically unnoticed, and training or preparation for such racial engagement is not regarded as essential.[6] Therefore, whether passively or directly, the concepts

---

investigate the cause and the underlying racial significance. I am also of ethnic-minority descent—African American and Mexican American—and I have experienced the racialized effects of several White evangelical outreach organizations throughout my career, both as an employee and a student.

[2]Even more dangerous, the leaders blamed the students for the turn in numbers; it was "their issue" and "problem." Critical inquiry and reflection on the organization's structure was not a priority. This is similar to other White short-term missionaries' reflections on the "numbers of those saved." The problem tended to rest solely on the person, and not their methods, theology, or missional practices. See Brian M. Howell, "Mission to Nowhere: Putting Short-Term Missions into Context," *International Bulletin of Missionary Research* 33, no. 4 (2009): 207; and Kraig Beyerlein, Jenny Trinitapoli, and Gary Adler, "The Effect of Religious Short-Term Mission Trips on Youth Civic Engagement," *Journal for the Scientific Study of Religion* 50, no. 4 (2011): 791-93.

[3]For an examination of this, see Kelly Brown Douglas, *Stand Your Ground: Black Bodies and the Justice of God* (Maryknoll, NY: Orbis Books, 2015); Samuel L. Perry, "Racial Habitus, Moral Conflict, and White Moral Hegemony Within Interracial Evangelical Organizations," *Qualitative Sociology* 35, no. 1 (2012): 89-108; and Willie James Jennings, *The Christian Imagination: Theology and the Origins of Race* (New Haven, CT: Yale University Press, 2010).

[4]The scope of this project does not allow me to expand on the issues surrounding religion and critical race theory. However, I strongly recommend Roy L. Brooks, *Racial Justice in the Age of Obama* (Princeton, NJ: Princeton University Press, 2009); J. Kameron Carter, *Race: A Theological Account* (New York: Oxford University Press, 2008); James H. Cone, *The Cross and the Lynching Tree* (Maryknoll, NY: Orbis Books, 2011); and Harry H. Singleton III, *White Religion and Black Humanity* (Lanham, MD: University Press of America, 2012). These authors bring to life the underlying racial element of this research.

[5]See Brian M. Howell, *Short-Term Mission: An Ethnography of Christian Travel Narrative and Experience* (Downers Grove, IL: IVP Academic, 2012).

[6]Paul Jeffrey, "Beyond Good Intentions: Short-Term Mission Trips," *Christian Century* 118, no. 34 (2001).

of Whiteness, power, patriarchy, and privilege are often projected onto the people groups encountered by these outreach organizations. While there have been numerous studies examining the personal effect of short-term missions and the response to issues such as justice, poverty, and ethnocentrism, there is a dearth of research on the racial effect White evangelical organizations has on multiethnic youth.[7] Accordingly, this chapter takes up an exploration of young adults who have both encountered and been a part of White evangelical outreach organizations (WEOO).[8]

This chapter employs the experiences of five ethnic-minority youth from the Los Angeles region who experienced and engaged with WEOOs and short-term mission (STM) groups over the period of five years.[9] Added narrative from emerging ethnic-minority adults is also applied to this research to discuss the effect, albeit on a specific region of the country, of STMs, which have become increasingly popular over the last decade.[10] The purpose of this chapter is to examine and explore the effects of WEOOs and STMs

---

[7]The following are prominent studies on short-term missions, their language, and societal effect: Brian Howell and Rachel Dorr, "Evangelical Pilgrimage: The Language of Short-Term Missions," *Journal of Communication & Religion* 30, no. 2 (2007); Jeffrey, "Beyond Good Intentions"; Daniel A. McFarland and Reuben J. Thomas, "Bowling Young: How Youth Voluntary Associations Influence Adult Political Participation," *American Sociological Review* 71, no. 3 (2006); Robert J. Priest and Joseph Paul Priest, "'They See Everything, and Understand Nothing': Short-Term Mission and Service Learning," *Missiology: An International Review* 36, no. 1 (2008); Robert J. Priest et al., "Researching the Short-Term Mission Movement," *Missiology: An International Review* 34, no. 4 (2006); Kurt Alan Ver Beek, "The Impact of Short-Term Missions: A Case Study of House Construction in Honduras after Hurricane Mitch," *Missiology: An International Review* 34, no. 4 (2006); Beyerlein, Trinitapoli, and Adler, "Effect of Religious Short-Term Mission Trips."

[8]This was determined by examining senior leadership in the organization—those who make policy and create the organizations culture—and if those in that position were majority White or of Euro-American descent, then it was considered a WEOO. Whites, however, do dominate in the evangelical outreach field; see Samuel L. Perry, "Social Capital, Race, and Personal Fundraising in Evangelical Outreach Ministries," *Journal for the Scientific Study of Religion* 52, no. 1 (2013); Perry, "Racial Habitus, Moral Conflict, and White Moral Hegemony within Interracial Evangelical Organizations."

[9]The use and engagement of ten additional informants was utilized to clarify findings and to correlate data summations. These were performed between 2007 and 2012 using unstructured interviews lasting ninety minutes. These interviews will be used throughout the chapter to support the findings. Grounded theory analysis was used during coding to arrive at themes, narrative patterns, and connections with race and ethnicity.

[10]This is based on my research that began when interviewing Hip Hoppers about their perspectives on Christians and church. See Daniel White Hodge, *The Soul of Hip Hop: Rims, Timbs and a Cultural Theology* (Downers Grove, IL: InterVarsity Press, 2010). See also Howell and Dorr, "Evangelical Pilgrimage"; Jenny Trinitapoli and Stephen Vaisey, "The Transformative Role of Religious Experience: The Case of Short-Term Missions," *Social Forces* 88, no. 1 (2009); Beyerlein, Trinitapoli, and Adler, "Effect of Religious Short-Term Mission Trips."

on the populations they serve. From the research findings, I will illustrate (1) subtle racism, microaggression, and patriarchy from WEOOs, and (2) allow the narrative of ethnic-minority experiences to chronicle their experience in these types of organizations.[11] Last, this chapter will examine alternatives and insights from the data gathered.

THE NARRATIVE AND VOICE OF YOUNG ADULTS

Sally was a model student and was responsible for bringing in three other students for this research. She was a young African American woman raised by her grandmother. She started attending a Christian ministry when she was thirteen. She says, "I thought it was cool at first. Everyone came at me like they wanted to get to know me. So, I was like, cool. They showed me love and treated me real nice. I never noticed, initially, the mess that was going on behind the scenes."

Sally became a mouthpiece for the ministry and helped populate the youth group with a great number of students. Sally continues, "I was like, damn, they serving us food and treating people nice. So, I'm gonna bring in my friends. I know, knew, a lot of people. So if I'm experiencing something good, then I'm gonna tell other people about that [*pauses and looks away*]. I'm not sure if I'd do that again knowing what I know now."

---

[11]I use *subtle racism* to describe a form of racism that is indirect, belittling, typically nonverbally communicated, and nonintentional. I make the case that with the gentrification of many urban cities in America, ethnic-minority students (predominantly Black and Latino) are making their presence known in what has been a traditionally White youth ministry settings in the suburbs. To examine this further, see Melvin M. Webber, "The Post-City Age," in *The City Reader*, ed. Richard T. Le Gates and Frederic Stout (New York: Routledge, 1996); Beyerlein, Trinitapoli, and Adler, "Effect of Religious Short-Term Mission Trips on Youth Civic Engagement," 780-95. With the mixture of these students in traditional youth ministry settings, the growing issues of racism, lack of intercultural communication skills, deficiency in diversity competencies, and a sheer lack of multicultural perspectives is creating a major rift in not just youth groups but also the wider Christian church. This increases an already large racial gap between ethnic groups and adds to the continuing chasm between the *unchurched* and *churched*. In turn, churches in suburban contexts are either on the brink of a multiethnic influx or are already there, and the once White, suburban, affluent church context will need to engage this rising cultural and ethnic change from a nonpatriarchal and nonprivileged position. This might include engaging issues such as the multiethnic Christ, the worth of Black life, lament from an ethnic-minority context, and embracing the growing racial divide among many churches. See Michael O. Smith and Christian Emerson, *Divided by Faith: Evangelical Religion and the Problem of Race in America* (New York: Oxford University Press, 2000).

Sally worked her way into the leadership of this ministry and became the "model minority" for the organization in videos and fundraising events.[12] Sally was also in several leadership programs in the community and within the organization. At one point, at least 45 percent of her schedule was "leadership training"; she was being prepped for "senior leadership."[13] None of the other students in the group were given as much attention, and far too often this caused tension among other younger students. As Pedro, a younger freshman who had grown up with parents who were ministers, stated, "She's not the only one that's a leader. You know? I can lead too!" This was a shared sentiment among several other younger students in the organization.

This tension was kept on the back burner among the inner group (Bob, Dave, Ann, and Kim) for the duration of high school. However, when the group graduated high school and several of the young women started living together, this tension revealed itself in the form of frustration and anger. The group had a falling out of sorts a year before I wrapped up my research. While they were able to work things out, the other members in the group felt Sally received favoritism throughout, which was reflected in comments such as "They always liked you," "You could never do anything wrong, even when you were wrong," "We know you; they [the White people] don't."[14]

---

[12]This is a common practice among well-intentioned yet interculturally unaware White/Euro-American leaders. One ethnic-minority student is typically utilized, and the story becomes focused on a gospelized version of the "American Dream," which in turn morphs into a pathway for other urban youth to follow, creating a form of tokenism.

[13]Local leadership development is crucial in working with youth and young adults. It is the life blood of a good youth ministry. I am not criticizing leader development; on the contrary, I praise it. However, Sally was singled out merely because she (1) "spoke well," (2) came off as "together," and (3) articulated her thoughts well, which in turn demonstrated to leadership teams that she was "leadership material." No other young person in the group was given as much attention as Sally in terms of "leadership potential." And she was made a "table piece," as she told me, at fundraising events. The use of ethnic-minority youth at fundraising events is what I term the *Pookie story effect*. In this sense, only the extreme parts of the story are used to sell the ministry and generate income; meanwhile there is no regard for the well-being or personhood of the individual. *Pookie* is an urban name given to those who have a rags-to-riches story. It is rooted in ghetto memes of poverty, welfare moms, and baby-mama-drama that many modern-day fundraising events tend to focus on.

[14]This is not an issue that solely finds itself in urban or WEOO contexts. Any time one person is given precedence over another, there is the possibility of tension and resentment. However, in an urban multiethnic context, it is extremely important to understand and be sensitive to the concept of "face" for young people. Face and social capital are about pride and respect. Often, when these are misunderstood or undervalued, contentious issues like this can be disastrous and create an even greater wedge between the youth and the organization. They can also create a wedge between the young person and their family, and ultimately between the young person

Sally felt that the tension and conflict "could have been dealt with much better." Because there was a lack of ethnic and cultural knowledge on the part of the WEOO, simplistic responses were given to Sally and her friends (e.g., "We'll be praying for you all" or "Allow God to work it out"). At times, those types of statements made things worse and created theological conundrums for Sally.

Sally was a strong leader, which made her stand out for other WEOOs coming into her neighborhood. Because she was bold, she was often photographed and made into a spokesperson for her ethnic group. Sometimes she was treated as if she were an object. She observes,

> You know, there were times when I felt like I was like being sold at, like, an auction. They didn't even want to know my name, really. They just wanted to either touch me, ask me a bunch of questions about Black people, or—which is what made me feel really freakin' weird—just have me like a silent doll. I can't really explain; it's like they didn't even want me to talk.

Sally was a centerpiece of this group and was often looked to for direction and leadership from the others. She was also seen as a "success story" by several of the STMs who came through her community. Because she was "well spoken," she was an easy Black woman to be around, as she explained to me, "There were moments—I mean, nobody told me this outright, but it was sure felt—that I was like, damn, I'm the safe Black person. [*laughing*] I'm really that person. Really? Really? Me? But, yup. That was me [*shakes her head and looks down*]."

Dave was a large African American male who dominated the room with his booming voice. Yet he was a teddy bear, as Sally referred to him, and had a heart for missions. He brought in thirty of his friends over the four years he attended the ministry. He says,

> Yeah man, those years were a trip. I always felt like I was a painting in some art gallery. The people would look and stare at me, never really connect, keep their distance, and love it when I performed for them. I never really fit in, but [*pauses*] where else was I gonna go? My mom and dad could care less, and that was the only place I found a space to be loved.

---

and their ability to navigate social relationships in their own community. This could lead to detrimental consequences and create a dependence on the WEOO.

In this particular interview, Dave relays the tension he felt between the good that was being done in the ministry and the racism he was feeling. This enigmatic feeling arises in many ethnic-minority youths in these situations.[15] There is good happening in the midst of a tough situation, but the feeling of acceptance and being a part of something is contrasted with racism and passive oppression. Dave, who lost his father and had a difficult time growing up, searched for community. So, when STMs came for the summer and people developed a relationship with him, he enjoyed the fellowship. But as he would put it, "The racism just got too much at times, and it wasn't even like they were calling me nigger or anything, just, like, small stuff." He is referring to microaggression, which in many regards can be worse than extreme racism.[16] Dave was perplexed by these relationships. On the one hand, he had some (temporary) friends; on the other, he had to deal with and engage with racist tendencies, comments, and actions that left him "angry" and "confused."

Dave would later tell me,

> I'm not sure if I can really say we were friends. I mean, they were cool and we actually had some good times. But the thing about race kept coming up in these little ways. And if I'd ever bring it up to them, they'd be like, "No Dave, no man, that's you; we're not racist at all." So it got hard trying to talk about things that affected me, racially speaking.

Because of Dave's large stature, he often put White males on the defense; they were cautious. His voice would often reverberate in small or large rooms, causing him to be noticed. That added to the way Dave felt around Whites. This too was a factor when Dave negotiated relationships among WEOOs.

Dave was able to use work and his hobby of playing video games to buffer some of the negative side effects he experienced. Simply being Black and large gave police and security guards reason to harass him; when Dave

---

[15]This issue has arisen in other interviews I have conducted around the country. See also Robert D. Lupton, *Toxic Charity: How Churches and Charities Hurt Those They Help (and How to Reverse It)* (New York: HarperOne, 2011).

[16]For more on microaggression's effects, see Eduardo Bonilla-Silva, *Racism Without Racists: Color-Blind Racism and the Persistence of Racial Inequality in America* (Lanham, MD: Rowman & Littlefield, 2013); Eduardo Bonilla-Silva, *White Supremacy and Racism in the Post–Civil Rights Era* (Boulder, CO: L. Rienner, 2001); Tim Wise, *White Like Me: Reflections on Race from a Privileged Son*, rev. ed. (Berkeley, CA: Soft Skull Press, 2008).

shared this with people from the WEOO or STMs, it was written off or be-littled. Dave usually would not push back and would retreat to his games or into silence. He told me that he often would be in a rage, but he knew he needed to "control himself," otherwise things would get ugly. He would often refer to the Incredible Hulk and say, "You won't like me when I'm angry!" Most of the students who came with the STMs used Dave as a "buddy" and liked to take selfies with him. All the while, Dave was aware of what was happening and the purpose of those selfies. "All they want to see is the big Black man and say they have a Black friend. I mean, is that all I'm good for?" Dave would often tell me of the anger he felt because of this, but he hid it well.

Kim was one of Sally's recruits and attended the youth ministry for only three years. She had to commute about an hour and a half via public transpor-tation. Developmentally (cognitively and emotionally), she was what some might call a "late bloomer."[17] She was also a type of leader in that she organized and created small groups around the issues of race and ethnicity. Kim says,

> It was hard as hell to be at that church. I was always looked at as the dumb one. You know? I hated that sh--. I couldn't take it anymore. Shoot, I left. [*laughs*] You know? Them White folks didn't know what the hell to do with me. I ain't sayin' that I didn't see a version of God, but, shoot, at what price? You know? I started telling my friends to avoid that place like the plague. I told 'em that we can find God on our own. I'm with Tupac on that one.

Kim was part Caribbean and White/Euro-American. Once she entered college, she ended up on the dean's list, led student groups, and created a strong voice for herself. Yet, while she was at this ministry organization, she was only seen as the angry Black woman.[18] Youth workers evaded her and used Sally as their communication piece to Kim. Kim says,

---

[17]This was one of the chief factors that worked against Kim. Any form of disability was seen as license for others to pity the person. This proved to be infuriating for those on the receiving end. Kim resented anyone asking her anything about her development.

[18]The concept of the "angry Black woman" is a multilayered one that deserves much more atten-tion than I can give here. Because of its new emergence in scholarship, most STMs and White-led urban youth ministries do not fully comprehend that caricature and how they have per-petuated it within their own organizations. For a more comprehensive look into how the angry Black woman issue and faith intersect with gender and race, I recommend Kelly Brown Douglas, *Sexuality and the Black Church: A Womanist Perspective* (Maryknoll, NY: Orbis, 1999); and Kelly Brown Douglas, *What's Faith Got to Do with It? Black Bodies/Christian Souls* (Maryknoll, NY: Orbis, 2005).

I love God. Period. There is no taking that away from me. But, I feel like I can't really find God when I'm told to worship and sing "this way" or "that way." I don't think God is like that. I think God is a God of variety. And I never felt at home in that church [*shakes her head*].

Kim was much more critical of the groups and the church ministry she was a part of. In the final year of interviews, she revealed to me that at times she faced hard financial problems and needed the aid of the WEOO she belonged to. She felt like she had to survive, and in order to do that, she had to take on "racist attitudes and racism" in order to live. This is often the position many socioeconomically disadvantaged ethnic minorities find themselves in. They are in need or can use some sort of help, but the baggage accompanied with that "help"—microaggressive behavior and racist ideologies—comes at a high cost; in some cases there is a loss of identity altogether. Kim added, "There were times I just had to take it because I needed some help. And you know, it wasn't like them White people were *trying* to be racist, but they couldn't help it. But it still hurt and made me feel like I was just some poor Black girl who would always be in need of White people."

Kim was not "easily moved" by a simple one-two-three process of salvation or Christianity either. She questioned faith, God, the Gospels, and even heaven. This made her a "project" among some of the STMs. Once, a young team attempted to argue with Kim for about two hours. Kim later told me that event showed her that religion was both "dumb" and "all about proving what is right and wrong so that they [Whites] could be right." Kim often challenged simplistic notions to Christianity and the myth that blessings are equal to accomplishment, monetary success, and a life with few problems. During her senior year of high school, two younger youth pastors attempted to convince Kim of "God's love for her." This was disastrous and led to a sequence of events that eventually pushed Kim away from the church and produced a negative view of anyone calling themselves a "missionary" or "Christian." Kim stayed in college and eventually completed a master's degree in counseling. In her final interview Kim said, "All I needed was someone to believe in me. I found that in people who weren't in no damn church." While keeping some contact with the rest of the group, she did not feel the same camaraderie the others did. After high school, Kim sought independence and creation of her own self-identity outside of what a WEOO or agency said it *should* be.

Ann was part Black and part Mexican American. She was extremely quiet, and interviewing her proved difficult in her early teen years. Ann was good friends with Sally and had a strong bond with her. The two were almost inseparable. Ann was often overlooked, and some in the WEOO mistakenly thought she was depressed, socially awkward, bipolar, or traumatized. To this, Ann says,

> I'm not depressed! I ain't sick neither! Just because I'm quiet don't mean I have problems. It just means I'm quiet. I like to check things out before I make a move. You know me too. I don't like to talk; I'll just sit in the back and see who's saying what. I wanna see what people are about. Once you get to know me though, you can't shut me up.

As Ann opened up more in later years, she revealed that when people tried to make her talk, she would make it a point to not talk or just give quick responses. She despised STMs and regarded them as "fake, tired [out of date or irrelevant], and exploitative." The urban youth ministry she was a part of was "okay" at the time, simply because it provided a safe place for her to live and be away from a hectic household.[19] Ann's silence proved to be a factor in how she was "ministered to," and it was indicative of her responses that would later come. In a rare moment, she opened up:

> I hate anyone making me do anything. But even more, someone making me talk. Them White folks always thought less of me 'cause I didn't talk when they wanted me to. Look, I pray. I know who God is, have a relationship with him and everything. Why I need to talk all about it? Tell me that. I hate it. Oh, I hate it when someone trying to "minister to me" [*uses air quotes*]. I can smell them from a mile way. They always come to me with like, "Hi, Miss Ann, how you doing?" And I'm like, "Get the f--- away from me, now"—in my mind, though! But my face will tell it all. Who like being "ministered to"? All they gonna do is go back and use it for some damn newsletter anyways, or try to prove to they friends how they led some little Black girl to God. Look, I ain't havin' it, and I know a lot of other kids feel that way too. Get to know me first. Then we can talk later about God. What make you think you know all about God and I

---

[19]Good does take place within these organizations. It is not all evil or bad, and often ethnic-minority students find some solace and worth in some of these mission agencies. Yet other interviewees suggested that these types of organizations should cease immediately, and if others are created, they should be much more inclusive and ethnically representative.

don't? You think you the only one God speak to? And I have to learn from you? What can you learn from me? I think I could be teaching them White leaders a thing too. But see, that would be too much for them. Shoot. Y'all ain't the only people that God talk to, White folks! God talk to me too. He just do it silently [*giggling*] 'cause God know me and know what I like—being quiet!

Ann was not alone in her silence. Many urban multiethnic young people and emerging adults can appear silent, aloof, out of sorts, and socially inaudible. And while youth workers need to be aware of and vigilant to the symptoms of depression, anomie, social withdraw, PTSD, and other mental health issues, the starting point of a relationship cannot be assuming the negative or trying to help. Ann and other students like her know more than they let on and often have a much more complex and informed position because of their silent observations. Ann's demeanor is not an anomaly and is much more common in urban and multiethnic settings. Students in those contexts are reserved and desire to get to know someone first rather than speak and talk.[20]

Ann later went to college. She continued in her faith and attended regular church services. Ann said she had a "strong faith," although when tragedy struck she did question and doubt the ultimate "power of God"—a common thread among many urban, rural, and suburban students. She wanted to settle down and have a family at some point. Ann's faith in God later took a turn toward a more complex nitty-gritty character, which involved integrating into herself much that was suppressed or unrecognized in her earlier part of life. Her self-certainty and conscious awareness of reality was much higher; this allowed Ann to have a much broader and complex faith.[21] Ann has developed an acute sense of who God is for her own life. Her faith, however, contained elements of popular culture, music, and forms of art most would deem as non-Christian—but these spoke God into her life. This caught my attention as an example of finding God in the sacred, secular, and profane.

Bob was first-generation Mexican American. His parents brought him to the United States when he was ten. With no citizenship papers, he is

---

[20]In post-soul contexts, traditional youth ministry approaches with upfront engagement, high-energy games, and extroverted activities needs to be contextualized. For some, a more introverted approach might be warranted.

[21]I argue that nitty-gritty 'hood theology—a more robust and complex faith than the simplistic "faith in God" or "faith in the unseen"—is necessary in post-soul contexts. Such faith embraces a much more pragmatic approach to theology and religion (Hodge, *Soul of Hip Hop*, 145-49).

"undocumented." Bob still attends this church ministry, which has led to ridicule from parts of his family, who are devout Catholics. At one point, Bob was part of a group of twelve students who were in similar situations (e.g., undocumented first-generation Mexican Americans). Of his friends, he alone remained in the ministry. He held leadership positions in the organization.[22] But eventually he was let go. Bob explains,

> This ministry is like my second home. There are some really good people here. But here's the deal: I'm like a freakin' fine piece of China to these people here. I was cool with them until I started asking for stuff that made them feel uncomfortable, like a job that paid, like helping me with my citizenship, like using me for more than just a film clip or good story in the main service.

Bob's statement connects with what I have called *contented ministry praxis*—ministry that is content until a more complex issue interrupts that simplicity. Bob was part of larger, more controversial issue in Southern California: the journey toward citizenship. What made things more volatile was that this ministry was politically conservative. Members of the church often made comments such as

- these people need to go back to Mexico;
- I'm not giving up my job for them;
- our country needs to return back to being American; and
- these people are ruining our country.[23]

Bob responds,

> So, what . . . I'm not good enough to sit next to you in the kingdom? But I'm good enough to clean your dishes, mow your lawn, and take care of your kids, right? As long as I'm serving you [White people] I'm okay. But the minute I want rights you've had all along, now I'm the enemy. What "America" are we going back to? My people owned this land before you all stole it from us!

Bob was asked to not comment openly on some comments made about him in a particular newsletter. He was asked to "take the higher road" and work

---

[22]These leadership positions were peer-oriented. The White/Euro-American leaders held all power and control; students like Sally and Bob were only able to "lead" their peers. Rarely were they asked to enter decision-making meetings or be involved in making policy.

[23]These are actual quotes from meetings, newsletters, and sermons.

toward "reconciliation" rather than "stoop to their level." Bob said to me, "Man, okay, so I don't have a voice now? They can talk all that smack, and I'm the one who is told to 'act right.' What's that about, man? I don't see much God in that."

Bob's anger was justifiable. At that time, the politicized issue of amnesty was widely debated. And because the issue of immigration was ethnically and racially charged, the group that felt the heat the most were Latino/as. Bob watched with intensity the debates and the political candidates who either dodged or opposed the issues. He was the most politically and socially aware student in the group. Bob's friends, who at first started to participate in my research but later opted out, also had a robust bent toward politics.

Bob wanted to vote in the 2008 election, but because he was not a citizen, could not. He was almost an anomaly for some WEOO workers.[24] On the one hand, they saw a human being with potential; on the other, they saw an "illegal alien" who could possibly, as two workers from an WEOO said, "mooch off the economy."[25] While Christian leaders did not directly tell him their opinions regarding immigration, he could feel them—much like Ann did when WEOO leaders attempted to minister to her. Bob says,

> Look, I'm human. I'm not some "alien" from outer space. I am human just like these other people. I wanna live just like the next person. But they make this issue of immigration like we are some evil people trying to take something from them. Who the hell wants to be cleaning tables and mopping floors? But I don't see no White folks lining up to do that work. So whose job am I taking? Mexicans are your problem now? How about the land you took from us? Can I talk about that now? It just don't make sense. And they want me to worship a God that supports me leaving America? I don't know man . . . don't make sense to me.

Bob struggled to comprehend a Republican, conservative, and very White God. These characteristics stood in opposition to his being and personhood. He was conflicted, and because his faith development was still evolving, he was not able to grasp the full scope and diversity of Christianity.

---

[24]Many WEOOs have a conservative base of supporters and subscribe to a conservative and even fundamentalist view of the Bible.

[25]This was said to me in passing as a group of protestors marched through the neighborhood we were in. At this time, California was in the heat of political, ideological, and theological debate regarding Latino immigration.

WEOOs presented only their perspective and version of Christianity—
stressing it as "truth" and the standard for Christian theology, therefore
marginalizing or even denying the existence of other narratives that move
away from the Western confinement of Christianity.[26]

Struggling to maintain steady employment—a common issue for those
who are undocumented—Bob turned to activism and advocacy. He wanted
to lead and help others who were in similar situations. And while his leadership skills were not noticed as quickly as Sally's, Bob eventually made it
into leadership. Bob did question the existence of God and what Christianity
meant for Mexicans and Chicanos. Bob could connect with a contextualized
version of Christianity until he read authors such as Justo González and
Gustavo Gutiérrez and could visualize a Brown Jesus. His later years in the
local urban youth ministry were "rough," as he put it. He said, "They were a
time when I questioned everything about God because I didn't know God
from my own land." Social and political activism helped shaped Bob's sense
of life and God. And while he still has many questions about Christianity,
he was able to find a place at the table for himself. He now desires to help
others to do the same.[27]

We will now turn to the significance of these narratives and their implications for missions.

MULTIFACETED INFERENCES

Though these stories represent a certain demographic and locality in the
United States, they present some problematic and troubling scenarios for
missiologists and Christian faith-based organizations alike. Over the last few
years, these types of stories have become increasingly common in many
urban and multiethnic enclaves around the United States as more WEOOs

---

[26]See Soong-Chan Rah, *The Next Evangelicalism: Freeing the Church from Western Cultural Captivity* (Downers Grove, IL: InterVarsity Press, 2009), 127-40.

[27]This was a difficult premise for the WEOO. They made continual efforts to discourage Bob from
"thinking this way" or from learning more about contextual Christianity. In all transparency, I
was Bob's mentor for several years and aided in helping create a strong community of caring
multiethnic adults who could mentor Bob. If it had not been for this effort, I believe Bob would
have succumbed to the pressure of the White leaders who suggested his search was "sinful." How
many other ethnic-minority youth who have dared to question White Jesus have been overwhelmed with "sin" talk such as this? How many more contextualized texts might we have if the
mind of a critical thinker was developed within their own context?

and STMs have had an uptick in "local outreach."[28] The impact, therefore, of WEOOs and STMs is significant and poses deeper critical interrogation. Five themes have emerged from this research:

1. Ethnic-minority youth tend to be treated as objects.

2. Ethnic-minority youth are forced into the American Dream meta-narrative of achievement, accomplishment, and success. Those that do not fit into such a model or do not follow it are often overlooked and labeled as "tough."

3. Anger and frustration are looked upon as "ungodly" and "sinful."

4. Diversity and racial competencies are not valued in senior leadership training, and those topics are often given an average of one hour at the end of training events.

5. Asians, fair-skinned Latinos, and model African American youth are valued.

These themes often force the issue of race and racism into the WEOOs' curriculum. Moreover, while Bob continued with this WEOO, the overall sentiment among ethnic-minority youth toward organized church and religion was disdain and apathy. Kim left the church altogether and considers herself "spiritual" but not "religious."[29] After her junior year, Kim did not stay in touch with her former youth group and was labeled "angry" and even a "backslider."

Bob too was labeled angry. But he learned how to corral that anger when he was with the White/Euro-American leaders of the ministry. The leaders then deemed him better, and he was able to be a part of the ministry as long as he was docile and calm. While Dave was frustrated and irritated with the racial intolerance of this ministry, he remained passive and quiet within the group. He was also a jokester, which gave him an advantage as the "funny Black guy." Dave said this "made the White folk feel comfortable."

---

[28]Howell and Dorr, "Evangelical Pilgrimage," 237.

[29]This is similar to the findings of Kenda Creasy Dean, *Almost Christian: What the Faith of Our Teenagers Is Telling the American Church* (New York: Oxford University Press, 2010); Christian Smith with Kari Christoffersen, Hilary Davidson, and Patricia Snell Herzog, *Lost in Transition: The Dark Side of Emerging Adulthood* (New York: Oxford University Press, 2011). Kim remained an open Christian, but the ministry she was a part of left a bad impression on her spiritual journey.

The leadership of the local WEOO attended multiethnic and diversity-focused conferences such as the Urban Youth Workers Institute and Christian Community Development Association, which had workshops and sessions on racial reconciliation. Yet even with this training, certain inferences arose that negatively affected ethnic minorities in these areas.[30] These were:

- Once a consensus of racial, cultural, and diversity knowledge was reached among the senior leadership team, the team felt as though they had "arrived" and issues of race and racial reconciliation were no longer addressed.

- If a critique about White/Euro-American privilege and power was too strong or "angry" in the training material, it was written off as "too secular" or "sinful."[31]

- Training was tolerated to retain employment—that is, the leader would attend racial-competency training just to say "I went," but the leader's attitude never changed.

- Ethnic minorities are used as good "stories" for financial and social purposes.

These themes were confirmed by Sally, Bob, Kim, Ann, and Dave. Further, they affirmed that it is crucial to engage these themes to overcome paternalism and racial intolerance in White/Euro-American–led youth ministry organizations. Sally states,

> I mean, I just don't see how this can be overcome unless someone in key positions of leadership are able to put down their damn pride. Otherwise, we, the Black and Mexican folk, are just left out. Shoot, we probably need to get our own organizations up and running. They [leaders in the youth ministry group] just ignorant. They don't understand me at all. I'm good and cool for a damn story or to raise money for your new chapel. But do you really know me? Do you really know where I'm coming from? Nope. You know what I'm sayin'?

---

[30]Ethnocentric views among youth who attended short-term mission trips was not significantly changed as a result of experiencing different cultures and ethnic groups (Beyerlein, Trinitapoli, and Adler, "Effect of Religious Short-Term Mission Trips," 783-84).

[31]Tim Wise refers to the "White Denial" of racism, White privilege, and White power domination in social structures. It is easy to ignore if you do not have to live it or deal with it on a daily basis. Tim Wise, *Between Barack and a Hard Place: Racism and White Denial in the Age of Obama*, Open Media Series (San Francisco: City Lights, 2009).

Sally, one of the more outspoken youth, was able to navigate some of these issues fairly well, partly because she had helped raise funds, participated in video clips that promoted the ministry, and, as she relayed to me, "knew when to tell them folk the truth and when to lie and make them feel good." It did not, however, always yield good results; she was part of a yearlong, contentious, ministry-wide dispute between a wealthy and powerful White/Euro-American donor of the ministry and a group of ethnic-minority students who were living with the ministry leaders.

In addition, WEOOs' lack of cultural and ethnic awareness creates a wider racial gap. Urban-ethnic minorities who encounter these WEOOs and STMs are also disgruntled with Christianity because it is viewed as a White religion disconnected from race.[32] This is especially true of the current racial tensions with White evangelicals who voted for Donald Trump—many Black millennials see him as a fascist and racist—and the Black community's concerns about police brutality, which includes the lack of respect for Black bodies.[33]

These bear a striking resemblance to a longstanding ideology around race, humanity, and being. Carl Linnaeus (1707–1778), a botanist, posited a taxonomy of races that elevated the European over all the others. In this sense, "scientific inquiry" was implemented to establish this racial ranking. Linnaeus's work was carried on and is entrenched in perceptions and worldviews.[34] This carried over into the justification of reprehensible and brutal enslavement of Africans. Linnaeus's work is just part of a line of scholarly thought suggesting European superiority:

---

[32]This increasing view is fodder for movements such as the Black Youth Project and Black Lives Matter, who distance themselves from Christianity, which is perceived to be both historically racist and colonialist. Rev. Sekou discusses this plainly when he asserts the question of "Who's God?" in regard to faith and spirituality at the intersection of race. See Osagyefo Uhuru Sekou, *Gods, Gays, and Guns: Essays on Religion and the Future of Democracy* (Cambridge, MA: Campbell & Cannon Press, 2011), 28-46.

[33]See Daniel Cox, Robert P. Jones, Betsy Cooper, and Rachel Lienesch, "The Divide over America's Future: 1950 or 2050?" (Washington, DC: Public Religion Research Institute, 2016), 20-26; and Douglas, *Stand Your Ground*, 50-89.

[34]The pseudo-science used to categorize races would eventually develop into justification for slavery and the supremacy of Europeans. This hierarchy is maintained to this day; one need only see a glimpse of the power in the United States and realize we, as a "civilized society," have not made much movement forward. See Jonathan Marks, "Racism: Scientific," in *Encyclopedia of Race and Racism*, ed. Patrick L. Mason (Detroit: Macmillan Reference, 2013), 446.

By the end of the eighteenth century, German zoologist and anthropologist Johann Friedrich Blumenbach had jettisoned the personality and cultural traits used by Linnaeus in favor of only physical traits. However, he also modified the Linnaean system by ranking, rather than simply listing, the races. Moreover, scholars at this time began to apply the previously informal term "race" (which had been used by the French naturalist Count de Buffon to refer to a local strain of people) to the formal Linnaean subspecies. The result was a parallel usage of the term, in which groups of people, diversely constituted, could be called "races," and their essences could be defined in accordance with whatever they were taken to be. Concurrently, the natures of large continental "races" could stand as formal taxonomic entities. Thus, races could exist within races, or they could crosscut other races. Because the attributes of the Irish, Italians, or Jews were Platonic essences taken to be inscribed in the very cores of the people in question—by virtue of simply being born into the group—it did not much matter what an individual representative looked like or acted like. These were not so much group-level generalizations, which have always existed as folk taxonomies, but group-level scientific definitions, which were something new.[35]

This type of categorization became law and gospel for missionaries heading into the New World.[36] Europeans were classified as the highest race, the one with the most intelligence, wisdom, and insight. Table 2.1 illustrates well the categories.

In this system, the European race is ruled by law, not caprice, opinion, or custom, and the other races must strive to emulate Europeans. Isaac de la Peyrère proposed a biblical justification of racial superiority:

> He suggested that certain biblical passages were consistent with multiple divine creations of people, of which the story related in Genesis was only one. These "Pre-Adamites" were the progenitors of the most divergent forms of people, who might thereby be considered to be different in both nature and origin, as they were the product of different creative acts by God. La Peyrère was subsequently invoked as the founder of a school called polygenism, which gained popularity in the nineteenth century as American scholars increasingly sought to justify the practice of slavery by recourse to science (although that had not been La Peyrère's intent).[37]

---

[35]Ibid., 447.

[36]Winthrop D. Jordan, *The White Man's Burden: Historical Origins of Racism in the United States* (London: Oxford University Press, 1980), Kindle ed., chaps. 4-5.

[37]Marks, "Racism: Scientific," 448.

Table 2.1. Linnaeus's categories of *Homo sapiens*

	American	**European**	**Asian**	**African**
Color	Red	White	Yellow	Black
Temperament	Irascible, impassive	Hearty, muscular	Melancholy, stern	Sluggish, lazy
Face	Thick, straight, black hair; broad nose; harsh appearance; chin beardless	Long blond hair, blue eyes	Black hair, dark eyes	Black kinky hair, silky skin, short nose, thick lips, females with genital flap, elongated breasts
Personality	Stubborn, happy, free	Sensitive, very smart, creative	Strict, contemptuous, greedy	Sly, slow, careless
Covered by	Fine red lines	Tight clothing	Loose garments	Grease
Ruled by	Custom	Law	Opinion	Caprice

Source: Jonathan Marks, "Racism: Scientific," in *Encyclopedia of Race and Racism*, ed. Patrick L. Mason (Detroit: Macmillan Reference, 2013), 446-47. Reprinted from *Systema Naturae*, 10th ed., 1758.

Today, we need only listen to urban/city missionaries speak of the populations they claim to serve as heathen, lost, sinful, immoral, unethical, and damned; these categories serve to create a superior position, which is often embedded in the mission and vision statement of their organization.

Once again, these racist views are pervasive throughout Western society. White is supreme, even in small numbers. Thus, it is safe to assume this worldview is present among some White missionaries, even if in a passive sense. The concept that Blacks are lazy and "less than" is nothing new. Take for example an infamous ad that illustrates the hard-working White man and the lazy Black man (see fig. 2.1).

Stereotypes like these were also applied to Asians, Native Americans, Latinx, and even Polish peoples (before they were categorized as White). While we cringe at the sight of such characterizations, they continue today. The 2016 presidential election season informed us that American society had "lost" its way and must be made "great again." This type of discourse echoes historical racist propaganda, which leads to the subjugation of all non-Whites.

Some North Americans want to believe that racism ended with the work of Dr. Martin Luther King Jr. Did it? What evidence is provided to demonstrate that it has ended? Future missiologists must contend with questions

Figure 2.1. Political poster showing the hard-working White man and the lazy Black man (1866)

like this as they train to enter the North American field. I will now summarize the effects of passive racism in North America.

THE EFFECTS OF PASSIVE RACISM

Before discussing broader inferences from this research, I should mention several limitations of this study. First, because the sample of ethnic-minority young people is small, caution must be used in generalizing the findings to the whole of evangelical outreach ministry (EOM) workers in the United States. Second, qualitative data for this study, even though performed over a period, were limited to essay-style narrative responses; a more quantitative study could reveal more complex findings on racism, microaggression, and White hegemony. Future studies on this topic should utilize these more rigorous quantitative methods.[38]

---

[38]Samuel L. Perry, "Diversity, Donations, and Disadvantage: The Implications of Personal Fundraising for Racial Diversity in Evangelical Outreach Ministries," *Review of Religious Research* 53, no. 4 (2012): 398.

From the research, here are findings on the effects of passive racism.

1. *The issues of race and ethnicity are important even if it is not an issue in a particular group.* From workers in WEOOs I received many responses that race is of no significance or that the problems of racism are only exacerbated when we talk about the issue and give it energy. This tends to be rooted in a position of privilege, which is derived from relatively historical nonoppressive conditions. Race was a key factor among all the interviewees and continues to remain a substantial factor in embracing Christianity by emerging ethnic-minority millennials.

2. *Belittlement.* Belittlement was ever-present in almost all the interactions between the WEOOs and ethnic-minority young adults I interviewed. While some organizations spend time training their workers on their use of language and nonverbal connotation, the interviewees overwhelmingly felt belittled in the "name of Christ." Language, including nonverbal language, is powerful. A look, a touch, the way someone positions themselves, tone, inflection, and eye contact (or the lack thereof) connote meaning. Bob and Sally said that in some cases it connoted a sense of superiority. One young man told me that it felt as if the White male missionaries were always looking for their next big conquest in the "name of God," and that White people from STMs, along with some ethnic minorities who had adopted White culture, saw the urban community as pitiful and lost. For ethnic minorities, language such as "at risk" or "lost" reinforces this perspective and suggests a paternalist presence.

3. *Microaggression.* Microaggression combined with belittlement offers a social brew of intolerance and disdain in passive form. Microaggression makes matters worse and creates a strong aversion not just for White Christians but for Christianity as well. Three ethnic-minority emerging adults relayed their antipathy toward Christianity after having been involved with White urban ministries. All were unsure of their faith and wondered whether God even existed. One older African American woman, who had worked for a STM and later resigned, said, "If a God does exist who allows White people to rule

and be in control, I'm not so sure I want anything to do with that kind of God." WEOOs are in dire need of doing the difficult yet important work of deconstructing their preconceived racial notions.

4. *Christianity and salvation in exchange for a person's ethnic soul.* This theme—trading your ethnic identity in order to become a Christian—emerged quite prevalently among many ethnic minorities I interviewed. In other words, if someone is going to become a Christian, then they must give up their culture and ethnic heritage because it is not compatible with White evangelical Christianity,[39] which is currently the dominant form of Christianity in the United States.[40] This is a result of the concentration of power and control of the Christian marketplace among White evangelicals—a hegemony constituting morality and values.[41] This hegemonic construct in turn produces White-based materials and curricula,[42] which then suggests to ethnic minorities that they can't be (1) Christian and (2) identify with their racial and ethnic heritage. Instead, they must adopt a White Christian cultural mantra to be a true Christian. Going back to nonverbal discourse, this is rarely expressed verbally but through subtle and microaggressive connotations (e.g., you can

---

[39]This is also supported by other scholars who have done research in White Christian organizations. See Judith Y. Weisinger and Paul F. Salipante, "A Grounded Theory for Building Ethnically Bridging Social Capital in Voluntary Organizations," *Nonprofit and Voluntary Sector Quarterly* 34, no. 1 (2005); Rick McClatchy, "Building a Multi-Cultural Organization in Texas," *Review & Expositor* 109, no. 1 (2012); Anthony B. Bradley, *Black Scholars in White Space: New Vistas in African American Studies from the Christian Academy* (Eugene, OR: Wipf & Stock, 2015); Anthony B. Bradley, *Aliens in the Promised Land: Why Minority Leadership Is Overlooked in White Christian Churches and Institutions* (Phillipsburg, NJ: P&R, 2013); Perry, "Diversity, Donations, and Disadvantage"; Perry, "Racial Habitus, Moral Conflict, and White Moral Hegemony"; and Marla Frederick McGlathery and Traci Griffin, "'Becoming Conservative, Becoming White?' Black Evangelicals and the Para-Church Movement," in *This Side of Heaven: Race, Ethnicity, and Christian Faith*, ed. Robert J. Priest and Alvaro L. Nieves (New York: Oxford University Press, 2007).

[40]William R. Jones, *Is God a White Racist? A Preamble to Black Theology* (Garden City, NY: Anchor, 1973); Jennings, *Christian Imagination*; and Douglas, *What's Faith Got to Do with It?*

[41]Samuel Perry asserts this notion of White Christian hegemony, which "refers to a form of domination maintained non-coercively through the instillation of the dominant group's values within the minority group and small concessions made by the dominant group without significantly altering the underlying systems of inequality" (Perry, "Racial Habitus, Moral Conflict, and White Moral Hegemony," 90).

[42]For a broader exploration into how this affects faith-based organizations, see Daniel White Hodge and Pablo Otaola, "Reconciling the Divide: The Need for Contextual and Just Models of Fundraising in Vocational Youth Ministry," *Journal of Youth Ministry* 15, no. 1 (2016).

avoid police brutality by being good; the gospel is the gospel so it transcends culture). This suggests a counterproductive ideology that ethnic-minority young adults could find difficult to embrace, thereby causing dissonance.

5. *White satisfaction amid ethnic-minority rage.* Many WEOO workers who came into the urban community left with a high sense of satisfaction, self-fulfillment, and greater sense of doing "God's work."[43] Ethnic-minority young people saw themselves as being "projects" or "newsletter stories," which created a sense of anger within them. The anger worsened among many ethnic-minority youths who felt belittled or ignored altogether. For the leaders in WEOOs, a sense of betterment for the greater good emerged. In other words, though race *may* be a factor, we are doing the best job for these kids because, after all, who else is doing it? This type of ethos was felt by all five students: Sally, Bob, Ann, Dave, and Kim. This might suggest what Perry defines as the racial habitus of White EOMs maintaining White domination within and throughout the organization.[44]

These narratives from ethnic-minority students represent a larger growing body of ethnic-minority students who are involved in WEOOs. As the demographics of the United States change, the growing populations of ethnic minorities will continue to affect both WEOOs and STMs. Furthermore, these narratives are only a glimpse of the possible damage done by well-intentioned yet interculturally challenged White evangelicals. More importantly, as the late Native American scholar and activist Richard Twiss reminds us, Christianity is not a white religion and cannot be "reduced to a systemized set of propositional truth statements."[45] More research in this area is needed on a broader scale to explore the effects of racism, microaggression, and patriarchy on the populations of ethnic minorities from WEOOs and STMs.

---

[43]This was documented in the numerous leadership meetings I attended with STM teams that came through the area. There were also meetings with STM students who expressed these tones as well.

[44]Perry, "Racial Habitus, Moral Conflict, and White Moral Hegemony," 90-91.

[45]Richard Twiss, *Rescuing the Gospel from the Cowboys: A Native American Expression of the Jesus Way* (Downers Grove, IL: InterVarsity Press, 2015), 59, 64.

PART 2

A CULTURAL EXEGESIS OF THE WILD

God is not a noun, that demands to be defined, God is a verb that invites us to live, to love and to be.

BISHOP SPONG

God is the one who offers the possibilities to the world, urging us to choose the paths that lead to a vision of the common good.

MONICA A. COLEMAN, *MAKING A WAY OUT OF NO WAY*

Why is it that Christianity seems impotent to deal radically, and therefore effectively, with the issues of discrimination and injustice on the basis of race, religion and national origin?

HOWARD THURMAN

If you got religion, show some sign.

GENEVA SMITHERMAN, *TESTIFYIN, SERMONIZIN, AND SIGNIFYIN*

Hip Hop is the last true folk art.

MOS DEF, IN *GQ*

Only God can judge me, so I'm gone. Either love me or leave me alone.

JAY-Z

THIS SECTION DISCUSSES a new method of interpreting God, Christianity, and Jesus in the wild. Much like *Star Wars: Episode IV*, this section brings new hope—hope for what can be and, for many in the post-soul context, what already is. This section attempts to give snapshots of what works and the complexities of God in a culture that desperately desires a new approach. What happens when we are wrestling with God in the presence of police terrorism? How might we begin to embrace a theology of suffering while being dislocated from our homes because of gentrification? And how might an ethnic-minority Christian process the culture of hate, racism, and sexism that someone like Donald Trump brings out within White American society?

This section then argues that Hip Hop theology does indeed create space for missiology to happen and for a richer and more robust form of Christianity to spring up. Chapter three continues my discussion of a Hip Hop theology and explores the God within it from a post–civil rights context, using artists and their art as a pathway forward. Chapter four examines Jesus within the context of Hip Hop and the profane. This is a real-time Jesus within a setting most missiological scholarship does not enter: the ghetto. What might Jesus be doing in the shadows and underbelly of life? Where does Jesus manifest his image in the midst of ever-present crying and dirges? Chapter five explores the narratives of emerging voices in a post-soul context. Using data gathered among ethnic-minority youth, the chapter explores a new paradigm of understanding Christianity and missiology. Let's begin with a sense of hope for the wild.[1]

---

[1]I have published the following works in a variety of places. What follows in these chapters is a reiteration of my findings as applied to a Hip Hop missiology.

3

GOD IN HIP HOP

A Conversation on Complexity

I WAS FILLED WITH PRIDE AND JOY for the work I had done. I had worked hard and long to create a paper that, in my mind, was pristine; it made a new argument for the theology of Hip Hop. I was in graduate school, and the professor who taught the course was especially tough and demanded a lot of his students. Nothing wrong with that. In fact, it was one of the main reasons I had worked so hard on this particular paper. The assignment called for a historical expository of a "Christian cultural movement" and the connection of that movement with current missiological issues. I knew what I needed to do and how to go about it. I would make the case for Hip Hop theology. So, I started out the way any student would: hit the academic search engines. I stumbled onto Tricia Rose's early work and saw the development of Cornel West's argument for the connection of the blues to Hip Hop. Then I read Michael Eric Dyson's work on Tupac Shakur and Jon Michael Spencer's journal of theomusicology; one issue was devoted entirely to Hip Hop. I was set. I had my sources and the history; I made a great case.

I turned in my paper, feeling pride and joy. I knew this was in fact one of the best graduate papers this professor would ever read. I felt like Ralphie in the 1983 film *A Christmas Story*. When he turned in a paper to his teacher, he knew *for sure* he would get an A-plus, plus, plus! I did too.

Well, to my shock, I did not get an A or even the C-plus Ralphie did. In fact, I had to do a total rewrite because my topic was rejected as invalid and "implausible as a Christian movement." As you can imagine, I was angry and a tad devastated. I cited my sources, gave evidence, and made a solid argument. Or so I thought. My pride was more damaged than anything. I then wrote a standard paper on a mission organization I cannot even recall now. I ended up with a B-minus. However, that rejected paper later paved the way for my early works, *Heaven Has a Ghetto* and *The Soul of Hip Hop*—all was not lost.

However, I've received a type of the professor's response over the years in reaction to my understanding, engaging, and involvement with Hip Hop theology. This misunderstanding has led to many overlooking the power of Hip Hop's spirituality and missiological significance. As I have presented papers at conferences, some have smirked when listening to the intricacies of Hip Hop's ecclesiology. When discussing the importance of lament in Hip Hop, colleagues have assumed I am giving a comedic monologue. Still others assume nothing in Hip Hop is good—it is all evil, and anyone who engages with it is assumed to be evil too. I do not fret or wander from my arguments in my earlier work, nor do I stray from the position in this book: Hip Hop provides a space for this generation of youth and emerging adults to (1) find God in a contextual manner, (2) have room for lament, ambiguity, doubt, and the profane, and (3) find diversity within Christianity and remain true to their own cultural heritage.

And so we pick up the conversation where *The Soul of Hip Hop* left off—at the crossroads of Jesus, the profane, and a post-9/11 America. This chapter converses with both the complexity within Hip Hop and the richness of its theological parameters. We will begin with a brief overview of the scholarship of Hip Hop culture. Maybe this is my way of saying "I told you so" to my former professor, but more than that, it is necessary to construct its significance and worth for future missiological scholarship.

THE FIELD OF HIP HOP STUDIES

The study of Hip Hop now spans more than two decades.[1] Scholars such as Tricia Rose, Michael Eric Dyson, Cornel West, Anthony Pinn, Jeff Chang,

---

[1]Portions of this section are adapted from Monica Miller, Daniel White Hodge, Jeffrey Coleman, and Cassandra D. Chaney, "The Hip in Hip Hop: Toward a Discipline of Hip Hop Studies," *Journal of Hip Hop Studies* 1, no. 1 (Spring 2014): 6-12; and Daniel White Hodge, *Hip Hop's Hostile Gospel: A Post-Soul Theological Exploration*, Center for Critical Research on Religion and Harvard University, ed. Warren Goldstein (Boston: Brill Academic, 2017), 9-26. This is an ongoing discussion and needs a much broader research prospectus, but the goal here is to provide the premise for Hip Hop studies.

Nelson George, Bakari Kitwana, and Murray Forman were among the first scholars to give Hip Hop academic legitimacy. Rose's work *Black Noise: Rap Music and Black Culture in Contemporary America* discussed the context and cultural attributes of Hip Hop culture and gave insight into the contextual elements of the culture and musical genre. Dan Charnas wrote one of the most exhaustive books on how Hip Hop developed into a commercial, transglobal, multibillion-dollar entity and gives direct insight into how Hip Hop "lost its soul and went corporate" over the last thirty-five years. He gives a powerful historical account of the culture from a socioeconomic position.[2]

Using Black popular culture as a backdrop, much of the scholarship engages the historical and sociopolitical areas of Hip Hop. Jeff Chang and Nelson George give accurate social portraits of the historical settings that gave rise to Hip Hop. They lay out Hip Hop's historical ontology and argue for the legitimacy of Hip Hop within the American pop culture scene.[3] Kitwana describes what the Hip Hop generation is and also does a cultural study on the attraction of Hip Hop for White adolescents.[4] Yvonne Bynoe continues this conversation and asserts both the political leadership within Hip Hop and the growing need for it within the young Black community.[5]

These works give a solid foundation to the field of Hip Hop studies and have legitimized it in academia.[6] Hip Hop studies, as coined by scholars such as Mark Anthony Neal and Michael Eric Dyson in the mid-2000s, is a field

---

[2]Dan Charnas, *The Big Payback: The History of the Business of Hip-Hop* (New York: New American Library, 2010).

[3]The mid- to late 1990s gave rise to a multitude of scholarship focused on Hip Hop culture. Scholars such as Russell A. Potter, *Spectacular Vernaculars: Hip-Hop and the Politics of Postmodernism* (New York: State University of New York Press, 1995); Michael Eric Dyson, *Between God and Gangsta Rap: Bearing Witness to Black Culture* (New York: Oxford University Press, 1996); Todd Boyd, *Am I Black Enough for You? Popular Culture from the 'Hood and Beyond* (Indianapolis: Indiana University Press, 1997); and Mark Anthony Neal, "Sold Out on Soul: The Corporate Annexation of Black Popular Music," *Popular Music and Society* 21, no. 3 (Fall 1997): 117; Mark Anthony Neal, *What the Music Said: Black Popular Music and Black Public Culture* (New York: Routledge, 1999), gave treatment to the multiple levels of Hip Hop within communication, cultural, and African American studies. These works were critical in understanding Hip Hop beyond its historical aspects.

[4]Bakari Kitwana, *Why White Kids Love Hip-Hop: Wankstas, Wiggers, Wannabes, and the New Reality of Race in America* (New York: Basic Civitas Books, 2005).

[5]Yvonne Bynoe, *Stand and Deliver: Political Activism, Leadership, and Hip Hop Culture* (Brooklyn, NY: Soft Skull Press, 2004).

[6]This of course is arguable, but in the last decade of Hip Hop scholarship, most academic professional associations have started a section or group on Hip Hop studies. This along with the growth of doctoral candidates doing their dissertations on or related to a Hip Hop issue is grounds to suggest that Hip Hop has in fact grown from merely a subcultural study.

that encompasses sociology, anthropology, communication studies, religious studies, cultural studies, critical race theory, missiological studies, and psychology.[7] It is a multidisciplinary area of study—much like the culture of Hip Hop. In its early phases, Dyson, West, and Pinn began the conversation of the socioreligious elements within Hip Hop and the dimensions of the quest for meaning in the lyrics of its artists.[8]

These studies, while groundbreaking in their right context, tended to focus on the lyrical features of artists and did not engage the broader social, religious, political, and cultural contexts. In 1991, Jon Michael Spencer published a special edition of *Black Sacred Music: A Journal of Theomusicology* titled "The Emergency of Black and the Emergence of Rap." In this issue the elements of Hip Hop's socioreligious context were examined. This pioneering work began to explore what protest and prophecy was like in Hip Hop. William Perkins wrote an essay on the Islamic elements within Hip Hop, and Angela Spence Nelson argued for the theological scopes of Hip Hop within the work of rap artists Kool Moe Dee and Public Enemy.[9] This work broke ground on the religious arenas of Hip Hop. Then, in 1996, Michael Eric Dyson forged new pathways at the height of the golden era of Hip Hop (1987–1996) with his book *Between God and Gangster Rap: Bearing Witness to Black Popular Culture*, which took elements of the Black religious experience and applied them to Hip Hop culture. An avant-garde work, Dyson follows this with his work on Tupac Shakur (see chap. 3). Anthony Pinn in 1995 digs even deeper with his work on suffering, pain, and evil within Black theology in *Why, Lord? Suffering and Evil in Black Theology*. This book also created fresh arguments around what it meant to be Black, to suffer, and still desire

---

[7]A little-known work published by Russell Potter in 1995 examines the rhetorical aspects of Hip Hop culture from the point of view of communications. His *Spectacular Vernaculars* was the first to argue that Hip Hop vernacular might in fact be part of the postmodern language.

[8]By *socioreligious*, I mean the conflation and connection between the religious and the sociological. In other words, the interaction between what is religious, spiritual, and faith sensibilities of a particular group, culture, people, musical genre, or geographic space. This can also embody the social constructs, social developments, and social conditions within that which is religious and spiritual; something especially helpful to comprehend for the missiologist. See Dyson, *Between God and Gangsta Rap*; Jon Michael Spencer, ed., "The Emergency of Black and the Emergence of Rap," special issue, *Black Sacred Music* 5, no. 1 (Spring 1991); Anthony B. Pinn, ed., *Noise and Spirit: The Religious and Spiritual Sensibilities of Rap Music* (New York: New York University Press, 2003).

[9]During the era known as the golden era of Hip Hop (1987–1996), a strong Muslim element existed within Hip Hop. Ice Cube was known to be part of the Nation of Islam and rap groups such as X-Clan and Gang Starr were associated with the Zulu Nation, which was connected to Islam.

some type of response from God. Pinn broke from the Black Christian lens that many scholars had taken. He peered deep into the issue of suffering within the Black community and challenged typical notions of Judeo-Christian suffering: how a good God could allow suffering for a specific group of people. In this work Pinn peers into what suffering looks like within a Hip Hop context by arguing for "nitty-gritty hermeneutics"—a hermeneutic for life that goes beyond a "just pray about it" worldview. This is the essence of Hip Hop. Pinn continued by publishing an edited volume in 2003, *Noise and Spirit: The Religious and Spiritual Sensibilities of Rap Music*, which was pioneering because it exclusively explored theological and spiritual elements within Hip Hop. This work was foundational for the study of religion in the Hip Hop context. It challenged the notions that the study of religion was limited to popularized music such as rock-and-roll, jazz, and metal. Works that explored music and religion often overlooked Hip Hop as a field of study[10] or worse, footnoted it as an "emerging culture" and disregarded it altogether.[11]

This type of disregard is typical for ethnic-minority arts and media. Hip Hop's bravado, hard-hitting social messages, and Black male power is often seen as a threat to hegemonic systems. Thus it is labeled evil, immoral, racist, or violent. In comparison, White male artists such as Insane Clown Posse are able to sing about death, killing others, and morbid fantasies of sex and "sin" and yet receive nowhere near the negative press that rap artists receive.[12] Therefore, Pinn's work was foundational in establishing links

---

[10]Raymond F. Betts, *A History of Popular Culture: More of Everything, Faster and Brighter* (New York: Routledge, 2004); and Robin Sylvan, *Traces of the Spirit: The Religious Dimensions of Popular Music* (New York: New York University Press, 2002).

[11]Lawrence Eugene Sullivan, ed., *Enchanting Powers: Music in the World's Religions*, Religions of the World (Cambridge, MA: Harvard University Press, 1997); Calvin R. Stapert, *My Only Comfort: Death, Deliverance, and Discipleship in the Music of Bach*, Calvin Institute of Christian Worship Liturgical Studies Series (Grand Rapids: Eerdmans, 2000); Davin Seay and Mary Neely, *Stairway to Heaven: The Spiritual Roots of Rock 'N' Roll, from the King and Little Richard to Prince and Amy Grant* (New York: Ballantine Books, 1986); Neil Leonard, *Jazz: Myth and Religion* (New York: Oxford University Press, 1987); Michael J. Gilmour, *Gods and Guitars: Seeking the Sacred in Post-1960s Popular Music* (Waco, TX: Baylor University Press, 2009).While these texts offer insight into religious quests within generalized and popular music, they do not give treatment to the Hip Hop context and tend to not mention Black music's religious experience and discourses.

[12]Note that groups such as 2 Live Crew received negative press regarding their lyrics and sexualized messages. One case went all the way to the Supreme Court. White male rock and metal groups such as Poison received none of the same treatment when, in videos, they openly engaged in sexualized imagery very similar to that of 2 Live Crew.

between rap and religion, the spiritual and the profane, and a quest for a contextual deity in Hip Hop contexts.

Related approaches to Hip Hop and religion have also emerged within the last decade. Christian perspectives on Hip Hop such as Efrem Smith and Phil Jackson's work *The Hip-Hop Church: Connecting with the Movement Shaping Our Culture* gives deference to Black youth and Hip Hop engagement from a Christian context. Smith and Jackson explore what a Hip Hop church may look like for a new approach to church. Alex Gee and John Teter created a Bible study text exploring the lyrics and theological stances within the work of Tupac and Lauryn Hill.[13] These works are crucial, although niche and focused largely on evangelistic tools for the study of Hip Hop and religion.[14]

Christina Zanfagna, an ethnomusicologist, investigated Hip Hop by understanding the people's responses, reactions, and worldviews within the culture of Hip Hop under an ethomusicological background. Zanfagna writes,

> While my study seeks to redefine the parameters of "spirituality"—that is, what is considered spiritual—it is not my intention to give a hard fast definition of hip-hop's spirituality or even define what kind of God-figure hip-hop music might point to, for such theological preoccupations would obscure the flexible, adaptive, ecumenical nature of hip-hop's anatomy of belief and the spiritual experience it produces.[15]

Here Zanfagna, also evoking the importance of a theomusicological study, begins to explore the profane nature within Hip Hop culture and pushes deeper than mere lyrical analysis. Zanfagna argues that the profane aspects of Hip Hop—connecting them back to Black musical genres such as the blues and jazz—offer theological insight once we move past the seemingly sinful façade.[16]

---

[13]Alex Gee and John Teter, *Jesus & the Hip-Hop Prophets: Spiritual Insights from Lauryn Hill and 2Pac* (Downers Grove, IL: InterVarsity Press, 2003).

[14]Pertaining specifically to Christian rap and Hip Hop theology, two scholarly articles and one book that delve deeper into religion and Hip Hop stand out: Garth Kasimu Baker-Fletcher, "African American Christian Rap: Facing 'Truth' and Resisting It," in Pinn, *Noise and Spirit*; and Cheryl Renee Gooch, "Rappin for the Lord: The Uses of Gospel Rap and Contemporary Music in Black Religious Communities," in *Religion and Mass Media: Audiences and Adaptations*, ed. Daniel A. Stout and Judith Mitchell Buddenbaum (Thousand Oaks, CA: Sage, 1996). Felicia M. Miyakawa's book *Five Percenter Rap: God Hop's Music, Message, and Black Muslim Mission* (Bloomington: Indiana University Press, 2005) gives a comprehensive overview of the relationship between Hip Hop and this Islamic sect.

[15]Christina Zanfagna, "Under the Blasphemous W(RAP): Locating the 'Spirit' in Hip-Hop," *Pacific Review of Ethnomusicology* 12 (2006): 2.

[16]Ibid., 3-4.

Recent works by Monica Miller, Ebony Utley, Andre Johnson, Emmitt Price, and Ralph Watkins offer a broader yet specific look into the dimensions of Hip Hop theology.[17] These works are more focused on critically examining the theology of Hip Hop and also provide a much needed outside perspective. Miller, for instance, comes from secular humanist space and offers critical insight into the study of Hip Hop's theology. We can stand to learn much from these perspectives as missiologists.

Miller offers a strong critique of Hip Hop's religious areas while challenging the notion that Hip Hop's religion is Christian centered. Miller explores Hip Hop's religion and pushes us to look beyond what Russell McCutcheon calls a "private affair" in religion when the narrative becomes a tradition and experience that is universalized in the world, and argues that we should not limit the religious narrative to just a singular phenomenon.[18] Miller also challenges the study of Hip Hop and religion by naming works that approach it from hegemonic studies, mainly within Christian contexts that limit the study of Hip Hop and religion broadly.[19] Miller plainly questions whether the religious is actually religious, or whether it is hyperimposed by creative authors wanting to find something that is not there. These are tough yet needed questions for us as Hip Hop scholars to wrestle with.

Johnson's reader provides what a construction of Hip Hop's spirituality looks like and creates a dialogue between religious expressions and the space they were created in. These essays provide a two-part focus on theoretical and methodical approaches—which, as the field of Hip Hop studies develops, is a much-needed conversation. How might one conduct extensive and longitudinal research specifically focused on its religious expressions? The second section examines Hip Hop and religion—what are the aspects of and dimensions within the religious in Hip Hop? Johnson provides a needed resource for Hip Hop studies by creating a reader to engage its religious spaces.

---

[17] Ralph Basui Watkins, *Hip-Hop Redemption: Finding God in the Rhythm and the Rhyme*, Engaging Culture (Grand Rapids: Baker Academic, 2011); Emmett G. Price III, ed., *The Black Church and Hip Hop Culture: Toward Bridging the Generational Divide* (New York: Scarecrow Press, 2011); Andre E. Johnson, ed., *Urban God Talk: Constructing a Hip Hop Spirituality* (Lanham, MD: Lexington Books, 2013); Ebony A. Utley, *Rap and Religion: Understanding the Gangsta's God* (Santa Barbara, CA: Praeger, 2012); and Monica R. Miller, *Religion and Hip Hop* (New York: Routledge, 2013).

[18] Miller, *Religion and Hip Hop*, 15-16.

[19] Ibid., 81-85.

Ebony Utley describes the "Gangsta's God" as a rhetorician's study into the sociospirituality of Hip Hop. Utley covers the racial implications of Biggie's "Jesus Piece" (a gold and diamond encrusted medallion of a personified White Jesus) within Hip Hop, where rappers tend to criticize White images of deity yet also connect with those images in the social market place of capital and social status.[20]

Watkins is creating a romantic view of Hip Hop and its theological and spiritual dimensions, which could be viewed negatively and prematurely given the newness of the emerging field of religion and Hip Hop. Watkins addresses such issues as Hip Hop's spiritual connection to the blues, theological truth in story, and the spiritual discourse within narratives of oppression.[21] Watkins's work provides a needed framework in understanding the *how* of Hip Hop's theological capacities.

And for those seeking a more concise reading in the field of Hip Hop and religion, in *The Hip Hop and Religion Reader*, Anthony Pinn and Monica Miller take an exhaustive look into the scholarship, both Christian and non-Christian alike, with Hip Hop at its core and context. This volume stands alone as the first anthology to examine Hip Hop from a religious perspective. It is joined by a reader, *Religion in Hip Hop: Mapping the New Terrain in the US*, edited by Miller, Pinn, and rapper Bun B, which delves into emerging scholarship and methodology in the field of Hip Hop studies. By using a rap artist as an editor, the scholarship is much sounder and provides that emic perspective for those seeking a broader understanding. Once again, this is crucial for any missiologist seeking to have knowledge about this generation and Hip Hop.

Works such as these have broadened the study of Hip Hop and religion and have thereby expanded Hip Hop studies. This volume picks up the conversation from within these studies. Theologically speaking, how does Hip Hop construct a theological discourse, and how was that theology formed? We will next examine the good within the paradoxes of Hip Hop's theology and why that paradox is needed.

---

[20]Utley, *Rap and Religion*, 64-67.
[21]Watkins, *Hip-Hop Redemption*, 39-65; chaps. 5-7.

THE VIRTUOUS IN THE PARADOX OF HIP HOP'S THEOLOGY

The obscure part of Hip Hop is its theology.[22] Would anyone other than scholars consider it to be theological? What is it? Moreover, what kind of theology is it? Is Hip Hop rooted in religion? Or is Hip Hop truly misunderstood by those professing to be pious and theological? Those who only see rap music through the media's eyes or who do not have an understanding of cultural matters tend to hear loud music, rough sounding lyrics, and deep bass; they see low-riding pants, long white T-shirts, and ominous facial expressions—all of which are in opposition to "God's plan." As I have interviewed those of an evangelical Christian heritage,[23] Hip Hop is as much of an enigma to them as, say, the New Age movement or Muslims. To them, Hip Hop appears worldly and secular. Yet artists such as Kanye West (see his *The College Dropout* album) argue that God loves the hustlers, pimps, killers, prostitutes, and people that society would otherwise not deal with.[24] Tupac questions if there is a heaven for real niggaz. He changed the letter *s* to *z* to indicate a deeper meaning of the word, suggesting a class or lower socioeconomic status rather than the more racialized term *nigger*. In this sense Tupac contextualized a word that was once was used negatively.[25] Big Syke asks if the church can even handle Hip Hoppers, while KRS-One has suggested that Hip Hoppers need to start their own church. The underlying assumption here is that God loves the Hip Hoppers.

Hip Hop is a powerful cultural phenomenon that has dominated the popular culture scene for over twenty years. Gordon Lynch argues that Hip Hop culture has permeated almost every facet of American mainstream culture.[26] Marketing executives try to sell just about anything using rap music. As scholar of rhetoric Ebony Utley suggests elsewhere, when Jay-Z made it

---

[22]Portions of this section are adapted from Daniel White Hodge, "Baptized in Dirty Water," in *See You at the Crossroads: Hip Hop Scholarship at the Intersections*, ed. Brad Porfilio, Debangshu Roychoudhury, and Lauren M. Gardner (Rotterdam: Sense Publishers, 2014).

[23]These evangelical Christians typically have a conservative and literal view of the Christian Bible and missions to non-Christians.

[24]Kanye presents a good and well-mannered complexity to religion. He moves beyond Western White approaches to Christianity and challenges the notions of "holy" and "Godly." These are areas we must engage in as we decolonize Christianity.

[25]Robin Kelly agrees and further suggests that the term can permeate skin color as well. Robin D. G. Kelley, *Race Rebels: Culture, Politics, and the Black Working Class* (New York: Free Press, 1994), 207-12.

[26]Gordon Lynch, *Understanding Theology and Popular Culture* (Malden, MA: Blackwell, 2005).

on *Oprah*, Hip Hop had truly arrived as a mainstream phenomenon. Further, Robin Sylvan argues that "music is one of the most powerful tools for conveying religious meaning known to humankind. Music and religion are intimately linked in almost every culture and in almost every historical period."[27] Rap is that music and Hip Hop is the culture in which it is housed. Historically, the last forty years have had many societal shifts.

Within almost any type of cultural genre in the West, the search for God or a type of God is inevitable.[28] Hip Hop is no different. First, I will define theology and how it will be used in this chapter. Theology, in its basic sense, is the study of God—the study of how God interacts, intercedes, speaks, lives, thinks, wants, and is.[29] In the West, God is a supernatural creator who shaped the universe and intercedes in the lives of humans for the betterment of society and a journey to a place called "heaven."[30] Therefore, by that definition we can see how God is constructed and developed in Hip Hop and within a post-soul urban context. This does not and will not assume that every person associated with Hip Hop culture is a God-like symbol. Nor does it presume that MCs—often thought of as God figures—are to be left out of the spiritual equation. In fact, it is the opposite. Most of the lyrics are from MCs creating a spiritual discourse. To take this a step further, I would suggest that Hip Hoppers reflect on divine action in community and in the proximity of pain and suffering. Hip Hop theology reveals that God "shows up" in the most unusual places and the most interesting locations—more often than not in the intersection of the sacred and the profane.[31] In

[27]Sylvan, *Traces of the Spirit*, 4.

[28]See Émile Durkheim, *The Elementary Forms of the Religious Life* (New York: Free Press, 1965), 21-23.

[29]It is important to note here that theology, as a formal academic discipline, focuses on the study of God in the Christian religion. While I will discuss Hip Hop's inclusion and expression of different religions, the main discussion of Hip Hop theology will make references to the Christian religion and Christian religious expression. Interrogating God is something reserved for another study. However, for this study, God will be, in a simplistic sense, a supernatural persona. Yet it could be argued from a gendered perspective that God is not just a *he* in the masculine sense but also embraces a feminine side. Most Hip Hoppers see God in a masculine form, and this does present problems for a more egalitarian approach to God and theology.

[30]While there are numerous versions of this story, for the purposes of this book and research, I will primarily refer to the Abrahamic God found in the three main monotheistic faiths: Islam, Christianity, and Judaism.

[31]This ideology of God at the center of theology is a changing conversation in the field of religious study. Anthony B. Pinn discusses this well in *The End of God-Talk: An African American Humanist Theology* (New York: Oxford University Press, 2012). While this is not the main focus of this

a post-soul context, those unusual and curious places need to be examined with both a missiological and hermeneutical lens; it is a part of life. In other words, violence, sexuality, "sin," and the nuancing of the secular is sought and taken into consideration—a difficult premise for evangelicalism. Therefore, Hip Hop theology is, in essence, the study of the Godhead (God, the Son or Daughter, and the Spirit)[32] in the post-soul urban context/environment in order to better understand the rich and complex manifestations of spirituality, divine interactions, God's presence, and the revelation of a contextualized God from within the Hip Hop community while being liberated from oppressive conditions. This is core.

While Hip Hop is not without its problems, as seen constantly in the media, and even some elements of it deal with the occult, it does not deserve the ridicule and scorn that many in the church—including those in academia—have given to it.[33] More importantly, it does not deserve the alienation that many religious institutions (Christian, Jewish, and some Muslim) have given it. What is even worse is when some Christian churches—who in all fairness believe they are doing right by Hip Hop—give up one Sunday service every quarter to the youth and believe that this reaches out to the community. This does not promote a true conversation and dialogue with the Hip Hop community.

Religion and theology in Hip Hop appears so vague to outsiders and scholars because its roots, history, and religious backgrounds have multiple and complex sources. We are dealing with a culture that originates in poor Black and Brown communities with multiple religious, spiritual, and faith

---

book, it deserves to be noted. This is not to assume that there are other forms of finding spirituality. For example, assuming that God would be at the center of a theological conversation is much different than assuming that a community of people is at the center of that theological conversation. MCs also facilitate much spiritual meaning and, in that sense, become a type of God for that space. These are all areas that need further study and research.

[32]In some manner, this might be seen as a Christian Hip Hop theology. While Christian theology does provide this type of sensibility, others do too. For example, in Zulu theologies there is room for a three-person Godhead. Moreover, the addition of a female presence is also accepted in many African versions of Christianity—the idea that God can only be a man and only have a son is a mere reflection of the patriarchy that has existed for too many ages in the Abrahamic faith traditions. Thus, it is good practice in the process of decolonizing Christianity to embrace different approaches to the Godhead; Hip Hop provides plenty of space for that.

[33]While the occult in Hip Hop is not the focus of this book, it does deserve mention. The occult connection is based on interviews over the last decade I have had with those who have stated they are dealing with the occult and "dark magic" while rapping.

backgrounds.[34] Many of those traditions, in turn, seep into Hip Hop—for example, employing christological symbolism is a regular custom for some rappers. Kanye, DMX, Tupac, and even Kendrick Lamar are fascinated with the deity, yet they claim no specific church affiliation. This presents many problems for scholars and laypeople attempting to deconstruct Hip Hop within a standard hermeneutical lens.[35] Hip Hop cannot be defined easily. Nor can Hip Hop be boxed into a five-step process in order to reach the culture—it is too complex.

One aspect of Hip Hop's complex theology is that it engages the nitty-gritty of life as it comes at us—in real time. Christina Zanfagna states,

> Mainstream hip-hop percolates with unlikely and multifaceted religious inclinations. Despite its inconsistent relationship to organized religion and its infamous mug of weed smoking, drug pushing, gun slinging, and curse spewing, rap music is not without moral or spiritual content. On the flip side, religious music continues to draw upon popular music idioms—a smart mission strategy to reach today's listeners.[36]

Therefore, Hip Hop presents a basic theology of life. This theological paradigm is not new.[37] Good and evil are common subject matters for the

---

[34]The core of Hip Hop's mores can be traced back to fifth- and sixth-century West Africa, with connections to traveling poets, musicians, and storytellers; and its core cultural attributes, which are consciousness, self-awareness, community, spirituality, unity, and love of God and self. Darlene Clark Hine, William C. Hine, and Stanley Harrold, *The African-American Odyssey*, 4th ed. (Upper Saddle River, NJ: Prentice Hall, 2010), vol. 1, chaps. 1-2.

[35]Most Christian pastors are classically trained and have a modernistic way of approaching sacred Scripture. The issue of salvation, for example, becomes mechanical, predictable, and efficient. In other words, these pastors rely on traditional methods of evangelism to reach the Hip Hop nation. This simply will not work within Hip Hop culture. Nor will traditional ways of approaching the Bible work. The Hip Hop culture loves Jesus but despises institutional religion. Most seminaries train their pastors to be a part of the local church while not understanding the community of the church in the wild, which goes beyond not only the four walls of the local church but also the programmatic aspect of church, such as camps, sermons, and events.

[36]Zanfagna, "Under the Blasphemous W(RAP)," 1.

[37]James H. Cone, *A Black Theology of Liberation*, 20th anniv. ed. (Maryknoll, NY: Orbis Books, 1990); James H. Cone, "The Blues: A Secular Spiritual," in *Sacred Music of the Secular City: From Blues to Rap*, ed. Jon Michael Spencer (Durham, NC: Duke University Press, 1992); James H. Cone, *The Spirituals and the Blues: An Interpretation* (Maryknoll, NY: Orbis Books, 1991); Michael Eric Dyson, *Holler If You Hear Me: Searching for Tupac Shakur*; Anthony B. Pinn, *Embodiment and the New Shape of Black Theology (Religion, Race, and Ethnicity)* (New York: New York University Press, 2010); Anthony B. Pinn, *Why Lord? Suffering and Evil in Black Theology* (New York: Continuum, 1995); Anthony B. Pinn, "Black Theology in Historical Perspective: Articulating the Quest for Subjectivity," in *The Ties That Bind: African American and Hispanic American/Latino/a Theologies in Dialogue*, ed. Anthony B. Pinn and Benjamin Valentin (New York: Continuum, 2001).

expressions of life in an urban popular culture.[38] Likewise, a new type of spiritual profundity is needed as society changes and people continue to wrestle with the problem of evil. It is a spirituality that takes into account

- racism within White patriarchal Christian traditions;
- suffering and pain from an ethnic-minority perspective;
- the potential and possibilities the Black church has for suffering, pain, and lament for Christianity; and
- the God of the secular, sacred, and profane all in real time.

Hip Hop has the space and historical complexity to deal with, for instance, someone questioning their faith or wondering how a God can exist in the face of continued suffering. Hip Hop theology does not offer up simplistic and elementary forms of theological responses. Instead, a Hip Hop theology wrestles with the individual, group, or situation; uses art and music as forms of therapy and coping mechanisms; fuses dance with faith; and allows issues, problems, or concerns to be held up together.

Descendants of Black musical traditions realize that there is more to the story for Hip Hop.[39] Hip Hop begins the complex theological discussion of how the profane, secular, and sacred meet at one place. Moreover, within Black musical traditions, there is an ideology that sees the sacred in the profane.[40] Spencer believes that the Black secular music of the masses, while still sinful, secular, evil, and corrupt, is not completely unreligious and might actually present a spirituality and theology for everyday life.[41] God is doing something within those secular, evil, and corrupt spaces, and in those spaces the possibility of the gospel actually doing what it is supposed

---

[38]For example, artists such as Aretha Franklin, Curtis Mayfield, Stevie Wonder, and Ray Charles provided a diverse spiritual message in their music. Ray Charles was considered "profane" and "unholy" in his time, yet his music is heard in many churches today. Jon M. Spencer argues that there is much protest within Black gospel music and that stories from the Bible were told through old Negro spirituals. Moreover, in the time of slavery, music became the message for church and life, and there was no delineation between sacred, profane, and secular—all were one. See Jon Michael Spencer, *Protest and Praise: Sacred Music of Black Religion* (Minneapolis: Fortress Press, 1990), 3-34.

[39]Cheryl Kirk-Duggan and Marlon F. Hall, *Wake Up! Hip-Hop, Christianity, and the Black Church* (Nashville: Abingdon, 2011), 89-115.

[40]Spencer, *Sacred Music of the Secular City*, vol. 6; and Zanfagna, "Under the Blasphemous W(RAP)."

[41]Spencer, "Introduction," in "Emergency of Black and the Emergence of Rap," 9.

to do can bloom and prosper. Teresa Reed reminds us that "James Brown captures the soulful spontaneity of the Sanctified church and the animated exhortation of the Sanctified preacher."[42]

This is a theological paradox not just for Hip Hop but also for those seeking answers when their theological highway has run out.[43] Could sin actually produce a theological paradigm? Could debauchery be a deep theological archetype? Could rappers such as Scarface and Geto Boys, with all their violent discourse and the stark viciousness of life they have lived in, actually be creating a space for God to enter and create new meanings? These areas need more exploration. There is no definitive word on this, but it does require us to investigate and not dismiss the pursuit of God in awkward, strange, and even disreputable places. Are we who study religion afraid to deal with the real nature of the profane? This requires an ecclesial commitment to justice in theological dialogue. Zanfagna observes, "To accept this presupposes that popular culture could be a sacred place—an arena in which one may encounter God even in the most unholy of places."[44] Hip Hop theology not only embraces the sacred, it also dines, sleeps, laughs, cries, loves, hates, and lives with the profane. It is part of everyday life. If we are to understand Hip Hop, then a basic theological worldview of the profane must exist.[45]

This theological oxymoron—theology of the profane—is not new.[46] If, for example, we investigate the life of Jesus, we must look at the controversy he created. We must look at the profane language Jesus used when describing

---

[42]Teresa Reed, *The Holy Profane: Religion in Black Popular Music* (Lexington: University Press of Kentucky, 2003), 15.

[43]Those who live in oppressive conditions seek a theology that "fits" within spaces in which normative theological inquires cease to exist. Issues such as violence confound theological inquiries that promote a peaceful message, but in the face of injustice (e.g., Ferguson and Baltimore), how does one respond when peace has failed? Could there be a theology of violence for Black and Brown youth who are brutally murdered by White police officers? Is David Walker's *Appeal* (see fig. 1.1) much more relevant now for the Black youth? Is Hip Hop part of that "appeal"?

[44]Zanfagna, "Under the Blasphemous W(RAP)," 1-2.

[45]William E. McCutcheon and Russell T. Arnal, *The Sacred Is the Profane: The Political Nature of "Religion"* (New York: Oxford University Press, 2013).

[46]In fact, theologians and church heroes such as Martin Luther assert that God meets us first in the profane, or "shit" of life. Therefore, only those who enter the "shit" can encounter the God of Jesus Christ. See, for example, Danielle Mead Skjelver, "German Hercules: The Impact of Scatology on the Definition of Martin Luther as a Man, 1483–1546," *Pittsburgh Undergraduate Review* 14, no. 1 (Summer 2009).

the Pharisees and Sadducees, and we must also contend with the fact that there were multiple messianic narratives of Jesus (some of which do not align with the current Judeo-Christian theological prototype).

Hip Hoppers can resonate with the eccentricities of many Bible characters: Noah, who was a drunk and cursed his kids; David, who was not only promiscuous but also double-crossed his "friend" in order to steal that friend's wife (e.g., placed Uriah on the front lines of the war so that he could be with Uriah's wife, Bathsheba [2 Sam 11]); and women in the Bible such as Mary, Martha, and Apphia who didn't get a book in the New Testament canon yet could have provided rich firsthand knowledge of Jesus. These are narratives Hip Hoppers can relate to, engage with, and connect to.

Hip Hop says, "Man, we're dealing with it all!" One of Tupac's greatest sins was that he called out his own "sin," which made others extremely uncomfortable. For example, at the same time he received an NAACP image award, Tupac confessed his active sex life and "love" for female "beauty." Black leaders such as Jessie Jackson strongly criticized the NAACP for their decision to give Tupac an award, yet Jackson reportedly has had several interactions with women other than his wife. Bill Cosby also was an outspoken critic of Tupac's "womanizing," yet Cosby has been accused of sexual misconduct by multiple women.[47] Artists such as Tupac continue to be problematic for many religious zealots who hold fundamentalist views of religion.

Hip Hop can be at least partially understood as being based on Anthony Pinn's five central themes of African American humanism as "a mode for religious orientation."[48] These principles derive from an ideology that rejects the God idea—in particular, the notion that God will or could break into history. A "controlled optimism" arises from a recognition that "we will

---

[47]Cosby has come under scorn and heated ridicule for those in the Hip Hop community. Because Cosby situated himself as a moral authority over poor and disenfranchised Blacks, and because Cosby's continued strong push for "moral" and "ethical" values for the Blacks, those in the Hip Hop community—and others too—have called out Cosby's hypocrisy and pharisaical behavior. They interrogate the morality of not just Cosby but also of those in the civil rights generation.

[48]These themes are taken from "Rap's Humanist Sensibilities," in Anthony B. Pinn, *Terror and Triumph: The Nature of Black Religion* (Minneapolis: Fortress Press, 2003), 8-88. Pinn's themes are focused on African American religious traditions, but I use these five themes to illustrate the connection between Hip Hop theology and culture. I am not arguing that Hip Hop is entirely humanistic. However, humanism is not without educational and theological positives. Part of Hip Hop's theology connects with Pinn's five themes, which is what this work is attempting to get at.

receive no help from God if we just wait." Thus, a portion of Hip Hoppers have taken a more gnostic position toward God. Yet I use these central themes to critique traditional modes of theological inquiry, that is, a more conservative approach to God and a bounded set of theological parameters that make the rules clear, normative, and standardized. Hip Hop creates an alternate way to find God, and many Hip Hoppers are on the journey to find a God that fits their circumstances. For the purpose of this study, I have reframed Pinn's central themes, which are as follows.

1. Understanding that humanity is fully (and solely) accountable and responsible for the human condition and the correction of its plight—especially as it pertains to social justice.

2. Suspicion toward or rejection of supernatural explanations and claims, combined with the understanding of humanity as an evolving part of the natural environment as opposed to a static, created being unable to change its path. This is one of the many reasons why traditional evangelistic tracts do not work with Hip Hoppers.

3. Appreciation for African American cultural artifacts and the perception of traditional forms of Black religiosity as having cultural importance as opposed to any type of cosmic or supernatural authority that remains unnamed and vague.

4. Commitment to individual and societal transformation. This is a key aspect of all Hip Hop culture, which reaches well into its theology.

5. Controlled optimism that recognizes human potential as well as human destructive activities while still leaving room for God (i.e., God would be able to intervene, at times, in the lives of humans).

I use Pinn's five elements to provide a theological premise in which to begin this conversation. These five elements are building blocks for the structure of Hip Hop's theology.

The irreverent spirituality infused with a sacred element of God in Hip Hop music is a proper subject for what Spencer calls theomusicology, "musicology as a theologically informed discipline."[49] The fact that Hip Hop music is theologically rooted is no coincidence. Hip Hop is about liberation,

---

[49]Spencer, *Protest and Praise*, vii.

authenticity, and freedom from the shackles of modernity. Spencer views Black gospel music as liberating for not only Blacks but also anyone from an oppressed context. Hip Hop is a contemporary response to oppression for this generation of urban people, including urban Whites.[50]

Artists such as DMX and Tupac argue that we can have a sacred relationship with Jesus, commune with Jesus, and even grow in community without ever setting foot in church. Tupac even asks and answers the question: "There's a heaven for a G [gangsta]."[51] For most, even asking this question is profane. But it raises the important question: If you can reach Jesus without the church, what good is the church? Hip Hop puts that and many other questions at our feet. Hip Hop questions the institutional church and challenges the moral fiber of pastors, reverends, deacons, and priests. This is one of the reasons an artist such as DMX can begin his album *Grand Champ* with illicit language regarding life and end the album in a prayer "thanking God for making me righteous."[52]

This neo-secular–sacred theology does three major things for Hip Hop:

1. It provides a basis for understanding life and not allowing simplistic answers to be used to explain pain, distress, suffering, anxieties, and evil acts.

2. It allows for everyday life, language, culture, and contexts to be given a fair examination. In other words, nothing is too sacred to talk about or deal with.

3. It gives room for rap music, one of the vehicles for Hip Hop's message, to give critical insight, pose deep theological questions, reject the current hegemonic powers, and allow for change in its music.

These three concepts are central. Many artists such as Common, Mos Def, Odd Thomas, Propaganda, and Tupac use these theological tenets in their music. In "Rap, Reggae, and Religion" Noel Leo Erskine says, "Rap theology . . . is intimately linked to notions of how society functions and who operates the levers of control."[53] Consequently, rappers become reporters—and in some cases preachers, if you will—of life, both the sacred and the profane.

[50]Ibid., 35-39.
[51]2Pac, "Life Goes On," *All Eyez on Me*, Death Row, 1996.
[52]DMX, "The Prayer V," *Grand Champ*, Ruff Ryders/Def Jam, 2003.
[53]Noel Leo Erskine, "Rap, Reggae, and Religion," in Pinn, *Noise and Spirit*, 78.

Erskine further states, "In rap theology, God takes sides and identifies with rappers in their attempt to confront violence with counter violence. Their God is the God of the Old Testament."[54] Rappers like Big Syke argue that God was both killer and all-loving; he takes the side of the marginalized to vindicate them and kill the oppressor.[55] While this may be a radical and even violent view for some, keep in mind that for many years God operated in this realm. Read the Old Testament books of Joshua, Deuteronomy, Judges, and Genesis to find this type of God. For many centuries scholars and laypeople alike argued that there were two different Gods—one of the Old Testament and one of the New Testament.[56] Similarly, artists such as GZA challenge the status quo and find alternate narratives they can relate to, especially in violent times—even more so when dominant culture pushes "reconciliation" and "forgiveness" even though it does not reciprocate. Hip Hoppers cannot and will not accept a mediocre theology that is biased and lifts up oppressors. They desire a God who will remove oppressive conditions and create space for lament and celebrating God. This is a paradox for a Christian faith that promotes a theology of celebration.[57]

These paradoxes make Hip Hop a fertile space to be engaged missiologically, not with the unbridled zeal of a missionary desiring to "evangelize the heathens," but in conversation and the desire to learn more about the living God.

Now we will look at a specific paradox within Hip Hop's theology: the hostility within the gospel from a Hip Hop perspective.

THE HOSTILITY OF THE GOSPEL

The rap artist Talib Kweli asserted that the gospel is hostile from the start. In his song titled "Hostile Gospel," he asserts that there are double standards and major issues ignored by mainstream American society:

Hip-Hop's the new WWF
What do you rap or do you wrestle? Niggas love to forget

---

[54]Ibid.

[55]Taken from Dyson's interview with Big Syke in Dyson, *Holler If You Hear Me*.

[56]See Robert Walter Funk, Roy W. Hoover, and the Jesus Seminar, *The Five Gospels: The Search for the Authentic Words of Jesus: New Translation and Commentary* (San Francisco: Harper-Collins, 1993).

[57]Soong-Chan Rah, *Prophetic Lament: A Call for Justice in Troubled Times* (Downers Grove, IL: IVP Academic, 2015), 21-26.

We got til it's gone, you think you on, you still hustling backwards
Your topical norm a tropical storm, it's a fuckin disaster
Back to the topic we on, it all started at Rawkus
They couldn't find the words to describe me so they resort to the shortcuts
Is he a backpacker? Is he a mad rapper?
An entertainer? or the author of the last chapter?
We living in these times of love and cholera
Synonymous with the apocalypse, look up the clouds is ominous
We got maybe ten years left say meteorologists, shit
We still waitin for the Congress to acknowledge this!

Here Kweli describes some of the current issues, which the dominant society is ignorant of. Kweli even argues that Hip Hop is the new WWF (World Wrestling Federation). In other words, the commercialization of Hip Hop has created a type of hostility—even from within the Hip Hop community—even though issues in the urban context continue to be ignored. Kweli continues,

In these tryin days and times
All I need is to be free
I can't do it on my own
Lord can you deliver me?
There are trials still to come
It's salvation that I need
So I'm reachin to the sky
Lord can you deliver me?
Deliver us . . .[58]

Asking for deliverance is fundamental in the face of hostility and suffering. Kweli asks God not only to deliver himself but also the community (us).

How does one deal with God in the face of such hostility? How, as Tupac asks, does one act like an angel when you are surrounded by devils? In the same sense, how can hostility be found in "good news"? The rapper and Hip Hopper living in the hostile urban context would say that even in "good times" there are hostile elements to life; even in the midst of good days, there is the possibility of being killed; even with a loving God, s--- still happens on a daily basis. Can God, devoid of White-dominant theology, deliver me

---

[58]Talib Kweli, "Hostile Gospel, Pt. 1," *Eardrum*, Blacksmith Music, 2007.

in my mess and this hostile context? Further, where can I find God in the hostility of life? Ralph Watkins says, "The heaven-and-hell debate drives this song—the premise being that hell is right here on earth. Do you know hell? Do you know what it feels like and looks like? Kweli says, 'If you ever walked through any ghetto, then you know it well.' Living in the ghetto is hell."[59] This type of theology is rooted in the reality of daily life existence right now—the ghetto reality.

In part two of "Hostile Gospel," Kweli asks for God's deliverance from this hostile context of economic, social, and theological inequality:

> Die on my feet before I live on my knees lord
> Deliver me from point A to B like livery
> Nothin is free, you got to be a hero to save
> They got you working like a slave from the crib to the grave
> A minimum wage can barely keep a job for a home
> A car or a phone, forget about gettin a loan
> You starting to moan, your bank account is getting withdrawn
> It's pitiful how we becomin slaves to things that we own
> They en-slavin the brains with the whips and the chains
> End up in the coffin chasing the fortune, chasing the fame
> Slave to the rhythm, slave to the night, slave to the day
> They hop aboard the Underground Railroad and run away
> Pray for the day niggas don't get taken away
> For makin a way to stop their baby's stomach aching today
> I sip a whiskey straight, no chase
> It's hard to take a man away from the sin when it's inside of him
> Please[60]

Hip Hop theology is about engaging this hostility and tension head-on. Watkins notes, "The God of hip-hop is a God who is found inside those who follow this God [the God of justice, equality and freedom]."[61]

What makes the world hostile is (1) the nefarious social conditions of the urban context, (2) oppressive conditions within urban areas that breed

---

[59]Watkins, *Hip-Hop Redemption*, 109.
[60]Talib Kweli, "Hostile Gospel, Pt. 2," *Eardrum*, Blacksmith Music, 2007.
[61]Watkins, *Hip-Hop Redemption*, 110.

frustration and hostility such that (3) Hip Hop creates a hostile form of theology that not only engages these issues but also demands a voice at the theological table. There it brings its frustration and hostility paired with "good news" of how to get out of the current situation. Kweli's point is less sophisticated and more blunt: the Christian gospel is hostile to people.

Carter Heyward captures the essence of this hostile gospel in relation to Jesus Christ:

> Most Christians expect Jesus to be all good, completely good, perfect, "without sin," as the tradition has taught us. Either we overlook and ignore things that he did and said about which, if it were anyone but Jesus, we might complain (cursing and killing a fig tree?), we learn to rationalize away the biblical record (he didn't really do this), or we find positive ways of looking at what only appear to be negative images (he's not really belittling his mother at the wedding; he's just trying to stretch and re-image his friends' understandings of "family"). We cannot seem to bear the notion of a Jesus who *didn't* always do or say the right thing.[62]

Our view of Jesus needs to fit into a nice, neat construct. When he does not, it is almost unbearable to fathom. In other words, if one of the central figures of the Christian faith has hostility in his life, is it not fair to suggest that Hip Hop can express the same in its approach to God?

The root meaning of *gospel* is "good news." Hip Hop's good news is not based in Christian values and theologies but in a much broader view of social justice, social awareness, social consciousness, community-mindedness, personal consciousness, and a journey to God, who can help and will provide shelter. This good news is part of what Hip Hop is attempting to bring to its community. Moreover, Hip Hop's gospel is not always a sacred quest; it is intertwined with the secular and profane—with weed, alcohol, sexuality, living a good life, and being successful. These appear to be anti-God and sinful in nature. Yet Hip Hop theology pushes us to hold these in tension with the good news in order for survival. It allows urban ethnic minorities to rise above the current situation—whatever that might be. There might be a spiritual presence within sin, the secular, and evil that can

---

[62]Carter Heyward, *Saving Jesus from Those Who Are Right: Rethinking What It Means to Be Christian* (Minneapolis: Fortress Press, 1999), 144-45.

lift a person into a transcendental plane. God in those spaces is good news for Hip Hoppers. To understand the post-soul culture, we cannot ignore or overlook the "sinful" and "wicked," for in these Hip Hoppers are searching for a theology. As Spencer argues, Black secular music such as Hip Hop can masquerade as sinful, sexual, and sonically evil yet represent a spiritualty for the everyday.[63] Hip Hop actually becomes the hermeneutic, or "word" and "truth," through its artists and culture—an aspect KRS-One has been promoting with his own work and activism.[64]

Within the tempest of issues that beset a Hip Hop post-soul community, God and God's gospel are still at the center of the storm (see fig. 3.1). Those issues, ever present and not disappearing simply because someone prays them away, are symbiotically connected to people. A new church program or short-term mission group cannot alleviate the problems of, say, police brutality, oppression from bureaucratic institutions, or daily violence. God is present in that tension and the experience of "sin." God's presence and the gospel are enmeshed in daily life and give meaning and hope to push forward and live. Often in situations such as these, the impetus is to simply survive. Therefore, it is within those domains of sin that God is recognized as even more beautiful and sacred. Sin actually causes God to be more immediate and whole for the person experiencing it. Instead of trying to avoid sin or do away with it— because in some cases, these issues are present and cannot be erased—the person is forced to live as is while still seeking God. In fact, sin in this sense can be seen as corporate and institutional—a view that Western evangelicalism often fails to understand. (Its focus is on the individual's sin.) Here, profane issues are seen along with God. While God is present, these issues are not something to avoid but to press in to and learn, develop, and grow from. And some sinful aspects may never go away—especially sex and sexuality.[65] In sin and wickedness, Hip Hoppers are searching for a theology with the space and width to deal with these issues. In some cases, this appears hostile.

---

[63]Jon Michael Spencer, *Theological Music: An Introduction to Theomusicology*, Contributions to the Study of Music and Dance (New York: Greenwood, 1991), 9-10.

[64]KRS-One, *The Gospel of Hip Hop: First Instrument* (Brooklyn, NY: powerHouse Books, 2009).

[65]I am not arguing here that one should just "sit with" heinous acts such as rape, incest, murder, and injustice. Just the opposite. We must seek justice in the face of those acts. Still, the event or residue of the event never leaves. And the aftereffects of such things—PTSD, anxiety, depression—are often overlooked or prayed away. For the Hip Hop community that is when the real work of God takes place, and in that work God is made even clearer and more present.

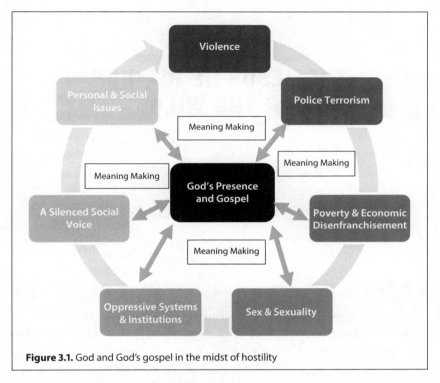

Figure 3.1. God and God's gospel in the midst of hostility

Finally, because Hip Hop is rooted in peace, love, joy, and unity, it is a post-soul context in which Christianity can provide space for those seeking a more robust understanding of God situated within the arts and media. Hip Hop creates space in which to dissent, question, doubt, rage, love, cry, laugh, love, eat, and feel without the constrictive control of dogmatic traditions. And while liturgy and cultural traditions are deeply respected by many, they are not held to by all. Within the hostility of Hip Hop's gospel, God emerges and engages this current generation living in the wild.

Rooted in hope, Hip Hop has potential for missiologists seeking to embrace a post-soul Christianity that embraces theology outside of Western evangelicalism rooted in White hegemony. But even more, Hip Hop is a community seeking God outside of traditional means and approaches. It provides space for this generation of youth and emerging adults to (1) find God in their own context, (2) have room for lament, ambiguity, doubt, and the profane, and (3) find the diversity within Christianity that will allow them to remain true to their cultural heritage.

4

THE JESUS OF HIP HOP
IN THE WILD

Race, Crisis, and the Pursuit of a Messiah

WHEN I SPEAK TO predominantly White evangelical audiences, I am
often asked what my relationship with Jesus is like—especially after
a talk on race, gender, or class. The assumption is that my relationship
with Jesus is lamentably poor or that I do not have one to begin with.
Sometimes there is a herd of White males in particular who question my
salvation, my relationship with Jesus, and my spiritual life. More often
than not, a young, zealous White male (with good intentions, I am sure)
wants to lecture me on either the Christian tenets of faith or what the
gospel really is. As a seasoned Christian secure in my walk with Christ, I
find this amusing. The core of these conversations (or rants) is focused on
Jesus—who he was and is, and what his gospel is. It seems there is a
standard way that I should interpret Jesus' life and teachings and manifest
his gospel in my life.

One summer I was speaking at a high school camp. It was a majority
White, conservative, evangelical crowd. However, the host group wanted to
mix things up a bit, so there were some Black and Latino students in the
crowd of about nine hundred. In my talk on the cross and the impact of Jesus'
life, I said Jesus was a social disrupter and used strong language, questionable methods, and resisted authorities. It was edgy but still within most
parameters of a camp talk. I went on to say that Jesus would have joined the
crowds in Ferguson protesting the death of Michael Brown and helping to

confront the injustice that many young Blacks face today in the United States. The Black and Latino groups erupted with clapping and cheers while the White students looked on in shock. A divide. I continued, saying that Jesus' language toward religious people could be taken to be the equivalent of the F-word but that such language was necessary because it called out dominate forces of oppression.

The Black and Latino groups loved it. Several leaders told me that they had been coming to this camp for years and had never seen a person of color up front. They were thrilled to hear about a Jesus that "wasn't a punk." As you can imagine, several White leaders tried to pull me aside and tell me I was wrong. One even went so far as to corner me in the lunch line to tell me, finger pointing and all, Jesus never did any such thing and I must be a "secular atheist." I challenged him by asking, "Have you ever read the language and historical narrative of Jesus? Are you aware of the strong nature of Jesus' language?" "No," he replied, "I need to do more research on that." Obviously.

My point is that typical White evangelical Christianity does not take into account the complexity, racial significance, or cultural worth of the historical Jesus. Further, there is a vast racial divide between how majority White Christians and those from oppressed or disenfranchised backgrounds view Jesus. It is time for the Hip Hop Jesus—a Jesus of and for the wild—to be seen, digested, and embraced. Missiologically, it is time to move away from traditional and domesticated versions of Jesus to explore a multiethnic, multiracial, and complex version of Jesus. This Jesus is, as Wilbert Shenk describes, messianic: "God is disclosed to be drawing near and entering redemptively into the human situation."[1] The Hip Hop Jesus contradicts the constructed systems of religion and rejects what humankind has built up. Shenk says, "The reign of God being manifested in Jesus the Messiah fundamentally contradicts the kingdom of the world."[2] Part of this "kingdom of the world" is rooted in race and dominance.

This chapter explores Jesus within a Hip Hop framework. First, I will discuss the complexities of race and ethnicity surrounding the Jesus figure,

---

[1]Wilbert R. Shenk, *Changing Frontiers of Mission*, American Society of Missiology Series 28 (Maryknoll, NY: Orbis Books, 1999), 11.
[2]Ibid.

arguing against the White archetype of Jesus. Then I will examine the Jesus of and in Hip Hop. Last, using a theomusicological framework, I will apply the Hip Hop Jesus to a specific song and argue for a contextualized embracement of the Hip Hop Jesus.

RACE, ETHNICITY, AND JESUS

Racial relations in the United States have been a muddied and turbulent road since the creation of the country.[3] White culture has been the dominant culture and racial group in the United States and has created intricate systems and institutions to reinforce its supremacy, including deity, religion, and faith.[4] The Euro-Western captivation of the Christian church has manipulated the image of Jesus into a blonde, White, blue-eyed deity who is irrelevant outside of those White contexts. This makes Christianity problematic for anyone attempting to find a racially and ethnically appropriate deity.[5] For some, Christianity cannot be redeemed because of the centuries of racism. The past is historically skewed toward Whiteness, and any attempt at reconciliation will result in the oppressed becoming more oppressed and disenfranchised.[6] Further, with a White image of Jesus, one is never able to appreciate fully the message of Jesus, because it will always be tainted with racialized imagery, which, for some scholars, distorts the Christology and gospel message within.[7] For scholars such as William Jones, "divine racism" takes place when an "in-group" and an "out-group" are created. Those who are outside of God's grace are hostile toward God, and in return God is

---

[3]Some content in this section was originally published in Daniel White Hodge, "Religion and Race," *Open Theology* 2, no. 1 (2016): 1033-35, https://doi.org/10.1515/opth-2016-0080.

[4]See Michael Battle, *The Black Church in America: African American Christian Spirituality*, Religious Life in America (Malden, MA: Blackwell, 2006); David Belton, "God in America," PBS, 2010; Lerone Bennett Jr., *The Shaping of Black America* (New York: Penguin Books, 1993); James H. Cone, *A Black Theology of Liberation*, 20th anniv. ed. (Maryknoll, NY: Orbis Books, 1990); Jay David and Elaine Forman Crane, *Living Black in White America* (New York: Morrow, 1971); and Ida B. Wells-Barnett, *On Lynchings: Southern Horrors, a Red Record, Mob Rule in New Orleans*, The American Negro, His History and Literature (New York: Arno Press, 1969).

[5]David Hempton, *Evangelical Disenchantment: Nine Portraits of Faith and Doubt* (New Haven, CT: Yale University Press, 2008); and Soong-Chan Rah, *The Next Evangelicalism: Freeing the Church from Western Cultural Captivity* (Downers Grove, IL: InterVarsity Press, 2009).

[6]William R. Jones, *Is God a White Racist? A Preamble to Black Theology*, C. Eric Lincoln Series on Black Religion (Garden City, NY: Anchor, 1973).

[7]James H. Cone, *Black Theology and Black Power*, 5th ed. (Maryknoll, NY: Orbis Books, 1997); James H. Cone, *God of the Oppressed* (Maryknoll, NY: Orbis Books, 1997); David and Crane, *Living Black in White America*; Jones, *Is God a White Racist?*; and Rah, *Next Evangelicalism*.

hostile toward them. In other words, God does not value all persons equally. Further, the out-group suffers more than the in-group, and God becomes indifferent toward their suffering as they are outside God's will. The racial and ethnic categorization is also crucial under divine racism, as it divides those who are blessed from those who are not. Constructs of a racial deity are conflated with sin, immorality, and debauchery. A pathology is created for those who are labeled sinners, immoral, and debauched.[8]

To see this more closely, Traci West writes compellingly that "for Christians of African descent in the United States, certain teachings about Jesus can advance their acceptance of white-supremacist ideas about their own black humanity."[9] In other words, the mere notion of having a White Jesus clouds, disrupts, and corrupts the theological pursuits of not only Blacks but also all ethnic minorities. West continues with a set of powerful questions:

> When missionaries who converted enslaved blacks in the Americas or colonized blacks in Africa taught a Christology informed by white dominance–black inferiority mythology, their evangelism confused truth with lies. How did such Christology rooted in confusion teach anti-black devaluation of embodied, human worth? Currently, what kinds of theo-ethical understandings of Jesus as Christ might assist Christians in disrupting racialized (and kindred heteropatriarichal) paradigms of human subjugation that continue to exist within Christian-dominated societies? In a contemporary liberationist Christian ethics that foments such anti-racist intervention, the varied permutations of anti-black racism interwoven for centuries into the Christology initially introduced to black converts would need to have been discarded—right?[10]

Centuries of seminary training, theological teaching, missions, and a colossal breadth of Sunday (and Saturday) morning sermons have created a Christology that places Whites at the top and Blacks—and ethnic minorities as a whole—near the bottom.[11] Even more problematic and troubling is that

---

[8]Jones, *Is God a White Racist?*, 3-6.

[9]Traci C. West, "When a White Man-God Is the Truth and the Way for Black Christians," in *Christology and Whiteness: What Would Jesus Do?*, ed. George Yancy (New York: Routledge 2012), 114.

[10]Ibid., 115.

[11]For example, Immanuel Kant writes that "humanity is at its greatest perfection in the race of the whites" (Immanuel Kant, lectures on "Physical Geography," in *Race and the Enlightenment: A Reader*, ed. Emmanuel Chukwudi Eze [Malden, MA: Blackwell, 1997], 64). Kantian ethics is taught in numerous classrooms, including some Christian churches. This White supremacist

some Black leaders and other ethnic-minority religious leaders continue the traditions of the White supremacist Jesus simply because it is true to them; established tradition and culture are far more convenient than a search for a more relevant Christology. This is in no way to undermined the excellent work that historical Black colleges, universities, and seminaries have provided in fostering critical thinking. Yet those voices often are moved to the margins or, even worse, branded as heretical. Howard Thurman argues,

> The significance of the religion of Jesus to the people who stand with their backs against the wall has always seemed to me to be crucial. It is one emphasis which has been lacking—except where it has been a part of a very unfortunate corruption of the missionary impulse, which is, in a sense, the very heartbeat of the Christian religion.[12]

Thurman is establishing parallels between the life of Jesus and the experiences of African Americans and all oppressed peoples who seek a contextual image of Jesus. William Hart says, "As a Jew, Jesus was shaped by his ethnicity, as were Black Americans; furthermore, he was poor and a member of a despised minority group dominated by a great imperial power."[13] Jesus' back was, using Thurman's metaphor, "against the wall." He too was oppressed and disenfranchised.

Tim Wise, noted antiracist and opponent of White privilege, recalls the first time he brought up the issue of Jesus' ethnicity to an all-White Catholic college. The audience was quick to insist that Jesus' ethnicity was irrelevant; they could not entertain the notion that Jesus could have been Black.[14] They had given in to the myth that Jesus' race is insignificant. But their failure of imagination and ensuing resistance to imagining a Black Jesus reveals just how deeply racial ideology has affected the Christian

---

worldview is in the North American social, cultural, and pedagogical DNA (Rah, *Next Evangelicalism*, 78-79). While this, I am sure, will raise concern with Kantian scholars—as well it should—this issue cannot be ignored and must be dealt with in context. Yes, Kant did not necessarily mention "race" in his formal ethical works, but the racial bell has been rung, and doing critical work on race, one cannot overlook this.

[12]Howard Thurman, *Jesus and the Disinherited* (Boston: Beacon Press, 1976), 7.

[13]William David Hart, "Jesus, Whiteness, and the Disinherited," in Yancy, *Christology and Whiteness*, 158.

[14]Ibid., 156-57.

imagination.[15] Jennifer Harvey states, "Traditional Christianity has committed this sin [not acknowledging and not embracing the Black Jesus] in its invention of the white Jesus."[16] Those mythological notions that Jesus was White, the downplaying of his ethnic background, the impression that he was Euro-centric, and his perceived inability to cope with minority groups has created a strong sense of contempt among Hip Hoppers toward most things Christian.[17]

James Cone argues that there must be continuity between the historical Jesus and the kerygmatic Christ. Kerygmatic theology is defined as the modern movement that seeks to orient scientific theology to Christian life and evangelistic activities, and thereby to bring about an interaction of theology, social, and apostolic action.[18] If not, then any community (especially those in power) might interpret "the kerygmatic according to its own existential situation," and craft Jesus in their own image.[19] Cone asserts that Black liberation theology is the appropriate ontological symbol for the divine because of the "white American inability to recognize humanity in persons of color. . . . Blackness, then, stands for all victims of oppression who realize that the survival of their humanity is bound up with liberation from whiteness."[20] If Blacks and ethnic minorities alike must seek their Christology from Whites, then the theological inquiry is already skewed and White models of perfection, morality, values, and living pure lives are already established from the initial setting.[21]

To complicate this further, Christian biblical interpretations of ethnicity have been hazy and obtuse at best. Africans brought over in the trans-Atlantic slave trade were baptized as Christians with the understanding that

---

[15]Tim J. Wise, *White Like Me: Reflections on Race from a Privileged Son*, rev. ed. (Berkeley, CA: Soft Skull Press, 2008), 54-56.

[16]Jennifer Harvey, "What Would Zacchaeus Do?," in Yancy, *Christology and Whiteness*, 90.

[17]Even though they distrust Christianity, artists have continued to reference Jesus as central to their faith expressions. Rap artists such as Kanye West, Nikki Minaj, Tupac, Lauryn Hill, Jay-Z, Big Syke, King T, DMX, and Geto Boys keep close connections with Jesus. But they see Jesus as suffering, Black, and disenfranchised, which they can relate to.

[18]E. F. Malone, "Kerygmatic Theology," in *New Catholic Encyclopedia* (Detroit: Gale, 2003), 158.

[19]Cone, *Black Theology of Liberation*, 113.

[20]Ibid., 7-8.

[21]Ibid.; Anthony B. Pinn, *Terror and Triumph: The Nature of Black Religion* (Minneapolis: Fortress Press, 2003); Thurman, *Jesus and the Disinherited*.

Eurocentric religion was "better for those savages."[22] Paul's letters in the New Testament were interpreted as an endorsement of slavery. Paul says, "Slaves, obey your earthly masters" (Col 3:22). In his letter to Philemon he encourages a slave is to return home to his master.[23] These erroneous biblical interpretations continued, and a sense of shame, guilt, and inferiority developed among Africans. In many ways, this continues to this day.[24] Cheryl Townsend Gilkes gives a richer picture of this phenomenon:

> When using the Bible as a tool for racial domination, white people in Europe, the United States, and South Africa assume that Jesus and the ancient Israelites are white. These readers have chosen and expanded upon selected portions of the Bible. Those selections sometimes refer to people of African descent, noted in English translations as Ethiopians or Cushites. The curse of Ham is actually non-existent. In Genesis 11, Noah's curse is placed upon Canaan, Ham's son. The other sons of Ham, who are the eponymous ancestors of Cush and Mizraim, are excluded from Noah's utterance. In order to argue that black people are cursed, white people have engaged in a massive misreading that reaches back to Ham in order to include Africans under that curse. Since the presumption of whiteness applies to everybody else in the Bible, whiteness is never specifically identified in biblical racial ideology—once again whiteness is silent. There is a problem with failing to acknowledge and identify whiteness in the Bible. Whenever white skin is specifically mentioned there is usually a terrible problem. Those biblical stories that could not be construed to be about whiteness are about leprosy, usually a curse from God.[25]

---

[22]See Andrew F. Walls, *The Cross-Cultural Process in Christian History: Studies in the Transmission and Appropriation of Faith* (Maryknoll, NY: Orbis Books, 2002).

[23]In turn, many Africans despised the epistles of the New Testament and focused largely on the message, life, and theology of Jesus. While Moses and the children of Israel were an important part of early African American Christianity, many Black slaves focused on Jesus and his message of liberation. See Peter J. Paris, *The Social Teaching of the Black Churches* (Philadelphia: Fortress Press, 1985); Andrew F. Walls, *The Missionary Movement in Christian History: Studies in the Transmission of Faith* (Maryknoll, NY: Orbis Books, 1996); and Walls, *Cross-Cultural Process in Christian History*.

[24]Nancy Pineda-Madrid, "In Search of a Theology of Suffering, Latinamente," in *The Ties That Bind: African American and Hispanic American/Latino/a Theologies in Dialogue*, ed. Anthony B. Pinn and Benjamin Valentin (New York: Continuum, 2001); Alphonso Pinkney, *Black Americans*, 5th ed. (Upper Saddle River, NJ: Prentice Hall, 2000); Anthony B. Pinn, *The Black Church in the Post–Civil Rights Era* (Maryknoll, NY: Orbis Books, 2002); Amos N. Wilder, *Early Christian Rhetoric: The Language of the Gospel* (Peabody, MA: Hendrickson, 1999).

[25]Cheryl Townsend Gilkes, "Jesus Must Needs Go Through Samaria: Disestablishing the Mountains of Race and the Hegemony of Whiteness," in Yancy, *Christology and Whiteness*, 71.

Gilkes's argument is profound; she illustrates the significance of interpretations, translation, and ultimately the construct of subservience, shame, guilt, and inferiority within religious and theological domains. Conflate these with centuries of teachings, and the image of Jesus is sullied under the guise of Whiteness.

Soong-Chan Rah also suggests that racism is at work within theological pursuits outside of Western White domains. He asserts,

> Because theology emerging from a Western, white context is considered normative, it places non-Western theology in an inferior position and elevates Western theology as the standard by which all other theological frameworks and points of view are measured. This bias stifles the theological dialogue between various cultures.[26]

As Rah suggests, race plays a central role when it pertains to matters of theological inquiry and standards of life.[27] The image of Jesus therefore becomes that of a White male who is indifferent to those who are not White. Individualized salvation, autonomous faith (e.g., a personal savior), and a "savior" represented as a White male is contentious for the Hip Hop community.[28] Rah links much of the racism within Christian theology to consumerism and materialism. Many White Christians desire more stuff and geographical safety. *Nice* and *safe* people and things are associated with Whiteness or docile and domesticated ethnic minorities.[29]

The "other" is created when cultures such as Hip Hop embrace a Jesus figure in their likeness. Black theology, liberation theology, third-eye

---

[26]Rah, *Next Evangelicalism*, 78.

[27]Alexis de Tocqueville notes that standardization, especially for politics and religion, is a dangerous brew. For him, it set up White (or Anglo-Americans) as "right" and "moral," creating a system that benefits them through policy, law, and ultimately religious belief structures. One can then conclude that a savior such as Jesus would in turn favor the White race. Alexis de Tocqueville, *Democracy in America*, ed. Tom Griffith, trans. Henry Reeve, Wordsworth Classics of World Literature (Ware, UK: Wordsworth Editions, 1998), 121-28.

[28]This includes the Christian Identity movement, which, according to Michael Barkun, has ties to such extreme White supremacist groups as the Ku Klux Klan, Nazis, and skinhead movements. Such hate associated with religion usually promotes a White "savior." Michael Barkun, *Religion and the Racist Right: The Origins of the Christian Identity Movement*, rev. ed. (Chapel Hill: University of North Carolina Press, 1997), 4-14.

[29]Rah, *Next Evangelicalism*, 46-63.

theology, Zulu Nation theologies, and Five Percenter theology are categorized by White, Western Christianity as "the other."[30] Regarding the historical context of otherness, Rah says,

> Creating "the other" allowed Western culture to express its power over non-Western cultures. Inferiority is inferred when a culture or people are categorized as "the other." . . . In the same way that Western culture diminishes non-Western culture through the creation of an "otherness," Western Christianity diminishes non-Western expressions of Christian theology and ecclesiology with the creation of "otherness."[31]

To this, Edward Said—whose reflections on otherness in connection to Arabic and Middle-Eastern cultures is similar—adds that "European culture gained strength and identity by setting itself off against the Orient as a sort of surrogate and even an underground self."[32] So, when Hip Hop is defined as secular, nonreligious, or profane, otherness is created, which gives permission to zealots such as G. Craig Lewis (who is Black himself) to call "all of Hip Hop satanic" and "worldly."[33] This is one example of how the "other" has spread beyond White Western Christianity.

Nevertheless, the Jesus figure, though racially controversial, remains a central piece of Hip Hop culture. For instance, Kanye West on a 2006 cover of *Rolling Stone* adorned himself with a crown of thorns, a beard,

---

[30]What makes this potent is that not only do White evangelicals believe and embrace this but also Blacks, Latinos, Asians, and the rising Christian populations in south and central Africa. This Western belief is intertwined with a typology of being right, moral, and correct. Andrew Walls, a noted African missiologist and Christian historian, argues that in contexts such as Ghana, Sierra Leone, Brazil, Argentina, and Kenya their own theologians are overlooked, devalued, and marginalized because White, Euro-tribal theologians continue to promote a White Western agenda in these settings (Walls, *Missionary Movement in Christian History*; and Walls, *Cross-Cultural Process in Christian History*).

[31]Rah, *Next Evangelicalism*, 78-79.

[32]Edward W. Said, *Orientalism*, 25th anniv. ed. (New York: Vintage Books, 2003), 3.

[33]G. Craig Lewis's DVD series "The Truth About Hip Hop" says Hip Hop is an agent of the devil. He informs his audience, who is majority Black, that demonic forces are at work within Hip Hop. When I approached his former ministry for a panel discussion or interview regarding Hip Hop, Lewis's staff refused and responded, "Minister Lewis does not debate. His word is from the mouth of God and that cannot be debated." Further, Lewis has continually ignored all attempts at dialogue from Christian rappers and other Christian pastors. He preaches solely to Black, religiously conservative audiences whose ages average forty-five and fifty-four, and who have largely become indoctrinated in a Western ethos of otherness. What better way to dehumanize someone than by labeling them evil, satanic, or demonic?

and bloody scars crisscrossing his face. His burlap cloth and the title "The Passion of Kanye West" immediately signals the appropriation of Christ by the rapper. The title of the article reflects Mel Gibson's 2004 film *The Passion of the Christ*, which graphically reenacted the crucifixion of Jesus. West takes on the persona of Jesus by asserting he is "crucified in the media" and "my misery is your pleasure."[34] West clearly feels as though he is a martyr.

The cross is representative of suffering, pain, disenfranchisement, and political oppression, and is a crucial element of and for the Hip Hop community. The cross represents these key aspects for the Hip Hop community:

- a savior
- victory over "death"
- redemption through suffering and pain
- the "devil," or evil presence, defeated
- victory over sin
- resurrection to a new life
- resurrection as a way of life
- pain for peace

These representations of Jesus in the Hip Hop community are critical, and Jesus, in turn, becomes a central figure for a culture and people who feel they are in similar situations. As Michael Eric Dyson notes, Hip Hoppers see a contextual Black Jesus as "the God who literally got beat down and hung up, the God who died a painful, shameful death, subject to capital punishment under political authority and attack, but who came back, and keeps coming back, in the form and flesh we least expect."[35] To this Ebony Utley adds, "The cross represents Jesus's victory over death. Cheating death makes Jesus the gangsta's hero. The cross as a symbol of death visually resurrects memories of unjust persecution from Jesus to ancestors who hung from lynching

---

[34]Kanye West, quoted in Lola Ogunnaike, "The Passion of Kanye West," *Rolling Stone*, February 9, 2006.
[35]Michael Eric Dyson, *Open Mike: Reflections on Philosophy, Race, Sex, Culture and Religion* (New York: Basic Civitas, 2003), 286.

trees."[36] Therefore, Jesus is much larger than a mere persona. For many who suffer under oppression, Jesus is representative of hope and aspirations for "a better life" and "brighter tomorrow," as Kelly, one of the interviewees from chapter one, states. Despite the racial connotations that Jesus carries, he is still powerful for rappers—especially Black rappers. He represents the struggles and psychological violence enacted to perpetuate slavery—even the modern slavery of the prison-industrial complex. Thus, West is evoking this historical imagery and connecting his life to that lineage.[37]

THE JESUZ IN AND OF HIP HOP

The Jesus symbol is a crucial part of the socioreligious sensibilities of Hip Hop communities. Hip Hop embraces various christological paradigms that fit in the Hip Hop setting. On one hand, we have a view of Jesus as liberator, embracing the social justice aspects of a messiah. On the other hand, we have a Karl Barth–like Jesus that sees Christ in the Trinity, having an ambiguous nature, being a mediator, being both elected by God and an elected man. Still, in other circles we have a Rudolf Bultmann–style Christ that sees Jesus through the lens of mythology, which breeds a wider, postmodern understanding of Jesus as a mythological hero. For artists such as Nas, Common, Lauryn Hill, and Erykah Badu, Jesus is Paul Tillich's Christ, who, much like these artists, engages the intellect, stirs the mind, and embraces deep theological study. From Tillich's perspective, Christ is no different from humankind in substance, just in degree, hence the term "degree Christology."[38] I will now examine variations of Jesus in the Hip Hop community that connect with aspects of the Zulu Nation and Five Percenter theology.

---

[36]Ebony A. Utley, *Rap and Religion: Understanding the Gangsta's God* (Santa Barbara, CA: Praeger, 2012), 57-58.

[37]To further understand West's theological construct, we must look at John 1:1-14, where Jesus introduces the Word who became flesh. West utilizes this, not as a blasphemous or heretical pursuit, but to reference both his connection to Jesus and his own personal suffering alongside Jesus. The cover of the magazine is representative of this and illustrates West's connection to this "flesh" from a secular context (Ogunnaike, *Rolling Stone*, 59-60).

[38]Paul Tillich, *Theology of Culture* (New York: Oxford University Press, 1959), 150.

The likenesses of the Hip Hop Jesus are vast and complex.[39] We will now reexamine the five likenesses a Hip Hop Jesus.[40]

1. Jesus abandons moralism and the authoritarian model of relationships. He does hold a moral standard but allows the community to grow in their faults, errors, and sins.

2. Jesus acts redemptively to bring the spiritual power of love and cohesion to the present moment while being aware of what it cost him and what it will cost us and the Hip Hop community.

3. Jesus accepts the true nature of people and intellectually, narratively, communally, and spiritually encourages them to change and continue the journey toward consciousness and healing.

4. Jesus rejects standardized and absolute messages of salvation, church, and religion while establishing new views of each.

5. Jesus challenges the status quo and argues for equal rights, justice, and cultural change in systems that oppress his people while still allowing for the people in these oppressive social structures/systems to change and follow him.[41]

Regardless of their faith background, Hip Hoppers can come together around these five likenesses of the Hip Hop Jesus. The following attributes together with a Hip Hop Jesus that focuses more on love and encourages the community of Hip Hop.[42] Jesus is seen as:

---

[39]The Hip Hop image of Jesus is a relational and contextual one. For some Hip Hoppers, even the name Jesus should be changed to *Jesuz*. Note the letter *s* has been dropped to demonstrate the contextualization of the Christ figure for the 'hood. And the letter *z* at the end of Jesus' name was added to give a portrait of a Jesus who could sympathize and connect with a downtrodden and broken people. The letter *z* is consistent with Hip Hop's tendency to change words and phrases to fit the context and annunciate words for a Hip Hop community. The *z* also represented a Jesus that is not only "above" but also "below," in reachable form. The *z* gives new dimensions to the portrait of Christ and validates the struggles, life, narrative, and spirituality of many Hip Hoppers. Tupac and the Outlawz use Jesuz to provide a more contextual application for their audience. See Daniel White Hodge, *The Soul of Hip Hop: Rims, Timbs and a Cultural Theology* (Downers Grove, IL: InterVarsity Press, 2010); and Daniel White Hodge, "No Church in the Wild: An Ontology of Hip Hop's Socio-Religious Discourse in Tupac's 'Black Jesuz,'" *Nomos*, March 23, 2013.

[40]Cf. Carter Heyward, *Saving Jesus from Those Who Are Right: Rethinking What It Means to Be a Christian* (Minneapolis: Fortress Press, 1999), 122-23. These are very similar to KRS-One's theological premise for Hip Hop as well. While he does not name Jesus outright as the deity, these likenesses are present throughout his discussion. See KRS-One, *The Gospel of Hip Hop: First Instrument* (Brooklyn, NY: powerHouse Books, 2009).

[41]Hodge, *Soul of Hip Hop*, 132-33.

[42]In *The Gospel of Hip Hop*, KRS-One has similar tenets and focuses largely on the peace, love, and

- liberating oppressed people and creatures

- healing personal wounds: ours, others', and the community's

- liberating the community of Hip Hop from fear, greed, lack of confidence, and low self-esteem

- healing peoples, nations, tribes, and earth of its ailments, sorrows, pain, and disorders

- loving others

- bringing peace and harmony to the community[43]

For those in the Hip Hop community who because of their environment tend to not subscribe to this "love and peace" message, another likeness of the Hip Hop Jesus is present—much like that of Trap Jesus.[44] The rough, tough, hypermasculine, rugged, and authoritative Hip Hop Jesus is particularly attractive to urban males.[45] A masculine Hip Hop Jesus is not necessarily unaware of his female followers, but he at least prefers a heteronormative posture much like that of Trap Jesus.[46] The Hip Hop Jesus has the following characteristics:

- He has fundamental attitudes regarding church, God, and Scripture.

- He supports male dominance and "man of the house" ideologies.

---

respect aspect of the gospel, which are also similar to this component of a Hip Hop Jesus.

[43]These are similar to the fifteen universal beliefs of the Zulu Nation, which present a broader, more accepting aspect of Jesus that moves outside of Judeo-Christian circles. See "Zulu Beliefs," Universal Zulu Nation, http://new.zulunation.com/zulu-beliefs/.

[44]Trap Jesus is a drug-dealing pimp who instills fear in his followers. From the mind of Lil Wayne, Trap Jesus represents the more violent and hypermasculine Jesus that many urban males— principally Black males—can relate to. Found on Spike Television's Adult Swim network, Trap Jesus, who lives a lavish lifestyle, is compassionate when the Sweet Tea Mobsters arrive (who are consequently arguing and bickering just as Jesus' disciples did) and offers them empathy and guidance. The rugged Trap Jesus gives the Sweet Tea Mobsters help. He is understanding and compassionate about the issues Black males face and exemplifies a brighter way while still living in the reality of the 'hood.

[45]Some female rappers have adopted the hypermasculine view of Jesus. Because there is a lack of female MCs in Hip Hop culture who can mentor these women in a female context, masculine traits become the norm for these women. Female rappers such as Lil' Kim and Foxy Brown have adopted male personas in their music. See Joan Morgan, *When Chickenheads Come Home to Roost: My Life as a Hip-Hop Feminist* (New York: Simon & Schuster, 1999); and T. Denean Sharpley-Whiting, *Pimps Up, Ho's Down: Hip Hop's Hold on Young Black Women* (New York: New York University Press, 2007).

[46]Thus, Trap Jesus becomes the secular articulation of a ghetto-appropriated Christ, who, as the author of the Hebrews passage suggests, "empathize[s] with our weaknesses" and was "tempted in every way, just as we are" (Heb 4:15).

- He "beats down" those who are in his way.

- He instills fear as a form of control and power.

- The devil is not only an entity but also a system and institution.

- Weakness is not tolerated.

- He is in control and powerful.

- The profane and secular parts of life are embraced and valued as sacred.[47]

This Hip Hop Jesus fits the ghetto context well and brings value and context to difficult geographic spaces. Rap artists such as Big Syke, King T, Geto Boys, Ice Cube, and Mobb Deep prefer this kind of Hip Hop Jesus. As we have seen with Trap Jesus, he is compassionate but has a street edge and wisdom. He will help, but first he will have his disciples hold you up at gunpoint to see if you are "for real." He can be generous but will tell you to "not f--- around, cuzz he watchin" just to make sure you will follow his ways. This Hip Hop Jesus is much more "street" and "ghetto," yet possesses elements of a messianic figure. Ebony Utley observes,

> If nothing else, Trap Jesus understands him [Black males] better because they are living the same life as black men facing obstacles while on their daily grind. His confinement is not a hindrance as much as it is a reality that black men can help each other overcome. Trap Jesus is trapped in the prison system because he was caught trapping (selling drugs) in the trap (hood). Both "traps" represent a cycle of impoverishment and imprisonment. Because Trap Jesus embodies this predicament, he is an accessible companion who looks and acts like his followers.[48]

However, these two likenesses of Jesus (loving and peace-based versus heteronormative) intersect at certain points:

- *True community.* Community that not only embraces each individual but also makes room for the community to learn from each other.

- *Open answers.* The historical Jesus was not moved when people challenged him, questioned him, or tried to anger him. He was bold

---

[47]Do not misread this as an endorsement of this style of Jesus. It is problematic on many levels and continues to promote heteronormativity within these circles.

[48]Utley, *Rap and Religion*, 55.

enough to handle doubt, questions, ambiguity, and mystery—key aspects to Hip Hop's post-soul theological constructs. Thus, the Hip Hop Jesus would be the same.

- *Embracing uniqueness.* The Hip Hop Jesus is not afraid to deal with people who do not look right, talk right, smell right, and believe right. He embraces the uniqueness of everyone. Yet he refuses to accept a person in their current state and looks beyond the obvious faults to what they could become—another aspect of Hip Hop culture's beliefs.

- *Rejection of the institutionalized church.* The historical Jesus had his strongest words for church folk and religious officials. In fact, some of his most pointed, charged, direct, and heated words were for people claiming to be religious. When Jesus did address "sinners," he did so in a respectful and enlightening manner, pointing them to a new consciousness, not condemning them to hell. The Hip Hop Jesus is about community that grows intellectually, spiritually, and theologically in a variety of modes and faith practices. The Hip Hop Jesus rejects the institutionalizing of dogmatic churches and aggressively advocates for unity and community in church-like settings.

- *Truth is a quest.* The argument over truth has disabled contemporary denominations and paralyzed many religious people. The Hip Hop Jesus knows that truth is relegated to the context, time period, and people seeking it. Moreover, the Hip Hop Jesus realizes that sacred words are open to interpretation. So, the Hip Hop Jesus searches for truth in a variety of places—another post-soul idea. For the Hip Hop Jesus, truth is a quest, not something to be conquered.

Unlike their relationship, or lack thereof, with the traditional, White, Western Jesus, Hip Hoppers embrace and love the Hip Hop Jesus. He is not concerned with church attendance numbers, tithes and offering totals, or which church has the biggest choir. The Hip Hop Jesus cares about the people and their quality of life. Therefore, Hip Hoppers are developing an ontological discourse—by which I mean a space and place for being your own cultural and ethnic heritage within the presence of God—regarding the cosmos, afterlife, death, pain, suffering, and relative social conditions similar to what Martin Luther, Karl Barth, Henri Nouwen, and Jürgen Moltmann have done for the Eurocentric Jesus.[49]

These elements of the Hip Hop Jesus constitute the *figura* of Christ in the Hip Hoppers' experience.[50] This has roots in African American Christology. The *figura* of Christ is part of the African American Jesus experience.[51] Jesus is seen as the liberator and mediator for Blacks. In essence, Hip Hop has taken that image of Jesus, contextualized it for themselves, and then remixed it for different ethnicities. The same basic principles apply and are all rooted in Black theology.[52] This concept can be applied to the Hip Hop Jesus. In the Black christological tradition, James Evans says,

> Jesus Christ was a figura in the sense that he was a cosmic reflection of Adam, the firstborn, the image of God, as well as the historical reflection of Joshua, who led the Israelites into the Promised Land. Jesus Christ was also a figura in the sense that he was a cosmic projection of "the new Adam," the image of God restored to its original state, as well as the historical projection of liberated humanity, evident in the mystical/concrete notions of the church as the "body of Christ" and "the people of God."[53]

The key element in understanding Christ for many Hip Hoppers is the difference between the traditional Western perception of Jesus and the likenesses of Jesus discussed thus far in this chapter. As other scholars and I have argued, theological pedagogy over the last millennia is rooted in a Euro-tribal view, which will be difficult to deconstruct or argue against.

---

[49]For an in-depth study into these racial pedagogies in theological settings, see J. Kameron Carter, *Race: A Theological Account* (Oxford: Oxford University Press, 2008).

[50]The *figura* of Christ is not a new concept. It is borrowed from Black Christology, which borrowed it from Greek and Roman thought to express "an idea of something that both reflects something that already exists as well as projects something yet to be" (Veli-Matti Kärkkäinen, *Christology: A Global Introduction* [Grand Rapids: Baker Academic, 2003], 206). The idea here is the cultural appropriation for contextualizing a deity figure in the Hip Hop context. The *figura* of Jesus for Hip Hoppers better connects them with the messianic narrative. As I have observed, within that narrative Hip Hoppers are able to grow spiritually and theologically. That narrative comes in many forms: the artists themselves, concerts and performances, the music, spoken poetry, silent times outside of urban centers, and community gatherings. A lot of the spiritual growth and development I observed took place in much smaller venues of less than two hundred people or with close-knit friends. Underground communities provide that space for this growth.

[51]James H. Evans Jr., *We Have Been Believers: An African-American Systematic Theology* (Minneapolis: Fortress, 1992).

[52]See Cone, *Black Theology and Black Power*.

[53]Evans, *We Have Been Believers*, 787.

This is one of the reasons why Tupac is so powerful; he embodies elements of the Jesus *figura* in not just his music but also his life. It is also why rappers/singers such as Erykah Badu, Paris, Mace, and Kendrick Lamar continue to have such a prominent effect on young audiences across the globe—they are the embodiment and external articulation of the Hip Hop Jesus. Veli-Matti Kärkkäinen observes that in this *figura* of the Hip Hop Jesus, "The Messiah was vested with the authority to usher in a new age in which the power structures of this world would be overturned and freedom would prevail."[54] The liberationist perspective is found in the Hip Hop Jesus.[55] Freedom for the Hip Hop Jesus means freedom from economic, social, political, educational, emotional, spiritual, theological, and familial oppression—expressly those oppressive conditions emanating from hegemonic institutions.

In this sense then, the Hip Hop Jesus becomes a type of messianic figure who brings voice, shelter, identity, hope, dreams, love, and passion to a community seeking a higher consciousness. He is a messianic figure who does not singularize pathways to them—rather, they are open to various pathways so long as the end result is a higher personal and social consciousness. Evans gives us an example of this in Black Christian contexts:

> The Messiah embodies the nationalistic hopes and dreams of an oppressed people. . . . It is noteworthy that continued oppression and travail did not destroy the messianic dream but intensified it. Indeed, the more evil abounded the more powerful the idea of the Messiah became. As the actual historical liberation of Israel seemed to recede into the remote provinces of probability, the Messiah became one capable not only of transforming the historical situation of the people, but of transforming history itself.[56]

Broadly, the Hip Hop Jesus lifts up people and gives them new hope. The Hip Hop Jesus then establishes a contextual and relevant theological framework for that community. This pushes past a Eurocentric image of Jesus and moves beyond the Western concepts of Jesus keeping this figure locked in one religious affiliation.

---

[54]Kärkkäinen, *Christology*, 207.
[55]Gustavo Gutiérrez, *On Job: God-Talk and the Suffering of the Innocent* (Maryknoll, NY: Orbis Books, 1987).
[56]Evans, *We Have Been Believers*, 79.

Given that the discourse about Jesus tends to be associated with the ste-reotypes of mainstream conservative Christians (homophobic, dogmatic, Western, judgmental), some in the Hip Hop community who religiously af-filiate closer to Zulu, Nation of Islam, Five Percenter, and Muslim spiritual practices might not be that closely tied with a Jesus *figura*. Ice Cube's 2006 song "Go to Church" scorns images of Jesus and marks him as weak, feeble, and incapable of being able to handle the reality of 'hood life.[57] The Hip Hop community cannot stomach this type of Jesus for very long. However, most spiritual guides and religions promote the qualities of the Hip Hop Jesus—peace, love, joy, and happiness. The name might be problematic for some, but the qualities are nonetheless important and valuable.

The *figura* of a Hip Hop Jesus is not a Jesus that is easily digestible. It is a hostile form of Jesus for those who see him only in singularities and con-strained theological proportions they have learned. The Hip Hop Jesus is filled with a multitude of problems, heresies, and blasphemy for them. Yet I argue that this type of Jesus is what Hip Hoppers are in search of. They desire to connect with such a messianic persona. The Hip Hop Jesus would be hostile to the traditions, teachings, training, and spirituality that have created spiritual prisons for so many. The Hip Hop Jesus would come to "set them free" from those types of religious bondage.

We will now examine a specific song to see how artists trudge on in this spiritual journey.

THE OUTLAWZ AND BLACK JESUZ

Hip Hop pushes past a socially constructed traditionalized White, blonde, blue-eyed, construct of Jesus and asks for a Jesus that smokes like we smoke, drinks like we drink, and acts like we act—a Jesus that we can relate to in the 'hood.[58] This type of Jesus also questions authority, seeks to increase

---

[57]While these are stereotypes within Hip Hop culture, they are still rooted in Western models of Jesus—a White and unrelatable Jesus who is impotent in real life. That is the main image rappers like Ice Cube are rebelling against.

[58]The traditional image of Jesus has been that of a bearded, long-haired, blue-eyed, White person (Cone, *God of the Oppressed*; Herbert O. Edwards, "Black Theology: Retrospect and Prospect," *Journal of Religious Thought*, no. 32 (1975); and Pinn, *The Black Church in the Post–Civil Rights Era*). The social reinforcement of this image from White-dominant culture has been problematic for many in the Hip Hop community, thus the push to have a form of Christ more contextual and relevant for the Hip Hop context (e.g., the ghetto and oppressive conditions from hegemonic systems).

social consciousness, validates and acknowledges social isolation as real to all in the 'hood, and every now and then "puts a foot in someone's ass to tell a motherf----- he real."[59] Continuing the analysis using Jon Michael Spencer's framework of theomusicology, I will analyze Tupac Shakur and the Outlawz's song "Black Jesuz" to argue that sensationalized images of Jesus are the missing pieces that mediate the growing gulf between traditional Christianity and Hip Hop culture, and that Hip Hop produces a more relevant and applicable theological mantra for Christianity.[60]

The dominant narrative of Jesus as a White, perfect image of deity is both problematic and offensive to rappers and the Hip Hop community.[61] Thus, a contextual, relevant, and appropriate Christ is needed to interpret deity and spirituality for the hood. In the song "Black Jesuz" by Tupac and the Outlawz, there is an attempt to make a god—who appeared too perfect, too nice, and too White—more accessible to the 'hood.

"Black Jesuz" tries to make life in the 'hood more understandable from a theological perspective. It is trying to create a space for the thug, the nigga, and the pimp to find God. It hopes for a Jesus who is not only Black but also Hip Hop. The intersection of Spencer's trinary construct is at work: where the sacred and the profane both reveal themselves in secular contexts—in this case, through Hip Hop artists.[62] Tupac and the Outlawz reverse the hermeneutical flow and use culture—in this case, Hip Hop—to interpret God in a hostile context.[63]

The song has three parts: (1) *doxology*, giving respect and acknowledgement; (2) *lament*, how life and love is done in this ghetto hell; and (3) *benediction* to Black Jesus as they search for the Jesus who is *for* us. Tupac opens the song with the doxology, a call out to the Jesus who can relate:

[59]Interviews in Daniel White Hodge, *Heaven Has a Ghetto: The Missiological Gospel and Theology of Tupac Amaru Shakur* (Saarbrucken, Germany: VDM Verlag Dr. Müller Academic, 2009).
[60]"Black Jesuz" was mentioned in the interviews I conducted as being instrumental in having the ability to see Jesus beyond the Western lens and White hegemonic structures.
[61]Cone, *God of the Oppressed*; Miller, *Religion and Hip Hop*; Pinn, *Why Lord?*; and Utley, *Rap and Religion*.
[62]Jon Michael Spencer, *Theological Music: An Introduction to Theomusicology*, Contributions to the Study of Music and Dance (New York: Greenwood Press, 1991).
[63]L. Joseph Kreitzer, *The New Testament in Fiction and Film: On Reversing the Hermeneutical Flow*, Biblical Seminar 17 (Sheffield, UK: JSOT Press, 1993); and L. Joseph Kreitzer, *The Old Testament in Fiction and Film: On Reversing the Hermeneutical Flow*, 24 (Sheffield, UK: Sheffield Academic Press, 1994).

Searching for Black Jesus
Oh yeah, sportin' jewels and shit, you know what I mean?
(Black Jesus; you can be Christian Baptist, Jehovah Witness)
[A God whose religious affiliation does not matter]
Straight tatted up, no doubt, no doubt
(Islamic, won't matter to me
I'm a thug; thugs, we praise Black Jesus, all day)
Young Kadafi in this bitch, set it off nigga, what?[64]

Once again, Christina Zanfagna reminds us that "Hip-hop wrestles with the ways in which the hedonistic body and the seeking soul can be fed and elevated in dynamic tension. This wrestling is often expressed through a dialectic of pleasure and pain or recreation and suffering."[65] From the Outlawz stance, "thug Jesus" is a needed deity figure and someone to be praised. Here, the search is clear; they are looking for a "blinging" Jesus without denominational affiliation who can relate to the suffering, pain, disenfranchisement, and historical oppression experienced by those in 'hood.

Kadafi, one of the Outlawz, exegetes his environment with laments to Jesus: (1) it is a nightmare, (2) times are desperate, (3) the form of religion does not relate, and (4) he questions whether God can relate:

Stuck in a nightmare, hopin' he might care
Though times is hard, up against all odds, I play my cards
Like I'm jailin,' shots hittin' up my spot like midnight rains hailin'
Got me bailin' to stacks more green

The visibility of pain and suffering is evident while the assertion to "survive" and make money is also evident. Can a God who loves everyone conjure a resolution within a "nightmare" situation? The ageless theological inquiry of doubt begins to manifest itself:

Gods ain't tryin' to be trapped on no block slangin'
No rocks like bean pies brainstorm on the beginnin'
Wonder how shit like the Qu'ran and the Bible was written
What is religion? God's words all cursed like crack
Shai-tan's way of gettin' us back or just another
One of my Black Jesus traps

---

[64]Tupac Shakur and The Outlawz, "Black Jesuz," *Still I Rise*, Interscope Records, 1999.
[65]Christina Zanfagna, "Under the Blasphemous W(RAP): Locating the 'Spirit' in Hip-Hop," *Pacific Review of Ethnomusicology* 12 (2006): 5.

Storm, another Outlawz member, follows and presents the following three questions:

1. Who has the guts to stand beside him in hell?

2. Can we meet at the intersection of the profane and sacred?

3. Is heaven a possibility or even a reality?

Who's got the heart to stand beside me?
I feel my enemies creepin' up in silence
Dark prayer, scream violence—demons all around me
Can't even bend my knees just a lost cloud, Black Jesus

Give me a reason to survive, in this earthly hell
'Cause I swear, they tryin' to break my well
I'm on the edge lookin' down at this volatile pit
Will it matter if I cease to exist? Black Jesus

Tupac, allowing members of the Outlawz to go first, then enters and creates a relatable Jesus—one who can affirm the social isolation and disinherited:

In times of war we need somebody raw, rally the troops
Like a Saint that we can trust to help to carry us through
Black Jesus, ha ha ha ha ha

He's like a Saint that we can trust to help to carry us through
Black Jesus

Tupac reminds Storm that surroundings in the 'hood are similar to warlike conditions, but there is a Saint who can "carry us through."

Outlawz member Young Noble begins the benediction—the fourth verse—affirming that race, culture, and religion are different in the 'hood:

Outlawz we got our own race, culture, religion
Rebellin' against the system

Young Noble keeps the lament tension intact while still begging Black Jesus to "please watch over my brother." This delicate treading between the sacred and the profane is similar to what Spencer refers to as "unreligious people's quest for the sacred."[66] Spencer argues that this is a way to understand the nature of irreligious music and the community that produces it.[67]

---

[66]Spencer, *Theological Music*, 16-17.
[67]Ibid., 161-62.

Thus, Young Noble, in an irreligious way, is in search of a God who does not flinch in the setting of blasphemy, heresy, and the sacrilegious.[68] He is engaging in a conversation with Black Jesus to which the answers of his pain are yet to be revealed. This is similar to David's prayers in Psalms: "Keep me safe, O God, for I have come to you for refuge" (Ps 16:1 NLT).

My God, my God, why have you abandoned me?
Why are you so far away when I groan for help?
Every day I call to you, my God, but you do not answer.
Every night I lift my voice, but I find no relief. (Ps 22:1-2 NLT)

These passages are similar to Noble's own apprehension, which he is laying before Black Jesus:

The President ain't even listenin' to the pain of the youth
We make music for eternity, forever the truth

Political prisoner, the two choices that they givin' us
Ride or die, for life they sentence us
Oh Black Jesus, please watch over my brother Shawn
Soon as the sky get bright, it's just another storm

Brothers gone, now labeled a statistic
Ain't no love for us ghetto kids, they call us nigglets
History repeats itself, nuttin' new in school I knew
E'rything I read wasn't true, Black Jesus

In the fifth verse, Tupac discusses the ill effects of a life within nefarious conditions:

To this click I'm dedicated, criminal orientated
An Outlaw initiated, blazed and faded
Made for terror, major league niggaz pray together
Bitches in they grave while my real niggaz play together

We die clutchin' glasses, filled with liquor bomblastic
Cremated, last wishes nigga smoke my ashes
High sigh why die wishin,' hopin' for possibilities
I'll mob on, why they copy me sloppily

---

[68]Monica Miller also argues that within these ostensibly profane areas, religious meaning is still constructed (*Religion and Hip Hop*).

> Cops patrol projects, hatin' the people livin' in them
> I was born an inmate, waitin' to escape the prison

In this verse, he exegetes the life of the thug, the pimp, and the pusher. Moreover, he asserts that those types of lifestyles produce drug abuse, hate, and distrust of systems. Church as an institution, for Tupac and the Outlawz, is no different. In their estimation, if the cops beat you, schools lie to you, and systems fail you, why would the church be any different? Tupac ends the verse with:

> Went to church but don't understand it, they underhanded
> God gave me these commandments, the world is scandalous
>
> Blast til they holy high; baptize they evil minds
> Wise, no longer blinded, watch me shine trick
> Which one of y'all wanna feel the degrees?
> Bitches freeze facin' Black Jesus

Michael Eric Dyson asserts that "Tupac was the secular external articulation of an ongoing religious debate about the possibility of identifying with a God who became what we are."[69] In other words, Tupac surmises that within the fallout of failed systems, promises, and theologies, there is a need for a Black Jesus; one in which "bitches freeze" when standing in his presence.[70]

Outlawz member Kastro finishes the last verse with a declaration to Jesus: we are hurting, please help. Kastro shows a Jesus who "walks through the valley"—a Jesus who can identify with hunger; a Jesus who realizes that this is not the intended mode of life for humans; a Jesus who, as Ebony Utley asserts, was gangsta, hung out with thieves and prostitutes, beat down some fools, used foul language to cast off religious leaders, and rejected the religiosity of his day:

> Jesus is the transitional God figure because, according to the Bible, God "out there" sent Jesus "down here" to sacrifice himself via death, burial, and resurrection to redeem humanity. The physical experience of walking the earth

---

[69]Michael Eric Dyson, quoted in "Tupac Vs.," directed by Ken Peters (USA: Concrete Treehouse Productions, 2002).

[70]In other words, individuals who are weak morally, ethically, and spiritually and pursue oppressive paths are not able to withstand the presence of a God who is for justice, reconciliation, ending oppression, and creating spaces in which people are valued over things (Watkins, *Hip-Hop Redemption*, chap. 6).

anchors Jesus to the human experience. . . . Only a God who walked among
humans could truly redeem them. This perspective is not lost on gangstas
who connect with Jesus' experience with haters (persecutors), murder (crucifixion), and resurrection (redemption). Jesus is familiar with suffering
because he suffered. Jesus is familiar with victory because his resurrection
conquered death.[71]

Kastro wants to see something better than the life he has experienced
thus far:

And it ain't hard to tell, we dwell in hell
Trapped, black, scarred and barred
Searching for truth, where it's hard to find God

I play the Pied Piper, and to this Thug Life, I'm a lifer
Proceed, to turn up the speed, just for stripes
My Black Jesus, walk through this valley with me
Where we, so used to hard times and casualties

Indeed, it hurt me deep to have to sleep on the streets
And haven't eaten' in weeks, so save a prayer for me
And all the young thugs, raised on drugs and guns
Blazed out and numb, slaves to this slums this ain't livin' Jesus

Kastro wants a deity that is "down here" and can redeem the mounting
negative experiences within the 'hood.

Finally, Tupac, in the last call of the song, tells us they are in search of the
Jesus who hurts like we hurt, smokes like we smoke, drinks like we drink,
and understands where we are coming from—a basic ontological hermeneutic for us all:

Searchin' for Black Jesus
It's hard, it's hard! We need help out here
So we searchin' for Black Jesus

It's like a Saint, that we pray to in the ghetto, to get us through
Somebody that understand our pain
You know, maybe not too perfect, you know
Somebody that hurt like we hurt

---

[71]Utley, *Rap and Religion*, 8.

Somebody that smoke like we smoke
Drink like we drink
That understand where we coming from
That's who we pray to, we need help y'all

Dyson tells us:

> Black Jesus for Tupac meant for him that figure that identities with the hurt,
> the downtrodden, and the downfallen. The Black Jesus is a new figure; both
> literally within the literary traditions of black response to suffering, but also
> religious responses to suffering. If this is the Black Jesus of history, it is the
> Jesus that has never been talked about and most people who talk about Jesus
> would never recognize.[72]

Tupac not only knew this but also embodied this in his work; in many of
his songs he argued for the contextualization of the gospel for the 'hood.
Tupac blurred the lines between the sacred and the profane. Tupac entered
into blasphemous zones and waded into heretical waters while searching for
this Black Jesus who could not only create a space for the thug and the nigga
to find deity but to redeem his context (the 'hood and inner-city spaces),
which most of society label as "bad places." Black Jesus attempts to bring a
type of 'hood redemption to nontraditional church members living within
the post-soul urban enclave called the ghetto.

TOWARD CONTEXTUALIZED IMAGES OF THE HIP HOP JESUS

Jesus was and still is a controversial person. He was neither one to mince words
nor miss an opportunity to connect with the disinherited. Utley observes that

> Jesus fraternized with sexually licentious women, cavorted with sinners,
> worked on the Sabbath, had a temper, used profane language with religious
> people, praised faithfulness over stilted forms of religious piety, and honored
> God more than the government. Gangstas respect Jesus because they see the
> parallels between his life and theirs.[73]

However, most of the critical, radical, and post-soul images of Jesus have been
lost and too often domesticated for either political or racial reasons. In other
words, the critical, radical, and post-soul image of Jesus that many Hip Hoppers

---

[72]Dyson, quoted in "Tupac Vs."
[73]Utley, *Rap and Religion*, 49.

could readily identify with are marred by the image of a quiet, turn-the-other-cheek, meek, and mild-mannered Jesus. Hip Hoppers in rough and rugged situations need a deity that can connect better with the rough and rugged.

Is it possible that seemingly blasphemous images of the Christ create spiritual awareness? Theologian Tom Beaudoin says, "Offensive images or practices may indicate a familiarity with deep religious truths."[74] One must understand the authority of church sacraments to devalorize them forcefully. Likewise, it takes a true believer in the power of worship to turn curses into praise and the word *nigga* into a term of high respect. The point here is not to promote degrading terms, but to acknowledge that such rhetorical devices are serious theological attempts at grasping a practice of inequality that is *very* real.[75]

Tupac and the Outlawz present Jesus as not only relatable but also able to connect with those who experience the inequalities of life. While most of "Black Jesuz" questions whether Jesus can connect, the subtext is that Jesus can relieve the burden of ghetto life. In the psalmist's terms, Jesus is a shepherd who causes those in dire straits to lie down in green pastures, who in a contemporary context is able to blow through the blunt, smoking persona and redeem those who hurt.

These contextualized images of Jesus are needed as they push beyond the traditional symbols and offer a contemporary Jesus for younger audiences.[76] More important, they are needed in Christian theology because many of these images get lost within the dominant American evangelical model of Christianity.[77] Suffering in context is nothing new. The search for meaning within that suffering is also nothing new.

---

[74]Tom Beaudoin, *Virtual Faith: The Irreverent Spiritual Quest of Generation X* (San Francisco: Jossey-Bass, 1998), 123.

[75]Cf. Don Cupitt, "Post-Christianity," in *Religion, Modernity and Postmodernity*, ed. Paul Heelas (Malden, MA: Blackwell, 1998).

[76]This is no different from what Jürgen Moltmann or Henri Nouwen argue when they discuss contextual Christologies that relate to and connect with current geographic spaces. Henri J. M. Nouwen, *In the Name of Jesus: Reflections on Christian Leadership* (New York: Crossroad, 1989); and Jürgen Moltmann, *The Way of Jesus Christ: Christology in Messianic Dimensions* (San Francisco: HarperSanFrancisco, 1990).

[77]Cf. Nelson George, *Post-Soul Nation: The Explosive, Contradictory, Triumphant, and Tragic 1980s as Experienced by African Americans (Previously Known as Blacks and Before That Negroes)* (New York: Viking, 2004); Paul C. Taylor, "Post-Black, Old Black," *African American Review* 41, no. 4 (Winter 2007): 625-40; Cornel West, *Prophetic Thought in Postmodern Times: Beyond Eurocentrism and Multiculturalism*, vol. 1 (Monroe, ME: Common Courage Press, 1993); J. Milton Yinger, *Religion, Society, and the Individual; An Introduction to the Sociology of Religion* (New York: Macmillan, 1957); Slavoj Žižek, *In Defense of Lost Causes* (New York: Verso, 2008).

Contextualized images of Jesus such as Aaron McGruder's Black Jesus, Lil Wayne's Trap Jesus, and Tupac's Black Jesuz represent an attempt to make deity and the sacred more accessible to those who typically do not grace church sanctuaries. They represent the fusing of the sacred and profane—a space that Spencer argues is misunderstood. They use culture to help interpret the sacred Scriptures and to remove some of the seriousness characteristically associated with Jesus.

Finally, they are more relevant and applicable to those from the post-soul, Hip Hop, and urban generation seeking Jesus. This generation is not interested in the God of multimillion dollar churches. They reject pastors who net more than their congregation makes in a year combined. They despise a church that limits their spiritual possibilities by telling them "this" is the "right way." They do not want a too-perfect Jesus. Tupac and the Outlawz present Jesus in human form for this generation.

Race continues to be a significant issue in the United States, and Hip Hop is well aware of the issues surrounding race and religion. Too often, a White, blonde, long-haired, Americanized Jesus is presented to Hip Hoppers; most ethnic minorities cannot relate.[78] Contextualized images such as McGruder's and Lil Wayne's Jesuses provide insight into a side of Jesus rarely seen. These sensationalized images provide stronger socioreligious connections for the Hip Hop community. A Hip Hop Jesus is given dimensions such as love and peace contextualized for the struggle of the Hip Hop community; he is truth-seeking and has a passion for community and personal growth. These characteristics are more relevant for the Hip Hop community. Tupac and the Outlawz demonstrate this in their song "Black Jesuz."

The contextual and relevant image of Jesus presented in this chapter is much needed for a missiology of and for the wild. It challenges the notion of the White Jesus and brings a more relevant one to the theological and religious table. The Hip Hop Jesus is hostile to those who see Jesus in a singular form. The Hip Hop Jesus is much more universal, holistic, and open to multireligious expressions. Thus, this Jesus is hostile toward a religion that claims him as solely their own. For Hip Hoppers seeking their

---

[78]This Jesus is also depicted as pro-war, patriotic, and against social programs.

own religious ideology, they would more likely be attracted to the Hip Hop Jesus, who is much more accessible and relevant than the traditional Western Jesus.

5

VIGNETTES OF
THE POST-SOUL VOICE

★

I REMEMBER THE EVENTS of Columbine, Colorado, quite well. I remember hearing about a school shooting and teenagers being killed. Horrible. I remember the airwaves being dominated by the tragic event—a steady stream of interviews, guesses as to what was happening, "experts" reporting on the event, and countless repetitions of the same footage. Again, this was a horrifying event for anyone, but when young lives are cut short by such senseless tragedies, it is even more devastating for a youth worker. I also remember during the fallout from the Columbine event, perpetrators Eric Harris and Dylan Klebold were obsessively analyzed by the media, pastors, and "experts" who wanted an answer as to why two seemingly "good boys" would commit such monstrous acts of violence. Talk shows such as *Oprah* debated and argued about why all of this was happening, and even more experts analyzed "this generation of youth." The millennials or Generation Y were receiving their first press hearing, and the outlook was bleak—at least during this time.

At the time, I was on staff with Young Life in the Bay Area, and we had a special time at our staff meeting to discuss the events. At our larger staff meeting, we spent half the day discussing Columbine and were told grief counselors would be on hand for our local areas to talk with students. So, I took them up on their offer. Specific directions were given to talk about this issue with our students, so I also did that. When I went to meet with my group of predominately Black and Latino students, I was met with disdain, noticeable eye rolls, and lip smacking, which could indicate only one thing:

things were not right. I assumed it was their grief over the events—but it was not. What they revealed to me started me on a path of critical inquiry that has not come to a halt since. They questioned whose tragedy is narrated, validated, and affirmed as "bad." Student after student in the group told me how offended they were at Young Life's gesture and that while they too felt bad about what happened at Columbine, what about their grief? One young woman told me about a recent school shooting in her school in which three people were killed, and there was no media coverage. A young man told me about the continual senseless killings of Black teens in the city, which, at that point, outnumbered the fifteen killed in Columbine. "Where is the national outcry for that? Tell me!" shouted one young man. After about three hours of listening, my staff and I realized there is a racial divide when it comes to national tragedy. I quickly realized that even in my high school, there had been school shootings that not once made the news. In fact, I kept a Glock 9mm, Beretta, and sawed-off double-barrel shotgun in various lockers at my high school for safety. Where was the coverage, experts, grief counselors, and help for my classmates and myself? Why do poor Black, Latinx, Asian, and disenfranchised White youth not receive the same coverage?

The racism here is almost overwhelming. One thing is clear: what happens to the dominant culture makes national headlines and is rendered important and crucial for the rest of society. This is reflected in major works on today's young people and emerging adults. In an NPR interview, Robert Putnam, religious scholar and researcher with the Pew Study on religion in America,[1] stated that the "none" factor—those having no religious affiliation—was connected much more to White teens than to Blacks and Latinos.[2] Christian Smith's landmark study *Souls in Transition: The Religious and Spiritual Lives of Emerging Adults* focuses on more affluent and White emerging adults than on urban, multiethnic, and intercultural ones.[3] David Kinnaman, whose text *You Lost Me: Why Young Christians Are Leaving Church . . . and Rethinking Faith*, a mandatory read in many

---

[1]Luis Logo et al., *"Nones" on the Rise: One-in-Five Adults Have No Religious Affiliation* (Washington, DC: Pew Forum on Religion & Public Life, 2012).

[2]Robert Putnam, "As Social Issues Drive Young from Church, Leaders Try to Keep Them," interview by David Greene, NPR, January 18, 2013, MP3, www.npr.org/series/169065270/losing-our-religion.

[3]See Christian Smith with Patricia Snell, *Souls in Transition: The Religious and Spiritual Lives of Emerging Adults* (Oxford: Oxford University Press, 2009), 33-87.

seminaries across the country, attempts to connect with the post-soul young person but does not fully transfer to the experience of Black millennials or those who are living in the wild.[4] Kara Powell and Chap Clark's now milestone text in youth ministry settings, *Sticky Faith: Everyday Ideas to Build Lasting Faith in Your Kids*, does not encompass research within the urban, post-soul context.[5] Many of the findings, while excellent in their own right, are for the average youth ministry context: suburban, two-parent families, intergenerationally mobile, and representative of the majority culture. In addition, large portions of youth ministry texts do not include, or have very little representation of, marginalized, Black, Latino, Hip Hop, or post-soul persons.[6] Could it be, much like with the Columbine incident, that there are other factors at work among multiethnic young people and emerging adults, and that the attention is focused too much on the majority culture? Could it be that the secular alarm has been sounded much too early as an entire subset of millennials have not been taken into account?[7] And could it be that Jenkins's warning about asserting "what Christians believe" or "how the church is changing" is impulsive, premature, and even inconclusive?[8]

Because we are dealing with the greatest population of young people in the United States, and because the next generation of Christian and missiological thought will come from them, it is imperative that we spend some time examining what makes this group of people tick. Some might argue that this chapter fits better in a youth ministry text, but I believe there is a great breach in the missiological literature in regard to young people. Moreover, I have found that many missiologists focus on international, not domestic, young people. This presents problems at multiple levels. This

---

[4]David Kinnaman and Aly Hawkins, *You Lost Me: Why Young Christians Are Leaving Church . . . and Rethinking Faith* (Grand Rapids: Baker, 2011), 19-35.

[5]Kara E. Powell and Chap Clark, *Sticky Faith: Everyday Ideas to Build Lasting Faith in Your Kids* (Grand Rapids: Zondervan, 2011).

[6]Many texts on youth ministry focus on suburban, affluent, highly educated parents, and economically mobile settings rather than the changing demographics and post-soul contexts.

[7]I use these texts as examples because they are some of the primary works being cited and utilized as evidence that this current generation is lost, wayward, or corrupt in some manner. And while Smith and Snell's work is research-based and nonjudgmental, their material has been used by some in the evangelical community to critique and judge.

[8]Philip Jenkins, *The Next Christendom: The Coming of Global Christianity* (New York: Oxford University Press, 2011), 3.

chapter, then, examines the spiritual and theological aspirations of the post-soul youth and emerging adults. Many North American Christians are frightened by this generation's faith and the future of the Christian church. But we might, in fact, be converging on a new understanding and knowledge of the gospel and Christianity—one rooted in a post-soul context. There is no doubt that something is different about this emerging group of young adults. What might this change mean for the North American church? Could this faith change signal a much richer faith experience for a generation who grew up on rules, ambiguity, and a White-dominated form of Christianity? I think so. This chapter will begin a much-needed conversation on multiethnic faith and spirituality.[9]

THREE WINDOWS ON FAITH IN THE WILD/POST-SOUL CONTEXT

Christian Smith begins *Souls in Transition* with the stories of three young people, which sets the tone and context of his research.[10] Similarly, in this section I will explore the stories of three young people I interviewed in my research. The purpose is to convey the themes that emerge from this generation and to argue away from the notion of the *nones*—that is, those considered to not have any religious affiliation—within the post-soul context. We begin with Nancy, a first-generation Chinese millennial born in the United States. Though she is fluent in Mandarin, she uses it only when talking to her non-English-speaking grandparents and father. Nancy attended a private evangelical Christian high school and college. Next is Javier, a Mexican American young person born in Mexico who was brought to the United States when he was five, along with his four sisters. He speaks Spanish, but it has become increasingly broken as he has learned English. Javier works many part-time jobs and desires to attend a Christian college because he would like to become a pastor. Last is Jessica, a White-and-Black mixed person who grew up in the suburbs. During her senior year in high school,

---

[9]This chapter is built on research that North Park University and North Park Theological Seminary are currently undertaking. Of course, this chapter is merely a snapshot of the urban post-soul millennial. This chapter's purpose is to illustrate that (1) there is another subset of the millennial and emerging-adult population that has been overlooked in the scholarship, and (2) the spirituality and theology created in those spaces are beneficial and helpful in the development and progress of Christianity in the twenty-first century.
[10]Smith, *Souls in Transition*, 10-32.

a geographic change shifted her toward a positive way of thinking about the poor. Jessica attended a Christian high school and went on several mission trips, which also shifted her view on race and God. She went to non-Christian college because she found Christian environments much too religious. We will now look at each student in more detail.

Nancy. The second time we met up, Nancy attempted to rush out the door, as she was late to an appointment. She stopped right before bursting out the door and exclaimed, "Sh--! I almost forgot the most important thing!" She ran back to the coffee table where she had almost forgotten her iPhone, which, as many scholars have concluded, is almost an appendage to the physical body for many millennials. "I can't do anything without this thing! It's how I live life!" she says. Nancy was often late and very event-oriented; a characteristic she says she inherited from her "American peoples." Nancy was the first in her family to be born in the United States, and, as a result, she bears the pressure to be fruitful, successful, and part of the "American Dream." To this, she says,

> Yeah, I'm always being told, "Nancy, you are the one who can make it" and I'm like, dang, can I just live my life [*laughs*]! I get it, though. My mom and dad had it rough and really just want me to succeed and live a better life. But, it's a lot, you know?

Nancy's parents instilled in her that to be successful, one needed an education. Notwithstanding stereotypes of Asians, Nancy excelled in academics in grade school all the way through college. Nancy also was given a lot of support from her parents to "succeed." With materials such as high-end laptops all the way to expensive calculators, Nancy had the "stuff," as she puts it, to succeed. "My parents would always tell me that they'd spare no expense for me in order for me to do better," she says. "I think my mom cared more about my grades than she did me at times!" Nancy's pressure to succeed was conveyed to me, and it was only matched by her parents' push to be "Christian."

Her parents were not of any particular faith prior to coming to the United States, but when they came to the United States, they quickly adopted Christianity. This is a trend of some Asian American families who want to assimilate quicker into United States society and culture; parents in turn raise their children as "evangelical Christians."[11] Nancy's upbringing confirmed some of this as she reflected on her faith growing up:

> As far back as I can remember, my parents were Christian. But, I know when I dug a little bit, I found that they were actually just like, you know, regular people back in China [*laughs*]. The United States gave them some religion. But, a lot of it had to do with fitting in. My dad wasn't always the "spiritual leader" he was supposed to be. I don't know, I mean . . . okay, it was like at times we were learning about God together.

For Nancy, faith was a part of her life, but the male-centered evangelicalism that ushers men to be "leaders" and "heads of household" was not for her. Often she did not feel a good direction for any faith.

Nancy went to a private Christian college but majored in global studies and sociology. This led her to a critical inquiry of society, religion, and even her upbringing. Her program immersed students in the city, made them take only public transportation, and helped them form critical insight into the social problems within the United States. This time period shook Nancy's faith. She says,

> Those were rough times for me. Everything in my world was torn apart. Everything that I thought was just normal. Right? I mean, everybody has a supportive mom and dad that gets them everything to succeed, right? I couldn't believe that God could allow such injustice for so long. And my experience at that college didn't make room for questions that fell outside the evangelical space.

Nancy's worldview began to change in college. Her faith was "quite strong" while in high school, but "trouble began" when she entered college, and she started to see the world from a different set of perspectives. While she attended a conservative Christian college, the program she was in contained a majority of more progressive voices that were both justice centered and socially oriented in approach. Nancy credits that program as being formative in her faith development while still being one that "wrecked" what she believed prior.

---

[11]Rebecca Y. Kim, "Made in the U.S.A.: Second-Generation Korean American Campus Evangelicals," in *Asian American Youth: Culture, Identity, & Ethnicity*, ed. Jennifer Lee and Min Zhou (New York: Routledge, 2004), 244-48.

Nancy's parents had a difficult time when she came home wanting to protest unfair land use, challenge more conservative political voices, and question the version of their Bible translation. Nancy quickly became estranged from her father, who, in her eyes, took it the hardest:

> I know he thought I was losing my faith and my religion. But I wasn't. I just was trying to find my own path. You know? My own way to God, and the way I was taught was the complete picture of who God is and was. I mean, I still have plenty of doubts. I still have a lot of questions, but I just don't think everything has to be worked out just now. I know my parents have a hard time with stuff like that. They want it to be neat and tidy. It ain't. It won't be.

Nancy's questioning and doubting was too much for her father. They remained in contact, but the relationship was strained. On several occasions he would send her Christian tracts on "returning to the faith." One was titled "Do you know you're saved?" This was insulting to Nancy; she remained fervent in her faith journey. She continues to work in the urban local context and speak for the marginalized. She was also an advocate for LGBT equality and fought against propositions that would prohibit same-sex marriage. Because of this, Nancy's father was angered and did not speak to her for over a year. Nancy struggled with her father's decision not to speak to her. "He thinks I'm lost just because I want to do the same work as Jesus," she told me over lunch when I asked her about her relationship with her father. She answered, "He and my mom are still living old school. I just think Jesus would be in the 'hood and part of those who society says are trash." Nancy says she finds faith in "strange places" and questions whether the God we have come to know, traditionally, exists. In other words, Nancy affirms that there might be other versions of God "out there," but that her faith remains "the same faith my parents taught me to have."

Nancy lives with her boyfriend and continues to work out her faith in community and with many tensions—her relationship with her parents and also the areas of her life that used to make sense and those current ones that make less sense. Church and religion are not priorities for her or her boyfriend. Church is more of a relic and a concept of the past rather than something she looks forward to. Religion is seen as oppressive and constructed for those who only want to follow and not question. For Nancy, God is made much more authentic when there is tension, pressure, and stress. She says that if it was not for those three elements, she is not sure God could work. "If it's always all good, why even have or need God? Why not just do it on my own? And trust me, there are plenty of times I think God is just someone who had a great self-help sales pitch. Maybe he was one helluva salesman!" [*laughs*]

Javier. Javier quickly unbuttoned his collared shirt to get to his L.A. Lakers T-shirt underneath, unknotted his black necktie, and threw them both over his shoulder. "Whew! I'm free! Thank God, I'm free at last!" he exclaimed. Javier had finished a double shift at a local high-end restaurant on a busy Saturday night when we met for the last round of interviews. "Them White folks was trippin' tonight man! Ya know? Damn. [*giggles*] It's all good though. I got paid!" Javier would typically be paid either daily or weekly, and always in cash. Most businesses do not have the bookkeeping margin to fill out the forms needed to hire an undocumented worker. Moreover, most businesses are looking for the highest return on their profit margin and will pay cash to avoid any extra fees or accountability to the federal government. Javier knew the ins and outs of this hustle all too well. Javier knew how to survive and was determined to "make it" out of the situation he was in. He says, "Man, I can't be doing this when I'm like fifty, man. You know? Shoot. I love my pops, but there ain't no way I'm gonna put my kids through this, know what I mean? I can't. I have to make it for them and for my family too. God will make a way."

Javier's work ethic was strong, and his drive to get out of his situation was keenly tuned to push forward. Javier's friends had grown up together and were all undocumented, but they had lived in the United States for at least a decade or more. Javier came from a big family, one that did not allow for too much variance from tradition. I knew Javier for almost two years before I convinced him to eat traditional US barbecue. When he finally did have some, he told me he could not believe how "stupid he was" to have waited so long to try "a piece of God's kitchen." While my barbecue typically garners that type of reaction from people, it did signal a strong adherence to all things Mexican for Javier and his family.

Javier's parents were strict and devoted Catholics, but they lived in a community that had several evangelical churches nearby. When he was in middle school Javier began attending one of those evangelical youth groups:

Ah, it was like a mistake, you know what I mean? I didn't really want to go to that group. But shoot, there was some fine ladies that went there, so I was like, shoot, I'm going. Me and the fellas went . . . every week too! [*laughs*] Those were the days. But God had different plans. What I thought was for me and my own sinful gain, he had for the better. Maybe those young ladies were part of God's plan. Yes, I do think they were, you know what I mean?

For Javier, the tradition youth group presented a version of God's message he had not received through his Catholic upbringing. Javier was attached to the evangelical youth group for many more reasons than the females who attended. To that he says, "No disrespect to my family at all. But I learned about God I had never heard about in my old church. The nuns didn't tell me about the gospel like how my youth pastor did. I was always learning new things about God in them young days of my youth."

For Javier, faith was central to his life. It would be tested as several political seasons came up and the issue of immigration was raised in a way that was racialized toward Latinos. During these times Javier felt alone, dislocated, and having anomie toward God. Javier had begun attending community college (they allow anyone to attend, documented or not), which caused stress between him and his father. His father, who was raised in a rural context in Mexico, did not fully comprehend the compulsion toward education in the United States. Often Javier was scorned for attending college because his parents wanted him to work the fields or take up a trade (e.g., carpentry or framing). "People keep telling me they want me to be a carpenter. Go to trade school and learn some trade. Man, I wanna be a pastor, dude. No disrespect to people who build houses, but I know God has a calling on my life."

Javier resisted counsel toward being a carpenter because he regarded that as stereotypical work Mexicans did. But for Javier, this type of resistance placed him at odds with not just his family and some friends—who were working trade jobs—but also his former youth group as they were encouraging him to take some of those same paths. This caused Javier to question his faith.

During this period, Javier turned to partying, alcohol use, and even questionable work in the underground economy. Javier identified with protestors and those who questioned the entire government structure of the United States. Since Javier lived in a border city, he attended many marches and protests. This put him at odds with those in his former youth group and youth pastors, who suggested that he was being sinful. When people, who were typically White, confronted him regarding his "sin" and isolation, Javier got mad and ignored them. "They act like just because I'm not there, I'm sinning. Damn." He added, "It's gonna be hard for them [meaning White people] to get it. They have their citizenship. I don't. I'm just trying to survive. I think God cares about that." This period was problematic for Javier, his family, and the members of the youth group he formerly was a part of. Javier was now attending a young adult service in the same church, but he says it was not much help and that the messages often were "anti-Mexican." Javier had a faith crisis.

Javier pressed on and continued in college, even though he failed most of his classes. However, he did have something going for him: several older ethnic-minority men from different faith communities began to mentor Javier. This made an enormous difference in his life:

> Life's tough when everything seems pointed at you. It's like you go to work, but they shady and wanna take advantage of you. My family didn't get what I was trying to do. It's like my dad, all he wants is for me to work in the fields, like him. I get it, but, like for that, I don't want to be like him. I know that's like no good for us as Mexicans, but I want to go to school. I know God's got a call on my life. But then you got these other Christians who think I'm all a sinner. I bet they don't think that when people like me are mowing their damn grass though. You know what I mean? Life's tough. If it wasn't for my mentors, I don't know where I'd be. They can handle my moods and me.[12]

Javier continued to develop, and by the time he reached his mid-twenties, a bill in Congress was proposed that gave people like him the pathway to citizenship and the ability to attain a United States green card (i.e., the Dream Act). This was a pivotal break for Javier, and he took it as a sign for him and his faith journey. "You see, God is looking out for us Mexicans! Now we can take part in the American dream too," he says. "This is God at

---

[12]Much like Bob (see chap. 3), Javier had a strong sense of justice, fairness, and equality. He could sniff out when someone was contradicting themselves on social issues such as immigration. If someone said they wanted "those immigrants to go back to Mexico," yet enjoyed cheap produce and manicured lawns, Javier would call them on the double standard. This is characteristic of those who are involved with justice work, and even how they interpret the Bible.

work and a lot of people working hard to get this through; God working through them!"

Javier's faith was coated with a sense of justice and community development. Javier's faith was more centrist, and at times more conservative, particularly when it came to issues such as sexuality and sexual orientation. Yet even on those issues he was politically liberal and sought out justice. Javier continued to question how God could allow such suffering in and by people, but that was couched in a strong sense of "God's plan" or "God's design," which in many regards connected Javier to the mystery and ambiguity of who God was for him and those like him.

Javier did not enjoy attending church, and his church attendance was very low. Yet he vigorously sought God through film, music, video, and Hip Hop artists such as Tupac, Kendrick Lamar, and Lauryn Hill. His faith matched that of the Black Hip Hopper, but he was still distinctly Mexican. For Javier, God was central to his beliefs about life, death, the afterlife, heaven, and beyond. He saw God much more pluralistically than he had when he was a young teenager. "If you had known me when I was thirteen, you would've thought I was going to be some Baptist preacher," he exclaimed. He continued,

> Things were so simple then, and the message of God seemed so basic. Now, it's complicated. That's how I'd say my relationship with God is—complicated. But that's okay because I see him so much clearer now. In the mess and in the good, he's there and he's with me. Just don't get me in no church that preaches all day!

Jessica. Jessica strolled into the coffee shop where we were supposed to meet, and if it had not been for me knowing who she was, I might have missed her. Quiet and soft spoken, Jessica had a real awareness for life, God, love, relationships, and her surroundings. "I try to live my life the way God intended. But we [humans] messed things up. So, I have to live in a messed-up way with how I think God might have wanted or wants." Jessica has been a cheerleader through high school and college. Her ethnic heritage is part Euro-American and African American. "My dad was Black, and my mom was White, and like blonde White and blue-eyed. All the stereotypes at once!" she says. Even after college, Jessica was still working out her own ethnic identity. By her own admission, she was often seen as White because of her fair skin and "good hair." Both Jessica's parents were missionaries who transitioned into education within Christian contexts. Jessica says,

> Yeah, I know all about those Bible verses. I know the right things to say, and I know the buzzwords that youth pastors, or, for that matter, any pastor wants to hear. I was living a double life for so long until I started to own my faith and religion. But, at the time, I was just the good girl who could get away with murder if I wanted to. My parents, who I love dearly, were wrapped up in trying to be good ministers and educators. We're better now though, I think.

Jessica had gone to private Christian schools for all her grade, middle, and high school years. But now she was done with "the religion of Christianity." However, Jessica was not done with God. In fact, she loved God and sought after him or her—as she would often say—through prayer, meditation, and the arts. Jessica's parents, who were now going through a divorce, had invested heavily in her Christian education, and she now questions whether that was a good decision:

> I don't know. I love both my mom and dad, but I think they worked so hard for me to be this saintly child that they missed out on their own relationship. I'm not sure that's what God intended. I know it's rough now for both of them. Their good Christian image is tarnished with divorce. But hey, do we really think God's sitting up there like, "ah man, you all just got a divorce, nope, no love for you!"

Jessica's uncanny sense of humor has helped her to better see God. And it is what kept her from "going clinically insane." Jessica, in her own estimation, was the model student who followed all the rules. Although, while attending a short-term missions trip during her sophomore summer, she began to question the impact of that type of work after she witnessed friends treating members of the small Guatemalan town, as she put it, "like zoo pets." It was then, as she recalls, that her "consciousness light" went on. "That trip left a bad taste in my Christian mouth. I couldn't believe that the people in this town were being looked at almost like zoo animals." Jessica began to question, albeit to herself, the impact of missions on people, race, and even White students. This particular event began a "chain reaction," as she would jokingly tell me, in which she was challenged to think more seriously on race, gender, class, and whether God was already working in the areas they traveled to.

During Jessica's junior year of high school the demographics of her once homogenous community began to change. One person she met, who later became one of her better friends, viewed God as much more freeing and open to questions, ideas, and doubt. This new belief came at a time when, as Jessica would put it, "my faith was at its zenith." For her, questions, ideas, and doubts outside accepted conventional notions was heresy and blasphemous. With this friend, she says,

> I know I used to argue all the time until I was purple in the face [*laughs*]. Maybe someone would think I was then Black, right? Ha! Okay, well, I would just be totally beside myself when she'd tell me that God was this open-ended deity. I was like, no he's not—I wasn't even tempted to refer to God by any-thing but a man—God's very clear on what's wrong and right. There is nothing gray; only black and white. Wow, was I young in my thinking! But that's how I was taught.

Jessica's friend helped reshape her view on God and life. She recalls that these intense and often argumentative conversations later became for-mative in her faith development. She also says this relationship came be-tween her and her parents because they were more fundamental in their beliefs: "I mean, my parents voted for Obama. I mean c'mon, my dad was Black! But they dang sure didn't like a God that was messy or chaotic." She says her faith would continue to be reshaped when a Hindu family moved down the street from her, and she later engaged them about death, life, and issues of justice. While difficult, those became times when Jessica saw a much more diverse God who had been at work much longer than her re-ligion had taught. At the same time, she remained the model student in school, even when teachers contradicted themselves theologically. She says, "I'd just be like, hey, you're wrong, dead wrong, but I'm not gonna say anything because I'm a good Christian lady." It would stand to reason that Jessica might become rebellious and critically interrogate issues like that, as was the case for Nancy. Jessica's protest came on tests, papers, and care-fully crafting arguments. She later told me she had to grow into her wom-anhood and find her voice.

Jessica's college years were marred by the execution of Troy Davis, and shooting deaths of Trayvon Martin and Michael Brown. She was confounded. On one hand, she had friends who supported law enforcement at all costs. On the other, she had family members who had been harassed and brutalized by the police. Her father had been profiled and was regularly pulled over. But she also had the privilege of light skin color. She says,

> I had to learn how to speak up and speak for the other side of my heritage, Black people. I didn't know how to do that. College helped. Friends helped. I knew that the way Trayvon died wasn't right. He didn't deserve that. I mean, no one does. I'm not even sure how God can continue to allow this, but, maybe there's some bigger plan for all of it. I know for me, it definitely got me off the bench and into the game; I was able to combine my faith into action and begin organizing. If his death was for that, then, shoot, I have to make it count then.

Jessica's faith in action was clear, and she adorned her body with tattoos reflecting Scriptures focused on justice, peace, and the gospel of Jesus. For Jessica, these were central to the gospel, but, like Nancy and Javier, church was optional. Community, yes; church, maybe. When asked about church and how she worked out her spirituality in community, she says,

> I mean, church is like a key to the Christian faith, right? I mean, any religion has their pope. But for me, and really, a lot of people like me, I just don't see it as relevant. Why do I need to attend a building just to seek God out? Why can't God meet us in our room, on the street corner, at the memorial in Ferguson where Michael Brown was killed? See, I think God's more about space and place than a specific location and church. I don't think God said we need a building for church. Religion says that.

Jessica also does not feel welcome at many churches because of her sexual orientation; she identifies as bisexual. And because she has witnessed a lot of her friends try to make "church work," she decided to avoid "the mess altogether." Jessica viewed LGBT rights as issues Jesus would take up, and she also sees the beauty "within the tension of the cross and her sexuality." This is characteristic of post-soul multiethnics. Sexuality and sexual orientation are areas that do not hinder or obstruct their view on God, theology, or spirituality. Increasingly, millennial multiethnics like Jessica are leading

social movements, uprisings, and political movements that attempt to keep
God in the "mess of it all."

This was one of the reasons that Jessica wanted to attend a non-Christian
college. She told me, "I had always gotten a good 'Christian' education, but
it was time for me to go out and see what else was out there and to see what
was at the end of that fence. You know?" Jessica's non-Christian college experience reinforced what she already knew: God was complex and faithful,
but also close to you in chaos. Jessica's move to a non-Christian college
capped an already strained relationship with her parents, and she often feels
guilty that this might be one of the main factors for their divorce. "I don't
think that was it, but, in my low days, I think that. And I'm like, damn, did
I break up my own parents?" she says. Her questioning resonates with a
growing number of post-soul millennials who hold dearly to ethics and
morality in their everyday actions while embracing deep family roots. Still,
Jessica says the non-Christian space was a good place to figure out her sexuality and find God within a multitude of views. Jessica did see herself as a
sort of missionary, and her missional sense, although crude in some manner,
was honed to "go forth" and present Jesus as nonjudgmental, loving, full of
grace, and comforting in time of suffering. Lament was important for Jessica,
and she told me she refined that while at college, away from the "Christian-
ese talk" that often enraged her.

Jessica, like Nancy and Javier, questions almost everything about the
Bible. Jessica's faith was found outside the Bible, and she has a strong
inclination toward the spiritual dimension and mysteries of God. She says,
"I know my sexuality just makes people uncomfortable. That's okay. I
think I'm more comfortable with that now. But please don't try and tell
me where my eternal place is, and whatever you do, don't try and convince me that God loves me any less for who I chose as a mate." Jessica
continues to work out her faith and is beginning to work toward a master's degree in divinity. Her relationship with her parents, while strained,
is "complicated but working." Jessica continues to seek God in the areas
of justice, equality, and social reformation. "That friend of mine in high
school really started something in me. A sense to question everything,
but I do know God exists out there. She's doing something great. I don't
know what, and it's very untidy and chaotic at times—things that drive

my parents insane—but I don't think it would be God if it wasn't at least somewhat crazy!" she says.

Building on these three narratives, we will now explore the spiritual taxonomies of this emerging group of millennials.[13]

SPIRITUAL TAXONOMIES OF URBAN, MULTIETHNIC, POST-SOUL YOUNG PEOPLE

To begin, let us look at what Christian Smith and Patricia Snell say regarding today's emerging adults:

> Our primary aim here is not to make value judgments, however, but rather to set a context for better understanding the religious and spiritual lives of emerging adults. The broad-brush picture we have just painted of the cultural worlds that most American emerging adults sustain and live in provides an expansive map of the large sociocultural terrain within which we can locate and better understand their religious and spiritual lives more specifically.[14]

Therefore, with this in mind, the impetus here is to explain this phenomenon and also contend that urban, multiethnic, post-soul young people are creating their brand, if you will, of faith and correlation to God.

---

[13]While these three windows provide a glimpse into post-soul millennial spirituality and faith, there are others that are worthy to note as well. Other significant motifs are developing, and while the research I am currently involved in is not complete, they are important. First, there are multiethnic post-soul millennials who, while once being connected to a strong faith community, now see it as both farcical and trivial because that faith cannot contend with the onslaught of police terrorism, racism, and economic inequality. For this group, God is created within the constructs of the oppressor and cannot be trusted. Typically viewed as a White man's religion, Christianity is corrupt and for foolish people who desire to pray about issues rather than act on them. Next is a group who find Christianity limiting because, once again, they see it as White and oppressive. Yet, rather than leaving faith altogether, they have returned to Afrocentric religions that embody spirit, land, body, food, and community. While there are traces of Christianity in their faith beliefs, the core focuses on a strong sense of Afrocentric deity (e.g., a Black God or Goddess) along with a critical sense toward anything White. A third group is apathetic toward God but also shaped by faith through human interaction. Having an almost humanist stance on life and religion, this group seeks out the best in humans rather than looking to God. For this group, God is socially constructed for those who are fearful of stepping into uncharted theological territory. And God is within all humans—very similar to Fiver Percenter theology in which God is seen within the humanity of people. There is a strong sense of community action and that "what counts" is what you do now.

[14]Smith, *Souls in Transition*, 75.

In figure 5.1 I have organized categories in boxes. The larger boxes are the areas much more likely to produce resistance and tension for some in more traditional Christianity. Nonetheless, they are similar to what some in the urban, multiethnic, post-soul context experience and are connected to as well.[15]

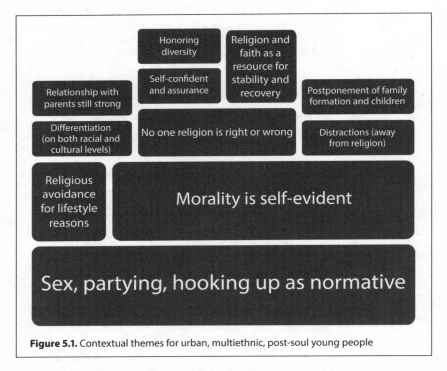

Figure 5.1. Contextual themes for urban, multiethnic, post-soul young people

As one might imagine, these are not typically associated with the traditional view of Western evangelicalism. With a growing number of sociocultural changes in family and demographics, such as employment security, rising costs of homeownership, student loan debt, and those under age twenty-eight living at home longer, the shift within religion and faith is pronounced. For example, going to college immediately after high school, attaining significant career employment after college, marrying, having kids, and buying a home are all typically associated with a stable religious life and is associated positively with religious involvement.[16] Yet these pathways have

---

[15]These categories are adapted from ibid., 75-87.
[16]Ibid., 327.

been interrupted, along with the changes already mentioned in chapter one, by a significant amount of fluctuations, such as

- post–9/11 America,

- an unsettled job market,

- the reconfiguration of US education for millennials,

- displacement of career employment, and

- disappearance of a middle class and blue-collar workforce.

And so the once-traditional pathway for a religious life connected to the American Dream is nonexistent.[17] Therefore, a younger generation is reluctant, and in some manner apathetic, as to what path is even right to begin with—and if that path will even work.

In addition, for many ethnic minorities—especially Black and Latino—the job market, pursuit of higher education, increasing institutional racism, and even hate crimes perpetuated against them have been the norm. Thus, the "traditional pathway" to success, the American Dream, and security has never been clear. Even before it was a Gen Y trend, many Black college grads, when they could or had the setting to do so, returned home after college and often supported their family.

Added to this, the popular notion that high school graduates "lost their faith" after high school does not hold true in many Black and Latino contexts. In fact, their faith often is made stronger because of college, questions, and doubt. And so I add to this the urban, multiethnic, post-soul emerging adult spiritual taxonomies to begin a new narrative on emerging adult faith in the United States. Figure 5.2 illustrates the taxonomies, and once again the larger boxes represent the more significant ones while the smaller represent those that are emerging.

---

[17]See Robert Wuthnow, *The Religious Dimension: New Directions in Quantitative Research* (New York: Academic Press, 1979); and Roger W. Stump, "Regional Migration and Religious Commitment in the United States," *Journal for the Scientific Study of Religion* 23, no. 3 (1984). One significant difference is in the Bible Belt of the Southern United States, where a strong adherence remains to conservative Christianity and its norms. See Christian Smith, David Sikkink, and Jason Bailey, "Devotion in Dixie and Beyond: A Test of the 'Shibley Thesis' on the Effects of Regional Origin and Migration on Individual Religiosity," *Journal for the Scientific Study of Religion* 37, no. 3 (1998).

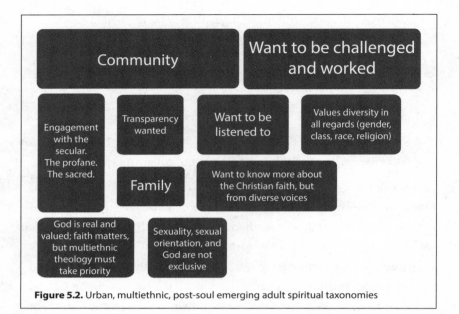

Figure 5.2. Urban, multiethnic, post-soul emerging adult spiritual taxonomies

These are also connected to a diverse set of quotes from interviews held between the years 2010 and 2015:

- Yo, I still love God, but all that preachin' be wearin' me out.

- What's the answer from the church to police brutality? Where that at? Huh? Other than wanting to have someone come to they damn programs.

- I think God loves me. I don't know about all that religion sh-- though.

- You gotta have God and Jesus out here in these streets.

- Give me a relationship. Not religion.

- While they in the church praying and talking about crap, we out here in these streets dying. Where is the action from Christians? Didn't Jesus stir sh-- up?

- So, I'm going to hell just because I love someone from the same gender? That's what God got? If so, I don't want anything to do with that.

- So, tell me, it's okay for male pastors to keep f---ing their parishioners, but for me, a woman, it's a sin to have sex with my faithful partner of eleven years?

- Okay, so my skirt is too high and my shirt too low. Okay. I see you. You wanna call me out on that. What about you [men] masturbating to women who look like me?

- I find it disturbing that many of these same Christian men who despise same-sex marriage oppose it on all accounts, yet would masturbate in a second to two women having sex on the Internet.

- God gotta be a strange cat, I mean, look, he made us, right?

- I still need a community that thinks like me and is trying to work out their faith.

These quotes are representative of the themes within this group of people. Moreover, the issue of sexuality continues to block those in the wild from traditionalists. Nevertheless, God is central to this generation. For many living in violent conditions and spaces, there is no option to doubt whether God exists. As one young woman put it to me, "You have to be shacked up with someone [God] out here in the streets. It's too difficult to do this mess on your own." The belief in God is crucial to this generation's faith.

Urban, multiethnic, post-soul young people are attempting to create a new understanding of Christianity, faith, God, and Jesus that is free of evangelical and dominant culture imprints. This, as one can imagine, causes many concerns, debates, and even excommunications. However, for the most part, the urban, multiethnic, post-soul person desires to stay connected to God—just on their terms. This, I believe, is no different from Martin Luther's attempt to differentiate his faith from the Roman Catholic Church or George Whitefield's move toward a more personal faith through "revival." These were approaches not heard of or embraced in their times, but they would later become staples in the faith. More often than not, young people are after a God that looks like them, talks like them, relates to them, and lives a life similar to them. This sounds like Stephen Bevans's transcendental model in the pursuit of God, in which it is an essential endeavor to wrestle with God in real time and in the sacred, secular, and profane. As Bevans contends, "A fundamental presupposition of the transcendental model is that one begins to theologize contextually not by focusing on the essence of the gospel message or the content of tradition as such." In this sense, this generation is attempting to "realize that as an individual, as a subject, one is determined at every turn by one's context: I am precisely who I am because I exist at this particular point in time, because I am a recipient of a particular national and cultural heritage."[18]

From a transcendental perspective, the post-soul millennial takes into account cultural, familial, ethnic, and racial heritages and begins to seek God without stripping those elements from their personhood.[19] Class, race, gender, sexual orientation, sexuality, ethnicity, family, and context are all held in tension. A simple "identity is Christ" is not necessarily the capstone of faith. More often than not, what is valued is identity in a Black or multi-ethnic Christ. The ambiguity of life and doubt about what may come is always a tension for the urban, multiethnic, post-soul young person. The constant fluctuation in the political, social, and cultural scene in the United States is always uneasy. Yet faith in God, even when a person is involved in a profane or secular context or activity, is essential. The construction of a view of God in this space is critical. For post-soul millennials, it is the genesis of a more robust faith that can encompass doubt, ambiguity, pain, suffering, and poverty, that is, "when things just aren't right."

While *nones* have no religious affiliation, those I have worked with and interviewed subscribed to a faith connected to God.[20] Ironically, liturgy and traditional Christian practices (e.g., Eucharist and Lent) were highly valued. In some regard, tradition is comforting and provides at least some contextual mapping of spirituality and faith.[21] Leaving the faith was not a typical course of action for this generation. For some, their faith was strengthened as they got older and were allowed to question, doubt, and lament more. Still others struggled through church services that were excruciatingly boring, irrelevant, or dull. This group tended toward an apathetic

---

[18]Stephen B. Bevans, *Models of Contextual Theology* (Maryknoll, NY: Orbis Books, 1992), 104.

[19]Ibid., 106-7.

[20]The "disconnectedness" that Kinnaman discusses was very low in relation to God, faith, and Jesus. While *nones* tend toward the six themes he lists as the phenomenon of disconnection (overprotective, shallow, antiscientific, repressive, exclusive, doubtless), they still have a sense of figuring out what to do in that space. They appear to be inclined to work through issues that previous generations (e.g., civil rights and Hip Hop Gen 1) could not figure out or left in ruin (Kinnaman and Hawkins, *You Lost Me*, 91-94).

[21]For example, a group practicing Communion might have a Tupac song such as "Hail Mary" or "So Many Tears" playing while the service is underway. Or they might use film or TV clips to connect, for example, the Lord's Prayer to a specific theme. The sacred, secular, and profane are in constant use within these contexts.

faith, but even in this apathy there were traces of faith and the desire to figure it out. In extreme cases, yes, some pushed away from God or denied God exists. Most of these individuals had experienced brutal trauma (e.g., rape or molestation) from another religious person, often from someone in a position of power. However, a critical interrogation of Western Christianity while maintaining a form of their own faith was the strongest view emerging within this group. This was and continues to be seen in millennials who are part of groups such as Black Lives Matter or the Black Youth Project. A sharp critique of White, male, heterosexual, conservative Christianity is part of the critical discourse.[22] And the voices of those who have been oppressed are held in high regard. But when that voice is not heard, the response is strong, sharp, and often expressed on social media—especially Twitter. For those who are even further marginalized (e.g., LGBT people), the critique of dominant culture goes much further than just White patriarchy. It also includes older ethnic minorities. And religion is at the heart of this—especially as the debate continues between conservative and progressive views on LGBT people.

The dearth of research and scholarship in and among urban multiethnic post-soul young people is painfully evident. Further, the deficiency of scholarship that deals with their spiritual and faith development is even greater. Thus, more investigation is needed into how this growing demographic sees, interprets, understands, and relates to God. For twenty-first century missiologists and youth workers, this will be critical to both ministry and personal development.

---

[22]I would add that this criticism is applied to other ethnic groups as well. For example, many Black millennials feel as though the older civil rights generation does not take their voice and narrative into account. So, in spaces like Ferguson, older Blacks are given the platform, while the youth are overlooked and not given space to discuss their narrative. Further, actions and policies are created without regard for those who live in Ferguson and other places like it. For Black millennials this is another example of patriarchy and oppression—even from your own people. The Black millennial voice is crucial, and many within this group feel overlooked and silenced in the presence of older people. The fight here is not just against White supremacy but also against the politics of respectability, Black heteronormative belief structures, and Black Christian male supremacy. It is a complex and difficult phenomenon.

PART 3

CHURCH IN THE WILD

Unconventional Missiology in the Twenty-First Century

I really hope there's a God out there bigger and different than what I've been shown here on earth. Because if the God that lives is the same that is here, I don't know man . . . I might have to go check out Satan!

MICHAEL, INTERVIEWEE

And to all future generations of Hip Hop, know this; it is this Love that has delivered this gospel to OUR PEOPLE for OUR correction and survival. This gospel comes to us as the physical manifestation of God's grace and love for Hip Hop.

KRS-ONE, *THE GOSPEL OF HIP HOP*

Often we view religion and science as having a zero-sum relationship. But for many sociologists, religion and science are both narratives that explain social reality—the former based on traditional authority and faith and the later on scientific methodology.

TOM KERSEN, "SOME THOUGHTS ON THE SOCIOLOGY OF RELIGION"

Evangelicalism has lost its way. In fact, it is no longer relevant for us [multiethnic millennials]. It is blasphemous and contentious. It favors the White oppressors and does not give us a space to even breathe, let alone speak.

MARCIA, INTERVIEWEE

The only place you will see Dr. King's "I have a dream" speech is in Hip Hop.

KRS-ONE

Not everything that is faced can be changed. But nothing can be changed until it is faced.

JAMES BALDWIN

THIS SECTION TAKES UP the latter part of this book's thesis: creating an unconventional missiological paradigm for community and missions. The previous two sections have been concerned with establishing the case for the wild, the urban, the post-soul, the sacred, the secular, and the profane as motifs that missiologists of the twenty-first century need to be concerned with. And so the next five chapters are focused on the *so what* of the previous two sections. Avoiding simplistic methodological and procedural stages, these chapters will focus on unconventional missions and the practical application of missions in the wild. These chapters will not establish exhaustive ideologies that will remain as the guiding pathways for missions in the twenty-first century. If anything, this book has merely begun to explore the post-soul and post–civil rights context. Therefore, a conclusive method would be both presumptuous and arrogant. The goal is to avoid the mistakes made by Christians of the past.

Chapter six begins with reimaging short-term missions by arguing that *short-term* must be deconstructed and reimagined. However, the experiential aspects of learning and personal growth must be retained. Chapter seven observes post-soul missiological persons Tupac Amaru Shakur and Kendrick Lamar, using them as a missiological paradigm. Chapter eight reasserts the importance and significance of race and ethnicity in missions. Chapter nine examines a theological space for protest and social disruption as missiology. Chapter ten concludes with concepts that might provide a future missiological space for the wild.

6

COMMUNAL CONNECTIONS IN THE WILD

From Short-Term Missions to Lifelong Relationships

MY FRIEND HAD SERVED in an urban Seattle community for close to twenty-five years. He had seen many young people develop into strong and mature adults. Further, he had strong networks within and outside the city. One of those networks was with a church just outside the city limits. Every summer the church had come into the city for their "mission experience." They would spend three weeks in the city with my friend's students, the neighborhood, the people, and the issues of the city. They would bring tutors, help restore buildings, and even provide monetary support for my friend's organization.

Many minds were challenged during those experiences, and a couple of young people emerged from that group who have gone on to do national and global work with and for marginalized groups. To that end, it was a success. What more could you ask for—minds and hearts being open to the Lord, and in turn those minds and hearts doing work in a missional setting?

But times and contexts change. The young people in my friend's urban group began to embody Christ's message. They started to grow into mature Christians who wanted to see their faith in action. Over time, this group took trips to cities such as Washington, DC, to push for policy change, meet with senators, and see bills passed that affected their community for the better. These young people also started developing the next generation by establishing a type of mentoring program!

Conversely, the suburban church youth group started seeing a decline in their attendance. Students in that group questioned God. Many disregarded their faith after high school and struggled to see anything good in Christianity.

As one summer approached, my friend reached out to this church and asked whether his group could come out to their church and work with their students. They could talk about their faith development, share how God was working in their lives, and spend a week in the suburbs creating relationships. After all, this church had been a support and blessing for him; the least he could do was to return some of that support, albeit not financially. To my friend's surprise, there was no response. So he decided to visit the church— maybe the emails and phone messages got lost. But that was not the case. In fact, when he arrived, my friend's longtime contact met him in the church's front office. "What's going on?" his friend asked. "Why are you here today?" My friend was taken aback and said, "Well, I'm here to meet with you and talk about the possibility of us coming to your church this summer." The pastor responded in disgust, "Why would we do that?" My friend suggested they talk more informally over lunch, but this pastor would not have it, and his anger grew. Eventually, the truth came out: "You don't come to us. We go to you. Why would you come here?" In other words, what can *we* learn from *you*? My friend was shocked. He tried to make a case but was quickly told the mere suggestion demonstrated his own "ignorance" and "inexperience." It was absurd.

To this day the two have not spoken—even after repeated attempts from my friend to reestablish their friendship.

"You don't help us. We help you." This situation and ideological structure reveals the core of thought from many short-term missionaries toward lower-income, marginalized, urban communities and people groups. The notion that an inner-city urban person cannot help someone of influential means typifies the colonialist mindset of not just institutions but also the people who manage those institutions.

The number of suburban churches in theological dire straits is growing. The "theological turn" has transformed many suburban church land- scapes and created a decline in church membership among mainline de- nominations.[1] In contrast, the urban multiethnic church context has grown

---

[1]On the theological turn, see Andrew Root and Kenda Creasy Dean, *The Theological Turn in Youth Ministry* (Downers Grove, IL: InterVarsity Press, 2011). Regarding church landscapes, see Robert

exponentially, and the *nones* category for emerging adults is not accurate (see chap. 5). But what makes this worse is (1) the colonialist worldview of suburban White churches toward urban multiethnic areas,[2] and (2) the devastating effect of those colonialist worldviews on multiethnic people, which could produce an even larger gap among ethnicities and races.

This chapter will suggest three ideas to alleviate, but not solve, these issues. We will begin to deconstruct racist, colonialist, sexist, and inequal mechanisms. Let's begin with ideas that will help in creating a missiology in the wild.

DEATH TO SHORT-TERM MISSIONS

I am not against learning experiences or the notion of missions. The short-term missions (STMs) that came to my friend's environment came with great intentions and did many good things. Lives were changed for the better, and suburban White youth saw the devastating effects of poverty, red-lining, and gentrification. No one from that suburban church entered the urban area with white hoods on their heads or swastikas on their arms. In other words, no one came with outright intense racism. I believe the experiential learning model—which most millennials thrive on—is vital and much needed.[3] Further, I stand with the idea that learning needs to take place onsite while engaging the issues—specifically in domestic settings. It is important to go to the urban context and learn about the issues—injustice and increasing inequality within the urban post-soul context—but those who go must know their own culture and understand their own ethnic heritage as

---

D. Putnam, *Bowling Alone: The Collapse and Revival of American Community* (New York: Simon & Schuster, 2000); Robert Wuthnow, *The Religious Dimension: New Directions in Quantitative Research* (New York: Academic Press, 1979); Kara E. Powell and Chap Clark, *Sticky Faith: Everyday Ideas to Build Lasting Faith in Your Kids* (Grand Rapids: Zondervan, 2011). On declining membership, see Gregory Smith, *America's Changing Religious Landscape* (Washington, DC: Pew Forum on Religion & Public Life, 2015).

[2]See Richard Twiss, *Rescuing the Gospel from the Cowboys: A Native American Expression of the Jesus Way* (Downers Grove, IL: InterVarsity Press, 2015); and Paul G. Hiebert, "Beyond Anti-Colonialism to Globalism," *Missiology* 19, no. 3 (1991).

[3]José Antonio Bowen suggests it is imperative to use experience and practical engagement with the younger millennial generation. He says that passive learning will not work and that the simple lecture, while still having a place, is not as effective as hands-on, active learning. I agree and suggest these principles can be applied to ministry, church, and missions. Therefore, the idea of learning while doing is critical, especially for homogenous and mono-ethnic areas. See José Antonio Bowen, *Teaching Naked: How Moving Technology out of Your College Classroom Will Improve Student Learning* (San Francisco: Jossey-Bass, 2012).

it relates to the area they are visiting. Jesus was not a short-termer when it came to relationships. I have yet to see where Jesus' ministry exhibited a short vision or a limited amount of investment in people, things, or places. Jesus took time. He understood the complexity of human life, behavior, interactions, and psyche. How many of us would walk with a person we knew would betray us? Jesus did. Day by day he invested in others and built relationships, even with those who would hurt him. This is where the real work of missiology is. Jesus knew this, and so did the early churches.[4] They tarried long with people and were not burdened with the Western construct of time management, numbers, and results. The goal is laid out in the Great Commission: to point people to Christ and his teachings.

However, the concept of short-term missions, which is having a short experience[5] rather than the more historical, long-term missional experience (in which culture, context, geographic location, and language is taken into account), is problematic and unsettling.[6] Brian Howell shows that STMs typically include research on tourism and pilgrimage, which reveals STMs as a cultural travel narrative.[7] And far too often STM trips to domestic urban and post-soul areas turn into self-indulgent tourism and sightseeing. This exacerbates the problems of (1) the lack of knowledge of the area, (2) failure to recognize the STM group's own racial and ethnic heritage, let alone that of those they are working with, and (3) theologies that encourage teaching "better decision making" and "stronger families"

---

[4]Much of the pressure to develop a short-term missions space has to do more with money, funding, and economics of the church than it does with actual mission. Churches funnel money into a specific area to "save souls" at any cost without accounting for their own ignorance of cultural, racial, gender, or sexual issues. Thus, many churches where I have interviewed or consulted people have a financial claim in doing short-term missions and feel the need to fulfill that economic mandate.

[5]I realize this is a simplistic definition of STMs, and that I am more focused on domestic, urban STMs and their effect, but overseas STMs are just as problematic. For a broader view of STMs, see Brian M. Howell, "Mission to Nowhere: Putting Short-Term Missions into Context," *International Bulletin of Missionary Research* 33, no. 4 (2009); Jenny Trinitapoli and Stephen Vaisey, "The Transformative Role of Religious Experience: The Case of Short-Term Missions," *Social Forces* 88, no. 1 (2009); and Kraig Beyerlein, Jenny Trinitapoli, and Gary Adler, "The Effect of Religious Short-Term Mission Trips on Youth Civic Engagement," *Journal for the Scientific Study of Religion* 50, no. 4 (2011).

[6]The scope of this book does not allow for a historical connection to short-term missions. Brian Howell's work, however, gives a historical account of the short-term missions movement that is invaluable. See Brian M. Howell, *Short-Term Mission: An Ethnography of Christian Travel Narrative and Experience* (Downers Grove, IL: IVP Academic, 2012).

[7]Ibid., 48.

without familiarity with the historical problems of that area or people.[8] Further, when people enter a community to change it or bring the Lord to it, cultural and racial damage is imminent.

Consequently, we need to put to death the term *short-term missions* and the concept surrounding it. In one regard, it may be as simple as removing the word *mission* from the title. *Mission* brings to mind several notions:

- God's mission
- The Great Commission
- Bringing the gospel to the lost
- Top-down theology (e.g., someone with knowledge and power bringing the gospel to those with less knowledge and power)
- God is not present in the location and needs an agent to reveal God's message[9]

Locals will translate these notions as follows:

- The White God's mission
- Whose "Great Commission"?
- Are we lost; who gets to define that?
- God is already at work; what new thing do you bring?
- God is already present

Removing the word *mission* may make a difference. At least it would remove some of the connotations and improve the translations by those on

---

[8]These ideological narratives typically stem from racist pathologies toward ethnic minorities that provide simplistic answers to complex problems. These types of bootstrap narratives damage relationships and do not account for the long history of inequality in urban contexts. Further, they are derivatives of a White-savior complex that many STMs come with into domestic urban missions. For further examination of these attitudes, see Willie James Jennings, *The Christian Imagination: Theology and the Origins of Race* (New Haven, CT: Yale University Press, 2010), 207-55.

[9]These are derived from my own research and from several other scholars who have helped me form ideas about colonialism, race, gender, sexuality, and missions. See, for example, Twiss, *Rescuing the Gospel from the Cowboys*; Philip Jenkins, *The Next Christendom: The Coming of Global Christianity* (New York: Oxford University Press, 2011); Wilbert R. Shenk, *Enlarging the Story: Perspectives on Writing World Christian History* (Maryknoll, NY: Orbis Books, 2002); Paul G. Hiebert, "Conversion, Culture and Cognitive Categories," *Gospel in Context* 1, no. 4 (1978); Stephen B. Bevans, *Models of Contextual Theology* (Maryknoll, NY: Orbis Books, 1992); Howard Thurman, *Jesus and the Disinherited* (Boston: Beacon Press, 1976); Trinitapoli and Vaisey, "The Transformative Role of Religious Experience."

the receiving end. Language is an important component of worldviews, and removing *mission* could create a new construct. Changing the word to something like short-term *excursion* or short-term *community engagement* might yield different attitudes from the people participating in those events. Over time, there might be enough momentum to remove *short-term* altogether and simply look at it as engagement—or, to be transparent, name it for what it is: *cultural or ethnic capacity building for the unaware*. Yet nothing is ever that simple.

Death to STMs may mean a complete overhaul of the concept. By *overhaul* I mean replacing or refurbishing the engine with a new one. Of course, this includes adding new items to make the engine run better and more efficiently. Though people are not as simple as a car engine, the idea is the same: a complete renovation of STMs to create a new space for learning, love, community, and engagement with the gospel by all, not just those with money and privilege.

The death of STMs means the word *mission* must be removed permanently. *Mission*—going forth and proclaiming the Word of God in an interculturally insensitive manner—is colonialist in nature and connotes a patriarchal hegemony that we must move away from. The death and overhaul of STMs will be a difficult reality for many and will not be simple.[10] Yet, if we are committed to a post-soul missiology, this is a natural step. Therefore, to achieve this death I propose the following:

- Empowerment of the people the group is working with—it may mean employment, protesting abusive and corrupt systems, or just listening without attempting to change people.

- Serious and in-depth interrogation of White privilege and White racism. Most of the lethal racism that comes from White people toward ethnic minorities is not from hate groups such as the KKK or neo-Nazis but from good, well-intentioned, moral White people who are ignorant of their own racial privileges and who blame ethnic minorities for their own circumstance and place in society.

---

[10]Millions of dollars are raised for and connected to STMs. Money is the one true god we pay attention to in the West. Thus, what I propose will come at a price and with a battle. I am not against taking trips to local areas to learn more or work with local groups (alongside them, not teaching them). But STMs do much more damage than good in ethnic-minority and post-soul communities.

- Reimagining a Christian worldview away from Western notions of Christianity. In other words, it is allowing the vastness and fullness of Christianity to exist or be developed in context without judgment.

- Empowerment of ethnic minorities to engage other ethnic minorities.

- Whites mentored and discipled by ethnic minorities. Soong-Chan Rah has suggested this on numerous occasions, but Whites having ethnic-minority mentors is of paramount importance for any White people desiring to do missional work.

- Fundraising models deconstructed and reimagined. One of the reasons STMs are majority White is because of the inequality that exists in fundraising.[11]

When my friend and colleague Austin Brown worked at Willow Creek Church near Chicago, a dynamic speaker was featured one Sunday morning. The speaker inspired the congregation to "get out" and "do God's work" among "the poor." And a large group of people wanted to do just that in nearby Chicago. Thinking quickly, she called a meeting with those interested and put training in place before any "work" could be done. The training consisted of racial/ethnic literacy, a history of Chicago, the culture of poverty, media literacy, and what reconciliation might look like from a White church in a multiethnic community. While some were upset and resisted (they wanted to "work" right away), the majority stayed for training. And what took place was a much more heartfelt and committed engagement rather than a quick, unthinking Christian response to doing God's "work." The idea was to stay in the community for the long term and see change through relationships rather than quick, newsletter-headline–generating activity. This is a great working example of what I am proposing.

Another example of having the notion of mission but doing the hard work of cultural, racial, ethnic, and geographic literacy comes from the Center for

---

[11]For an excellent study of the racism and exclusion associated with fundraising models within Christian evangelical associations, see Samuel L. Perry, "Diversity, Donations, and Disadvantage: The Implications of Personal Fundraising for Racial Diversity in Evangelical Outreach Ministries," *Review of Religious Research* 53, no. 4 (2012); Samuel L. Perry, "Racial Habitus, Moral Conflict, and White Moral Hegemony Within Interracial Evangelical Organizations," *Qualitative Sociology* 35, no. 1 (2012); and Marla Frederick McGlathery and Traci Griffin, "'Becoming Conservative, Becoming White?' Black Evangelicals and the Para-Church Movement," in *This Side of Heaven: Race, Ethnicity, and Christian Faith*, ed. Robert J. Priest and Alvaro L. Nieves (New York: Oxford University Press, 2007).

Student Mission (CSM) Chicago group.[12] CSM Chicago, which is a majority White organization, brings college-age people to the city during the summer. But they first train the young people for the context they are headed into. Further, the CSM Chicago leaders have themselves been through training and are open to further development of their racial and ethnic knowledge— a crucial step for missional organizations.[13] Moreover, CSM comes alongside ministries and organizations doing work in the city to enhance their effectiveness. This is a great example of racial humility while still helping and creating a learning space for those who are ignorant of a large city's issues. While not perfect, there is still a space to learn, grow, educate, and assist.

We will now turn to the discourse of mission. The language of missions tends to be problematic and reveals a certain perspective that often is hostile to ethnic-minority communities.

THE PROBLEMS ASSOCIATED WITH THE DISCOURSE OF MISSIONS

My old friend and colleague Richard Twiss often talked about the word *mission* and its negative subtext with Native American peoples. Twiss regularly discussed how, for many Native Americans, missional language connoted a sense of superiority, Manifest Destiny, exceptionalism, and White dominance using Christianity as a vehicle. He told me that many First Nation groups cringed at the mere utterance of the word and that words such as *commissioned, commission, called, God's mission,* and the *mission of God* were regarded as hostile and antagonistic. Language is powerful, and it comes with historical references. Further, language produces division when it is not regarded as vital or when its historical relevance is ignored or overlooked. There are many problems associated with the discourse of mission.

First, for many in the urban multiethnic community, it connotes a sense of imperial conquest: the 'hood is something to be *reached* and *conquered*

---

[12]The majority of young adults from CSM are White. CSM has continued to reach out to ethnic-minority groups, but funding continues to be a racial divider. I mention CSM to illustrate the point that a predominately White group has the potential to do good work, but it takes commitment and being humble to figure out the needs of a community.

[13]White people must continually educate themselves to be allies of ethnic minorities. Since the power differential is in their favor, it is imperative that Whites learn to frequently deconstruct their Whiteness and power. Being White will never go away, but its effects can be lessened when racial humility is exhibited in combination with persistent racial- and ethnic-literacy training.

for God's kingdom. The discourse of missions reflects a sense of superiority, and those who are inferior are subjected to evangelistic rigor rooted in a colonial spirit that sees those in the urban post-soul context as exotic objects. This conquest spirit utilizes racial categories to create a power structure subject only to "God's rule." For many, the racial categories are part of the worldview of engagement when it comes to missions.

This racial hierarchy sees the different ethnicities in order as listed in figure 6.1. Skin tone is taken into account (e.g., lighter skin is valued over darker skin, thereby having more privilege in the hierarchy). Thus Asians, typically the model minority, are at the top and are safer than most other ethnicities. This type of racism and colonialism is passive, and it comes from people who hold high moral Christian values. It is embedded in how a group prepares and how they view the people of certain communities. And because this has been practiced and carried out over decades, it has become institutionalized.

White Christianity becomes the driving narrative behind all authority, theology, and "the Christian way." And this narrative trickles down to the lower levels. Other narratives of God, Jesus, and Christianity are not valued and are sometimes seen as heretical. When a construct such as Black liberation theology is presented, it often is suspect and not valued. This is problematic. First, the White Christian narrative is adopted by many as *the way* for theology. And those who question that narrative are accused of sin and

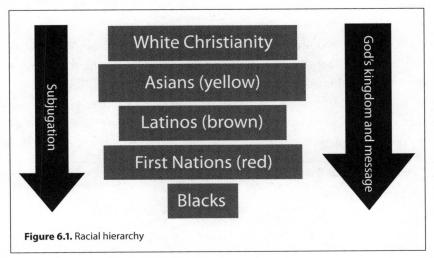

Figure 6.1. Racial hierarchy

threatened with the loss of salvation. This is important, because so many STM programs are developed with White Christian narratives that have no regard for an intercultural perspective on Christianity. Because many White Christians have little intercultural competence, it is less likely they will embrace someone else's culture and will insist on their way as *the right way* to practice Christianity. While removing the verbiage of *mission* will not completely solve this, the deconstruction of this term will help to reduce the idea of a superior group bringing the Word to an inferior group.

Second, the verbiage of *mission* typically overlooks the time it takes and extensive processes needed to develop communities, relationships, and people. Western culture is driven by efficiency. The need to stay plugged in is constant. Moreover, efficiency is always in action; it does not halt at the door of the church. Thus, ministry is practiced the same way: efficient and calculable.[14] Much leadership management is rooted in the idea of getting more things done better and quicker. But when it comes to missions and people, this is not feasible.

People and their relationships are messy; efficiency should not be applied to human interaction. Yet quick results and marked, and measured outcomes are used in missions. People are seen as something to "win" and "save," while real people and the context of their humanity are often disregarded. At the same time, strangely enough, feeling good about a mission is placed above the actual work within a community. In other words, selfies, Instagram likes, and Facebook posts take precedent over the actual ministry and work. People involved in STMs often feel and know this, even though it is communicated nonverbally.[15] While extended time is needed to build relationships, *short-term* demonstrates that time is not valued. So, STMs must be reconsidered and, if at all possible, regarded as a relic of the past.

The rhetoric of missions is problematic in many regards. We will now turn to the power of relationships and establishing connections rooted in tension and growth.

---

[14]This is part of George Ritzer's McDonaldization thesis, which I regard as a good framework for the way STM is done. George Ritzer, *The McDonaldization of Society* (Thousand Oaks, CA: Pine Forge Press, 2004), 13-20.

[15]Nonverbal communication is a large part of the communication process and often is more effective than verbal communication. See Donald K. Smith, *Creating Understanding: A Handbook for Christian Communication Across Cultural Landscapes* (Grand Rapids: Zondervan, 1992); and Charles H. Kraft, *Communication Theory for Christian Witness* (Maryknoll, NY: Orbis Books, 1991).

LIFELONG RELATIONSHIPS: BEYOND RECONCILIATION

Reconciliation is a popular word among many White evangelical (and some ethnic-minority) churches. Often, it is embraced with a warm, fuzzy, and nostalgic notion of "being brothers and sisters in Christ." But it overlooks historical racism, White supremacy, and systemic inequality. As a rule, when terms such as *reconciliation* become popular and are used in mainstream settings, this tends to mean that it has lost most of its root significance and power. It is co-opted by the dominant culture. And while I am in strong favor of reconciliation that deals primarily with White racism, I am not in favor of reconciliation that overlooks the difficult parts of race, ethnicity, class, gender, and systemic oppression. We cannot just "hug it out" and think that things will be okay. A much broader and complex understanding of reconciliation is needed. As an ethnic minority I do not have the freedom to "be of good cheer" while systematic oppression is being thrown at me. Reconciliation cannot happen. It is time we begin to dismantle this rhetoric.

The conversation about reconciliation will be a difficult for Whites in particular. True reconciliation cannot be attained simply by reading a book, attending a conference, or completing some certificate. *If* it is to come into reality, it will require relationships rooted in long-time commitments and regard for the other person or community. Such relationships must be eye-to-eye, on the same level, and not top-down. Whites interested in developing relationships with ethnic minorities will listen to and empower the other person. These relationships do not plateau after experiencing warm feelings or some kind of breakthrough is achieved. Whites and ethnic minorities regard each other highly and work with each other in community. This will be difficult for any organization or ministry driven by numbers, fundraising, a feel-good sense of helping others, and a mono-ethnic worldview. Power is put down and privilege is challenged. In this work, relationships are crucial and part of the process. The journey and the tension are parts of the ultimate pathway forward to a better relationship. This kind of an encounter (formerly called *missions*) means that we begin by knowing the other and living by Jesus' second greatest commandment: love your neighbor as yourself.

Relational tension is often overlooked and avoided; most in the Western context have looked on relationships from either a utilitarian context, an intimate partner context, or an enemy context. The Western mindset views tension as bad and to be circumvented—there must be something wrong with the relationship if there is tension. However, tension is precisely where a good relationship grows. Both parties are responsible to work through that tension and create a better relationship. The messiness makes it a stronger relationship and creates a sense of ownership by both parties. This deconstructs a planned and methodical progression that typically comes with some type of mile marker to ensure things are going right. Happiness and warm feelings are not the chief concern of relationships. Rather, the centerpiece is the betterment of the other person and their community.

How might this look then for those wanting to come to the urban post-soul context? I suggest a two-part structure for relational connections. The first is to come alongside already-existing organizations and ministries. The other is to create long-lasting and meaningful relationships with people different from you in race, ethnicity, religion, culture, class, or gender. However, it takes time for any of this to happen. In a hyper-paced, hyper–results-oriented culture, time is both overlooked and devalued. We have come to adore the McDonaldization process of efficiency, calculability, control, and predictability.[16] This continues the legacy of supremacy and does not empower the other.

Here is what I suggest for those who want to build genuine relationships[17]:

1. Begin with an open heart and the desire to know the people in that community better without pushing them to change anything.

2. Learn about the community and the people. What is their history? What is their context? What have been their greatest achievements, and where have there been great inequalities? Learn about the environment that the people live in. This will take time. It cannot be done rapidly.

---

[16]The effects of McDonaldization on discipleship and mentoring cannot be overlooked (Ritzer, *McDonaldization of Society*, 163-200). It seems churches and ministries turn out replicas of the previous generation by creating protégés rather than critically thinking and culturally aware individuals. See John William Drane, *The McDonaldization of the Church: Spirituality, Creativity, and the Future of the Church* (London: Darton Longman & Todd, 2000); and his follow-up text *After McDonaldization: Mission, Ministry, and Christian Discipleship in an Age of Uncertainty* (Grand Rapids: Baker Academic, 2008).

[17]These are beginnings, and not the finalized approaches. I am not sure there is a final method to any of this. Please do not assume that by "doing" this, you have now overcome racism and/or any other "ism," for that matter. These are merely suggestions.

3. If you are White, seek mentorship or discipline from an ethnic minority. This is crucial. It creates space for intimate conversations in which a White person submits to an ethnic minority in a learning posture.

4. Know who is doing what and how they are doing it; never assume that your way is the right or best way. White evangelicals often insist on doing something their way because they "know how to do it." If there is a legitimate concern and cause for correction, good communication skills are necessary in order to avoid a paternal position. But even in that, it is important to take the time to figure out how things are done for that context. For example, time management may not be as highly regarded by others as it is in your context.

5. Use social media lightly. Continually monitor yourself as to why you are posting something. Does it need to be posted? Pictures of Whites doing good work in Africa are difficult enough for many ethnic minorities, but when that is done domestically, it creates anger and a disconnect with the essence of the gospel. Moreover, it is just wrong and immoral to regard people as zoo projects.

6. Establish criteria for how you will help with issues beyond fence building and drywall plastering. This means engaging with the social, political, educational, and economic problems that face the specific community.[18] It means doing a community assessment to figure out what is needed and to use influence and power for good and change.

7. Plan on the long haul; stay for a while. Do away with the discourse of *short-term* and begin to look at actual relationships with the people and their community. It will take plenty of patience to do this. Realize that your privilege means turning over power to those in the community and allowing them to lead. Seek the development of that community through fair housing, access to affordable healthcare, employment, economic development, access to materials only reserved for the privileged (e.g., SAT/PSAT tutoring), and the creation of a community that seeks the peace of the city.

---

[18]For some, this may appear much too liberal or progressive. While I value different perspectives on God, the Bible, and faith, I ask, What did Jesus do in these kinds of situations? And is a liberal perspective that bad? Will it corrupt everyone? Love is expressed while acting on unjust laws, polices, and systems.

For those desiring a lifelong relationship, I suggest the following:

1. Do life together. The grind of daily living quickly gets past the surface elements of a relationship. Life together allows us to see the faults, the beauty, the crap, the love, the hate, the joy, the depression, and the God of a person. Over time, this is achievable. For some, this may mean intentional community living.[19] For others, this may mean a weekly relationship that involves doing an activity or event together. Relationships are messy; the goal is not to prescribe a process but to engage in that messiness.

2. Allow people time to develop. Many of us have a diverse set of issues, problems, and behavioral idiosyncrasies that are either not seen or not valued when seen. While we should not tolerate passive-aggressive or dysfunctional behavior, we should look at the effects that the bumps, bruises, imperfections, and nuances of personality have on both an individual and a community. Allowing people to develop over time is merciful and gives strength to the relationship.

3. Create room for listening among those who differ in age. This requires involvement in someone's life and attending to what is important to them. A friend once told me that it was of utmost importance for young people to listen to him, but he did not reciprocate. Many older adults make this mistake. They have something to tell "those young people," who had better listen. This mistake is often compounded when speaking of religion. Two people must listen to each other and participate in each others' lives. When this is done right, lifelong relationships are cemented and the space to grow with each other is revealed.

4. As the relationship develops, embrace the tension. This is difficult because most of us tend to avoid tension and conflict. I am not suggesting we seek conflict and tension—there is enough of that in our world already. Tension and conflict come naturally in a relationship. We are all different, and those differences will begin to annoy us at

---

[19]Many of these spaces have been co-opted and gentrified by White, well-intentioned, young adults. But they do more damage than good as a result of their racial, cultural, and ethnic illiteracy. I realize that intentional community requires a level of privilege that some do not have.

some point. Arguing is part of a relationship. Discuss that, embrace it, and learn from it. Doing this, however, might require professional counseling and therapy. We learn both the good and the bad habits of communication from our family. Professionally trained therapists are able to help deconstruct what makes us upset and where it originated from. That space allows for health and growth. There is no growth without tension pushing it forward.

5. Reconciliation will be messy. For White people it will mean the deconstruction of power, privilege, and access to their Whiteness as a resource. This may prove too difficult for some. Colonialism runs deep and becomes part of one's mental and emotional DNA. A serious and honest look at Whiteness often turns a person's worldview inside out. This can cause conflict, disassociation of identity, anomie, and even depression. Though difficult, within the confines of a relationship the detox of Whiteness is achievable and worthwhile. Reconciliation then has space to develop and be experienced in full.

Lifelong relationships are difficult. They require commitment to communication and embracing tension. This should take the place of STMs. It will create a community based on an eye-to-eye connection with God and God's mission—not ours. In order for lifelong relationships to develop, STM organizations need to dismantle their power and embrace transparency. In relationships, God is revealed when the sacred, profane, and secular are allowed to intersect.

We will now turn to the gospel of Tupac Amaru Shakur. Tupac presents a missiological premise crucial for anyone desiring to engage the wild and post-soul era. I situate Tupac in the post-soul context as not just a voice but also a symbol for the sacred, secular, and profane. Within this, we will begin to create a missiology for the present context and era.

7

BAPTIZED IN DIRTY WATER

*Learning from the Post-Soul Missiologists
Tupac Amaru Shakur and Kendrick Lamar*

Here on Earth, tell me what's a black life worth?
A bottle of juice is no excuse, the truth hurts
And even when you take the shit
Move counties, get a lawyer, you can shake the shit
Ask Rodney, LaTasha, and many more
It's been goin' on for years, there's plenty more
When they ask me, "When will the violence cease?"
When your troops stop shootin' niggaz down in the street
Niggaz had enough time to make a difference
Bear witness, on our own business
Word to God, 'cause it's hard tryin' to make ends meet[1]

Tupac in Compton, man! To kids, even grown men, he was like a superhero.
I don't know what gave him this aura but he had something else. Now I'm old
enough to say I don't think even he knew it.[2]

Tupac Amaru Shakur. Even the name causes many Hip Hoppers like Kendrick Lamar to pause for a moment.[3] When asked what he did on hearing

---

[1]Tupac, "I Wonder if Heaven Got a Ghetto?," *R U Still Down? Remember Me*, Interscope Records, 1997.
[2]Kendrick Lamar, quoted in Dorian Lynskey, "Kendrick Lamar: 'I Am Trayvon Martin. I'm All of These Kids,'" *The Guardian*, June 21, 2015, www.theguardian.com/music/2015/jun/21/kendrick-lamar-interview-to-pimp-a-butterfly-trayvon-martin.
[3]Fifteen of the interviewees noted that Biggie Smalls was also considered a prophet and Hip Hop spiritualist. Only releasing a total of four albums (which pales in comparison to Tupac's arsenal

the news of Tupac's death, Marlon Wayans stated that he cried like his momma cried when Marvin Gaye was murdered. Young girls and boys who were not even alive during Tupac's life remember and adore him as if they had grown up in his era. Further, even mildly liberal parents today (who were teens in the 1990s) pause and think about the effect Tupac had on their own lives.[4] Tupac is iconic. Recalling Tupac's accomplishments, Quincy Jones states that if Martin Luther King Jr. had died when he was only twenty-five, he would have been just a struggling Black Baptist minister. Malcolm X would have been just a street hustler, and Jones himself would have been just a struggling trumpet player. When Tupac died at twenty-five, he left a legacy of life, love, rage, pain—and theology. "Tupac was touched by God, not very many people are touched by the hand of God,"[5] Jones said.

Conversely, Kendrick Lamar *is* the post-soul rapper.[6] A West Coast rapper who raps like an East Coast lyricist, Lamar is able to create space to talk about life, death, love, sex, hate, rage, racism, social inequality, and God—all in the same album. Lamar embodies the sacred, secular, and profane and has the ability to create a dialogue with and about God that one can digest while still leaving room for complexity. Lamar does not deal with binaries in theology (e.g., good and evil) as many theologians do; rather, he is able to pick up the Tupac-ian mantle and continue the complex conversation about police brutality, and around Brenda, the fictional character Tupac created in his work who is homeless, in poverty, and with child. Lamar has the power to set a banquet for the oppressed and marginalized in the dirty water itself.

There is interplay between Tupac and Lamar. Not only does Lamar use and interview Tupac in his album *To Pimp a Butterfly*, but he has been commissioned

---

of albums), Biggie is still noted as one of Hip Hop's moguls who attempted to work out the profane and secular in sacred spaces. More research is needed on the spiritual significance of Biggie.

[4] As seen in my 2004–2008 interviews on Tupac's theological mystique in Daniel White Hodge, *Heaven Has a Ghetto: The Missiological Gospel and Theology of Tupac Amaru Shakur* (Saarbrucken, Germany: VDM Verlag Dr. Müller Academic, 2009).

[5] Quincy Jones, cited in *Thug Angel: The Life of an Outlaw*, directed by Peter Spirer, 2002. This paragraph is adapted from Daniel White Hodge, "Baptized in Dirty Water: Locating the Gospel of Tupac Amaru Shakur in the Post-Soul Context," in *Secular Music and Sacred Theology*, ed. Tom Beaudoin (Collegeville, MN: Liturgical Press, 2013).

[6] This emerges from my research in Daniel White Hodge, *Hip Hop's Hostile Gospel: A Post-Soul Theological Exploration*, ed. Warren Goldstein, Studies on Critical Research in Religion (Boston: Brill Academic, 2017), 6.

by Hip Hop legends such as Dr. Dre and Snoop Dogg to be a socio-spiritual leader within Hip Hop culture. If Tupac is Hip Hop's saint, Lamar is its theologian. They represent two different eras of post-soul culture. They are able to create the necessary critical intellect needed in the post-soul context.

So, what makes such an iconic figure? What makes Tupac what some scholars call an urban theologian?[7] What makes Tupac's music, life, and poetry continue to ring true twenty years after his death? Is there something deeper and more meaningful in Tupac's lyrics, which are infused with a type of ghetto spiritual essence and urban contextualized spiritual authority entrenched in the murky waters of the profane and the sacred?[8] How does Lamar pick up that mantle and create a new space for the post-soulist? This chapter will explore these questions.

SITUATING TUPAC IN THE POST-SOUL CONTEXT

To begin, we must situate four terms related to Tupac and the post-soul context. First, post-soul in the *macro* sense of an entire culture differs somewhat from *micro* post-soul as applied to Tupac as a singular individual. Tupac, as this chapter will argue, is a post-soul personification of the rejection of norms, hegemonic authority, and dominant religious structures that inhibit community building.[9] The post-soul era began in the late 1960s and early 1970s, and it rejected dominant structures, systems, and metanarratives that tended to exclude ethnic minorities, particularly those in the

---

[7]Michael Eric Dyson, *Holler If You Hear Me: Searching for Tupac Shakur* (New York: Basic Civitas, 2001); Daniel White Hodge, *The Soul of Hip Hop: Rims, Timbs and a Cultural Theology* (Downers Grove, IL: InterVarsity Press, 2010); and Ralph Basui Watkins, *Hip-Hop Redemption: Finding God in the Rhythm and the Rhyme*, Engaging Culture (Grand Rapids: Baker Academic, 2011).

[8]For too long religious discourse and rhetoric has had a polarized stance on good and evil, the sacred and the profane. However, a third area has emerged in the post-soul context—that which is between good and evil, sacred and profane. Thus this ground is quite murky and diluted, which is the world where Tupac found God. For further review see Esther Iverem, "The Politics of 'Fuck It' and the Passion to Be a Free Black," in *Tough Love: The Life and Death of Tupac Shakur*, ed. Michael Datcher and Kwame Alexander (Alexandria, VA: Black Words Books, 1997); Jack Miles, *Christ: A Crisis in the Life of God* (New York: Alfred A. Knopf, 2001); Anthony B. Pinn, *The Black Church in the Post–Civil Rights Era* (Maryknoll, NY: Orbis Books, 2002); and Teresa L. Reed, *The Holy Profane: Religion in Black Popular Music* (Lexington: University Press of Kentucky, 2003).

[9]Garth Alper, "Making Sense Out of Postmodern Music?," *Popular Music and Society* 24, no. 4 (Winter 2000): Zygmunt Bauman, "Postmodern Religion?," in *Religion, Modernity and Postmodernity*, ed. Paul Heelas (Malden, MA: Blackwell, 1998); Harvey Cox, *Religion in the Secular City: Toward a Postmodern Theology* (New York: Simon & Schuster, 1984); and Don Cupitt, "Post-Christianity," in Heelas, *Religion, Modernity and Postmodernity*.

'hood. The post-soul era rejects linear functional mantras and embraces communal approaches to life, love, and God.[10] The post-soul context was formed in the cocoon of a social shift that broke open the dam to the questioning of authority, challenging the status quo, asserting one's self-identity in the public sphere, and questioning group leaders.[11] The post-soul embodies a more urban, ethnic-minority, Hip Hop worldview. Therefore, while still recognizing the societal shift that occurred during those years, the post-soul is a more multicultural, multiethnic approach to postmodernity and the issues it raises.[12]

Second, post-soul theology prioritizes the connection with the God of the oppressed and disenfranchised. Post-soul theology seeks to better understand God in the profane, the blasphemous, and the irreverent. Moreover, it makes God accessible to humans in a multiethnic and inclusive way while still recognizing the atrocities committed in the name of religion.[13]

Third, many renowned evangelical theologians argue that we live in a secular culture. However, within the post-soul context, spirituality re-emerges and seeks to discover God in the ordinary. This pathway is foreign to traditional soteriologies. The neo-secular is a mixture of sacred and profane spiritual journeys pursuing God in a space outside traditional forms of worship.

---

[10]Linear functional mantras comprise sequential-based reasoning, linear worldviews (first this, then that), and simplistic answers.

[11]See Nelson George, *Hip Hop America* (New York: Penguin Books, 1998); Hodge, *Soul of Hip Hop*; Mark Anthony Neal, *What the Music Said: Black Popular Music and Black Public Culture*; Mark Anthony Neal, *Soul Babies: Black Popular Culture and the Post-Soul Aesthetic* (New York: Routledge, 2002); Anthony B. Pinn, *Black Church in the Post–Civil Rights Era*; Anthony B. Pinn, *Embodiment and the New Shape of Black Theology* (New York: New York University Press, 2010).

[12]For example, books such as Steven Best and Douglas Kellner, *Postmodern Theory: Critical Interrogations* (New York: Guilford, 1991), fall short of mentioning the social, religious, and cultural shift that the civil rights movement brought to the American public sphere. Moreover, Raymond F. Betts, *A History of Popular Culture: More of Everything, Faster and Brighter* (New York: Routledge, 2004), does not mention the contributions of Hip Hop and Rap moguls. In the work of Scott Lash, "Postmodernism as Humanism? Urban Space and Social Theory," in *Theories of Modernity and Postmodernity*, ed. Bryan S. Turner (Thousand Oaks, CA: Sage, 1990); and Lash, *Sociology of Postmodernism* (New York: Routledge, 1990), Gil Scott-Heron, Ray Charles, and even the television show *Fresh Prince of Bel-Air* were never mentioned in the literature. While each of these represent major changes and social shifts, they were not engaged. The post-soul, as argued in chapter one, is therefore a parallel conceptual framework that includes those excluded voices, and it creates space for artists like Tupac. Tupac asserted time after time that race played a role in the historical discourse of people, and the post-soul aids in filling that void.

[13]Daniel White Hodge, "No Church in the Wild: An Ontology of Hip Hop's Socio-Religious Discourse in Tupac's 'Black Jesuz,'" *Nomos*, March 23, 2013.

Fourth, neo-sacred is rooted in the post-soul theological context. This sacred space embodies city corners, alleyways, clubrooms, cocktail lounges, and spaces/places that are extraneous to many who call themselves Christian. The neo-sacred is Tupac's message to pimps, hookers, thugs, niggas, and those overlooked by society, missionaries, and many churchgoers. The neo-sacred is concerned with finding God in the post-soul socioecological landscape and making God accessible for all.

Tupac was more than just a fad or an estranged artist. He had a mission and message that few are able to embrace. The cost is high: your life. Tupac saw life and culture beyond the routine and ordinary; he approached life full of passion, rage, anger, love, thoughtfulness, and even carelessness. He was the product of a post-soul society and was groomed on the ambiguous consumer culture of the 1980s.[14] In this consumer culture, Tupac became a popular critical pundit for the Hip Hop community. He was a byproduct of the postrevolutionary Black spirit alive in the early 1970s.[15] He was the voice of the ghetto, the marginalized, the oppressed, and the downtrodden, connecting God to a people who would never imagine gracing the pristine hallways of a church.[16] He related God, culture, Hip Hop, life, pain, and even "sin" to Jesus, and forced the listener to deal with those issues while offering an accessible pathway and access to a God not marred with blonde hair and blue eyes. Tupac's God was the God of the 'hood. As Cheryl Kirk-Duggan so eloquently states of Tupac, "Amid his deep hurt and alienation, he often expressed profound religious sensibilities—a kind of street spirituality that invokes traditional faith categories [and] ranging from irony and sarcasm to humility and sincerity, aware of the life and death issues that people face daily on the street."[17]

---

[14]Tawnya Adkins Covert, "Consumption and Citizenship During the Second World War," *Journal of Consumer Culture*, November 1, 2003.

[15]See also Pinn, *Black Church in the Post–Civil Rights Era*, in which he discusses the effects of the civil rights movement, post-soul creations, and postrevolutionary elements for the Black church and Black theology.

[16]While this was Tupac's main audience, numerous suburban, wealthy, White people have connected with Tupac's message simply because they were marginalized, oppressed, and or downtrodden by parents and or other structural forces similar to that of the urban poor.

[17]Cheryl A. Kirk-Duggan, "The Theo-Poetic Theological Ethics of Lauryn Hill and Tupac Shakur," in *Creating Ourselves: African Americans and Hispanic Americans on Popular Culture and Religious Expression*, ed. Anthony B. Pinn and Benjamín Valentín (Durham, NC: Duke University Press, 2009), 214.

Tupac was also the product of his mother's upbringing in the Black church framework, which was connected to protest and praise. His mom, Afeni Shakur, gave Tupac his foundation and provided the theological foundation for his later life, including Afrocentric thinking and theologizing. This gave Tupac the context in which to create and think about not just the *missio Dei* in his own life but also for the community. Tupac continually emphasized that work needed to be done in order to benefit the community; if it did not, it was not worth the work.

Tupac provided an alternative space for those who do not fit the White evangelical model of finding God; he allowed people to *seek* God within a missional framework in post-soul space.[18] Therefore, there are five major eras that shaped Tupac's life music, poetry, and theological themes. Those five eras are:

1. Military mind (1971–1980)

2. Criminal grind (1981–1988)

3. The ghetto is destiny (1989–1992)

4. Outlaw (1992–1995)

5. Ghetto saint (1996–present)[19]

---

[18]Tupac did have his issues. He was aware of these personal failures as it related to his own anger, hurts, and pain. Moreover, Tupac struggled with the positive and the negative in his life. On one hand there was the hopefulness of the African American community; on the other there were elements of his life that blocked that hopefulness. That said, this chapter illuminates the gospel message of Tupac. There is more than enough negative press on Tupac as a negative Black male. However, Tupac creates theological space for those who have been overlooked so they can connect with God. I am not asserting that we accept Tupac as a perfected person; he was human and had his faults. However, within those faults we find God and Christ at a deeper level, a level many of us are not willing to go to because it involves elements of the blasphemous. This chapter utilizes ethnolifehistory, which is a method that charts the varying peaks within a person's life that can then be translated into potential periods, eras, and stages by focusing on (1) the creation of life eras and their development and transition from one major event to the next, (2) key moments that help to shift one era to the next, (3) transitional effects on the subject from one era to the next, and (4) how these eras, shifts, and the effects of such changes impact the cultural products under study. I am persuaded that ethnolifehistory make it a promising method for religion and Hip Hop studies. Ethnolifehistory not only pushes religion and Hip Hop studies beyond lyrical and aesthetic analysis but also includes close ethnographic attention to underutilized sources in the current terrain of religion and Hip Hop studies. Attention beyond a sole focus on the lyrical and aesthetic dimensions to consider the lived realities and geography of an artist's life seldom considered might offer a more expansive window into how and why meaning or religion is constructed and plays particular roles, taking on different shapes at certain moments in an artist's life. For more, see Daniel White Hodge, "Hip Hop's Prophetic: Exploring Tupac and Lauryn Hill Using Ethnolifehistory," in *Religion in Hip Hop* ("the Volume"), ed. Monica Miller, Bernard Freeman, and Anthony B. Pinn (London: Bloomsbury Academic, 2015).

[19]For a comprehensive review of each life era and how I arrived at these eras see my *Soul of Hip*

Tupac, much like Lamar, weaved a strand of theology through the intersections of the sacred, secular, and profane—where Tupac resided daily and found meaning pursuing the numinous. It was a space outside the traditional environment of church. Tupac was creating a neo-sacred theology, which was a contextualized spirituality of and for the urban post-soul community.[20] Tupac gave the broader American media outlets a view into the 'hood, implying that there is much to engage with and learn from at the intersections of the sacred, profane, and secular, and within the apparently blasphemous.[21]

In the face of severe economic, social, and political disparities, Tupac believed a new type of theological discourse was needed. For example, in one of his first songs, "Panther Power," Tupac bellows:

As real as it seems the American Dream
Ain't nothing but another calculated scheme
To get us locked up shot up back in chains
To deny us of the future rob our names
Kept my history of mystery but now I see
The American Dream wasn't meant for me
Cause lady liberty's a hypocrite she lied to me[22]

Tupac calls out the very fabric of the American Dream (home ownership, education, affordable health care, and day care),[23] and on behalf of the

Hop, which examines Tupac's missiological gospel and his discussion of the major changes from era to era and how he emerged and defined himself through each one.

[20]Neo-sacred theology defines the intersection of the profane and the sacred, a space that has elements of both deity and sin. It points to divine edification in the midst of chaos, pain, blasphemy, and irreverence.

[21]This takes up the argument begun by Benjamín Valentín in regard to sketching cultural theology and the importance of relevant cultural figures within a theological space. While Valentín argues for a Latino cultural theology, I believe that Tupac is part of that process even though he was African American. Many young Latinos saw Tupac as part of their own cultural geography. For instance, Valentín asserts that Latino youth realize culture matters. They are being oppressed in more ways than simply economics: cultural imperialism, racism, and sexism. Tupac covered these in his music and felt connected to this type of critical cultural discourse. See Benjamín Valentín, "Tracings: Sketching the Cultural Geographies of Latino/a Theology," in Pinn and Valentín, *Creating Ourselves*, 39-40.

[22]Tupac Shakur, "Panther Power," *Beginnings: The Lost Tapes (1988–1991)*, Koch Records, 2007.

[23]These four elements are what Fred Block describes as the four main constructs of the American Dream. The exponential increase in cost of all those areas between 1973 and 2003 have almost eliminated the middle class. For Tupac, and many other Black scholars, the poor, the ghettoized, and African Americans are at the bottom of this avalanche of misery. These are also building blocks for Western evangelical Christianity and used as part of Christian exceptionalism. Fred Block et al., "The Compassion Gap in American Poverty Policy," *Contexts* 5, no. 2 (2006).

ghetto poor, he challenges its apparent mythology. Where is God in all of this? Where is justice for those who do not live the commercialized "good life"? Tupac asserts the neo-sacred within this pain and disillusionment in a song titled "Lord Knows":

I smoke a blunt to take the pain out
And if I wasn't high, I'd probably try to blow my brains out
I'm hopeless, they shoulda killed me as a baby
And now they got me trapped in the storm, I'm goin' crazy

Forgive me, they wanna see me in my casket
And if I don't blast, I'll be the victim of them bastards
I'm losin' hope, they got me stressin', can the Lord forgive me
Got the spirit of a thug in me[24]

At the same time, Tupac realizes that this is not the way life was supposed to be. He is fully aware that God has not intended people to behave in an inhumane fashion. He calls out to God in a post-soul style, decrying his lifestyle:

Fuck the friendships, I ride alone
Destination Death Row, finally found a home
Plus all my homies wanna die, call it euthanasia
Dear Lord, look how sick this ghetto made us, sincerely
Yours I'm a thug, the product of a broken home[25]

In these lyrics Tupac does what he has to in order to survive these types of injustices while still asking the poignant theological questions of God in the face of suffering. Tupac presents a voice to engage culture, deal with conflict, create cohesive narrative, generate community, dispel traditional powers, and call people to a different level of engagement with God. Cheryl Kirk-Duggan says that, "like James Baldwin, Shakur confronted black suffering with a moral ire."[26] For those who argue that this type of approach to life is vile, immoral, and sinful, Tupac replies that only God can judge him:

---

[24]Tupac Shakur, "Lord Knows," *Me Against the World*, Interscope Records, 1995.
[25]Tupac Shakur and The Outlawz, "Letter to the President," *Still I Rise*, Interscope Records, 1999.
[26]Kirk-Duggan, "Theo-Poetic Theological Ethics," 219.

Oh my Lord, tell me what I'm livin' for
Everybody's droppin', got me knockin' on Heaven's door
And all my memories, of seein' brothers bleed
And everybody grieves, but still nobody sees
Recollect your thoughts, don't get caught up in the mix
'Cause the media is full of dirty tricks
Only God can judge me[27]

Blues music had a similar sensibility. Contextual, relevant, gritty, and with reflections of Black lives in the White supremacist South, many White conservatives and religious Blacks dismissed the blues as evil, sinful, and vile. Teresa Reed reminds us that, "blues singing was associated with the brothel, the juke joint, and the dregs of black-American society."[28] Still, despite the stench of "sin," Reed argues that the

> religious commentary is salient in the blues text. . . . These lyrics treat religion in a way that yields two important kinds of information: . . . blacks integrated secular thought with sacred . . . [and] the postbellum shift in black-American religious consciousness.[29]

Tupac's music is merely a continuation of this postbellum shift, now with rap music.[30]

A great example of part of this shift came in the late 1960s and early 1970s with a heated debate about whether Black theology had any relevance or merely reflected an "angry" and "hateful" message from Blacks.[31] Black theologian Herbert Edwards, in response to claims from some White theologians that Black theology was not a valid theological approach, argued that Black theology provided contextualization, a voice, for those who had previously been either dismissed by White evangelicals or forcibly assimilated to their tradition. Tupac begins to create such a Black theological space.[32]

---

[27]Tupac Shakur, "Only God Can Judge Me," *All Eyez on Me*, Death Row Records, 1996.

[28]Reed, *Holy Profane*, 39.

[29]Ibid., 39-40.

[30]Hodge, *Soul of Hip Hop*.

[31]See, for example, James H. Cone, *Black Theology and Black Power*, 5th ed. (Maryknoll, NY: Orbis Books, 1997).

[32]Edwards argues that in order for theologies to have a concrete basis they must prove the inadequacy of the preceding theologies, establish and prove their own adequacy for the present, and establish continuity with the primordial, normative expressions of the faith. See Herbert O. Edwards, "Black Theology: Retrospect and Prospect," *Journal of Religious Thought* 32, no. 2 (1975): 46-47.

Tupac calls out the inadequacy of the previous and existing theologies for the present crisis: poverty, recidivism rates for young urban males, racism, and classism. Tupac never once questioned, blasphemed, or cursed the name of God or Jesus. But he called out religious officials, traditional churches (churches practicing hypertraditionalism and adherence to the "letter of the law"), conventional forms of religion, irrelevant theologies, and current methods of evangelism.

Tupac was not a formally trained theologian, pastor, or evangelist.[33] He did not have the eloquence of T. D. Jakes or the patois of a Baptist preacher. Still, Tupac was able to connect God to the streets and give those who had never heard of God a vision for what their life could be. For Tupac and others like him, lacking formal seminary training never disqualified him from doing "God's work." Still, Tupac never developed solid conclusions about a theology of the 'hood. He began the discussion, but because of his early death, he never finished a ghetto gospel:

> We pro'ly in Hell, already, our dumb asses not knowin'
> Everybody kissin' ass to go to Heaven ain't goin'
> Put my soul on it, I'm fightin' devil niggas daily
> Plus the media be crucifyin' brothers severely[34]

This aptly titled song "Blasphemy" was a rejection of a form of Black theology that places the pastor at the center of the church in which he creates a pious stature (and it is typically a *him*) and discourages honest questions and doubts emerging from the congregation.[35] Tupac not only challenges but shatters the status quo by placing context and reality into his message within this song. He further states:

> The preacher want me buried, why? 'Cause I know he a liar
> Have you ever seen a crackhead? That's eternal fire
> Why you got these kids' minds, thinkin' that they evil?
> While the preacher bein' freaky, you say, "honor God's people"

---

[33]In my 2008 research, nineteen of the twenty of the interviews stated that Tupac was their "pastor" and had a connection to theology. They said Tupac was a prophet because of the way he could interpret theological matters and make it clear for them. See Hodge, *Soul of Hip Hop*.

[34]Tupac Shakur (Makaveli), "Blasphemy," *The Don Killuminati: The 7 Day Theory*, Death Row Records, 1996.

[35]Pinn, *Embodiment and the New Shape of Black Theology*, 101-23.

Should we cry, when the Pope die? My request:
We should cry if they cried when we buried Malcolm X
Mama tell me: Am I wrong? Is God just another cop
Waitin' to beat my ass if I don't go pop?[36]

Tupac continues shattering the status quo of nice theological answers by offering up metaphorical comparisons:

They ask us why we mutilate each other like we do
And wonder why we hold such little worth for human life
(Facing all this drama)
To ask us why we turn from bad to worse, is to ignore from which we came
You see, you wouldn't ask why the rose that grew from the concrete had
Damaged petals
On the contrary, we would all celebrate its tenacity
We would all love its will to reach the sun
Well, we are the roses
This is the concrete
And these are my damaged petals
Don't ask me why
Thank God, nigga
Ask me how[37]

In one of his greatest theological songs, "So Many Tears," Tupac pushes past the "milk" theology, described by the apostle Paul in 1 Corinthians 3:2, and into a mature theological stance that embraces the realties of death, depression, suicide, and the failures of life:

Now that I'm strugglin' in this business, by any means
Label me greedy getting' green, but seldom seen
And fuck the world 'cause I'm cursed, I'm havin' visions
Of leavin' here in a hearse, God can you feel me?
Take me away from all the pressure, and all the pain
Show me some happiness again, I'm goin' blind
I spend my time in this cell, ain't livin' well

---

[36]Tupac, "Blasphemy." In this verse we can also see Tupac connecting with mainstream theological thought by asking the serious questions of God. In other words, is God just another White, conservative Republican wanting me to fit in and wear suits and ties? Is there a place for the real nigga and thug in heaven?

[37]Tupac Shakur, "Mama's Just a Little Girl," *Better Dayz*, Interscope Records, 2002.

I know my destiny is Hell, where did I fail?
My life is in denial and when I die
Baptized in eternal fire I'll shed so many tears

Lord, I suffered through the years, and shed so many tears[38]

The post-soul context requires one to disembody and deconstruct current theological mantras that continually hold up tradition. Pain, injustice, and racism force the post-soulist to look beyond the "standard" and ask God for more. Simplistic answers are rejected and despised: it lets God off the hook too easily to say "just pray about it." But in times of pain and injustice, everything needs to be on the hook, including God.[39] The procedure is quite simple: have a conversation with God, be real, and do not be afraid to use strong language to describe your pain—a crucial element of a missiology at the intersections of the sacred, profane, and secular:

Was it my fault Papa didn't plan it out?
Broke out, left me to be the man of the house
I couldn't take it, had to make a profit
Down the block, got a Glock, and I clock grips
Makin' G's was my mission
Movin' enough of this shit to get my mama out the kitchen
And why must I sock a fella?
Just to live large like Rockefeller?
First you didn't give a fuck, but you're learnin' now
If you don't respect the town then we'll burn you down
Goddamn it's a motherfuckin' riot . . .

I see no changes, all I see is racist faces
Misplaced hate makes disgrace to races
We under, I wonder what it take to make this
One better place, let's erase the wasted
Take the evil out the people, they'll be actin' right
'Cause both black and white are smokin' crack tonight
And only time we deal is when we kill each other

---

[38]Tupac Shakur, "So Many Tears," *Me Against the World*, Out Da Gutter Records, 1995.
[39]Pinn describes this type of theological process as nitty-gritty hermeneutics, pushing past the basics of theology and into the depths of life to ask God "tougher questions." Acceptance of pain is put into context, and the hermeneutic moves into the "nitty-gritty" of life. Anthony B. Pinn, *Why Lord? Suffering and Evil in Black Theology* (New York: Continuum, 1995), 113-38.

It takes skill to be real, time to heal each other . . .
Pull a trigger, kill a nigga, he's a hero
Mo' nigga, mo' nigga, mo' niggas
Rather I'd be dead than a po' nigga
Let the Lord judge the criminals
If I die, I wonder if Heaven got a ghetto[40]

The goal was to create a manner in which a portion of society who had been forgotten, those living in urban enclaves, could still be human and have meaning. In his song "Searching for Black Jesuz," Tupac and the Outlawz search for a deity that can relate to them, one who "smokes like we smoke, drink like we drink."[41] In the song "Picture Me Rolling" Tupac questions whether or not God can forgive him; he asks, "Will God forgive me for all the dirt a nigga did to feed his kids?"[42] In this neo-sacred element, Tupac begins to ask the longstanding theological question: What does forgiveness really look like for sinners?

For the urban post-soulist, this process of searching for God in the mystery, the hurt, and the pain, and then finding God in that heinous mixture is a welcome breath of fresh air compared to the facile three-point sermons characteristic of so much evangelical theology. This space is at the heart of dialogue and the very place God is experienced. In fact, almost anyone who has experienced deep loss and pain can relate. For example, "White Man's World" combines Tupac's request for heavenly favor and reprisal in a process similar to the psalms: "God bless me, please / . . . Makin' all my enemies bleed."[43] Within those statements much more is at work—a fundamental attempt to make God accessible in a social structure that has been forgotten and left for dead.

More of the neo-sacred and post-soul theology arises in songs such as "Hail Mary." The song suggests a liturgical prayer, beseeching listeners to follow God and to "Follow me! Eat my flesh."[44] While it might appear that Tupac is asking his listeners to see him as God, in fact Tupac was acting as a type of pastoral go-between. In several interviews from the early 1990s, he

---

[40]Tupac Shakur, "I Wonder if Heaven Got a Ghetto," *R U Still Down*, Interscope Records, 1997.
[41]Tupac Shakur and the Outlawz, "Black Jesus," *Still I Rise*, Interscope Records, 1999.
[42]Tupac Shakur, "Picture Me Rollin'," *All Eyez on Me*.
[43]Tupac Shakur, "White Man's World," *Don Killuminati*.
[44]Tupac Shakur, "Hail Mary," *Don Killuminati*.

made reference to people in the 'hood not always having a clear path to God, and that in that absence of such a path, if he was the only pathway, then so be it.[45] Tupac made it clear he was not God or Jesus, but merely a conduit and a beacon to a contextualized Jesuz.

Tupac fills part of the vacancy for those who doubt. In the song "Po Nigga Blues," Tupac poses a question to God that oozes with spiritual doubt: "I wonder if the Lord ever heard of me, huh / I need loot, so I'm doin' what I do."[46] In other words, will God really forgive me when I am practicing socially unapproved standards of living? Dyson reminds us that "Tupac's religious ideas were complex and unorthodox, perhaps even contradictory, though that would not make him unique among his believers."[47] Part of that vacancy felt in the 'hood also comes with images of heaven: streets of gold, mansions, pearly gates, and a God who is perfect—these may be too much for the person living on streets riddled with potholes, in project housing with broken gates, and with White racist images of God. Paulo Freire boldly states that within situations of oppression, the main goal of the oppressed should be to "liberate themselves from their oppressor."[48] Tupac was helping to create the pathway to liberation.[49]

Tupac had a post-soul theological gospel message for his fans, community, and society, embodying both the sacred and the profane. Tupac owned a lot of his own "sins" and shortcomings, which in post-soul contexts creates a kind of transparency and authenticity. His listeners could identify with a marred, scarred, profanity-ridden, and broken ghetto "preacher." Within that profanity, an attempt to create honest communication between God and humankind is at work. In the song "The Uppercut," Tupac and E.D.I. contend that "I'm a product of the pimp, the pusher, and the reverend / . . . We all lost

[45]Tupac Shakur, interview with *Vibe* magazine, approximately 1995; accessed on YouTube.

[46]Tupac, "Po Nigga Blues," *Loyal to the Game*, Amaru Interscope Records, 2004.

[47]Dyson, *Holler If You Hear Me*, 204.

[48]Paulo Freire, *Pedagogy of the Oppressed*, trans. Myra Bergman Ramos, 30th anniv. ed. (New York: Continuum, 2000), 28.

[49]Within my interviews, a theme of liberation from traditional church arose. "To move away from," "get out from under," and "move out" were phrases used by the respondents when asked "How has Tupac's music, poetry, and spirituality affected you theologically?" These phrases were part of a larger discussion on how contemporary religion had become corrupted and lost its edge in life. Whether or not race was a factor in this response was not analyzed. But here is a clear implication that the interviewees felt they needed to move out from their current theological situation and that Tupac helped them to do just that.

souls tryna find our way to heaven."[50] What would a missiology look like if it began with that premise? How might we then entreat Black Lives Matter in the church?

Dyson asserts that, "Tupac aimed to enhance awareness of the divine, of spiritual reality, by means of challenging orthodox beliefs and traditional religious practices."[51] Tupac's "gospel," in essence, was a mature one that sought to better apprehend God in a world gone askew—critical to a missiology in the wild.

KENDRICK LAMAR IN POST-SOUL CONVERSATION

Kendrick Lamar is a recent addition to the Hip Hop scene. Yet many view him as a sort of secular, profane, and sacred Hip Hop icon.

Lamar has risen to the top of Hip Hop in a relatively short time. At the age of thirty (in 2017), Lamar has, as many of the interviewees exclaimed, "picked up the Tupac mantle" and carried it on. Lamar's "Tammy's Song" and "Keisha's Song" continue Tupac's conversation in "Brenda Has a Baby" and give greater and more graphic details to the struggles of many abandoned and disenfranchised Black women living in urban regions. Lamar, as Kelly stated in a summer 2012 interview with me, is "the future of Hip Hop. He is a breath of fresh air, ya know? I mean, he's still got some songs in there that dog women out, but, for the most part he could be someone who could really be a voice for women in this male-run game called Hip Hop." Kelly's thoughts were shared by other interviewees as well. Lamar brings youthfulness, energy, and a message that generally deviates from the norm in contemporary commercialized rap (money, hoes, and sex). Lamar also combines the sacred, profane, and secular in a tightly woven social knot that creates a type of nitty-gritty hermeneutic his audience is able to relate to and engage with.

Lamar is a post-soul rapper who came of age during the late 1990s when rap music and Hip Hop was at the end of its golden era. Lamar was raised in a post–9/11 America and has benefited from the use of technology and the Internet.[52] Lamar legacy was assured with the help of pioneers such as

---

[50]Tupac Shakur, "The Uppercut," *Loyal to the Game.*

[51]Dyson, *Holler If You Hear Me,* 204.

[52]This is not to suggest that Lamar is the only rapper who came of age during this period or that he is a lone rapper without the community of the underground in Hip Hop. However, Lamar is one of the few commercialized rappers (having been on MTV, BET, and consistently

Dr. Dre, Snoop Dogg, Ice Cube, and MC Eiht, among others. They symbolically passed the mantle onto Lamar in a closed meeting and ushered him in as the new Hip Hop Don—a title typically reserved for veteran rappers and Hip Hoppers.[53] Lamar adds a taste of reality and new dimensions to the West Coast musical genre.

Lamar is a product of the post–golden era shift when Hip Hop became more commercial and in pursuit of economic prosperity.[54] Moreover, in this era, much of the elements (spirituality, knowledge, self-consciousness) of Hip Hop have eroded, according to some scholars.[55] Yet Lamar brings in a new wave of engagement with family, racial issues, God, and a new vision of what a theological purist might look like within the post–9/11 landscape. In his body of work, Lamar begins to deconstruct and challenge what Monica Miller refers to as the Black church and the "spirit of market maintenance."[56] Lamar does not "otherize" those who do not fit but look more like normal spiritual and theological persons. Even more than that, he takes a different approach to beefs with other rappers. In a 2015 interview he says, "It's just about balance. I don't fault other artists. I don't say this person should be doing that. As conscious as my music sounds, I would never point the finger because every day I make mistakes."[57] Like Tupac, Lamar welcomes the conversation yet delivers a critical sociopolitical critique in both his music and life.

Songs such as "Heaven & Hell," "Ronald Reagan Era (His Evils)," "Overly Dedicated," "The Heart Pt. 2," and "Growing Apart (from Everything)" wade into the issues of sex, religion, and human life. Let's examine the opening verse in "The Heart Pt. 2":

---

selling top ten albums) who is able to connect theological queries with real life and still maintain an audience.

[53]Sources stated that the gathering was small and that Lamar was at the center. It was almost as if the group were laying hands on him and "commissioning" him to "go forth."

[54]S. Craig Watkins, *Hip Hop Matters: Politics, Pop Culture, and the Struggle for the Soul of a Movement* (Boston: Beacon, 2005).

[55]See Neal, *Soul Babies*; George Nelson, *Where Did Our Love Go? The Rise and Fall of the Motown Sound*, Music in the American Life, 2nd ed. (Chicago: University of Illinois Press, 2007); and Tricia Rose, *The Hip Hop Wars: What We Talk About When We Talk About Hip Hop—and Why It Matters* (New York: Basic Civitas, 2008).

[56]Monica R. Miller, *Religion and Hip Hop* (New York: Routledge, 2013), 77-81.

[57]Kendrick Lamar, quoted in Dorian Lynskey, "Kendrick Lamar: 'I Am Trayvon Martin. I'm All of These Kids,'" *The Guardian*, June 21, 2015, www.theguardian.com/music/2015/jun/21/kendrick-lamar-interview-to-pimp-a-butterfly-trayvon-martin.

Sitting in the studio thinking about which mood would go
Right now, freestyle or write down, whatever
It still come up clever
I just need to free my thoughts, and Lord knows that I know better
But I ain't perfect, I ain't seen too many churches
Or know them Testament verses
You should either hear me now or go deaf
Or end up dead, die trying and know death
Might end up dead, swallow blood, swallow my breath
Fuck a funeral, just make sure you pay my music respect nigga
I mean that from the bottom of my heart
You see my art, is all I have
And victory tastes sweet, even when an enemy can throw salt
Still knock 'em out the park like a fucking tow car
Let bygones be bygones, but where I'm from
We buy guns and more guns to give to the young[58]

Lamar is being transparent in this song while acknowledging the social issues plaguing the community. Coming from South Los Angeles, Lamar is accustomed to the violence in urban centers. However, this song in particular acknowledges the humanity within religious experience and gives space for imperfect personalities to create congruence.

Lamar, having been raised in a Black Christian home, is accustomed to many of the Black Christian traditions but is also aware of the realities of the human condition, which he labels "sin." Thus, in several regards, he is following Miller's critique of the Black church and "market maintenance," and asking why Black churches do what they do in the manner they do it. Lamar also, like Tupac, criticizes the Black church for the money it takes from its people, especially in low-income communities.[59] In a post-soul sense, this critique is often met with resistance and suspicion from those of the civil rights generation. Yet, for those under the age of twenty-five who are Black or of another other ethnic minority, they have grown up with this critique

---

[58]Kendrick Lamar, "The Heart Pt. 2," *Overly Dedicated*, Top Dawg Entertainment, 2010.
[59]Two informants close to Lamar said that Lamar is "pissed off" at the Black church for what he calls a "misfortune of events" in regard to what Black pastors have created in the 'hood. The pastors drive lavish cars while their parishioners are kept in economic bondage. This information was only made available for this research, and I have kept the informants' identities hidden.

and often use it themselves. So it is fitting to hear from an artist such as Lamar asking difficult questions of the Black church.

Lamar's work is paramount in this era of Trayvon Martin, Mike Brown, and so many other Black bodies that fall to violence. Lamar stands as a rapper on the cusp of the commercial rap industry, yet he possesses the fortitude to critically engage the issues without completely sinking to sex, women, and partying. To that he says, "These are issues that if you come from that environment it's inevitable to speak on. . . . It's already in your blood because I am Trayvon Martin, you know. I'm all of these kids. It's already implanted in your brain to come out your mouth as soon as you've seen it on the TV. I had that track way before that, from the beginning to the end, and the incident just snapped it for me."[60] This nuanced sociopolitical critique is much desired in this post-soul era. Lamar's critique of systemic racism, overt oppression, and inequality speaks truth to his age group and era. Lamar is able to hold in tension his faith, his upbringing, the commitment to his community, the reality of being young, and what God may be attempting to do.

Take, for instance, the cover art on Lamar's 2011 album, *Section.80* (see fig. 7.1). The album's title is in focus, but in the upper-right-hand corner is a Bible that has a blunt and cigarette lighter on top of it, with more books underneath. To the left of that is a loaded gun clip, condoms, lipstick, a stack of money, and a faded-out lamp. To the front of that is a pipe and a medicinal marijuana container next to the paper, which states the album's title. Lamar's use of sacred, profane, and secular imagery is well balanced. Sex, drugs, religion, violence, and pleasure all in one album cover reveals that Lamar is contemplating serious issues.

Figure 7.1. Album cover of Kendrick Lamar's *Section.80*

---

[60]Lamar, quoted in Lynskey, "Kendrick Lamar."

The album itself is no less an engagement with those issues. From a post-soul sense, this is the wild. This is where God emerges. This is the space and place in which the gospel is the richest and truest. Away from the outward appearance of sainthood, a post-soulist like Lamar is about what is now and contemporary in terms of problems and pain.

Lamar's 2015 album, *To Pimp a Butterfly*, is a mixture of soul, funk, jazz, the spoken word, and rap connected to the golden era of Hip Hop. This album holds in tension good, evil, sin, and the sacred; it is a well-balanced album for the theomusicologist. The ending has a poignant and moving interview with Tupac. It is edited in a manner that puts Tupac and Lamar in the same room discussing social issues relevant in 2015: the injustice toward young Blacks, racism, and the tension as to what defines a Black male.[61] *To Pimp a Butterfly* is a masterful album dancing on the platform of evil, which it names "Lucy." Lamar creates a post-soul conversation and allows the listener to wrestle with that as well. He says this album was created in the wake of Ferguson, Missouri, and Trayvon Martin.[62] Lamar says,

> Lucy is all the [things] that I was thinking of that I know can be detrimental to not only me but the people around me, and still be tempted by them. That's some scary shit. It's like looking at a bullet inside of a gun, knowing you can kill yourself with it, but you're still picking it up and playing with it. Everything that we glorified in the hood—smoking, drinking, women, violence—was at my feet times 10. All of it's there. In the neighborhood we wanted to have power and with success comes power. That is temptation at its highest.[63]

Lamar also keeps in tension evil and ways to look at it from an urban post-soul perspective. Regarding his friends, he says,

> I don't think people are evil. My homeboys, they're not evil. These are good-hearted people who just want to hang around and see the good things in life. But when you're around negativity, that's where the negative spirits dwell. And those spirits get inside you. I know it's true. We always wonder why people act the way they're acting. We put the statistics in it and we put history behind

---

[61]That particular interview from Tupac is believed to have been conducted in late 1995 by an unknown interviewer from *Vibe* magazine.

[62]Micah Singleton, "To Pimp a Butterfly: Kendrick Lamar's New Album Is Perfect," *The Verge*, March 19, 2015, www.theverge.com/2015/3/19/8257319/kendrick-lamar-album-review-to-pimp -a-butterfly.

[63]Lamar, quoted in Lynskey, "Kendrick Lamar."

it, but we're missing God in the equation. The devil is real and he's alive. Nobody ever brings that shit up.[64]

Still, in a post-soul sense, we need to discuss the fact that both Lamar and Tupac are plagued when it comes to gender and sexuality; we are challenged with references to women solely as sexual objects and inferior in the human species. Hip Hoppers, men in general, have a difficult time straying away from the objectification of women, which is no different than Western Christianity. Many Hip Hoppers were raised in urban, working-class, blue-collar communities that tend to be fairly conventional and inelastic regarding gender roles, gender behaviors, sexual orientation, and moral values. These cultural codes are embedded in religious customs (which are typically Christian, although Islamic religions tend to prescribe strict moral codes for women and men). They are often negotiated through behaviors that must fall within the cited norms of the given context, which are often stacked against women.[65] Lamar, and many like him, is simply following the customs of his upbringing, which is socially, politically, educationally, and economically progressive. This progressive stance, however, typically ends with gender and sexual orientation, which contradicts their broader position regarding equality and justice.[66] This is no different than the position of women in the Black church, who are present in large numbers yet hold few key roles and little power in the church.

Women in a male-dominated culture such as rap music have difficulty establishing a pro-women agenda—let alone a feminist one—and are often overlooked and labeled as a "dyke" or "lesbian" for confronting misogynistic behaviors and lyrics.[67] Hip Hoppers and rappers like Tupac

---

[64]In this particular point in the interview, the author is talking with Lamar about evil and how he views sin; the interesting point is that Lamar is very aware and lucid about his response and the development of his argument is true for both his era and context (ibid.).

[65]Marcella Althaus-Reid, *Indecent Theology: Theological Perversions in Sex, Gender, and Politics* (New York: Routledge, 2000); and Althaus-Reid, *From Feminist Theology to Indecent Theology: Readings on Poverty, Sexual Identity and God* (London: SCM Press, 2004).

[66]Pittsburgh underground rapper Jasiri X is beginning to engage gender and sexual-orientation issues. While the scope of this book does not allow me to expand on many underground rappers, it is important to note such Hip Hop male rappers who are taking up such issues, often with little commercial airplay.

[67]*Hip Hop: Beyond Beats and Rhymes*, directed by Byron Hurt (Northampton, MA: Media Education Foundation, 2006); and Mark Anthony Neal, *New Black Man* (New York: Routledge, 2005).

and Lamar did not invent misogyny.[68] This is as American as a painting of White, blonde Jesus hanging in church hallways. Therefore, the bigger and more contentious issue is: How do we deal with gender and sexual-orientation inequality, inequity, and oppression? These crucial questions cannot be overlooked. The post-soul movement of Black Lives Matter agrees and continues to usher forth a *her*story as a counter narrative in the public sphere. Given their intellect, I believe both Tupac and Lamar would agree this is needed.

We will now turn to the location of Tupac and Lamar's missiological gospel essence.

LOCATING TUPAC AND LAMAR'S MISSIOLOGICAL GOSPEL ESSENCE

Lamar presents a post-soul epistemology of hope rooted in the mire of racism, sexism, patriarchy, and the dominant culture. What type of hope is that? Lamar works this out in his album "Damn" (2017). It is not easy to take in the elements of social, political, and racial inequality and then just have it eroded away by a singular phrase, "God is in control." Lamar identifies the nitty-gritty 'hood theology that many have to experience and he wrestles with areas of doubt and uncertainty, which are relevant for an era etched with hate, overt racism, and the disregard for Black bodies. Lamar, in that sense, places these issues at the altar but without trying to create a solution rooted in a mythic imagination of harmony, accord, and unity so often given to those in impoverished conditions. No, Lamar takes all of those issues and holds them next to God and begins asking: Why? How long? Can we ever see peace? He also walks with the listener on a journey of fearing death, love, hate, violence, and ultimately God.

---

[68]It is interesting to note that Lamar has touted a strong relationship to his fiancée and high school sweetheart, Whitney Alford. This is a break away from Tupac's numerous encounters with women and a break from rap culture's notorious polygamy, which is often bragged about. In recent years Lamar has reconsidered the use of terms such as "bitch" and "ho," and evidences growth in this way. Will it prove to make a difference? Time will tell. See Lauren Weigle, "Whitney Alford, Kendrick Lamar's Fiancée: 5 Fast Facts You Need to Know," *Heavy*, http://heavy.com/entertainment/2016/02/whitney-alford-kendrick-lamar-fiancee-girlfriend-wife-dating-who-is-net-worth-ring.

Lamar follows the same line of critique that Tupac took on organized religion and becoming churched.[69] For Lamar, a churched mindset creates problems: people become locked into the same patterns of belief without any growth whatsoever. Beyond his music, Lamar is after spiritual growth and development. Yet he is not satisfied with the mere face or look of spirituality. In a 2017 response to an article written about him, Lamar says,

> I went to a local church some time ago, and it appalled me that the same program was in practice. A program that I seen as a kid the few times I was in service. Praise, dance. Worship. (Which is beautiful.) Pastor spewing the idea of someone's season is approaching. The idea of hope. So on and so forth.[70]

Lamar's post-soul analysis speaks to post–civil rights movements such as Black Lives Matter, which critique church life, attendance, and rules. Groups such as BLM hold their meetings on Sunday mornings instead of going to church, mainly because they have seen the uselessness of church attendance. Lamar galvanizes these sentiments while still holding a robust desire for God and spiritual growth. He continues,

> As a child, I always felt this Sermon had an emptiness about it. Kinda one-sided, in what I felt in my heart. Fast forward. After being heavily in my studies these past few years, I've finally figured out why I left those services feeling spiritually unsatisfied as a child. I discovered more truth. But simple truth. Our God is a loving God. Yes. He's a merciful God. Yes. But he's even more so a God of DISCIPLINE. OBEDIENCE. A JEALOUS God. And for every conscious choice of sin, will be corrected through his discipline. Whether physical or mental. Direct or indirect. Through your sufferings, or someone that's close to [sic] ken. It will be corrected.[71]

---

[69]Becoming habitualized to church attendance, worship, and the physiological effect of church on the body produces an addictive state. This phenomenon has fostered a traditional mindset toward church life. Rigid church life is assumed to be normative for worship and life. This mindset is carried into missions as well. For an exploration of the economics of church attendance as connected to spatial-location models, see Laurence R. Iannaccone, "Religious Practice: A Human Capital Approach," *Journal for the Scientific Study of Religion* 29, no. 3 (1990): 299-312. Also see Pedro Pita Barros and Nuno Garoupa, "An Economic Theory of Church Strictness," *Economic Journal* 112, no. 481 (2002).

[70]Kendrick Lamar, quoted in DJZ, "Kendrick Lamar Responded to Our Article About His Fear of God," *DJBooth*, May 9, 2017, http://djbooth.net/news/entry/2017-04-28-kendrick-lamar-god-response.

[71]Ibid.

Lamar is pursuing a mature faith, one that moves beyond the milk of the gospel and into the dark, mystical complexity of a faith much deeper than once-a-week church attendance, good music, and loud preaching. Lamar seeks social, cultural, societal, and spiritual renewal. Often rappers are criticized for not revering God and faith and, of course, for embracing sin. Lamar does not shy away:

> I feel it's my calling to share the joy of God, but with exclamation, more so, the FEAR OF GOD. The balance. Knowing the power in what he can build, and also what he can destroy. At any given moment.
>
> I love when artists sing about what makes Him happy. My balance is to tell you what will make Him extinguish you. Personally, once that idea of real fear registered in my mind, it made me try harder at choosing my battles wisely. Which will forever be tough, because I'm still of flesh. I wanna spread this truth to my listeners. It's a journey, but it will be my key to the Kingdom. And theirs as well. I briefly touched on it in this album, but when he tells me to react, I will take deeper action.[72]

Fear is something that is not discussed much among young, postindustrial Black males. Yet here is Lamar placing fear in the context of God.

Something rarely mentioned in the gospel of Jesus is the tension of doubt situated against hope. Arguably the most referenced Scriptures of Jesus grappling with hope and doubt are Matthew 26:36-46, Mark 14:32-42, and Luke 22:39-46, in which Jesus is in deep prayer right before the events leading to his crucifixion. We see Jesus grappling with the weight of the cross and the strain of what was before him. In these passages he is identifying with humanity's deep doubt that arises during times of stress, pain, and fear. In many regards, it is difficult to imagine Jesus dealing with fear and doubt. So much of Western Christianity sees deity in the form of male strength and power. Jesus is rarely seen as being afraid during the most difficult moment in life. Yet Jesus depended on God, saying he wanted God's will to be done. Lamar is in that space of asking God, Can you do it? Can you actually be what "I really need"? Lamar reflects post-soul ideology when he wonders why so much evil still exists when we have had churches for so long. Think about the dozens of churches on one block of the Austin neighborhood, a

---

[72]Ibid.

west-side community of Chicago. They often do not communicate with one another. The post-soulist sees the contradiction between church talk about love and unity and what is actually lived out. Thus, Lamar addresses it. He inserts issues in his album, posing them as questions but also statements. Lamar has openly talked about his depression and suicidal thoughts—something that is an ongoing problem for many young Black adults. He is building on the neo-sacred–secular ontology that Tupac created space for, but Lamar does it in a twenty-first-century way by making us aware of it in not just his music but through social media as well.[73]

I believe Jesus was just like this. When we read Jesus though the lens of a post-soul theological construct, we see his fragile nature. Jesus is tired. He is often short with people. We already know he uses strong language. He was a troublemaker. He spoke out. He was a brawler who stood up for the new gospel he was announcing. (We often forget or overlook this aspect of Jesus.) He was a deity that hung out with the "sinners" and "losers" of the day. What type of God does that? What type of God comes to the earth as a human? The theological shift Jesus presented is often missed because Western evangelicalism has domesticated him. Lamar is bringing back that disruptive and unruly Jesus. He troubles the theological waters by presenting Jesus as "a crisis in the life of God."[74]

Tupac's "good news," conversely, is about life in a post-soul context that is a type of "indecent theology."[75] As grand narratives of God have collapsed in mainstream society, creating contextual and relatable parallel narratives is crucial and desired by post-soulists. Tupac's gospel, at its core, seeks to give marginalized urban dwellers (and poor Whites as well) a voice to address God and a place to find meaning in unbearable conditions. For Lamar, it is about the tension of grappling with depression, dead friends, and racism, and keeping God in focus through all of that. Tupac is an indirect "theologian," bringing a neo-secular message of God's love to the people and contextualizing epistemological processes—in other words, constructing new knowledge—for a generation raised in the crack cocaine milieu. Jamal

---

[73]Hodge, *Hip Hop's Hostile Gospel*, 21-22.

[74]See Jack Miles, *Christ: A Crisis in the Life of God* (New York: Vintage eBooks, 2011).

[75]Marcella Althaus-Reid discusses an "indecent" approach to theology by questioning religious authority figures and allowing new voices to emerge (in her case, a feminist perspective on religion). Althaus-Reid, *From Feminist Theology to Indecent Theology*.

Joseph notes that Tupac had a huge heart for people to understand a better way of living, to know positive role models, and to be critical thinkers.[76] Lamar is a contradiction within a saintly modality. He is able to authentically communicate the struggles of his own life while still invoking the spirit of Jesus in protest. Thus, there are three gospel messages within both of their works: the gospel of "hold on," the gospel of "keep ya head up," and the gospel of "heaven has a ghetto."

First, the gospel of "hold on" encourages those who have given up or are about to give up on life, including other people.[77] Tupac encourages his listener to see there is hope for a brighter tomorrow:

> When I was alone, and had nothing
> I asked for a friend to help me bear the pain
> No one came, except God
> When I needed a breath to rise, from my sleep
> No one could help me except God
>
> When all I saw was sadness, and I needed answers
> No one heard me, except God
>
> So when I'm asked who I give my unconditional love to?
> I look for no other name, except God[78]

In this poem, titled "God," Tupac calls out to God and asks for a conduit. He finds it in the midst of hurt. James Cone calls this type of process "revelation" and argues, "For black theology, revelation is not just a past event or a contemporary event in which it is difficult to recognize the activity of God. Revelation is a black event."[79] In this poem, Tupac receives the revelation and looks for no one else but God.

In the song "So Many Tears," Tupac begs God not to forget a nigga: "Lord I suffered through the years / And shed so many tears . . . / Dear God, please let me in."[80] There is a paradoxical optimism in the midst of extreme pain,

---

[76]Jamal Joseph, *Tupac Shakur: Legacy* (New York: Atria Books, 2006), 16-23.

[77]See, e.g., Iverem, "The Politics of 'Fuck It.'"

[78]Rev. Run reading Tupac Shakur's "God," in *The Rose That Grew from Concrete*, vol. 1, Interscope Records, 2000.

[79]James H. Cone, *A Black Theology of Liberation*, 20th anniv. ed. (Maryknoll, NY: Orbis Books, 1990), 30.

[80]Tupac Shakur, "So Many Tears," *Me Against the World*, Amaru/Interscope/Jive Records, 1995. This mindset is no different than what slaves had to deal with and their vision that God would

despair, and violence.[81] Tupac calls the person to seek a better way and higher level of understanding.

The gospel of keeping your head up was a frequent theme in Tupac's discourse. Howard Thurman states that one of the ingenuities of Black slave culture was the ability to not allow immediate experience to diminish ones hopes, dreams, or visions. The immediate experience may by hurtful, problematic, nefarious, and abusive, but one must foster and encourage a future vision that allows one to escape the immediate consequences. Hopelessness occurs when one has the inability to imagine a different future.[82] In this gospel Tupac is essentially making sense of immediate pain and suffering. Tupac would say, "Yes, I'm holding on, but where do I look?"

Tupac wanted his fans to know that the ideology of "keeping ya head up" was not in vain. In the face of extreme opposition and hurt, there was still a way to move forward. Even when things seemed as though they could not get any better, Tupac told his fans that there was a better way. Life did not end on the experience of the immediate event; errors and successes were not necessarily defining moments:[83]

> If I upset you, don't stress, never forget
> That God isn't finished with me yet
> I feel his hand on my brain
> When I write rhymes I go blind and let the Lord do his thing
> But am I less holy
> 'Cause I chose to puff a blunt and drink a beer with my homies?
> Before we find world peace
> We gotta find peace and end the war in the streets
> My ghetto gospel[84]

---

eventually help them. Luke Powery asserts that the spirit of lament is combined with celebration and that they go hand in hand. Luke A. Powery, *Spirit Speech: Lament and Celebration in Preaching* (Nashville: Abingdon Press, 2009).

[81] This ideology connects with Rudolph Otto's "mysterium tremendum" (Rudolph Otto, *The Idea of the Holy*, 2nd ed. [London: Oxford University Press, 1950], 12-24). What God did in spite of an appalling situation is mysterious. For Otto, "a God comprehended is no God" (ibid., 25). In other words, holding on does not always mean that it will make sense or will even feel right. This idea helped Tupac deal with the bigger picture of sin and the brokenness of humankind.

[82] See Howard Thurman, *Jesus and the Disinherited* (Boston: Beacon Press, 1976).

[83] Cone, *Black Theology and Black Power*; Cone, *God of the Oppressed*; and Kain & Abel, with Master P., "Black Jesus," *The 7 Sins*, Priority Records, 1996.

[84] Tupac Shakur, "Ghetto Gospel," *Loyal to the Game*, Amaru Entertainment/Interscope Records, 2004.

Tupac attempted to bring a pragmatic type of hope through his music instead of traditional hymns. Tupac replaced hymns with the "thug life" mantra and his message of encouragement in hard times.[85]

Regarding the authority of what is from God and what is not, Dyson writes,

> Countless sacred narratives are hardly distinguishable from contemporary rap. . . . The prophet Jeremiah belched despair from the belly of his relentless pessimism. And the Psalms are full of midnight and bad cheer. This is not to argue that the contrasting moral frameworks of rap and religion do not color our interpretation of their often-opposing creeds. But we must not forget that unpopular and unacceptable views are sometimes later regarded as prophetic. It is a central moral contention of Christianity that God may be disguised in the clothing—and maybe even the rap—of society's most despised members.[86]

Tupac was part of this long tradition of lament, praise, and life in the secular, or what James Cone calls the "secular spiritual."[87]

In the song "Hold Ya Head," Tupac encourages those who are in prison, in pain, and lost to hold on and keep their head up in times of trouble. Through weed, alcohol, and even illicit sex, a post-soul theology arises:[88]

The weed got me tweakin in my mind, I'm thinkin'

God bless the child that can hold his own
Indeed, enemies bleed when I hold my chrome
Let these words be the last to my unborn seeds
Hope to raise my young nation in this world of greed
Currency means nothin' if you still ain't free
Money breeds jealousy, take the game from me
I hope for better days, trouble comes naturally
Runnin' from authorities 'til they capture me
And my aim is to spread mo' smiles than tears

---

[85]Hodge, *Heaven Has a Ghetto*, 278-84. This was one of the reasons Tupac was so calm, almost at peace, with the knowledge of his imminent death (Joseph, *Tupac Shakur*). Tupac was fully aware that life did not end here. There was a better place in heaven for him.

[86]Dyson, *Holler If You Hear Me*, 208-9.

[87]James H. Cone, "The Blues: A Secular Spiritual," in *Sacred Music of the Secular City: From Blues to Rap*, ed. Jon Michael Spencer (Durham, NC: Duke University Press, 1992), 68-97.

[88]Moralists' confined view looks on the outside to see if a person is righteous. Thus Jesus was considered a heretic, a blasphemer, and a profane individual for his views on spiritual matters. Cf. Miles, *Christ.*

Utilize lessons learned from my childhood years
Maybe Mama had it all right, rest yo' head
Tradin' conversation all night, bless the dead
To the homies that I used to have that no longer roll
Catch a brother at the crossroads
Plus nobody knows my soul, watchin' time pass
Through the glass of my drop-top Rolls; hold ya head![89]

In the song "Still I Rise," Tupac laments to the Lord that the struggle is almost too much to bear; pain and misery parade through his life, and the journey seems as if it will never end. Yet, in the end, still I rise. "Tupac sounds out that in times of trouble, God is with you, so keep your head up. Even the words in that phrase, 'head up' is meant to persuade one to look unto the Heavens from which our help comes."[90]

Finally, the gospel of heaven having a ghetto was a recurring thought in Tupac's worldview, contextualizing heaven and making it accessible for people who do not subscribe to Western theology. Tupac even calls himself the "ghetto missionary." In an interview on BET, Tupac states,

> If I can't be free, if I can't live with the same respect as the next man, then I don't wanna be here. Because God has cursed me to see what life should be like. If God had wanted me to be this person, to be happy here, he wouldn't let me feel so oppressed. He wouldn't let me feel so trampled on; you know what I'm saying? He wouldn't let me think the things I think. So, I feel like I'm doing God's work, you know what I'm saying? Just because I don't have nothing to pass around for people to put in the bucket don't mean I'm not doing God's work; I feel like I'm doing God's work. Because, these ghetto kids ain't God's children? And I don't see no missionaries coming through there. So I'm doing God's work. While Reverend Jackson do his shit up in the middle class and he go to the White House and have dinner and pray over the president, I'm up in the 'hood doing my work with my folks.[91]

Here Tupac expresses not only the divisions of class within Black society but also within its theological walls.[92] Tupac knows it is his mission to bring the

---

[89]Tupac Shakur, "Hold Ya Head," *Don Killuminati*.
[90]Hodge, *Heaven Has a Ghetto*, 264.
[91]Tupac Shakur, interview by Ed Gordon, *BET*, 1994, www.bet.com/music/2016/09/15/tupac-bet-interview-1994.html.
[92]This is an ongoing debate within Black culture and the Black church. For further discussion see

gospel to those who have been left out and have not been invited to the heavenly party with its clean streets. The thought, then, is this: if life continues as is, heaven will have cops waiting to "beat our ass" the minute we walk through the gates. Therefore, Tupac decided to ask, Does heaven have a ghetto? In other words, can I be accepted in this realm that has continually told me I am neither worthy nor acceptable? Can I be accepted as I am, or do I have to enter through the back door so as to not disturb the residents or mar the fine linen?[93]

The great writer, mystic, and theologian Howard Thurman asks the relevant and almost irreligious question regarding religion and its message to the poor and disheveled: "What does our religion say to them?"[94] Thurman says,

> I can count on the fingers of one hand the number of times that I have heard a sermon on the meaning of religion, on Christianity, to the man who stands with his back against the wall. It is urgent that my meaning be crystal clear. The masses of men live with their backs constantly against the wall. They are the poor, the disinherited, the dispossessed. What does our religion say to them?[95]

Tupac took the challenge and made an attempt to create a gospel message for the poor, disinherited, and dispossessed peoples living in the urban enclaves: the ghetto. He created a transcendental space in which the thug, the nigga, and the pimp can find God.

Tupac's answer to his own question, "Does heaven got a ghetto?" is yes! However, not in the literal sense. Tupac never said that there is poverty,

---

Michael Eric Dyson, *Is Bill Cosby Right? Or Has the Black Middle Class Lost Its Mind?* (New York: Basic Civitas Books, 2005); C. Eric Lincoln and Lawrence H. Mamiya, *The Black Church in the African American Experience* (Durham, NC: Duke University Press, 1990); and Pinn, *Black Church in the Post–Civil Rights Era.*

[93]These types of questions create theological conundrums in contemporary evangelical theology, which echo vagueness and ambiguity regarding God's love for marginalized peoples. Therefore, the Hip Hopper, the ghetto person, and Tupac himself pose a new question: If social structures and systems have failed us, won't the church and religion follow suit? Tupac could no longer sit by and accept a traditional view of Jesus or Christianity. He needed a stronger theology than that, a Christ who could accept the thug and the marginalized person. This was the outcry in songs like "I Wonder if Heaven Got a Ghetto?" and "Black Jesuz." These were expressions of a deeper search for God and spirituality. These were also fundamental questions of who God really is—questions that many of us ask ourselves, such as are we really saved? See Hodge, *Heaven Has a Ghetto,* 264-65.

[94]Thurman, *Jesus and the Disinherited,* 13.

[95]Ibid.

crime, gentrification, and homelessness in God's kingdom. The term is used figuratively and symbolically, as if to ask, Is the gospel big enough to fit everyone who wants to fit in, and can God handle me if he really created me? Tupac said yes. He encouraged his audience, as a pastor would his flock, to see that there is a different image of heaven and that there is room for those who do not fit in a traditional evangelical theology:[96]

> Who's got the heart to stand beside me?
> I feel my enemies creepin' up in silence
> Dark prayer, scream violence—demons all around me
> Can't even bend my knees just a lost cloud; Black Jesus
> Give me a reason to survive, in this earthly hell
> 'Cause I swear, they tryin' to break my well
> I'm on the edge lookin' down at this volatile pit
> Will it matter if I cease to exist? Black Jesus[97]

TOWARD A MISSIOLOGY OF POST-SOUL PROPHETS

Tupac was not perfect. He was baptized in the dirty waters of marketing, social representations of blackness, stereotypes of the gangsta and the tattooed thug, and the poor Black child. He was not Jesus incarnate, nor was he the perfect role model for everyone. Before he left for prison, he told Jada Pinkett Smith that he wanted to quit thuggin' and give up on rap and solely do acting.[98] However, Tupac ended up embodying the same Black male image he had fought so hard against for so long: the cyclical prison inmate, the nihilistic Black male, and the paranoid, pessimistic urbanite.

Lamar, by contrast, has openly said he wants to avoid the pitfalls and perils he has seen overcome Hip Hoppers like Tupac. Lamar wants to remain alive long enough to create something that has yet to be done—to build a space for the post-soul intellectual rooted in God. Tupac was after that, but his life was cut short of that goal. Lamar realizes the pressures of fame, money, and a constant stream of consumption could overtake him. So he reveals those pressures in his music and openly shares his humanness.

---

[96]This is also something I discuss at length in my chapter on engaging the theology of the profane in *Soul of Hip Hop* (159-64).
[97]Tupac and The Outlawz, "Black Jesus."
[98]Dyson, *Holler If You Hear Me*, 215-16.

Lamar brings a refreshing space in commercial Hip Hop, which is all too often filled with a singularized mantra of sex, misogyny, drugs, and nihilism. However, Lamar does not shy away from sexuality. He holds it in tension. Tension is a key element within the post-soul faith.

The paradox between the sacred and the profane arises within these conflicts. Tupac embodied both sin and deity; Lamar wrestles with the way forward. Within this contradiction, there is both good and evil, sin and salvation, dirt and cleanliness. All work at and have the ability to create a fuller faith, one that is honest about both the good and the bad. This is the human struggle. Tupac, in this sense, was no different from Paul. While Tupac knew what was right and how to do the right thing, he did not do it because his flesh was weak (Rom 7:7-24). Still, within that weakness, he sought space to find God and Jesuz. This is a large part of post-soul theology. Tupac and Lamar let us know that *they* are not the way; they are only pointing the way to Jesuz.[99]

Wilbert Shenk says,

> When the church lives in conscious response to the reign of God, its life is governed by only one criterion. Indeed, the power of the church's witness depends on the extent to which God's kingdom defines and shapes that witness. When the church attempts to make its ministry relevant by rendering "respectable" service, it has adopted an alien criterion and it becomes merely mundane.[100]

Thus, Tupac and Lamar present a post-soul missiology for several reasons.

1. They live a transparent life and are able to identify with their own sin, shortcomings, and deficiencies. Neither run from them or hide them. As humans, this is our reality. As Christians, this is our reality. Missiologically, those who are able to come "as is" are much easier to engage. Tupac insisted that people should not reduce their hopes, dreams, and visions to the level of the event. For someone living in the inner city, this means the vile living conditions they are in at the time. For others, that might be poverty or a broken home. Whatever it is, Tupac insisted that people keep their heads up, and Lamar

---

[99]This connects to John the Baptist in the Gospel of John 1:19-32, where John denies that he is the One and that the one who comes after him—Jesus—gives life eternally.
[100]Shenk, *Changing Frontiers of Mission*, 16.

continues that existential ideology. Hopelessness occurs when one cannot imagine a different future. Tupac encouraged his audience to keep believing in a better day and that heaven itself might have a ghetto. Simply put, there is a place that will accept us as we are.

2. They both seek God's face in the midst of tension, ambiguity, and doubt. Tupac's song "So Many Tears" is the perfect example of this. The sin of his past life, the hurt of his current life, and the ambiguity of his future are held in tension. Death could be immanent, but Tupac pleads his case with God, and even in his chaos, he offers a "sinner's prayer" throughout the track.[101] Lamar's song "The Heart Pt. 2" places this reality in full view. Here, Lamar admits to not "being too perfect," but he still seeks God. This profound sociotheological statement is in pursuit of a theology that fits the context from which it originated.

3. Both Tupac and Lamar see themselves as leaders, but as leaders that are in the mix of problems, not from on high. Tupac struggled with his position as a leader—he was not the typical older, gray adult that most expect to see as a leader. This created a conundrum for Tupac and older adults. The same is true of Lamar; he is too young to lead, right? No. Tupac and Lamar do missiology by creating space to learn, grow, and develop with God in the post-soul context. They both lead in thought and push for the better. Yet they realize their own fragility in leadership and allow other voices to come alongside.

4. Both allow doubt, ambiguity, and a mysterious God to exist. For many in the post-soul context, there is no assurance or guarantee of a bright future. Moreover, theologies of celebration are unacceptable, invalid, and in some cases worthless for a post-soulist. Moving into the twenty-first century, a missiological framework that emphasizes doubt, ambiguity, and a mysterious God is key. A God who is solvable, answerable, and quantifiable is not worth seeking or following. If we have answers and power, why would we need God?

5. Tupac and Lamar create the space needed to question traditional, normative, and stilted forms of spirituality that have created an

---

[101] This is isolated in the background of the song and can be heard during the second and third chorus.

ossified Christian faith. The church must be the beacon of light that opens the door and reinvites people to engage from their context and not from a preimagined space of salvation. Tupac, utilizing Hip Hop, had the ability to allow questions to flow. Often he instigated the questioning. For too long Christianity has been a symbol of distrust, corruption, lies, sexual misconduct, and misappropriating Christ. Tupac says, Let's start there and acknowledge the atrocities, seek forgiveness, and create a new way—together. A solid missional church opens doors and helps the community in their midst; they do not decide *for* the community or act in the place of God within it but allow people to think for themselves, critically. To think for oneself, though, means to question. It is time we go there, and Lamar can lead the way.

Tupac and Lamar are some of the only rappers within the Hip Hop cultural continuum who have earned, at least at the present time, the title of "ghetto saint" and "urban prophet." Tupac's music pursues God through sexuality, manhood, pain, violence, revenge, hate, anger, love, hope, and nihilism. Lamar questions the church, deals with aspects of the fear of God and yet pushes the Hip Hop community forward. Tupac was the externalized secular discussion of transmediated discourses of religious pursuits within the Hip Hop community. Lamar picked up that mantle and continues the dialogue for a post-soul age. Tupac is a prophetic and totemic symbol within Hip Hop and urban communities.

Tupac was human and at times contradictory to his own belief system. He wanted peace yet was in a feud with Biggie Smalls, Sean Puffy Combs, and Nas—claiming on several occasions that he had "f---ed Biggie's wife." Moreover, his own personal demons of insecurity, lack of self-worth, and instability gave Tupac the image of a thug. What he embodied is not tolerated in many Christian contexts, yet at its core Tupac's message was a Judeo-Christian one. Where then does that leave us?

Even within this seemingly contradictory and even hypocritical life, Tupac remains prophetic to many. His work creates a post-soul space for an unconventional missiology to take place. Because he was so transparent with his faults and shortcomings, he has become one of Hip Hop's most respected artists and voices. Perhaps his intertwining of God (the sacred), his own life (the secular), and a realist form of life in urban context (the profane) made him the ghetto theologian he is now seen to be. Tupac's painful past might have given him the artistic insights to create music and poetry that relates to his audience within the Hip Hop community. Lamar is pursing the future Tupac foresaw: a post-soul theology rooted in faith and tension. Can a post-soul missiology embrace this and allow it to develop further?

8

BEYOND RECONCILIATION IN THE WILD

The Importance of Engagement with the Intricacies of Race and Ethnicities in Missions and Missiology

I HAVE SO MUCH TROUBLE talking about race and ethnicity with him," she said to my mentor. "I just don't know where to begin," she went on. "I mean, I guess, race is still a problem, but it's really only a problem when we keep talking about it." The conversation continued. "Can we just talk about race, racism, or whatever the issue is without the anger? Can't you just separate that?"

This conversation took place with a former supervisor of mine who, in all regards, is an internationally recognized speaker and author, and is considered a ministry expert. And while White women tend to be able to better understand the plight of ethnic minorities than White men, the difficulties of privilege, ignorance, and personal racial neglect cannot be overlooked or avoided. This conversation took place when another good friend and mentor of mine intervened in a conversation about race I was having with my boss. At this point, I was still young in my career, and, like many Blacks in an all-White environment, I had to choose my battles wisely.[1] The slightest move

---

[1]This is not a "made up" phenomena. For some, this is merely an overreaction and an emotional response, yet that perspective typically comes from ignorance and a privileged racial position. For a further investigation into this issue, especially within Christian ministries, and to explore the effects of being an ethnic minority in White space, see Anthony B. Bradley, *Black Scholars in White Space: New Vistas in African American Studies from the Christian Academy* (Eugene, OR: Wipf & Stock,2015); and Bradley, ed., *Aliens in the Promised Land: Why Minority Leadership Is Overlooked in White Christian Churches and Institutions* (Phillipsburg, NJ: P&R, 2013).

toward a threatening posture could ruin not only my career but also my reputation. I was walking a thin line. But I could not take the racist over-tones anymore; I had had enough. I needed to say something. So, after careful thought, counsel, prayer, and preparation, I decided to talk this over with her and asked a witness, my mentor—who was also a woman—to be present while this conversation happened.[2]

I wanted to confront the issue of being ignored, talked down to, and being the only person of color on the entire staff in an organization that claimed to be "about the kingdom." I had prepared well and had carefully thought through what I wanted to say. My mentor and I had worked to-gether to get my points clear and avoid any hint of anger, which proved to be much more difficult than I had imagined. About a quarter of the way through the conversation with my boss, I was making a point about feeling invisible and being talked down to. Up until this point, we were having a decent exchange. But then my boss took a deep breath, looked away, and interrupted me, "Daniel, I think what you're feeling is valid, but I just don't see where I have any part in this. I've never looked at you as a color, nor do I hold any prejudices against you. So, I'm not sure where I fit into this equation." My mentor attempted to speak up and interpret what I was saying to my boss, to no avail. I grew impatient. The belittling remarks over my time there had grown overwhelmingly difficult to deal with. All of the passive racist nature of ignoring my thoughts on Black or Latino theolo-gians swelled me with anger, and the passive nature of her privilege, which in turn ignored my experience, created a sense of injustice in me. She said, "I'd love to talk to you about race, but can we do that without the anger? I don't see the gospel in your anger, and it is difficult to talk with you when you're mad. You're very off-putting."

---

[2]A Black man confronting a White woman carries with it historical overtones of rape, carnage, and Black male violence. When entering these situations, I have learned to have a witness and position myself carefully to avoid the "brutal Black man" syndrome that so often comes with being a bald, large, loud Black man in America. For privileged and racially unconscious White women, I tend to fall into one of three categories: (1) pervasively sexual and exotic, (2) violent and threatening, or (3) comedic or neutral (typical for younger Black males). And so, with those racial overtones, I must navigate those environments carefully to avoid land mines that could put me in jail or, even worse, get me killed. See bell hooks, *Yearning: Race, Gender, and Cultural Politics* (Boston: South End Press, 1990), 51-56, 193-200; Traci C. West, "When a White Man-God Is the Truth and the Way for Black Christians," in *Christology and Whiteness: What Would Jesus Do?*, ed. George Yancy (New York: Routledge, 2012), 117-30.

No, you can't separate the anger from the experience. No, you can't separate the anger from the racism. No, you cannot micromanage an ethnic minority's experience and narrative. No.

I have come to learn that is a quite frequent experience. White supervisors in Christian ministries, who are ignorant and unconscious of their own race, culture, and ethnic position, proceed to prescribe what is right and just for other ethnic minorities. Moreover, they assume a position of dominance and prescribe treatment based on White hegemonic experience and narrative, particularly White men. They are ignorant of both what is and what was in terms of race and ethnicity. This is ever present in missions. Whites ignore the issue of race and only pursue the gospel or God's kingdom while trampling the framework of race. We need to recognize that this is outdated. The ideological construct surrounding reconciliation is based on a White supremacy myth that states we "all have the problem of racism." It does not recognize the history of systemic violence of White racism in the United States. For me, the term *reconciliation* has no meaning other than marketable charm—much like the word *justice*. Often (and even more after the 2016 election) White Christians say they want reconciliation—until the matter of race comes up, and then it becomes an uncomfortable theological issue. "Jesus sees no color," "God is the God of everyone," "Don't be political regarding race," or "You're a race baiter" is often said. Racial reconciliation cannot happen—at least not yet. Reconciliation is too often reduced to "feeling good" about another race. But that's not accurate. Further, we in the ethnic-minority community have been asking for reconciliation for decades, even centuries. Yet a known racist and anti-Semite, Stephen Bannon, was an adviser to the president in 2017. What then does that say to us as people of color? What does it say when the highest office in the land is occupied by people hostile to the existence of ethnic-minority life? And what does it say about American Christianity when a majority of White evangelicals supported a presidential candidate who goes against almost all that they say is "biblically important"? Reconciliation, then, is just a word.

Therefore, we need to dismantle and deconstruct issues on race, which this chapter attempts to do. If you are not convinced by the scholarship dealing with race, ethnicity, racism, White privilege, and its effect on

Christian theology, then this chapter will not make any difference for you.[3] But if you are wondering, questioning, or possibly attempting to figure out what next steps you should take to move forward in your mission organization, then these precepts will help to begin the conversations and construct a new path toward racial, ethnic, and cultural literacy, primarily for Euro-Americans.[4] I offer three imperative starters that, while not eliminating racism and White supremacy, will prayerfully limit their sting for ethnic minorities.

THE DEATH OF AND MOVEMENT AWAY FROM RESPECTABILITY AND BOOTSTRAP NARRATIVES

Jesus' life was grounded on the importance of ethnicity and cultural heritage. Why else would Matthew spend so much time describing Jesus' lineage, which is the first thing we read in the New Testament? Even more than that, Jesus knew the reality of both his time and context. He did not provide simplistic answers regarding life, love, death, or even sorrow. In other words, Jesus had a complex view of life, society, and his era. In fact, in many stories in the Gospels, Jesus shatters respectable norms (see Mt 5–7; Mk 2:1-12; 3:1-6; Lk 7:36-50; Jn 6). Jesus was not concerned with saying the right things, being

---

[3]The following are a few of the key works that have influenced my work: hooks, *Yearning*; West, "When a White Man-God Is the Truth"; Eduardo Bonilla-Silva, *Racism Without Racists: Color-Blind Racism and the Persistence of Racial Inequality in America* (Lanham, MD: Rowman & Littlefield, 2013); Eduardo Bonilla-Silva, *White Supremacy and Racism in the Post–Civil Rights Era* (Boulder, CO: L. Rienner, 2001); Tim J. Wise, *White Like Me: Reflections on Race from a Privileged Son*, rev. ed. (Berkeley, CA: Soft Skull Press, 2008); Ronald J. Ercoli, "Institutional Racism, the White Image of Jesus Christ, and Its Psychological Impact on African Americans" (PhD diss., Illinois School of Professional Psychology, 1996); Michael Eric Dyson, *Is Bill Cosby Right? Or Has the Black Middle Class Lost Its Mind?* (New York: Basic Civitas Books, 2005); Mark Anthony Neal, *New Black Man* (New York: Routledge, 2005); Anthony B. Pinn, *Terror and Triumph: The Nature of Black Religion* (Minneapolis: Fortress Press, 2003); Alphonso Pinkney, *Black Americans*, 5th ed. (Upper Saddle River, NJ: Prentice Hall, 2000); Franklin E. Frazier and Nathan Glazer, *The Negro Family in the United States* (Chicago: University of Chicago Press, 1966); Andrew F. Walls, *The Cross-Cultural Process in Christian History: Studies in the Transmission and Appropriation of Faith* (Maryknoll, NY: Orbis Books, 2002); Amos Yong, "Race and Racialization in a Post-Racist Evangelicalism: A View from Asian America," in Bradley, *Aliens in the Promised Land*; Soong-Chan Rah, *The Next Evangelicalism: Freeing the Church from Western Cultural Captivity* (Downers Grove, IL: InterVarsity Press, 2009); Howard Thurman, *Jesus and the Disinherited* (Boston: Beacon, 1976).

[4]This is important because, as an ethnic minority, I have "changed" as much as I can racially. All of my life I have had to submit, readjust, conform, resubmit, and suppress my way of life for Whites and White culture. Further, ethnic minorities also have to conform to White culture within missional situations; therefore, it is imperative that Whites begin to do the same difficult work it takes to be interculturally literate for not just their own lives but also for the work of the kingdom.

the right person, or dressing a certain way to win followers and notoriety.[5] Therefore, it is imperative to note his example when dealing with our need for respectability and bootstrap narratives, which have harmed not just ethnic minorities but, as we see from the November 2016 election, also harmed poor, lower-middle-class Whites.[6]

"Just be good." "Dress nicely." "Always do what the police officer asks." "Follow orders." "Respect them, and you'll gain their respect." These are components and markers of the politics of respectability.[7] They are rooted in bootstrap narratives and meritocracy:[8] if you simply work hard enough, look good enough, talk well enough, and show respect long enough, you will gain the respect of Whites and be able to pull yourself up by your own bootstraps and succeed. But I ask: Will someone tell that to the countless number of ethnic minorities who have been laid off, fired, or even killed following those mantras? Ask Alton Sterling if that worked. Talk to Trayvon Martin, and tell him to pull his pants up; maybe that would have kept him alive. Write a letter to Sandra Bland and let her know how much she needs to respect White police officers. And maybe if Walter Scott had just stood still, he would have gained the White officer's respect. Bootstrap narratives simply do not work. The notion that you will succeed if you are good enough and respectable

---

[5]This does not give permission to or sanction the politics of correctness. Often political correctness is used negatively among some Christians; that is, they feel they have to say certain words regarding ethnic minorities, women, or of sexual orientation. Some argue that we need to return to a more honest way of talking to each other and avoid political correctness. I believe Jesus was not about the politics of respectability in the sense of being liked for the sake of being liked. His "correctness" made sure the marginalized felt welcomed, loved, and cared for no matter who or what they were.

[6]Jabari Bodrick says, "The bootstrap narrative is essentially the belief that a person in the United States who works hard, assumes personal responsibility, and maintains a strong moral center can accomplish anything. Unfortunately for many students from low-income families, this narrative does not reflect their experiences." Jabari Bodrick, "The Myth of the Bootstrap," *Socioeconomic and Class Issues in Higher Education*, 2015, www.naspa.org/constituent-groups/posts/the-myth-of-the-bootstrap.

[7]This is the framework that desires to maintain respect, at almost any costs, over the dignity of ethnic minorities and any confrontation of Whiteness and White racism; it is the act of respecting Whiteness while submitting to Whiteness. Historically, it was how "African American elites sought to develop independent institutions that would enable free people of color to 'uplift' themselves to conditions of respectability." Jeffrey R. Williams, "Racial Uplift," in *American History Through Literature 1870–1920*, ed. Tom Quirk and Gary Scharnhorst (Detroit: Charles Scribner's, 2006), 933.

[8]"Meritocracy refers to a social system in which individuals advance and earn rewards in direct proportion to their individual abilities and efforts." "Meritocracy," in *International Encyclopedia of the Social Sciences*, ed. William A. Darity Jr. (Detroit: Macmillan Reference, 2008), 98.

enough needs to be rooted out of our vocabulary. Behind it is White culture demanding that ethnic minorities act right so all will be made right.

However, these notions often are promoted passively and through a screen of unknowing maltreatment. In other words, most Whites are not consciously exhibiting racist behavior; it occurs through socially constructed, passive, and sometimes repressed memory.[9] Whites assume their dominance because their history books and curriculum asserts it this way. Whites assume their governance because the majority of political leaders in the United States reflect their race. Whites assume their theological authority because seminaries and mission schools and their curricula reflect While authority. Racism and White supremacy is in the theological DNA of Christianity in the United States. In other words, if you ask a fish what water is, it will not know because it has always been submersed in water. It is the same with White supremacy. It has always been there for Whites; it is assumed as the "invisible knapsack," as Peggy McIntosh puts it:

> I think whites are carefully taught not to recognize white privilege, as males are taught not to recognize male privilege. So I have begun in an untutored way to ask what it is like to have white privilege. I have come to see white privilege as an invisible package of unearned assets that I can count on cashing in each day, but about which I was "meant" to remain oblivious. White privilege is like an invisible weightless knapsack of special provisions, maps, passports, codebooks, visas, clothes, tools, and blank checks.[10]

Whiteness and White privilege are unseen and not recognized. As with my former supervisor, Whiteness is invisible and weightless to many White people. So, that ignorance creates a "right way" of presenting the gospel, God, Jesus, and Christianity. It leaves little room for openness and

---

[9]Though, as the Trump election campaign has revealed, White hate for ethnic minorities is quite pervasive, and the conservative White evangelical framework has left little room to disagree with a White notion of God, life, family, marriage, society, and especially the language to communicate. Therefore, I doubt that this hate is absent within missional societies or Christian ministries. And so I, along with other ethnic minorities, are confronted with the reality that long before Donald Trump this type of hate has entered communities, cities, and countries masked as Christian love but rooted in a deep hate for "those people" when they question or disrupt Whiteness. For a broader view of this point, see William R. Jones, *Is God a White Racist? A Preamble to Black Theology*, C. Eric Lincoln Series on Black Religion (Garden City, NY: Anchor, 1973).

[10]Peggy McIntosh, "White Privilege: Unpacking the Invisible Knapsack," *Independent School* 49, no. 2 (1990): 33.

discussion outside of what has already been branded as the right way to do things. McIntosh continues,

> My schooling gave me no training in seeing myself as an oppressor, as an unfairly advantaged person, or as a participant in a damaged culture. I was taught to see myself as an individual whose moral state depended on her individual moral will. My schooling followed the pattern my colleague Elizabeth Minnich has pointed out: whites are taught to think of their lives as morally neutral, normative, and average, and also ideal, so that when we work to benefit others, this is seen as work that will allow "them" to be more like "us."[11]

Training and schooling is crucial here. Training done within a homogenous perspective will continue the legacy of White supremacy in missions and missiology. Therefore, the death of bootstrap narratives and movement away from maintaining respectability are vital in order to begin dismantling White privilege.[12] McIntosh contends,

> One factor seems clear about all of the interlocking oppressions. They take both active forms, which we can see, and embedded forms, which as a member of the dominant group one is taught not to see. In my class and place, I did not see myself as a racist because I was taught to recognize racism only in individual acts of meanness by members of my group, never in invisible systems conferring unsought racial dominance on my group from birth.
>
> Disapproving of the systems won't be enough to change them. I was taught to think that racism could end if white individuals changed their attitudes. But a "white" skin in the United States opens many doors for whites whether or not we approve of the way dominance has been conferred on us. Individual acts can palliate, but cannot end, these problems.[13]

In other words, simply acknowledging individual racism is not enough. Simply saying racism exists or, even worse, *existed* creates a way out of acknowledging systemic racism and White supremacy. McIntosh is correct in

---

[11]Ibid., 32.
[12]This is not a singular solution. In other words, if you solve this, then you will have solved that. I am suggesting a start. The start is not the end, and Whites must do the difficult work of intercultural competence. Ethnic minorities cannot be the teachers in this journey either. Whites will have to seek other conscious Whites to help them; they will have to do the historical analysis of their own Whiteness and complicity in racism. This is overwhelming for many. It's like being shoved out of a warm bed into frigid waters. The shock can be overwhelming for Whites.
[13]McIntosh, "White Privilege," 35.

her statement: individual acts can be of use, but we cannot end there. The dismantling of systems, protocols, and governance must be undertaken. On a national level, this could prove to be impossible, but on a domestic missiological level it could be enacted, albeit with tension.

For this dismantling to happen, several steps need to occur first, which will be difficult, and even impossible in some cases.

- White leaders first need to take a step back to examine their own power, privilege, and position. This will not be easy or stress free. Examining historical, familial, and social contexts is crucial. Learning about these issues is a must. This can be done through multitude methods, but learning and education are key.[14]

- White leaders must educate themselves through exposure to intercultural values and norms. In North Park University's program called Sankofa, participants are matched up with people from different ethnic and cultural backgrounds, spend at least six months in training, and then take an intensive four- to five-day trip in the South touring places of significant civil rights history. They end in Ferguson, Missouri. This creates a genuine sense of accountability for attitudes regarding race and ethnicity. Most who participate are changed for a lifetime. This is an example of what is needed.

- We should embrace Black post-soul voices in constructing new pathways for mission. This means allowing those on the margins, those who have been overlooked, and those whose perspective could be seen as radical to be included in our missiological perspectives. We must embrace the tension and conflict that comes with sexuality, sexual orientation, and gender identity. The issue of oppression cannot

---

[14]I suggest reading and fully digesting Robin DiAngelo's work on White fragility. This is important because it affects how White missionaries operate and engage with ethnic-minority groups. Moreover, it affects aspects of resources, access, and power, which also impact the way missions are done. DiAngelo states, "White Fragility is a state in which even a minimum amount of racial stress becomes intolerable, triggering a range of defensive moves. These moves include the outward display of emotions such as anger, fear, and guilt, and behaviors such as argumentation, silence, and leaving the stress-inducing situation. These behaviors, in turn, function to reinstate white racial equilibrium." This aspect of White fragility affects how the story of Jesus is told and how the components of ethnicity are embraced. Thus, DiAngelo is not to be ignored. See Robin DiAngelo, "White Fragility," *International Journal of Critical Pedagogy* 3, no. 3 (2011): 54.

end at the border of race and ethnicity. While we may disagree with someone's sexual orientation, it does not make it right or just to turn them away, ignore them, undermine them, passively try to save them, or simply write them off. Often, those voices provide direction to enter into spaces our own voices could not go. And I believe Jesus will be right there moving forward with us.

- We should embrace tension as a theological standard. Good news— the gospel—appears within tension. The messier and more difficult things get, the more Jesus' commandments have a chance to take hold. The uglier it gets, the more space is created for Jesus' love to move in. The more that tension rises, the more God can be seen, if God is sought. Tension for tension's sake can be an impossible scheme, but tension seeking God can be productive. Thus, when it comes to issues of race and ethnicity, tension is the heat that can burn through the walls of hostility to the other side (see Eph 2:14). I cannot imagine the disciples of Jesus never having an argument with him; all of those cats were too passionate about their work and lives to not have had at least one verbal altercation with him. Do you think that Jesus never truly ticked off someone to the point of frustration? The gospel, when seen and embraced without social filters, is sharp and cutting. It forces us to introspectively see the nature of ourselves and purge those areas not fitting as a follower of Jesus—the ones that are truly difficult and full of tension. Therefore, a theology of tension is needed. Most Christians avoid theological tension at all costs and might even contend that it is sinful. However, I believe tension is essential for growth and development. It will be at the center of our breakthrough on race and ethnicity.

These are areas we must begin to consider for a paradigm shift in missiology. The old ways are not working. It is time to shed the old skin, much like a snake does, and create new skins of thought, worldview, and theology in relation to race and ethnicity. It is time to put to death bootstrap narratives and the politics of respectability.

We will now look at the second imperative to begin dismantling racism within missions.

THE DEATH OF AND MOVEMENT AWAY FROM
WHITE DOMINANCE IN MISSIONS

In an era of demographic change that favors an intercultural perspective, the prevalence of Whiteness in missionary settings is problematic.[15] Further, the image seared into the minds of non-Christians is that of White Christians joyfully doing the work of God in other countries or working among the "at risk" youth in inner cities. Couple that with social media representations of these groups amid ethnic minorities that assumes dominance, declares victory, and asserts the dominance of White values. All of these make missions a "White thing." These images must cease.

Predominately White church plants in ethnic-minority communities are problematic as well. Many times this type of gentrification unknowingly destroys any indigenous or local voice in the community. Churches springing up in the new urban landscape are often ignorant of that particular community and typically upset the community's socioeconomic balance.[16] A common scenario is when a White suburban megachurch enters an urban context to teach those in that context to do missions using White suburban methods, practices, and theology.[17] A partner of our center at North Park from south side Chicago runs one of the largest Black youth ministries in

---

[15]Jones notes that White ignorance of social injustices experienced by ethnic minorities is grand. He says, "America's still-segregated modern life is marked by three realities. First, geographic segregation has meant that—although places like Ferguson and Baltimore may seem like extreme examples—most white Americans continue to live in locales that insulate them from the obstacles facing many majority-black communities. Second, this legacy, compounded by social self-segregation, has led to a stark result: the overwhelming majority of white Americans don't have a single close relationship with a person who isn't white. Third, there are virtually no American institutions positioned to resolve these persistent problems of systemic and social segregation" (Robert P. Jones, *The End of White Christian America* [New York: Simon & Schuster, 2016], Kindle ed., loc. 2049). This is highly problematic for those same White Christians desiring to enter predominantly ethnic-minority communities to do missions and bring the gospel.

[16]Urban environments are quickly changing in the United States. High rents and stratospheric real estate have created a type of new urban center. The once-feared inner city is developing into a White, affluent, and green space, which have erased many relics of local history. It is as if the Apple store and Starbucks have always existed and the ugliness of displacement and inequality never happened. Scholars of urban studies agree that the term *urban* is rapidly changing. See Edward W. Soja, *Postmetropolis: Critical Studies of Cities and Regions* (New York: Blackwell, 2000); William E. Thompson and Joseph V. Hickey, *Society in Focus*, 7th ed. (New York: Pearson Books, 2011); and William H. Whyte, "The Design of Spaces," in *The City Reader*, ed. Richard T. Le Gates and Frederic Stout (New York: Routledge, 1996).

[17]This comes from a position of dominance rather than out of a genuine call from God. It reflects the superiority to "teach" others without asking, learning, and collaborating with the people of that community, who often are doing great work.

the city. They have been a cornerstone of that community for decades. A White suburban church approached them desiring to train them on how to do missions and outreach in their community—for a fee, of course.[18] The church was looking to expand by working in the city. My friend said they talked, but in the end they lovingly yet firmly rejected the proposal. If anything, my friend's church could have taught the suburban church how to develop intercultural and multiethnic relationships, how to create a Christian Community Development model, and how to live with and among people, even if they never change.[19] This is an example of the imperialism that has continued to plague missions and missional approaches to community engagement.

The White gaze upon multiethnic contexts needs redirection and reconstruction. Willie Jennings explains that the movement away from White dominance entails doing Christian theology differently: "Christian intellectual identity that is compelling and attractive, embodying not simply the cunning of reason but the power of love that constantly gestures toward joining, toward the desire to hear, to know, and to embrace."[20] No one would plot a course across the country without consulting a map and acquiring the necessary knowledge prior to departure. The same is true for engagement with an unfamiliar context. We cannot assume God is not doing God's work in a specific context long before we arrive. To assume we are saviors or rescuers creates an imperial status of dominance in that context. This is why we must move away from White dominance in any missional settings.

The death of White dominance means that fundraising strategies and models will be overhauled. Mission donors tend to be White and affluent,

---

[18]The monetizing of Christian ministry is troublesome on many levels. I support honorariums, pastors' salaries, and the professional component of ministry, yet the how-to market is treacherous to navigate and the expertise of many Christian consultants is questionable. Monica Miller contends that the focus is on money and profit rather than on people—a recipe for disaster and exploitation (Monica R. Miller, *Religion and Hip Hop* [New York: Routledge, 2013], 6-7).

[19]The Christian Community Development model is based on John Perkins's now-famed model of the three Rs: restoration, relocation, and reconciliation. This model focuses on developing the community holistically and not placing the sole emphasis on salvation and church attendance. It is about community and working with the people already in a space and place. See John Perkins, *With Justice for All* (Ventura, CA: Regal Books, 1982).

[20]Willie James Jennings, *The Christian Imagination: Theology and the Origins of Race* (New Haven, CT: Yale University Press, 2010), 291.

and they tend to fund other Whites. And mission organizations reflect that White dominance. Christian mission organizations lack diversity and engagement with diverse perspectives. Volunteer organizations and evangelical outreach ministries (EOMs) are likewise racially homogenous; most EOMs are led by White evangelicals.[21] In his study of social capital and fundraising within EOMs, Samuel Perry found that Whites dominate the ministry landscape: 84.8 percent White, 4.8 percent Black, 8.3 percent Asian, and 2.2 percent Latino.[22] We see similar numbers among young ministry organizations. These numbers present several problematic variables. Whites tend to be unware of much of the history of race in the United States.[23] Because these Whites lead or are in supervisorial roles at EOMs, it is likely that they will dismiss or minimize racial identity and racism within the EOM, and appear unsympathetic toward the deaths of young Black bodies (e.g., Trayvon Martin). On the second front, it is difficult for subordinates to discuss issues of racism and racial inequality with their supervisors—even more so if the issue is *with* their supervisor.

Thus, fundraising becomes problematic when issues of social capital are factoring into the context. As Marla Fredrick McGlathery and Traci Griffin remind us:

> Further complicating this problem is that upon becoming a part of contemporary interracial evangelical mission organizations, many workers do not know the history of African American evangelical missions or the struggle of the black church in America. Without this knowledge, the appeal of white-conversion Christianity can appear unproblematic. Those who want to share the gospel with the world and be held accountable for living lives of more

---

[21]Michael D Lindsay and Robert Wuthnow, "Financing Faith: Religion and Strategic Philanthropy," *Journal for the Scientific Study of Religion* 49, no. 1 (2010): 87.

[22]Samuel L. Perry, "Social Capital, Race, and Personal Fundraising in Evangelical Outreach Ministries," *Journal for the Scientific Study of Religion* 52, no. 1 (2013): 164.

[23]Michael O. Emerson, *People of the Dream: Multiracial Congregations in the United States* (Princeton: Princeton University Press, 2010); Antony W. Alumkal, "American Evangelicalism in the Post–Civil Rights Era: A Racial Formation Theory Analysis," *Sociology of Religion* 65, no. 3 (2004); Wilbert R. Shenk, *Changing Frontiers of Mission* (Maryknoll, NY: Orbis Books, 1999); Tim J. Wise, *Little White Lies: The Truth About Affirmative Action and "Reverse Discrimination,"* Blueprint for Social Justice (New Orleans: Twomey Center for Peace Through Justice, Loyola University, 1995); Tim J. Wise, *Colorblind: The Rise of Post-Racial Politics and the Retreat from Racial Equity*, Open Media Series (San Francisco: City Lights Books, 2010); Tim J. Wise, *Between Barack and a Hard Place: Racism and White Denial in the Age of Obama*, Open Media Series (San Francisco: City Lights Books, 2009).

integrity would "naturally" become part of such an organization. . . . [This] immediately places them in a position that requires them to work against the stigma within African American communities regarding the racist history of white missionary organizations in places like the United States, Africa, and South America.[24]

Lack of diversity presents difficulties for ethnic minorities attempting to raise funds. When I was a young area director with Young Life on the Central Coast of California, my metro area director (supervisor), who was Black, lost 75 percent of his funding within the first two months of assuming the leadership role. Further, parents did not want to send their children to our weekly club meetings for fear of the new "urban youth ministry" component, and within the next three months he lost over half of his parental support and committee members. While he and I lamented these issues, his supervisors were unsympathetic to the situation and even suggested that he change his approach to "be more like them." Conforming to the dominant culture is often a struggle for ethnic-minority youth workers in EOMs. The mere fact of being an ethnic minority in an EOM can place them in an adversarial stance. The ethnic minority who works for an EOM will likely have to give up their ethnic identity and heritage to fit in with their White counterparts, presenting more issues for fundraising.[25]

This is not an isolated occurrence. As I have interviewed other ethnic-minority youth workers in EOMs, they relayed the following tropes told to them by their White supervisors:

- Race is something of the past; let's leave it there.

- Social problems are not our concern; preaching the gospel is.

- The reason there are still race problems is because we keep talking about racism.

[24]Marla Frederick McGlathery and Traci Griffin, "'Becoming Conservative, Becoming White?' Black Evangelicals and the Para-Church Movement," in *This Side of Heaven: Race, Ethnicity, and Christian Faith*, ed. Robert J. Priest and Alvaro L. Nieves (New York: Oxford University Press, 2007).

[25]Micah Singleton, "To Pimp a Butterfly: Kendrick Lamar's New Album Is Perfect," *The Verge*, March 19, 2015, www.theverge.com/2015/3/19/8257319/kendrick-lamar-album-review-to-pimp-a-butterfly; Emerson, *People of the Dream*; and Samuel L. Perry, "Racial Habitus, Moral Conflict, and White Moral Hegemony Within Interracial Evangelical Organizations," *Qualitative Sociology* 35, no. 1 (2012).

- I don't think racism is at play here in this situation.

- You're making more out of this than is really there.

Often, ethnic-minority staff are cross-examined when they relay narratives of racism within EOMs and are told their experience is invalid or inadequate. Having an ethnic-minority leader in senior leadership is needed. Samuel Bell correctly observes that

> Recent research on race relations within evangelical institutions suggests that white evangelicals, like white Americans in general, tend to embody a complex of covert racial ideologies, attitudes, and practices collectively labeled "white racial identity" or "whiteness" that serve to legitimize and reproduce white structural and cultural dominance within evangelical institutions.[26]

Thus, it becomes difficult when *one* ethnic minority is hired; they are faced with a myriad of issues in regard to race and ethnicity. This Whiteness that Bell refers to complicates the fundraising process and facilitates fundraising models not suitable for ethnic-minority contexts.

Learning the history of racism, inequality, and oppression toward US ethnic minorities could alleviate some of these problems. When we are aware of our own ethnic heritage and become knowledgeable of the continuing significance of race in the United States, we are better able to listen to others' narratives and life experiences.[27] Further, a diverse staff means diverse views and approaches to Christian theology and the gospel within respective contexts. However, ethnic minorities are typically siloed within EOMs. For them, the only way to organize is at once-a-year national events sponsored by Christian Community Development Association or Urban Youth Workers Institute.

White supremacists do not like to be in discomfort. Moreover, they will not allow themselves to be in distress over racial issues. Whites continually comment on how uncomfortable they became the first time they realized they are a minority. Whites feel stressed, anxious, and even angry being the "other." Exclude a White person from something, and they will let you know

---

[26]Samuel L. Perry, "Diversity, Donations, and Disadvantage: The Implications of Personal Fundraising for Racial Diversity in Evangelical Outreach Ministries," *Review of Religious Research* 53, no. 4 (2012): 398.

[27]Alvaro L. Nieves, "An Applied Research Strategy for Christian Organizations," in Priest and Nieves, *This Side of Heaven*, 310-11.

immediately. Any perceived injustice leads to a claim of "reverse racism." Yet many Whites remain passive while ethnic minorities experience discomfort, stress, anxiety, and even fear of death.

Just because there is ethnic inclusion does not mean there will be ethnic unity. If we learned anything from the 2016 election, it is that the dream of a multiethnic future is yet to be realized; the hope of having the minority vote triumph over a person like Donald Trump was a myth. This is true when EOMs hire an ethnic minority—the hope is that somehow the evil of racism will suddenly end, and the organization will be reconciled. But, in fact, most White organizations do not realize their racism and bigotry until an ethnic minority is present. Therefore, the presence of one, while good, often causes more problems. If that person wants to change the mission statement to reflect a more interculturally sensitive perception, how will the organization react? If that person wants to hire more women and ethnic minorities to positions of power, will donors withdraw their support? If that person suggests the cross has connections to the lynching tree, will that organization have the strength to engage, or will it wither into a mythical land of "unity" and White fragility? In each case, the latter is often the course of action, and White voices remain in control.

To overcome this, power and control must be yielded. That is easier said than done, especially when those in control fear the ascendancy of ethnic minorities and the retreat of White hegemony.[28] I am not convinced that by hiring someone of ethnic-minority descent the organization will somehow become inclusive. If anything, the organization has just begun that process and might not be able to survive if that person is freed to be culturally ethnic.

I long for a different route that allows the voices of ethnic minorities to be heard. I desire much broader perspectives and different voices within

---

[28]Fear is what drives many Whites. The 2016 election of Donald Trump was no different. Fear of immigrants. Fear of losing control. Fear of Blacks. Fear that somehow the United States is becoming more multicultural—and that is a problem. This type of fear is embedded deep within the American Christian imagination, and the threat of anything other than Whiteness presents a clear and present danger to a supremacy that many Whites simply do not and care not see. Thus, it is with ease that many White people dismiss a candidate for an evangelical outreach ministry position by openly saying race had nothing to do with it, yet power and control remains with Whites. It is also easy for Whites to dismiss anyone who suggests racism is at work. See Brenda Major, Alison Blodorn, and Gregory Major Blascovich, "The Threat of Increasing Diversity: Why Many White Americans Support Trump in the 2016 Presidential Election," *Group Processes & Intergroup Relations*, October 20, 2016.

Christian theology—especially in missiology. My goal here is to present new ideas that resist White dominance in missions. However, I do not believe that if and when my ideas and actions are accepted, White supremacy will end and racism will stop. This is a much more complex problem that cannot be written off as "the fall of humanity" (e.g., sin). I am not hopeful that Whites will turn over their power to ethnic minorities. I am not ambitious enough to believe that somehow God will sprinkle magic dust on US Christianity, and things will work out.

Deep divisions and hurts exist—especially within the ethnic-minority community. Those hurts have gone unaddressed for far too long. When a known racist is in the highest position of the land, it is neither a hopeful nor joyful time. It is a time of lament. A time for sorrow. And a time for action. I am not convinced that White people can partake in that action for justice. While I believe some, if very few, Whites "get it" and are allies, the vast majority—especially those in positions of power in EOMs—cannot undo their supremacist nature.[29] Thus, the next and final imperative is to nurture and nourish doubt and ambiguity in missiology as we dismantle and move away from White dominion in missions.

NURTURING DOUBT AND AMBIGUITY IN MISSIOLOGY

Doubt is essential for faith development. Without it, we grow stagnant and set in our worldview. Doubt creates a sense of ambiguity, which when embraced can bring about new understandings of God. Most of us are used to being in control. We seek order and not chaos. As Christians, we have lost the sense of the wildness so entrenched in the biblical narratives. We seek that which is known, secure, and safe. Western culture has lost its sense of the wild. Economic stability is a measure of success and social status, and with it come accolades and social capital. After all, no one seeks advice from someone who is in the unemployment line, buried in debt, or without secure social moorings. Most of the legendary voices who write leadership texts come from affluent contexts. We see success all around us, which is typically

---

[29]I realize this is a strong statement to make. But it is not much different from James Baldwin, W. E. B. DuBois, or Angela Davis in their understanding of how Whiteness works. White supremacy, in their estimation, is like a disease, and thus without the proper treatment (e.g., continual intercultural engagement and training) it will be impossible for those Whites to move away from it. It is a difficult realization.

neat and tidy. And all of this is closely tied to our faith—good Christians are successful and possess a certain amount of wealth. Home ownership, good education, upward mobility, stability in lifestyle, healthy eating, and faith in God are touted as the right stuff for Western life. I refer to this by the acronym RAP: resources, access, and power. But despite the illusion of control and stability, in reality, life for humans is messy. It always has been. Somehow Christians have twisted the narratives of the Bible to mean "success equals control times wealth," which means God's blessing. Friends, this is a lie.

In the pursuit of control, Western Whites have overlooked the human element—humans are imperfect and uncontrollable. The veneer of control is easily removed. After the horrific events of 9/11, many Americans felt unsafe, insecure, and threatened by forces they did not think could breach our borders. Then came the Great Recession of 2008. What was once "secure" turned out to be a mirage. Doubt crept in. As new research emerged on millennials and Gen Ys regarding their religious and spiritual sensibilities, we began to doubt the future of Christianity. Instead of embracing doubt and confusion, we create ideologies and theologies that soothe us. For example, after 9/11, there was a resurgence of American exceptionalism, and when we went to war in 2003, the idea that the United States is "God's nation" reemerged. However, God has not declared the United States as his "chosen nation." Rather, it would be more appropriate to question those mantras. We must critique those ideological structures and disrupt the flow of thought that no longer functions in the wild. That is what embracing doubt and ambiguity requires.

For missiologists, this means giving up control of the newsletter headline declaring "Those Saved This Week." It means embracing that fact that not all will fall into line behind a simplistic gospel message. Simply listening to a passive sermon causes the Gen Y community to question whether the pastor is trustworthy; making a faith commitment is almost out of question. Doubt is about leaning on God, much like the disciples had to do.

John 6 gives us a clear picture of what this doubt looks like in real time. The passage opens with Jesus feeding the multitudes and generating food from a small bag of fish and bread.[30] This established Jesus as a true miracle

---

[30]Although the number is typically referred to as five thousand, most scholars agree that the number was closer to fifteen thousand, and some render it as large as eighteen thousand when women, children, and the disabled are included.

worker. Of course, he had already performed a miraculous Sabbath healing at a pool in Jerusalem (Jn 5) and had turned water into wine at the wedding in Cana (Jn 2). And prior to feeding the multitudes, he had walked on water (Jn 6:16-21). Though these signs and wonders were amazing, they did not convince everyone about Jesus.

The Jews challenged Jesus' authority (Jn 6:22-59): Where did it come from? And where did he come from? They asked Jesus for a sign that they might believe (vv. 30-31). But Jesus knew where these questions were coming from. Moreover, he knew the hearts of these people. He said he was the "bread of life" (vv. 35-40). In response, many grumbled and complained (v. 41).

Rather than sitting with the tension Jesus created and realizing their own theological highway had ended, they pressed on. Rather than doubting their theological training, they resisted. They argued with Jesus. But Jesus did not waver; he used some of the most direct, strong, and even profane language with his critics. In John 6:51 and 54-59, Jesus told his questioners that he was the way to God the Father, and to get there they had to drink his blood and eat his flesh—this was the bread of life. In that context, Jesus had broken every rule. A zombie-like savior? *No! This is not the way; nor is it even theological! This conversation has shifted from contentious to blasphemous!*

Rather than sitting with their tension and doubt, and rather than struggling with Jesus' hard message, they pushed back toward assurance. But Jesus gave no earthly assurances and made no outlandish promises of security. Even in that context, people sought a concrete understanding of who and what Jesus was. They found Jesus' words tough, hard, stern, and even dangerous (v. 60). Jesus, not missing a beat, asks, "Do you take offense at this?" (v. 61). The grumbling and pushback continued to a breaking point: "After this many of his disciples turned back and no longer walked with him" (Jn 6:66 ESV).

I am convinced many of those who walked with Jesus at some point probably felt as though Jesus was their pal. Yet without the messiness and tension of what a relationship brings, that notion was never tested—until then. Again, doubt is messy. Ambiguity is too much for many. Jesus knew this and even turned to the Twelve and asked them if they too were going to leave (v. 67).

This story reveals the true nature of where unengaged and unchallenged doubt can lead. Yes, engage in the debate. Yes, embrace the tension and conflict. Yes, seek wise counsel and wisdom. And yes, continue to seek God, by all means. But we must learn to sit with that ambiguity. We must, for example, nurture doubt and ambiguity in an era when a known racist has become the president of the United States. And while we do that, we must also seek out and nurture a multiethnic perspective on God.

While Western evangelicalism did establish pillars on which many people have stood on, it is not the be-all and end-all of Christianity in the twenty-first century. Western evangelicalism has run its course. There is not much we can salvage from it. Hip Hop theology creates space for multiethnic voices to imagine God and heaven while filled with doubt. It allows us to live in ambiguity while still seeking the face of God. Hip Hop theology gives credence to love, unity, peace, and fellowship with God from the context of a multiethnic and intercultural perspective. This is where missiology needs to go, and together we can begin to reconstruct what Christianity looks like in the wild for a generation seeking new and fresh symbols of Jesus.

The problems facing missiologists in the twenty-first century are vast and complex. There is no simple fix. The issue of race remains significant, especially in the West. The 2016 presidential election exposed the fact that hate mongering, xenophobia, fascism, and racism run deep in Christian evangelical circles.[31]

---

[31]The nefarious stew of racism woven with Christian ideology and the mythology of "God's country" was evident when Donald Trump ran for president in 2016. Trump gave conservative evangelicals permission to come out of the closet and be a racist. Trump did not create what he was peddling, however. He was merely the catalyst and the conduit that, for some, revealed this nation's racist and hateful past. For those of us in ethnic-minority communities who study religion and race, this is nothing new. Problematic was the endorsement of Trump by so many evangelicals—both Black and White—and their silence when violence spilled into Trump's rallies.

9

A THEOLOGY FOR THE WILD

Protest and Civil Disruption as Missiology

APRIL 29, 1992: A DATE THAT will live in infamy, in my mind. For those of you who are too young to remember (or have forgotten), that was the day the jury rendered their verdict on the now infamous Rodney King police-brutality case. The trial, which predated the O. J. Simpson case, set a precedent in which high-profile court cases keep audiences fastened to their TVs. In my community, it was known all too well that the police were not there to protect and serve. If we had a problem, the police were the last resort for help. The police were brutal, callous, and violent toward young Black and Latinx people. Law enforcement was bringing violence to Black and Latinx neighborhoods. This was a time before cell phone videos of police brutality and shootings hit the media—not that they make a difference for Black lives. All we had were narratives of police violence. Those narratives, from mostly Brown and Black people, were quickly dismissed as fictional accounts. Moreover, a counter narrative suggested Black and Latinx people were resisting arrest—if we would just comply, we would not have to endure violence. After all, the officers were merely doing their job (another type of respectability narrative). This was not the case, however. Often someone could have been wearing the wrong hat at the wrong time in the wrong place at the moment a police officer wanted to release some tension. They were then subject to the cop's rage and anger, all in the name of the law. We had endured this for years—so when we saw the video of Rodney King being beaten, while we felt for him and his suffering, we were relieved that someone had recorded it and that it was now a national issue.

When the trial was moved out of Los Angeles to a then-predominantly White, affluent neighborhood in Simi Valley, red flags went up. But given the solid evidence, this was a sure win. The day of April 29 dawned with blue skies. I was in an English class, which was right before lunch. I was sitting in the second seat of the outer row next to the door. Our teacher, Ms. Williams, had a closed-circuit television in our classroom and decided we should watch the verdict. I did not pay much attention, because this was an open-and-shut case. The officers who brutally beat King were obviously guilty of abusing their power. I remember talking to a friend about what we were going to do over the weekend. Then, the lead juror appeared on the screen. The class was suddenly silent as if to suggest this was a moment of truth. The typical courtroom jargon was exchanged as we watched intensely. Here it came . . . not guilty. My senses were overwhelmed. My classmates were obviously equally as stunned. Dumbfounded, I asked my teacher, "What did they just say?" In a quick response, as if to agree with the verdict, she responded, "Oh, they said not guilty."

I saw red. Literally.

From what I can remember of that day, I marched out of the classroom, along with half of the class, and I started knocking on classroom doors and disrupting instruction, because that day's lesson was about to go into the streets. "Not guilty!" I proclaimed. The student body gathered at the Greek Center, the central part of the school, and started protesting. As if on cue, a good friend of mine pulled out an American flag and started burning it. We were enraged. I thought about all the work of our elders in the civil rights movement—for what? This moment stands out in my mind to this day. What does it mean to be an ethnic minority and Christian? How does this ambiguous mix play out in real-time American society?

I took part in the uprisings that day and for the next two. By definition, an uprising is protesting social hardships, legal inequalities, and police mistreatment.[1] A riot is more unorganized and unplanned. We knew what we were doing. For the first time in my life I was ready to die rather than merely

---

[1] See "Uprising," *Encyclopedia of African American Cultural History*, ed. Colin A. Palmer, 2nd ed. (Detroit: Macmillan Reference, 2006), 5:1951-57.

exist as a young man. I realize that sounds strange to some of you because you may not have faced such oppressive conditions or felt like your only way of being heard was to violently burn down hegemonic structures.[2] I do not regret most of my actions from those days.

I know that there are many Christians who watched this event on TV and probably wondered what was going on: How could they be burning their communities, and, as King later said, why can't we "get along"?

Where is God in the uprising? How do we see Jesus in the Black Lives Matter marches all over the country? Missiologically speaking, how does a church in the wild disrupt conventional Christian thought and protest hegemonic voices? Does it even want to?

The church has been domesticated by Western evangelicalism and White supremacy. We are told that violence is never an option and that we should forgive. Yet the United States, often in God's name, readily kills combatants, insurgents, or enemies of the state. Without batting an eyelash, the "right to bear arms" is at the center of many evangelical conversations. Why do we need guns? For protection by violent means. Does this not also apply to ethnic minorities? Often, no. And so countless bodies of Blacks lay strewn across the nation. We are counseled by outsiders about how we should have acted or what we should have or have not said to the murdering officers. It is time we embrace a disruptive missiology, much like Jesus did. Jesus would be in Ferguson. Jesus would stand with Freddie Gray's family. Jesus would be pushing for the deconstruction of the prison-industrial complex. Jesus would be disrupting the traditional mindset that spews empty counsel on to people it does not understand. Jesus would be saddened by the love of empire that so much of Christianity has fallen prey to.

Therefore, this chapter addresses protest and civil disruption as missiology. Violence is not a starting point and should not be looked at as such. However, in the face of hyperoppressive conditions and extreme social,

---

[2]The only thing I had remorse for was the ethnic-minority property that we knowingly destroyed. Resentment had built up between Korean Americans and Blacks during this time. The powder keg's fuse was lit when Latasha Harlins was shot in the back by Soon Ja Du, a Korean American store owner, who received no prison time for her actions. While that was wrong, it was exacerbated by the White supremacist logic of interethnic racism built upon centuries of ethnic infighting. Thus, for years after, I dedicated a lot of my time to restoring those places and working much closer with Korean Americans.

economic, and racial inequality, what are those who bear the brunt of these heinous issues to do? What do we do after we have followed due process and still receive no justice? This chapter then will argue to push past the "wait on God" premise often given to ethnic minorities seeking justice. When all other options have been exhausted, I assert that violence is a viable option and still remains biblically rooted. I end the chapter with a preview of missiology in the wild. I will first begin with the American Christian love of empire.

REIMAGINING KING NEBUCHADNEZZAR
IN THE CONTEXT OF EMPIRE

The Old Testament is filled with rich and complex narratives about the human experience. One of the stories that stands out is found in the book of Daniel. Daniel and three other young Hebrews refuse to bow to a statue of King Nebuchadnezzar. In Sunday school we are told about Daniel's three friends being thrown into a furnace, and then a mysterious fourth person appears with them. They are miraculously saved. Daniel and his friends' acts of disruption eventually led the king to God. We are regaled with their heroism, but we often fail to realize the implication of their actions: what it means to protest and create social and cultural controversy. Few have contemplated the notion of empire and what it took to stand up to the emperor, King Nebuchadnezzar. It took much more than courage—it took a disruptive spirit bent on doing the right thing.

The story picks up in the latter part of Daniel 2, when the king is humbled by Daniel's interpretation of his dreams:

> Then the king placed Daniel in a high position and lavished many gifts on him. He made him ruler over the entire province of Babylon and placed him in charge of all its wise men. Moreover, at Daniel's request the king appointed Shadrach, Meshach and Abednego administrators over the province of Babylon, while Daniel himself remained at the royal court. (Dan 2:48-49)

It would appear the story ends well. Not exactly, as we will see in chapter three of Daniel. But first, let's look into who Nebuchadnezzar was.[3] The king

---

[3]There is mixed opinion regarding Nebuchadnezzar. Some see him as a hero and a great leader. Others make him out to be evil and self-centered. I'm simply providing context and background to his kingdom.

was known for land development. He was known to bring cities back to life. Clever in warfare, Nebuchadnezzar did not treat his enemies well, but his wrath was limited to the leaders he had conquered. Nebuchadnezzar was fully aware that if he killed everyone, there would be no one left to build up his new kingdom.

Nebuchadnezzar paid good wages and built up a solid middle class in the Babylonian Empire. He stabilized the economy, created jobs, and established the infrastructure to keep the empire secure. He put his newly acquired people to work rather than imprisoning them or making them into slaves, which was customary. Nebuchadnezzar gave them a new identity. This in turn engendered loyalty, trust, and a willingness to overlook the king's flaws. Women had work equal to that of men in his economy.[4] He had a system of taxes and tolls, which, in turn, built the city, stabilized the outer walls, and created wealth. Some people climbed into the upper-middle class. Under his rule, his subjects experienced stability and peace. Nebuchadnezzar had created a system people were happy to be a part of.[5]

Because Nebuchadnezzar constructed a new identity for Babylon, created economic stability, fashioned state-of-the-art infrastructure, built up conquered people rather than tearing them down, and empowered a workforce socially and financially, Babylon stood as a model to other cities and rulers. Nebuchadnezzar, therefore, was rather popular. In situations like this, much like now, leaders who produce for their people can in turn hide many indiscretions. And when people are fed, paid, and safe, any revealed indiscretions are minimized.

Nebuchadnezzar was not as philanthropic as he seemed. He just knew how to make an economy work. (Some suggest he developed a rough version of a free market.) But he could be vicious. And many narratives reveal that he was self-consumed, which is evident throughout the opening chapters of the book of Daniel. Nebuchadnezzar was full of himself. He had fallen in love with not only himself but also certain ideologies. Ideologies and philosophies tend to be well-ordered and neat. They look good on paper. They present a model of the way things *should be*. But they do not encompass the human messiness of relationships and day-to-day life. People mess up utopias.

---

[4]However, women received less pay, and laws continued to favor men.
[5]Conquered subjects were grateful that the king did not kill, imprison, or enslave them.

Nebuchadnezzar had fallen prey to his own hype, a trap that catches many powerful leaders. He had built a city out of ruins, conquered a people, and created a great economic system. His subjects not only praised him but also thanked him for the work, and he relished it all. Thus, Nebuchadnezzar's idea of what *should be* was growing.

Empire, as the Oxford English Dictionary defines it, is a realm or domain having an absolute ruler, an extensive territory under the control of a supreme ruler (typically an emperor), or an oligarchy. It is difficult to imagine that Nebuchadnezzar was not aware of the sociological and psychological constructs that would induce people to gladly fall into compliance. Babylon was an empire, and Nebuchadnezzar was making full use of all the means at his disposal to increase his realm. Love of empire creates a stilted utopian perception of life. Adding religion to the mix creates a passively destructive pathology in which justifications for heinous and nefarious actions are not only accepted but also demanded because God or the gods have commanded it.

Love for empire takes on a persona; it is the talk and the life of a culture. To go against empire makes a person the enemy and places them outside the parameters of accepted social life. Complacency is chief among the side effects of love of empire, and it leads subjects to agree with what the empire wants. People agree so long as their own safety or wealth is not jeopardized. That agreeableness, then, is directly related to luxury and comfort. A sense of hatred is developed toward anything or anyone who attempts to take them away. Once people have luxury and comfort, the love of empire is almost complete. What seals this love is enculturation to the "way it is": the tropes, cultural mores, social constructs, and leader's rule. Enculturation is the glue that kept together the disparate parts of the Babylonian empire.

Nebuchadnezzar was not omnipresent. In his absence, the enculturated people policed themselves. They didn't want change; they selfishly protected what they had, defending the empire to the death. They saw things from a simple, black-and-white perspective, and they used violence to protect the empire's creedal framework and ideological construct. Nebuchadnezzar had created something exclusive and exceptional.

With this in mind, it makes what Hananiah (Shadrach), Mishael (Meshach), and Azariah (Abednego) did so much greater than what we are told in common narrative of the account. The social pressure, cultural isolation, and ridicule they had to endure for not bowing to the idol had to have been immense (Dan 3:8-12). Imagine the taunts, jeers, and negativity thrown at them for standing up while everyone else was bowing down. We might even say they silently protested against empire, much like some Black professional athletes of today. The implication is that they disrupted the empire because of God's call on their life. The king's authority was not absolute. They stood firm even when Nebuchadnezzar angrily called them in and gave them one more chance to bow (Dan 3:13-15). They disrupted ideological frameworks and the love of empire, which enraged Nebuchadnezzar, who gave them a death sentence. And even with death looming, they persisted. Imagine what might have crossed their minds as they approached the furnace. Dead bodies may have littered the pathway—imminent death is a deterrent for many. Yet they persisted. We know the rest of the story: the king yielded to this disruption only after he saw God in the fire with them; their garments were not so much as singed.

Are we that bold? Is our missiology that bold? Do we have the courage to persist in our resistance? Can we look at our faith and what Jesus has called each of us to do without any regard for our own life? It is difficult because empire is so appealing to those that comply. Perhaps some people who bowed to Nebuchadnezzar's statue also felt it was over the top; they may have felt disgusted with what was happening. But what were they to do? After all, it is the king; you cannot fight city hall. Yet they bowed.

Empire places barricades that impede Christian growth and theological development.[6] Empire creates constructs that give the impression of piety while remaining a god to those who comply. So many bowed to this image because they felt it was their duty; some were fearful or silent as they complied, but that silence made them complicit.

But, as we know, it does not work out that nicely for many—especially Black bodies that disrupt. They are openly put to death, just like in

---

[6]The greed for security, power, and wealth has poisoned the hearts of many White evangelicals. They have lost their way. Empire is more suitable to them than Jesus and the Scriptures' teachings about idolatry. The idol has blinded them to justice, mercy, and love, and empire has set boundaries for those who do not fit or comply with the empire's demands. As the threat of diversity looms, White evangelicals have all but sold their souls to maintain control of their White property and White nation. Thus, the story found in Daniel is as relevant today as it was in the past. It warns those who continue to bow to the image of White supremacy.

Babylon, for the crowds to see. I am certain that there were people in the crowd around Daniel and his friends that said, "If they'd only listened and complied, they'd be alive." Or, "Look, I don't really agree with Nebuchadnezzar, but he takes care of me. They should just bow down!" There were jeers, I am sure, from the crowd: "Hey, if I gotta bow, you should too." "Why aren't they kneeling? They're being disrespectful." "This is for our kingdom, respect it!" Our society sees Black disruption on any level as a threat to be immediately shut down. Almost all of the organizations created by Blacks to help and support Blacks have been destroyed, and with newly released FBI files, we now know the depth of FBI surveillance of Dr. Martin Luther King Jr.'s life. So, what does disruption look like? Can we learn to disrupt empire from Shadrach, Meshack, and Abednego? In a time of "alternate facts," it will take a village to summon the strength to overcome and outpower the love of empire. We will now turn our attention to theological disruption in which violence is not ruled out.

A THEOLOGICAL PARADIGM OF VIOLENCE AND CIVIL DISRUPTION

Jesus would be on the streets of Ferguson protesting the senseless death of Michael Brown. Jesus would have been with the people who lamented Tamir Rice's death. Jesus would insist on dismantling the prison-industrial complex. Jesus was just that type of person. While he could not take up every issue of his day, the Gospels indicate that he would still be controversial, upset by what is happening in the church, and persisting in the *missio Dei*. Jesus was a civil disrupter, which is seen as he aggressively and violently disrupted commerce in a church setting that was blaspheming his Father. Civil disruption was part of his worldview structure, but we have lost that image of Jesus. Besides having European features, our Jesus is docile, passive, and nonthreatening. If this were true of the real Jesus (and of his disciples), the Christian movement would have been halted at its beginning. Jesus disrupted almost everything first-century people thought about deity. He was in solidarity with those who were suffering, oppressed, marginalized, and disenfranchised. A nonpolitical Jesus is both absurd and fictional. The Western Jesus has been made in the image of Whiteness. It is time to disrupt that image and engage with the Jesus of civil, social, political, and theological disruption. Here, we have a missiology for the wild.

Consequently, it is important to discuss how and when violence is used and when that violence is justified, especially when religion is invoked.[7] Violence and responses to violence are labeled "just" and "unjust" by the groups within societal structures. Violence in response to what a state defines as a "just cause" is not only acceptable but also may be deemed moral or even holy. More importantly, once the public or society has deemed war and violence as just, the line connected to God becomes visible.[8] For example, following the attacks of 9/11, the war on Al-Qaeda and the Taliban was deemed a "holy war" by certain media outlets. To compound that, President George W. Bush repeatedly stated that he had "prayed" about and "asked God" for wisdom regarding his decision to invade Iraq. This type of socioreligious discourse aids in accepting the murder of children and innocent bystanders as a result of this "holy" war. "God's will" is further used to enact violence against religious groups such as Muslims. Violence, in this sense, is seen as a form of justice against "those people." Further, Wade Clark Roof reminds us that civil religious rhetoric can be just as dangerous as the violence itself, because it involves both nationalism and constructs of identity.[9] This union of religious and political rhetoric creates myths within the public arena in which God is "on our side" and "with us." These myths are powerful ideological vehicles for promoting violence through military force.[10]

A type of social mythology is used by a nation-state to take "just" actions when it is harmed or threatened. When combined with God and religion,

---

[7]Some content in this section is adapted from Daniel White Hodge, "The Pedagogy of Hip Hop in Teaching Missiology: Exploring a Project Based Learning Environment Using Elements of Hip Hop Culture as the Curriculum," in *Transforming Teaching for Mission: Educational Theory and Practice* (Wilmore, KY: First Fruits, 2014).

[8]Joseph S. Tuman, *Communicating Terror: The Rhetorical Dimensions of Terrorism*, 2nd ed. (Thousand Oaks, CA: Sage, 2010), 67-72.

[9]Wade Clark Roof, "American Presidential Rhetoric from Ronald Reagan to George W. Bush: Another Look at Civil Religion," *Social Compass* 56, no. 2 (2009). Also see Kevin Coe and David Domke, "Petitioners or Prophets? Presidential Discourse, God, and the Ascendancy of Religious Conservatives," *Journal of Communication* 56 (2006); Tuman, *Communicating Terror*, 122-26. We look at presidents here because, arguably, they have some of the biggest influence over political, religious, and economic rhetoric. As noted in Coe and Domke's as well as Tuman's works, presidents greatly influence how a nation-state recognizes not just terrorism and its evils but also to the extent the people within that system will agree to violence, war, and death to those who oppose "God's nation."

[10]Roof, "American Presidential Rhetoric."

this mythology suggests that "God's nation" is given the right to invoke war on those that persecute it. Roof says,

> The myth of a Chosen Nation arises out of the Hebrew Bible and suggests that Americans are exceptional in having a covenant with God: they are the New Israel in the language of the early Puritans. A second myth of origin—Nature's Nation, emerging out of the Enlightenment and Deism—gave rise to the notion that the United States arose out of the natural order, and that the country reflects the way God had intended things to be from the beginning of time. Building upon both of these foundational myths, the Millennial Nation myth implies that God chose America to bless the nations of the world with the unfolding of a golden age. The last two are obviously complementary: one looking to the beginning of time, the other looking to the end of time.[11]

When a people believes they are "God's nation," that nation's actions are thought to be sanctioned by God. Further, any suffering inflicted on the "other side" is overlooked and considered just.

Myth, in this sense, is dangerous: it typically leads to more violence. However, it touches on one's identity, and we have learned from the American Religious Identification Survey that religion and personal identity are tied closely together. And when a nation's leader, who is "God's servant," uses socioreligious rhetoric at a time of fear, panic, and social threats, the acceptance of violence and suffering is increased. Roof observes,

> Myths are the means by which a nation affirms its deepest identities and frames its rationale for political action; they are the elementary, yet profound, stories giving meaning and purpose to the collective life of a people; they evoke the imagination, so crucial to national self-understanding. Functioning largely at the unconscious level in the minds of citizens, they are activated though ritual, and particularly during times of national threat.[12]

A nation's mythology encourages the public to look at national threats as a threat to God. Moreover, when leaders embrace the ideas of "how it should be" and "what God wants," the instinct to kill, murder, and destroy "the other" becomes powerful. Roof says, "In such moments myths are easily absolutized, or turned into hardened, reified realities taken to be literally

---

[11]Ibid., 288.
[12]Ibid., 287.

true." As historian Richard T. Hughes points out, in such moments of fear and panic the myth can be a comfort for citizens.[13]

Recently, religious rhetoric has been used increasingly by US presidents. Roger Smith notes that "George W. Bush has used more religious rhetoric than his predecessors and has used it in distinct ways."[14] More specifically,

> Ronald Reagan initiated a new era in which "God" references per presidential address more than doubled compared to presidents from FDR through Jimmy Carter. George W. Bush ranks highest in references per address and references per 1,000 words, exceeding even Reagan. In contrast, though Bill Clinton and George H. W. Bush invoked God more often per address than pre-Reagan presidents, their rate per 1,000 words was roughly that of those predecessors. The second Bush and Reagan also adopted the prophetic posture in 47% of their addresses, compared to 0% for pre-Reagan Democrats, 5% for pre-Reagan Republicans, and 15% for the first Bush and Clinton, all statistically significant differences. Both presidents, but especially Bush, made prophetic statements most often in relation to the role of the United States in promoting freedom in the world.[15]

This type of rhetoric and public discourse flirts dangerously with what Coe and Domke call the "Divine vision for US foreign policy."[16] Because the president is the "head of the nation," public opinion often follows the president's lead. The mix of politics and religion, however, is nothing new in the United States. Billy Graham is noted as one of the first Western Christian evangelicals to begin urging presidents to "convert" and "choose a religion" for the "moral state of the nation."[17] This picked up speed during the 1960s when Roman Catholic John Kennedy was elected as president (a controversy at the time). It continued throughout various presidential terms, bringing this rhetoric into the present where we see little to no line dividing church and state. The socioreligious rhetoric runs dangerously

---

[13]Richard T. Hughes, *Myths Americans Live By* (Champaign: University of Illinois Press, 2003).

[14]Rogers M. Smith, "Religious Rhetoric and the Ethics of Public Discourse," *Political Theory* 36, no. 2 (2008): 279.

[15]Ibid., 280. For an even broader examination of socioreligious rhetoric in the context of justified violence, see also Kevin Coe and David Domke's work on presidential discourse and the ascendancy of religious conservatives (Coe and Domke, "Petitioners or Prophets?").

[16]Ibid.

[17]See documentary *God in America*, in which noted scholars document the rise of Billy Graham and examines the connections between church and state (David Belton, "God in America," PBS, 2010).

close to that of countries such as Iran and Afghanistan, where religion, state, country, and Allah are interrelated. Thus, it has become simpler for presiding presidents to invoke "prayer," "war," and "God" while still having most of the nation support them in that decision.

On a macro level, people want payback and retribution when they feel wronged or attacked. This sense of payback often takes the form of maximum revenge, particularly after national events such as 9/11, ISIS attacks on US citizens, and events labeled as "terrorism." In other words, the people want revenge, and they want it immediately. This vengeance is justified when "innocent lives" are taken and especially when dominant society is struck at the center of what they believe to be sacred (e.g., economic and religious symbols). The notion of an "eye for an eye" is warranted, and the public wants it used against any who would come against "us" or attempt to destroy "us." Rhetoric such as "freedom," "take back," "never forget," "one nation," "proud American," "God's country," and "our nation" appeal to the public's religious formation and identity. These, in turn, encourage mob rule, which after the events of 9/11 has created a "new world" in which violence against "bad guys" is accepted and at times required.[18] More importantly, the Brown skin of those accused of "terrorism" and having a "savage lifestyle" give the public even more of a license to kill, murder, and seek retribution.[19]

Violence is expected and even desired in response to violent acts against "us." While some were outraged over the war in Iraq, the public largely supported the war because it was "just" in the sense that the United States, "God's country," was retaliating against an aggressor. The ensuing logic was that the aggressors were, in fact, attacking God. This type of violence is accepted and even required by the public.

These worldviews and ideologies are troubling, vexing, and problematic, to say the least—especially for missiologists. It benefits those in dominant structures and encourages those in positions of racial dominance to act

---

[18]For example, bumper stickers and T-shirts that read "Terrorist Hunting License" or "The Marines: We Arrange a Meeting Between Terrorists and God" are typical discourses that skirt the lines of socioreligious rhetoric and, tinged with humor, give license to kill those who are bad.
[19]Hughes, *Myths Americans Live By*; Coe and Domke, "Petitioners or Prophets?"; and Tuman, *Communicating Terror*.

violently in the name of God. They ignore truth and, under a religious guise, grant absolute certainty to myths.

Yet when those in urban communities suffer similar violence, it is neither seen nor valued as important by the public at large. In the face of violence against them, Blacks and urban ethnic minorities are encouraged to be non-violent. Still, the broader United States uses violence as a means of establishing "peace" and legitimizes that violence as normative. In extreme examples such as 9/11, it is part of God's retribution toward enemies. As is the case in the Baltimore uprisings, cries of "stop the violence" and "we need peace in our city" were heard, yet rarely are these directed toward the police and systems that produce pain and death, as in the cases of Freddie Gray, Tamir Rice, Trayvon Martin, and Laquan McDonald.

Whose pain, suffering, and story is valued, told, supported, and avenged? Is it wrong that gang members engage in some of the same retaliatory methods that the US military uses when one of their own is killed? Is it morally wrong to say that one death is valued over another? How do we contend with a God who appears to be on one side? Because of this double standard, voices within Hip Hop culture and rap music call out this injustice. Tricia Rose tells us that "Rap arose in a postindustrial city context in which artists and listeners are able to shape their own social community through the music."[20] Rose also says that Hip Hop is a source of alternative identity formation and social status for youth in a community with "war like conditions."[21] Michael Eric Dyson argues that Hip Hoppers are able to conjure up a certain type of capital from the misery and pain of inner-city living. Dyson contends that "Hip-hoppers joined pleasure and rage while turning the details of their difficult lives into craft and capital."[22] Hip Hoppers have called attention to the ghetto and argued that it too is valid, real, and worthy of the same retribution and vindication as the broader United States, even if it means getting revenge by violent means.

---

[20]Tricia Rose, *The Hip Hop Wars: What We Talk About When We Talk About Hip Hop—and Why It Matters* (New York: Basic Civitas, 2008), 78-85.

[21]Ibid., 34.

[22]Michael Eric Dyson, *Between God and Gangsta Rap: Bearing Witness to Black Culture* (New York: Oxford University Press, 1996), 177.

Ice Cube intones:

It's time to take a trip to the suburbs
Let 'em see a nigga invasion
Point blank on a Caucasian
Cock the hammer didn't crack no smile
Take me to your house, pal[23]

In this song, Ice Cube describes what might happen if ignoring such issues continues. As noted in chapter two, in Ice Cube's third album he converts to Nation of Islam and acts as God's agent within his songs to bring "death to all White Devils" who are nonbelievers of Allah. To the naked eye and ear, one might consider this to be "obscene" and "too violent." Yet these are similar discourses to those of Ronald Reagan, George H. W. Bush, and George W. Bush in describing the "insurgents" who invaded "our country."[24] One must ask, What is the difference?

Such narratives closely resemble the violence in patriotic speech in which attacking and killing is celebrated through religious discourse. In other words, hegemonic violence is celebrated and glorified, but insurgent and urban violence is not. The uprisings that took place in Baltimore after the death of Freddie Gray are an example. Pastors, celebrities, and pundits on both sides of the aisle had a set of prescribed messages for the Baltimore protesters. "Why are you doing this," "Stop the violence," and "You don't get nothing out of violence" types of comments were sent to the protestors. Former NFL player Ray Lewis even recorded a video pleading with "his people" to "stop the violence" and that "this is not the way." Were the same messages sent to the Baltimore police department? Where were there national outcry and prescribed directives for the armed security units attacking peaceful protestors?

The US military has killed thousands of Iraqi civilians, and that is defended and branded as heroic. But when White American civilians die, it is an atrocity. Moreover, if the police gun down unarmed Black youth, it is regarded as okay; if rappers talk about anger and revenge, they are "animals" and "predators"—a threat to public safety. What's the difference? There is none. And the Hip Hop community, along with many others in

---

[23]Ice Cube, "AmeriKKKa's Most Wanted," *AmeriKKKa's Most Wanted*, Greene Street Studios, 1990.
[24]Smith, "Religious Rhetoric and the Ethics of Public Discourse"; Coe and Domke, "Petitioners or Prophets?"

socially conscious communities, sees and have experienced this. We live in a racist, hierarchical society. Kelly Brown Douglas observes, "That which practically convicts a black person for her or his own murder is an 'element' of stand-your ground culture. It is a deadly secretion, replete with religious legitimation, generated by America's surreptitious narrative of Anglo-Saxon exceptionalism."[25]

What then is violence? It would seem that mainstream America has developed their own canon for violence when it justifies their own pain and suffering. Should it not also, however, be the case for those who have suffered under oppressive and racist conditions for centuries? This is a difficult question to contend with, partly because it assumes a type of power that most Christians, including some ethnic minorities, are unwilling or afraid to deal with. It involves taking back power for the purpose of safety and justification. It is the same power that David Walker, Nat Turner, and Toussaint Louverture took up in the past and used as a theological means of justice, freedom, and righteousness for their people.

Historically, we praise White men who did the same thing: George Washington, Ulysses Grant, Abraham Lincoln, Franklin Roosevelt. At some point these men employed Christian ideology to use violence to benefit Americans and advance American exceptionalism. Yet ethnic minorities are told to keep the peace, forgive our enemies, turn the other cheek, not repay violence with violence, and ignore the bloodshed. Where is God in this? What do we do when there is no justice because the system has failed? How long would America hold out if ISIS continually killed people in this country? Could we forgive Osama bin Laden? These difficult questions are dealt with accurately in the Bible—if we are willing to remove our ideological blinders.

Far too often White supremacy demands that minorities avoid conflict at all costs. Whites in key leadership positions in mission agencies fear open conflict; when someone raises an issue that causes discomfort, the response is to blame the person raising the issue rather than to look at the issue itself. Characteristically, the emphasis is on being polite; dealing with an issue is considered impolite, rude, or out of line—in some cases leading

---

[25]Kelly Brown Douglas, *Stand Your Ground: Black Bodies and the Justice of God* (Maryknoll, NY: Orbis Books, 2015), 49.

to the termination of that person's employment.[26] This of course leads to more destructive relationships and continuing racism. However, if a macro issue, such as terrorism or illegal immigration, is raised by a White authority, it's okay to eliminate the conflict or threat at any cost and by any means necessary. This confounding double standard on violence does not make sense; nor is it justified. Nonviolence is derived from a privileged and typically sheltered position. Some will ask, What about Martin Luther King Jr.? Didn't he advocate for nonviolence? Yes, but violence was necessary to reach certain goals. Here is what King said at a speech to the American Psychological Association in Washington, DC, in 1967:

> Urban riots must now be recognized as durable social phenomena. They may be deplored, but they are there and should be understood. Urban riots are a special form of violence. They are not insurrections. The rioters are not seeking to seize territory or to attain control of institutions. They are mainly intended to shock the white community. They are a distorted form of social protest. The looting which is their principal feature serves many functions. It enables the most enraged and deprived Negro to take hold of consumer goods with the ease the white man does by using his purse. Often the Negro does not even want what he takes; he wants the experience of taking. But most of all, alienated from society and knowing that this society cherishes property above people, he is shocking it by abusing property rights. There are thus elements of emotional catharsis in the violent act. This may explain why most cities in which riots have occurred have not had a repetition, even though the causative conditions remain. It is also noteworthy that the amount of physical harm done to white people other than police is infinitesimal and in Detroit whites and Negroes looted in unity. . . .
>
>   The policymakers of the white society have caused the darkness; they create discrimination; they structured slums; and they perpetuate unemployment, ignorance and poverty. It is incontestable and deplorable that Negroes have committed crimes; but they are derivative crimes. They are born of the greater crimes of the white society. When we ask Negroes to abide by the law, let us also demand that the white man abide by law in the ghettos.[27]

---

[26]Kenneth Jones and Tema Okun, *Dismantling Racism: A Workbook for Social Change Groups* (Amherst, MA: Peace Development Fund, 2001).

[27]Martin Luther King Jr., "The Role of the Behavioral Scientist in the Civil Rights Movement," speech to the American Psychological Association, Washington, DC, 1967, www.apa.org/monitor/features/king-challenge.

King also questioned the framework of the "dream." He wondered what Blacks were coming into and whether it was enough to demand equality with White America. These are typically not the quotes we see from the popularized MLK figure in contemporary American society. Once again, Whites do not want to deal with the conflict of their own racism and a legacy of hate that emanates from their own communities.

Violence should not be a goal. Violence is not the answer. Violence should never be the first action taken. However, though our society lives by those words, it does not abide by those principles in practice. Ethnic minorities, in particular Blacks, have had to endure the hard heel of White violence, and in turn they are asked to be patient while that heel digs itself into their bodies, their families, their finances, and even their lives. What then does justice look like in that realm? This is what groups such as Black Lives Matter are after. In reality it is not much different than what the civil rights movement was asking for six decades ago. We must reflect on these uncomfortable questions theologically and then create a praxiological response if we truly seek justice. As activist and sociologist Keeanga-Yamahtta Taylor lets us know,

> Police brutality has been a consistent badge of inferiority and second-class citizenship. When the police enforce the law inconsistently and become the agents of lawlessness and disorder, it serves as a tangible reminder of the incompleteness of formal equality. You cannot truly be free when the police are able to set upon you at will, for no particular reason at all.[28]

Part of having a theology of the wild is looking at something like evangelism not as proselytizing but as social protest in the wild (e.g., oppressive systems). It is about having an evangelism that disrupts the principalities and powers that sustain economic inequality, racial injustice, and the marginalization of those who do not conform to enforced social norms. Jesus is manifested in protest. Much of what Jesus did was a protest against his era. It is important to take on that spirit of protest and disruption, which does not just challenge or call out injustice but does something about it, even if it means death. In that spirit, in the wild, we begin to see what that type of

---

[28]Keeanga-Yamahtta Taylor, *From #BlackLivesMatter to Black Liberation* (Chicago: Haymarket Books, 2016), 108.

evangelism might mean for ethnic minorities and how they are included in the narrative of Jesus. Taking on police brutality and state-sponsored violence against Black bodies is not easy. But if Christians do nothing, who will take the challenge and bear the weight? Who will carry on in the spirit of the three Hebrew men?

FINAL REFLECTIONS ON A MISSIOLOGY IN THE WILD FOR WHITE SISTERS AND BROTHERS

In 2015, Kelly Brown Douglas boldly stated,

> Today, the Manifest Destiny stand-your-ground-culture war is fueled by the presence of a black man living in the White House. There is no greater challenge to America's grand narrative of Anglo-Saxon exceptionalism than a black president. This represents a complete encroachment upon the space reserved for cherished white property. It is no surprise, therefore that stand-your-ground culture has asserted itself in an aggressive and unrelenting manner.[29]

When it comes to White power in ministry organizations, it is common to hear statements such as, "She is a good White person; she is trying, at least, but she's still not there." In this era of sociopolitical contention, that is both unacceptable and cowardly. Thus, it is difficult for many Whites to lay down their power and fathom a true power shift toward ethnic minorities. It is even more difficult for White cisgender, heterosexual, Christian evangelical males to embrace intercultural competence—especially in a space rooted in protest and disruption. We presently are in a polarizing age. If you are reading and tracking with this text, you are either (1) an ethnic minority sitting in a seminary class that has been dominated by White theologians, or (2) a self-aware White person who is trying to undo your White supremacist notions. I have been told that the people who actually need this kind of information typically check out early. I am okay with that. They need to leave. I do not want to sound callous, but they will probably live the rest of their lives in racial, cultural, and White ignorance.

This text is designed to help racially diverse people converse and think through what Christian protest and social disruption looks like within a

---

[29]Douglas, *Stand Your Ground*, 130-31.

missiological context. If it is your first introduction to dealing with race and ethnicity, this text can be rough. It is not meant to be *the* guide for the future but one of many emerging voices in this generation. This section is for those White sisters and brothers who are socially, culturally, and racially conscious and want to continue to learn and do the hard work of justice. Here is a space for those who identify as racially White or ethnically Euro-American to think through what a missiology in the wild *might* be. Part of the beginning to this journey is the ability and strength to lay down power and listen to marginalized voices.

Many ethnic-minority authors, pastors, directors, filmmakers, and leaders have yelled this from the mountaintops. I make no new case for this action. If you are still in a place where you question the relevance of critical race theory, the reality of a multiethnic understanding of deity, and the significance of ethnic-minority narratives, I am going spend some time exploring these elements and why they are still an issue. While I am all for inclusion and unity, I am not for unity that neglects ethnic-minority voices, position, and power. If this means ethnic people groups have to start with few White people in leadership, that is okay. We are in a time of crisis, and the time to be nice has passed.

A White missiology for the wild might begin with (1) relationships, (2) the ability to lament, (3) the capacity for doubt and ambiguity, and (4) a trinitarian framework that reflects suffering, contextual relevance, lament, and ethnic value in protest. This includes an understanding of God as multifaceted and complex. A missiology for the wild cherishes *missio Dei* and makes Jesus central. For the most part, though, this Jesus will not be recognizable by typical standards. As Tupac and The Outlawz contend, we're talking about a Jesus who "smokes like we smoke" and "drinks like we drink."[30] A blunt-smoking Jesus? That is not the catechesis of the irreverent— it is pure blasphemy! Yet within *that* blasphemy, something much larger is at work, a fundamental attempt to make a Jesus, who has been Westernized and Americanized, as Stephen Bevans has contended, much more contextual and biblically centered.[31]

This construct, while nothing revolutionary, includes two central themes: *capacity* and *margin*. First, *capacity* is the ability to receive or contain. It is the

---

[30]Tupac Shakur and The Outlawz, "Black Jesus," *Still I Rise*, Interscope Records, 1999.
[31]Stephen B. Bevans, *Models of Contextual Theology* (Maryknoll, NY: Orbis Books, 1992), 10-11.

ability to allow space for the nitty-gritty of life, God, theology, and Christianity. It is the capability to imagine beyond what has been taught and to reimagine what could be, might be, and is. It is in many regards the space to converse and communicate, to debate, to challenge, to build, to tear down, to grow, to remain still, and to connect with a God who can be much more mighty and diverse (in every regard) than we could ever imagine or dream. Capacity is the missiological primer for those seeking a Christ-following community.

Capacity, likewise, is a space of receiving. A central premise of a missiology for the wild is receiving those in the wild as well as those who appear to be tame. For the most part, missiologists have had the capacity to take in various aspects of different cultures as part of their central training.[32] Yet they have faltered in receiving those cultural differences as their own and for seeing God within those non-Western cultures.[33] Thus missionally minded persons must have the capacity to receive not just knowledge but also change, reform, and edification. They will be open to receiving those who traditionally have been rejected in the Christian context,[34] and to receiving those who would in other circles be labeled as troublemakers for questioning, challenging, and disrupting the "elders." A missiology in the wild has the capacity for receiving individuals such as these. It will receive and embrace a culture like Hip Hop, with all its nefarious behavior and illicit sexuality, as a whole, not merely for a special "Hip Hop Sunday" worship service.

Capacity also means patience. Within a church of capacity, patience is crucial because it is the red blood cells that enrich the bloodlines of the

---

[32]David J. Bosch, *Transforming Mission: Paradigm Shifts in Theology of Mission*, American Society of Missiology Series (Maryknoll, NY: Orbis Books, 1991); Robert Hall Glover and J. Herbert Kane, *The Progress of World-Wide Missions*, rev. ed. (New York: Harper, 1960); Glenn Rogers, *A Basic Introduction to Missions and Missiology* (Bedford, TX: Mission and Ministry Resources, 2003).

[33]Soong-Chan Rah, *The Next Evangelicalism: Freeing the Church from Western Cultural Captivity* (Downers Grove, IL: InterVarsity Press, 2009), 77-83; Amos Yong, "Race and Racialization in a Post-Racist Evangelicalism: A View from Asian America," in *Aliens in the Promised Land: Why Minority Leadership Is Overlooked in White Christian Churches and Institutions*, ed. Anthony B. Bradley (Phillipsburg, NJ: P&R, 2013), 53-55; and Andrew F. Walls, *The Cross-Cultural Process in Christian History: Studies in the Transmission and Appropriation of Faith* (Maryknoll, NY: Orbis Books, 2002), 177-91.

[34]One of the crucial elements of post–civil rights emerging adults' critique of the older generation is that there is no room, that is, capacity, for people like a transgender Black male, a lesbian Latina, or a strong-language-using Black woman who interrupts Black civil rights male preachers at a democratic speech. Missiologists of the wild not only need to make room for such people also but create platforms for them so God can work through them.

community. It means having space to disagree with someone yet respect and value who they are and what they believe. It is the patience to engage with tough issues and not walk away, split up, or turn to violence (unless those are the only options remaining because the issue, person, or worldview have become dangerous to people). It is the patience to move away from absolutes and have the capacity to entertain a more robust view of multiplicity. A missiology of and in the wild will be a place that has the bandwidth large enough to sit amid the strains of disagreement and ideological differences. It might mean lengthy and at times volatile discussions and engagement with issues such as the prison-industrial complex, police terrorism, and colonialism within missions. We need to have a large enough capacity to withstand the pressures and conflicts these types of topics can create. This is a missiology in the wild.

Second, building on capacity, a missiology of the wild will have margin. *Margin* is defined as the extreme point of a boundary. I want to be clear that there *are* boundaries. What I am describing here, which is, for that matter, the premise of this book, is not that there are no boundaries or limits to how we engage culture. But, much like Hiebert's bounded- and centered-set frameworks, we must not begin with the tight margins of the past century of Christianity (e.g., a centered set is a much more applicable approach).[35]

Margin gives space the needed space to be what it is. In contextual terms, it allows people to have time in dealing with an issue. Margin disrupts the love of ideological structures and absolutes, because margin allows people to be human without regard to what a particular creed may require them to do. That is, margin begins with where people are, not with where we, or the leadership, want them to be. It gives slack to the humanness of life. It allows room for mistakes and setbacks. But a missiology of margin also means that tradition is not overlooked or destroyed.[36] In fact, in many regards, tradition is part of the hybrid engine that drives a new pathway forward. The old must be interwoven with the new.

---

[35]Paul G. Hiebert, "Conversion, Culture, and Cognitive Categories," *Gospel in Context* 1, no. 4 (1978): 26.

[36]For many post-soul and post–civil rights young people, liturgy and a connection to tradition is crucial in their faith development. So, while traditions that have no margin or capacity push away those who are younger, a fixture on contextualizing traditions (e.g. communion, singing of hymns, Christmas carols) is needed and desired.

Taking all this into account, I advocate for protest and disruption at all levels. Protest and disruption does not always manifest itself as a group of people holding banners or posters in a downtown area. In fact, while that still has its place, the most effective disruption comes when you, as a White person, are told a "joke" about ethnic minorities and choose to push back, challenge that racism, and help instruct that individual. You will be a disrupter for justice when you protest a policy that will adversely affect your ethnic-minority coworkers. You will be a protester when you fight a Christian tradition that hurts people of color. You will disrupt when you yield your spot on a conference stage. Those are elements of protest and disruption that can help, not solve, the issues of injustice and inequality. None of this is easy. Diversity is difficult to maintain. It means actually doing work. Homogeneity is popular because it is much simpler and neater. I invite you into the mess; I invite you into the wild to join us in the mire of racism, sexism, populism, White racism, and White supremacy.[37]

---

[37]When I visited Ferguson, Missouri, White activists told me (1) they will not or cannot lead the movement, and (2) they use their privilege to surround Black residents when police officers approach the scene during a protest. They told me that they use body cameras to film the police officers and that the police do not like using violent methods on Whites. Thus, they help in the protest by leveraging their White privilege.

10

CONCLUSIONS

Toward a Missiology of the Wild and the Secular, Sacred, and Profane

IN THIS BOOK **I** ARGUE FOR missiological engagement within post–civil rights contexts in the United States and focus on Hip Hop theology as a missiological tool for radical engagement of emerging adult populations in the wild. I have suggested new conceptual models for domestic missions within an ever-growing multiethnic demographic. My argument is based on three disciplines: missiology, Hip Hop studies, and youth ministry.

Engaging with and developing innovative pathways will be neither easy nor simple. Yet that should not stop us. Nothing good is within easy grasp or comes without tedious labor. So I would like to propose some dream-making moves for the future—dreams of what might and could be. Some of these dreams are already turning into reality; others are still off in the distance. So, where are we, and where do we need to go?

Hip Hop provides the space to dream. It allows space for dissent, questions, and doubt. So much of our Christian faith is built on a foundation of certainty and knowledge. Moreover, Western Christianity tries to defend God when God needs no defense. Apologetics is not what Jesus had in mind when he laid out the Great Commission. Questions are for those who need a stronger walk with God or for those who are on a quest for God. When space is created for dissent and disruption, faith grows. That space exists in my church, LaSalle Street Church in Chicago. Dissent is not only allowed but also encouraged. It is part of the ethos of the church. Conservatives, centrists, progressives, and liberals all gather under one roof. The community spectrum in ideology is wide—it is not homogeneous by any stretch of the imagination. Hip Hop creates space to have that dissent and openly question aspects of faith that do not make sense or have errors in them. Part of this dissent and disruption will also mean dismantling the dominion of absolute truth and policies.

Embracing Hip Hop means working as a community in the process of seeking truth and knowledge. Knowledge and truth, then, are owned by the community, not an individual. For faith to develop, we must own our faith for ourselves. Far too often, knowledge and truth come from the pastoral team without any connection to what it means for the messy life of the person in the pew. I am not suggesting a revival of individualism; I'm suggesting that our knowledge of truth is evolving with Jesus at the center of it all. Hip Hop theology moves us in that direction. In some cases, Hip Hop theology includes conflict, tension, and communication in one package. Tension is sure to come, but that is part of the deal. There is no fuzzy, kumbaya feeling about doing the difficult work of faith development in the wild. Yes, we should strive for equality. Yes, we should not always focus on the serious. But in relationships, the messier it gets, the more opportunity there is for the gospel to be seen and relationships to grow.

Hip Hop theology is also a place to *experience* rather than merely know. For too long the Christian faith has emphasized knowing and having the assurance of being right. Hip Hop theology shakes those foundations while still allowing Jesus to remain central. Further, it creates the opportunity for experiencing intimacy rather than just knowing what's theologically or ethically correct. Experiential components of faith development are a central aspect of urban, post-soul, millennial pedagogy; passive learning in churches—a pastor delivering knowledge from up front and then assuming all is well—is nonexistent for this group. Further, there has been no embracing, thought development, or interaction with the people or engagement with active learning. I am not suggesting the elimination of all sermons—in certain contexts they can be used as a starting point in faith development.

Hip Hop theology lives out the sacred, the secular, and the profane, all of which are important for a missiology and church in the wild. I return to the opening lyrics of Kanye and Jay-Z's track "No Church in the Wild," in which this question is posed: "What's a god to a nonbeliever? / Who don't believe in anything?"[1] The answer: nothing. But if that God is shown to be the God of the Bible (loving, forgiving, challenging, mysterious, and ambiguous at times), then the post-soul generation might be willing to listen. There is the possibility of having a relationship with the God who has been hidden from the wild spaces. The God who exists in a space of questions and dissent. A God like that is different than a God who is a perfectionist. And while I am not asserting we dumb down God or create a god who is not God, I am suggesting we show the God of the Bible. The God who can be bargained with. The God who chooses a liar (Abraham) to begin a nation. The God who allows the story of Jonah to end on a miserable note. The God who invites sorcerers (the magi who came to Jesus) into Jesus' story. The God who includes women in all areas of the biblical narrative. The God who sent Jesus to disrupt all religious structures and ideologies of his day. That God. I would like to get to know that God. And I know that God could begin the conversation with a person in the wild. The goal here is not to convert that nonbeliever but to have a relationship of meaning and significance rooted in God. Allow God to do the work—not you, not the church, not knowledge, and not absolute truth. God through Jesus, using Hip Hop as a vehicle, is part of that process.

For too long the "gospel presentation" has outweighed other components of ministry and missiology. For example, an organization that feeds the homeless might want to present the gospel prior to feeding the people. The organization has a captive audience—they are hungry and will stay to hear a message. This is a manipulative way to present Jesus; the communication myth is that the truth is the truth no matter the style or space it is communicated in. Or a short-term mission might ignore systemic racism or structural oppression in a community by sending prayers and well wishes to them rather than action. After all, God will somehow miraculously work it out. These approaches are faulty and defective, and they do more harm than good. I dream of a missiology that puts into use Abraham Maslow's hierarchy of needs but nevertheless keeps the gospel message throughout its approach.[2]

---

[1]Jay-Z and Kanye West featuring Frank Ocean, "No Church in the Wild," *Watch the Throne*, Roc-A-Fella, Roc Nation, Def Jam, 2012.

[2]Other stages were added in later works. I use this adapted model to illustrate an engagement process similar to Maslow's original model as a potential means of engagement for ministry

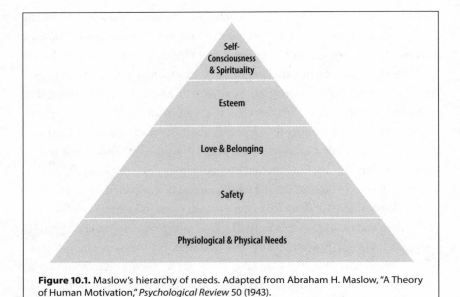

Figure 10.1. Maslow's hierarchy of needs. Adapted from Abraham H. Maslow, "A Theory of Human Motivation," *Psychological Review* 50 (1943).

Meeting physiological and physical needs is the starting point of approach and engagement (see fig. 10.1).[3] Physiological needs are basic for a person or an entire community to flourish: air, food, clean accessible water, monetary accessibility, shelter, and sleep. Unfortunately, these are not being met for some in the urban post-soul context (e.g., Flint, Michigan). When basic needs are not being met, it is difficult to pay attention to the gospel message. In these situations, God seems to care only about numbers and not people.

Once physiology and physical needs are met, safety is crucial. For example, getting to school is troublesome for some young people because they need to cross gang territories. A young Latino told me, "Who wants to go to school once you've gotten your ass kicked? I don't. They can suspend me all day for absences—my safety is important." One solution is having leaders and volunteers pick up and drop off the students. This will ensure the students arrive at school on time without being harassed or even beaten. Safety is crucial in missiological engagement.

organizations. See Maslow's hierarchy of needs in Abraham H. Maslow, "A Theory of Human Motivation," *Psychological Review* 50 (1943).

[3]This model is done well within CCD models or when Christians use holistic principles in their ministries, seeing people as more than numbers and prospects for salvation.

The next level in Maslow's hierarchy is love. Christians often have difficulty loving "the other" because we assume we are commanded to judge, critique, and call out "sin." This is erroneous and does nothing to bring people closer to God. Love is critical to engaging those in dire need. Love means putting aside our own thoughts, worldviews, beliefs, and hopes and accepting others as they are, much like Jesus does with us.

Love means bringing people such as our LGBT brothers and sisters into the fold even though they might not measure up to what we think a Christian should be. Too often we want to debate, criticize, and hate rather than love. Love is central; it makes things happen for God. Creating spaces for love means deconstructing our concepts of Christianity and the Christian lifestyle. We must accept people for who they are right now, not for what we hope them to become. This is at the core of being part of something and feeling like you belong.

LaSalle Street Church creates spaces to love others and build a sense of belonging. During the week, families located throughout the city host other church members for potluck dinners. The goal is to be together as a church family. The church's mission statement places Jesus' life and teachings at the center; everything else is open to interpretation. This creates space for dialogue and community while belonging.

The next step in the hierarchy of needs is esteem, which is critical. Esteem involves the empowerment and personal development of people in and among community. Prestige is important as well. Far too often a person's voice is lost, especially among oppressed peoples (e.g., women and ethnic minorities). A multiethnic perspective is needed. This means empowering those from the dominant culture to train, educate, and help those who have no voice to do greater things than the privileged do. This process is not to be done in a top-down, authoritarian manner but rather in tandem with the person. I dream of a ministry that listens to what is needed for a person's esteem and then is a catalyst in helping meet those needs. I dream of an organization that sits with and supports people as they grow in both their personal and community esteem.

Self-consciousness and spirituality are the final needs in Maslow's hierarchy. Though many want to begin with these, I suggest that these needs should be addressed only when the other needs are met. Most seminaries begin here and have little regard for the previous areas. This is detrimental to a person's spiritual development. In the Hip Hop community, other areas of life must be dealt with before a person connects with their deeper consciousness and spirituality. Once all other needs have been met, space is opened to hear the gospel and how it might work in a person's life. This is fundamental to missiology.

Through this process, the *missio Dei* is seen and embraced. This is the process of bringing the gospel—the good news—to those in need in a contextual, interculturally appropriate, ethnically rooted, and decolonized manner. The good Samaritan Bible Story reveals that all of these other areas of need must be met prior to the stereotypical gospel presentation. I dream of seeing ethnic minorities being part of this process. I dream of White Christians deconstructing racial dominions of power. The messiness within the *missio Dei* is good.

We will end by examining one last area for developing a missiology in the wild: the neo-secular sacred. Within the gray and blurred areas between the sacred and the profane lies what I call the "neo-secular sacred" within Hip Hop.[4] The neo-secular sacred concept comes directly out of the theology of the profane. It is the area in which the day-to-day, nitty-gritty aspects of life in hostile contexts come together yet still find connections with God. I contend that God, from whatever faith tradition, is able to love and comfort the individual in this state. God is not worried about dogmatic norms or liturgical traditions—only the heart of the individual. God's *love* of the sinful nature of humanity draws God close to the person. There are moments in Hip Hoppers' lives when they decide to engage and embrace the profane element of life and give up any sign of being sacred. The neo-secular sacred is exactly that: the ability to be loved in that mess and funk, accept life as it is, yet still approach God with an as-you-are ethos rather than an attempt to get it right prior to engaging God. The neo-secular sacred searches for

---

[4]This concept is derived from my doctoral research on Tupac's gospel message, and it has loosely and indirectly been discussed by scholars such as Craig Detweiler and Barry Taylor, *A Matrix of Meanings: Finding God in Pop Culture* (Grand Rapids: Baker Academic, 2003); Tom Beaudoin, *Virtual Faith: The Irreverent Spiritual Quest of Generation X* (San Francisco: Jossey-Bass, 1998); David Dark, *Everyday Apocalypse: The Sacred Revealed in Radiohead, the Simpsons, and Other Pop Culture Icons* (Grand Rapids: Brazos Press, 2002); and John Drane, *The McDonaldization of the Church: Spirituality, Creativity, and the Future of the Church* (London: Darton, Longman & Todd, 2000).

deeper meaning in life and embraces the not-so-perfect aspects of life. The neo-secular sacred embraces the quirks, idiosyncrasies, peculiarities, oddities, bad sides, and rough nature of urban living. In other words, without sin, there is nothing to love; with sin, we are made to be loved by God.

Inside this theological paradigm, there is the opportunity to be human and authentic with ourselves and God. The neo-secular sacred within Hip Hop has existed from its inception as both a culture and musical genre, yet it is more fully revealed in artists such as Tupac who possess contradictions in their lives. For Hip Hop, the neo-secular sacred answers some of the questions they have regarding pain and suffering, but is also gives hope in something beyond this life. It also allows for human contradictions to be acknowledged and exhibited as they work out the details with God. Christina Zanfagna states that "hip-hop's spirituality—its mystical allusions, contradictory images, and profaned exterior—can be 'tricky' and elusive to the average outsider not born or 'baptized' in the streets."[5]

Overall, the neo-secular sacred within Hip Hop is about finding a transcendental force in the most obscure places of life—the profane. The neo-secular sacred has three major elements that take shape within Hip Hop:

1. *It has panentheistic characteristics.* The term *panentheism* (not *pantheism*)[6] was first coined by K. C. F. Krause (1781–1832) for the view that God is in all things, while at the same time God is greater than all things. This particular element of the neo-secular sacred sees the world and God as interdependent for their fulfillment and to create a better earth. In other words, God needs imperfect humans to fulfill God's ultimate *missio Dei*—which for Hip Hoppers is largely a message of hope and peace. This means that God acknowledges the profane within life and uses it to promote that same life, because that is the nitty-gritty of real life. This also means that God can use

---

[5]Zanfagna further states, "It follows that rap music embodies the pluralism of current religious energies as well as the spiritual touchstones of hip-hop's exalted predecessors, such as James Brown's wails for black power, the 'sexual healing' of Marvin Gaye, Stevie Wonder's prophetic preaching, the meditative bedroom lamentations of Al Green, and Prince's lyrics of erotic deliverance." Christina Zanfagna, "Under the Blasphemous W(RAP): Locating the 'Spirit' in Hip-Hop," *Pacific Review of Ethnomusicology* 12 (2006): 3-4.

[6]Pantheism views God as in all, and all as in God. It believes that all religions contain some truth; God is too big to be enclosed in any one religion.

anything God so chooses to use in order to broaden the message of love and peace. So, if God is in all things, that must include the secular, or that which is supposedly devoid of God—even things that are not so pretty. This fits nicely into an omnipresent theological paradigm that sees God in everything, including things most people care not to talk about. Panentheism, therefore, begins to find God in the oddest places: the murk, the mire, and the sludge of life. This is a key element of the neo-secular sacred theological concept.

2. *Life has good and bad elements.* In this view, life is seen as both evil and good; both are always present. Whether we choose evil or good, or a mixture of both, is an ongoing element to life. From the neo-secular sacred theological position, both are present in our lives, and all of us are capable of ultimate good and ultimate evil. If we deny one or the other, we essentially deny ourselves. The secular—which the Oxford Dictionary defines as "Of or pertaining to the world"—is a constant within all of us (unless we remove ourselves from contemporary society). The neo-secular sacred is this: embracing these two conflicting forces in our lives. They are what make us "tick."

3. *It rejects religionism as the only form of reaching God.* Religionism is the belief and ritualistic practice of dogmatic and rigorous religious traditions. Religionism believes that God is found at a higher level within those rituals. Religionism is either-or, never both-and or maybe. Religionism, when practiced, produces simplistic outcomes for many people, and the neo-secular sacred rejects it as the only way of attaining a direct line with God. Religionism, for many Hip Hoppers, covers up reality and fosters inauthentic behaviors. For Hip Hop, religionism explains away life, problems, hurts, hopes, and dreams. It systematizes God and makes God into an iconic idol that no one can reach. Within religionism, rational answers are preferred over the ambiguous and indefinite conclusions of neo-secular sacred theology. For the Hip Hopper, when religion turns systematic, rigid, and impractical, it renders itself useless. Regarding religion, Paul Tillich observes:

> Religion opens up the depth of man's spiritual life which is usually covered by the dust of our daily life and the noise of our secular work.

> It gives us the experience of the Holy, of the something which is un-touchable, awe-inspiring, an ultimate meaning, the source of ultimate courage. This is the glory of what we call religion. But beside the glory lies its shame. It makes itself the ultimate and despises the secular realm. It makes its myths and doctrines, its rites and laws into ultimates and persecutes those who do not subject themselves to it. It forgets that its own existence is a result of man's tragic estrangement from his true being. It forgets its own emergency character.[7]

The neo-secular sacred ultimately remembers its "emergency character" while also making room for Tillich's glory of the Holy. These two worlds co-exist within humans. This causes confusion for many, denial for others, and, for a few, acceptance of who we truly are: fallible yet capable of great deeds.

The neo-secular sacred within Hip Hop does not constrain people within narrow religious and doctrinal boundaries. Instead, it makes much more room for people to expand their knowledge about God. Thus, the neo-secular sacred is a better approach to spirituality by using Hip Hop as one of its vehicles. It allows the yin and yang of life to flow more naturally than religionism's guilt, shame, and rules, which no one can live up to.

Let's continue this conversation, explore new pathways, dismantle White supremacy, and use Hip Hop as the vehicle for missiological transformation, a missiology in the wild for twenty-first-century Christianity.

The time is now. God is at work in areas we cannot see with the naked eye. Our culture is ready. It's time for a church and missiology in the wild!

---

[7]Paul Tillich, *Theology of Culture* (New York: Oxford University Press, 1959), 9.

AFTERWORD

Wilbert R. Shenk

HIP **HOP CULTURE** presents a dynamic opportunity that ought to elicit ready response from missiologists. Of all the academic fields associated with the theology, faith, and history of the Christian movement, missiology is the one dedicated to working along the fault line between faith and unfaith that is always present in every culture. We see this fault line most readily in the new and uncharted "wild" places in contemporary culture. To test this assertion, I propose that we review the what, why, and how of missiology.

WHAT IS MISSIOLOGY?

Among academic fields of research and study, missiology probably is in early adulthood. Although we can find examples of missiological reflection from the early years of the nineteenth century, when the modern mission movement was emerging, it was at best tentative and provisional. Essentially, these early writings consisted of reports by missionaries on their daily life and experiences that could be used in mission magazines to acquaint supporters with their work. But critical reflection on missionary activity was rare. At the end of the nineteenth century, a German scholar-pastor named Gustav Warneck wrote the first missiology textbook. Within twenty years several academic journals devoted to mission studies were published in various languages and books about missionary work were produced. Across the twentieth century mission studies have gained academic recognition. Since 1965 schools of world mission or intercultural studies, attached to graduate seminaries or universities, have been founded in North America.

Missiology can be called an academic hybrid. It maintains its academic vitality only by staying connected to mission action. It draws on resources from multiple sources. The following analogy may help clarify the kind of training needed to become a missiologist. We take for granted that a medical doctor is trained through a combination of classroom study, laboratory work, and supervised internship in a hospital. The training to become a missiologist follows a similar pattern. To become a missiologist a person must study theology, history, anthropology, and linguistics—fields that are relevant to missionary work—and devote several years to reflecting on field experience combined with learning from the experience of other practitioners. Missiology detached from actual experience is of doubtful value.

WHY MISSIOLOGY?

While missiology is a relative newcomer in terms of academic study, we ought to recognize that the first reflection on mission is found in the New Testament. The Acts of the Apostles is made up of a series of crises that resulted from the first wave of missionary activity following Pentecost. Fundamental questions were being raised as traditional Jews encountered Gentiles. Their cultures clashed. It soon became evident that crosscultural evangelization was a big challenge. Indeed, the controversy engendered by those who insisted on maintaining the Jewish foundation versus the apostle Paul who championed evangelization of the Gentiles almost split the infant church. Jesus Christ clearly mandated his disciples to "go into all the world" with the gospel, but he did not warn the disciples that they would face difficult questions about culture and religious practice. If the mission of Jesus Christ was to be carried to "the Gentiles" as well as the Jews, the only way forward was the hard work of apostolic discernment and decision. All of this is further expounded in the Pauline Epistles. From this perspective missiological reflection is as old as the New Testament itself. Tragically, this integral relationship and vital interaction between church and mission did not last.

Church history shows that after the fourth century CE, *church* was increasingly separated from *mission*. In other words, the church came to be understood as the place where the "souls" of its members were nurtured and protected so that at death they would enter heaven. The local church was understood as having no direct connection with mission. Special people and religious orders engaged in "missionary work" beyond territorial Christendom. Members of the local congregation stayed home.

Groundbreaking work in New Testament and theological studies in the last half of the twentieth century has challenged this traditional understanding. It is now generally acknowledged that for the past two centuries we had a fundamentally wrong understanding of mission. It was asserted that the church is the source of mission, and missions are like appendages of the church. This is not consistent with the New Testament. For example, the Gospel of John emphasizes that God is the source of mission. The New Testament describes mission in trinitarian terms: God sends the Son into the world in the power of the Holy Spirit. Jesus sends his body, the church, empowered by the Holy Spirit to continue his mission to the whole world. *Sending* is integral to the nature of God.

Missiology has been leading the way in envisioning and implementing an understanding of mission based on the *missio Dei*, that is, the mission of God. This vision of a *missional church* is increasingly accepted as normative. But an enormous amount of work remains to be done to turn concept into reality. It is not easy to reverse course after more than fifteen centuries, during which a static understanding of the church was accepted as the norm. But we must not rest so long as the vast majority of local congregations across the world are not set free from this debilitating model.

HOW IS THE WORK OF MISSIOLOGY DONE?

Dutch missiologist Johannes Verkuyl said that the function of missiology could be compared to the service station. We depend on service stations to keep our cars, trucks, vans, and motorcycles running. A driver must stop periodically when a vehicle needs a new supply of fuel or requires an oil change. Everyone who drives a vehicle depends on the service station to provide the services every vehicle requires. Missiology plays a similar role. It produces and makes available the resources required to keep missions "on the road"—fuel, lubrication, repairs, information about road conditions, and maps. This metaphor is useful but not wholly adequate.

As demonstrated powerfully by this book, emerging new cultures—represented here by Hip Hop—are essentially unmapped territory. A first task when entering a strange area—whether that is geographical, cultural, or intellectual—is to conduct a reconnaissance survey and mark out paths that will assist those who wish to engage with this culture effectively. This will be followed by careful, accurate, and respectful descriptions of the cultural terrain, the languages spoken, cultural values, worldview, and folkways that define this people group. In other words, a careful ethnographic description must be developed. Special attention will be paid to the religious sensibilities of the people of this culture by engaging in sympathetic observation and dialogue with them.

Missiology as an academic field is always at risk. It will remain vital only so long as it stays engaged with missional frontiers. Daniel White Hodge has provided us with a map of the challenging terrain called Hip Hop culture. I pray that many others will join in the task of continuing exploration and missiological interpretation of this dynamic field. And may the fruits of these labors contribute to the continuing vitality of mission studies and the extension of the reign of God.

BIBLIOGRAPHY

Alper, Garth. "Making Sense Out of Postmodern Music?" *Popular Music and Society* 24, no. 4 (Winter 2000): 1.

Althaus-Reid, Marcella. *From Feminist Theology to Indecent Theology: Readings on Poverty, Sexual Identity and God.* London: SCM Press, 2004.

————. *Indecent Theology: Theological Perversions in Sex, Gender, and Politics.* New York: Routledge, 2000.

Alumkal, Antony W. "American Evangelicalism in the Post–Civil Rights Era: A Racial Formation Theory Analysis." *Sociology of Religion* 65, no. 3 (2004).

Arnal, William E., and Russell T. McCutcheon. *The Sacred Is the Profane: The Political Nature of "Religion."* New York: Oxford University Press, 2013.

Banks, L. William. *The Black Church in the U.S.: Its Origin, Growth, Contribution, & Outlook.* Chicago: Moody Press, 1972.

Barker, Greg. "God in America: How Religious Liberty Shaped America." DVD. New York: Corporation for Public Broadcasting, 2010.

Barkun, Michael. *Religion and the Racist Right: The Origins of the Christian Identity Movement.* Rev. ed. Chapel Hill: University of North Carolina Press, 1997.

Barros, Pedro Pita, and Nuno Garoupa. "An Economic Theory of Church Strictness." *The Economic Journal* 112, no. 481 (2002).

Battle, Michael. *The Black Church in America: African American Christian Spirituality.* Religious Life in America. Malden, MA: Blackwell, 2006.

Bauman, Zygmunt. "Postmodern Religion?" In *Religion, Modernity and Postmodernity,* edited by Paul Heelas. Malden, MA: Blackwell, 1998.

Beaudoin, Tom. *Virtual Faith: The Irreverent Spiritual Quest of Generation X.* San Francisco: Jossey Bass, 1998.

Bell, Daniel. *The Coming of a Post-Industrial Society: A Venture in Social Forecasting.* New York: Basic Books, 1973.

Belton, David. "God in America: How Religious Liberty Shaped America." DVD. New York: Corporation for Public Broadcasting, 2010.

Bennett, Lerone, Jr. *The Shaping of Black America*. New York: Penguin Books, 1993.

Best, Steven, and Douglas Kellner. *Postmodern Theory: Critical Interrogations*. New York: Guilford Press, 1991.

Betts, Raymond F. *A History of Popular Culture: More of Everything, Faster and Brighter*. New York: Routledge, 2004.

Bevans, Stephen B. *Models of Contextual Theology*. Maryknoll, NY: Orbis Books, 1992.

Bevans, Stephen B., and Roger P. Schroeder. *Constants in Context: A Theology of Mission for Today*. Maryknoll, NY: Orbis Books, 2004.

Beyerlein, Kraig, Jenny Trinitapoli, and Gary Adler. "The Effect of Religious Short-Term Mission Trips on Youth Civic Engagement." *Journal for the Scientific Study of Religion* 50, no. 4 (2011).

Block, Fred, Anna C. Korteweg, Kerry Woodward, Zach Schiller, and Imrul Mazid. "The Compassion Gap in American Poverty Policy." *Contexts* 5, no. 2 (2006).

Bodrick, Jabari. "The Myth of the Bootstrap." *Socioeconomic and Class Issues in Higher Education* (2015). www.naspa.org/constituent-groups/posts/the-myth-of-the-bootstrap.

Bonilla-Silva, Eduardo. *Racism Without Racists: Color-Blind Racism and the Persistence of Racial Inequality in America*. Lanham, MD: Rowman & Littlefield, 2013.

———. *White Supremacy and Racism in the Post–Civil Rights Era*. Boulder, CO: L. Rienner, 2001.

Bosch, David J. *Transforming Mission: Paradigm Shifts in Theology of Mission*. American Society of Missiology Series. Maryknoll, NY: Orbis Books, 1991.

Bowen, José Antonio. *Teaching Naked: How Moving Technology Out of Your College Classroom Will Improve Student Learning*. San Francisco: Jossey-Bass, 2012.

Boyd, Todd. *Am I Black Enough for You? Popular Culture from the 'Hood and Beyond*. Bloomington: Indiana University Press, 1997.

Bradley, Anthony B., ed. *Aliens in the Promised Land: Why Minority Leadership Is Overlooked in White Christian Churches and Institutions*. Phillipsburg, NJ: P&R, 2013.

———. *Black Scholars in White Space: New Vistas in African American Studies from the Christian Academy*. Eugene, OR: Wipf & Stock, 2015.

Brooks, Roy L. *Racial Justice in the Age of Obama*. Princeton, NJ: Princeton University Press, 2009.

Bynoe, Yvonne. *Stand and Deliver: Political Activism, Leadership, and Hip Hop Culture*. Brooklyn, NY: Soft Skull Press, 2004.

Carter, J. Kameron. *Race: A Theological Account*. New York: Oxford University Press, 2008.

Chang, Jeff. *Total Chaos: The Art and Aesthetics of Hip-Hop*. New York: Basic-Civitas Books, 2006.

Charnas, Dan. *The Big Payback: The History of the Business of Hip-Hop*. New York: New American Library, 2010.

Coe, Kevin, and David Domke. "Petitioners or Prophets? Presidential Discourse, God, and the Ascendancy of Religious Conservatives." *Journal of Communication* 56 (2006).

Cone, James H. *Black Theology and Black Power*. 5th ed. Maryknoll, NY: Orbis Books, 1997.

———. *A Black Theology of Liberation*. 20th anniv. ed. Maryknoll, NY: Orbis Books, 1990.

———. "The Blues: A Secular Spiritual." In *Sacred Music of the Secular City: From Blues to Rap*, edited by Jon Michael Spencer. Durham, NC: Duke University Press, 1992.

———. *The Cross and the Lynching Tree*. Maryknoll, NY: Orbis Books, 2011.

———. *God of the Oppressed*. Maryknoll, NY: Orbis Books, 1997.

———. *The Spirituals and the Blues: An Interpretation*. Maryknoll, NY: Orbis Books, 1991.

Conn, Harvie M. *Reaching the Unreached: The Old-New Challenge*. Phillipsburg, NJ: P&R, 1984.

Costen, Melva Wilson. Review of *Protest and Praise: Sacred Music of Black Religion*, by Jon Michael Spencer. *Theology Today* 48, no. 3 (1991).

Covert, Tawnya Adkins. "Consumption and Citizenship During the Second World War." *Journal of Consumer Culture* 3 (2003).

Cox, Harvey. *Religion in the Secular City: Toward a Postmodern Theology*. New York: Simon & Schuster, 1984.

Crandall, Ronald K. "Church Growth Movement." In *Contemporary American Religion*, edited by Wade Clark Roof. New York: Macmillan Reference, 1999.

Cupitt, Don. "Post-Christianity." In *Religion, Modernity and Postmodernity*, edited by Paul Heelas. Malden, MA: Blackwell, 1998.

Darity, William A., Jr. "Ethnomusicology." In *International Encyclopedia of the Social Sciences*, edited by William A. Darity Jr. Detroit: Macmillan Reference, 2008.

———. "Suburban Sprawl." In *International Encyclopedia of the Social Sciences*, edited by William A. Darity Jr. Detroit: Macmillan Reference, 2008.

Dark, David. *Everyday Apocalypse: The Sacred Revealed in Radiohead, the Simpsons, and Other Pop Culture Icons*. Grand Rapids: Brazos Press, 2002.

David, Jay, and Elaine Forman Crane. *Living Black in White America*. New York: Morrow, 1971.

Dean, Kenda Creasy. *Almost Christian: What the Faith of Our Teenagers Is Telling the American Church*. New York: Oxford University Press, 2010.

Delgado, Richard, and Jean Stefancic. "Critical Race Theory." In *New Dictionary of the History of Ideas*, edited by Maryanne Cline Horowitz. Detroit: Charles Scribner's, 2005.

Denzin, Norman K. *Images of Postmodern Society: Social Theory and Contemporary Cinema*. Thousand Oaks, CA: Sage, 1991.

Detweiler, Craig. *iGods: How Technology Shapes Our Spiritual and Social Lives*. Grand Rapids: Brazos Press, 2014.

Detweiler, Craig, and Barry Taylor. *A Matrix of Meanings: Finding God in Pop Culture*. Grand Rapids: Baker Academic, 2003.

DiAngelo, Robin. "White Fragility." *International Journal of Critical Pedagogy* 3, no. 3 (2011).

DJZ. "Kendrick Lamar Responded to Our Article About His Fear of God." *DJBooth*, May 9, 2017. http://djbooth.net/news/entry/2017-04-28-kendrick-lamar-god-response.

Douglas, Kelly Brown. *Sexuality and the Black Church: A Womanist Perspective*. Maryknoll, NY: Orbis Books, 1999.

———. *Stand Your Ground: Black Bodies and the Justice of God*. Maryknoll, NY: Orbis Books, 2015.

———. *What's Faith Got to Do with It? Black Bodies/Christian Souls*. Maryknoll, NY: Orbis Books, 2005.

Drane, John William. *After McDonaldization: Mission, Ministry, and Christian Discipleship in an Age of Uncertainty*. Grand Rapids: Baker Academic, 2008.

———. *The McDonaldization of the Church: Spirituality, Creativity, and the Future of the Church*. London: Darton, Longman & Todd, 2000.

Durkheim, Émile. *The Elementary Forms of the Religious Life*. New York: Free Press, 1965.

Dyson, Michael Eric. *Between God and Gangsta Rap: Bearing Witness to Black Culture*. New York: Oxford University Press, 1996.

———. *Holler If You Hear Me: Searching for Tupac Shakur*. New York: Basic Civitas, 2001.

———. *Is Bill Cosby Right? Or Has the Black Middle Class Lost Its Mind?* New York: Basic Civitas Books, 2005.

———. *Open Mike: Reflections on Philosophy, Race, Sex, Culture, and Religion.* New York: Basic Civitas, 2003.

Edwards, Herbert O. "Black Theology: Retrospect and Prospect." *Journal of Religious Thought*, no. 32 (1975).

Emerson, Michael O. *People of the Dream: Multiracial Congregations in the United States.* Princeton: Princeton University Press, 2010.

Emerson, Michael O., and Christian Smith. *Divided by Faith: Evangelical Religion and the Problem of Race in America.* New York: Oxford University Press, 2000.

Epstein, Heidi. "Re-Vamping the Cross: Diamanda Galas's Musical Mnemonic of Promiscuity." *Theology and Sexuality* 8, no. 15 (2001).

Ercoli, Ronald J. "Institutional Racism, the White Image of Jesus Christ, and Its Psychological Impact on African Americans." PhD diss., Illinois School of Professional Psychology, 1996.

Erskine, Noel Leo. "Rap, Reggae, and Religion." In *Noise and Spirit: The Religious and Spiritual Sensibilities of Rap Music*, edited by Anthony Pinn. New York: New York University Press, 2003.

Escobar, D. "Amos and Postmodernity: A Contemporary Critical and Reflective Perspective on the Interdependency of Ethics and Spirituality in the Latino-Hispanic American Reality." *Journal of Business Ethics* 103, no. 1 (2011).

Evans, James E. *We Have Been Believers: An African American Systematic Theology.* Minneapolis: Fortress Press, 1992.

Faulkner, Sandra L. "Concern with Craft: Using Ars Poetica as Criteria for Reading Research Poetry." *Qualitative Inquiry* 13, no. 2 (2007).

Franklin, John Hope, and Alfred A. Moss Jr. *From Slavery to Freedom: A History of African Americans.* 8th ed. New York: McGraw Hill, 2000.

Frazier, Franklin E., and Nathan Glazer. *The Negro Family in the United States.* Chicago: University of Chicago Press, 1966.

Freire, Paulo. *Pedagogy of the Oppressed.* Translated by Myra Bergman Ramos. 30th anniv. ed. New York: Continuum, 2000.

Funk, Robert Walter. *The Five Gospels: The Search for the Authentic Words of Jesus: New Translation and Commentary.* San Francisco: Harper Collins, 1993.

George, Nelson. *Buppies, B-Boys, Baps and Bohos: Notes on Post-Soul Black Culture.* New York: HarperCollins, 1992.

———. *Hip Hop America.* New York: Viking, 1998.

———. *Post-Soul Nation: The Explosive, Contradictory, Triumphant, and Tragic 1980s as Experienced by African Americans.* New York: Viking, 2004.

Gilkes, Cheryl Townsend. "Jesus Must Needs Go Through Samaria: Disestablishing the Mountains of Race and the Hegemony of Whiteness." In *Christology and Whiteness: What Would Jesus Do?*, edited by George Yancy. New York: Routledge, 2012.

Gilmour, Michael J. *Gods and Guitars: Seeking the Sacred in Post-1960s Popular Music.* Waco, TX: Baylor University Press, 2009.

Glover, Robert Hall, and J. Herbert Kane. *The Progress of World-Wide Missions.* New York: Harper, 1960.

Gutiérrez, Gustavo. *On Job: God-Talk and the Suffering of the Innocent.* Maryknoll, NY: Orbis Books, 1987.

Hailey, Foster. "Billy Graham Urges Restraint in Sit-Ins." *New York Times*, April 18, 1963.

Hart, William David. "Jesus, Whiteness, and the Disinherited." In *Christology and Whiteness: What Would Jesus Do?*, edited by George Yancy. New York: Routledge, 2012.

Harvey, Jennifer. "What Would Zacchaeus Do?" In *Christology and Whiteness: What Would Jesus Do?*, edited by George Yancy. New York: Routledge, 2012.

Hattery, Angela J, and Earl Smith. *African American Families.* Thousand Oaks, CA: Sage, 2007.

Hebdige, Dick. "Postmodernism and 'the Other Side.'" In *Cultural Theory and Popular Culture: A Reader*, edited by John Storey. London: Pearson Prentice Hall, 1998.

Heelas, Paul, Martin David, and Paul Morris. *Religion, Modernity and Postmodernity.* Religion and Modernity. Malden, MA: Blackwell 1998.

Hempton, David. *Evangelical Disenchantment: Nine Portraits of Faith and Doubt.* New Haven: Yale University Press, 2008.

Heyward, Carter. *Saving Jesus from Those Who Are Right: Rethinking What It Means to Be a Christian.* Minneapolis: Fortress Press, 1999.

Hiebert, Paul G. "Beyond Anti-Colonialism to Globalism." *Missiology* 19, no. 3 (1991).

———. "Conversion, Culture, and Cognitive Categories." *Gospel in Context* 1, no. 4 (1978).

Hine, Darlene Clark, William C Hine, and Stanley Harrold. *The African American Odyssey.* Vol. 1. 4th ed. Upper Saddle River, NJ: Prentice Hall, 2010.

———. *African Americans: A Concise History.* 5th ed. Upper Saddle River, NJ: Pearson, 2014.

Hocking, William Ernest. *Re-Thinking Missions: A Laymen's Inquiry After One Hundred Years.* New York: Harper, 1932.

Hodge, Daniel White. *Heaven Has a Ghetto: The Missiological Gospel and Theology of Tupac Amaru Shakur*. Saarbrucken, Germany: VDM Verlag Dr. Müller Academic, 2009.

———. *Hip Hop's Hostile Gospel: A Post-Soul Theological Exploration*. Edited by Warren Goldstein. Studies on Critical Research in Religion 6. Boston: Brill Academic, 2017.

———. "Hip Hop's Prophetic: Exploring Tupac and Lauryn Hill Using Ethnolifehistory." In *Religion in Hip Hop ("the Volume")*, edited by Monica Miller, Bernard "Bun B" Freeman, and Anthony B. Pinn. London: Bloomsbury Academic, 2015.

———. "No Church in the Wild: An Ontology of Hip Hop's Socio-Religious Discourse in Tupac's 'Black Jesuz.'" *Nomos* 10 (2013).

———. "No Church in the Wild: Hip Hop Theology and Mission." *Missiology: An International Review* 41, no. 1 (2013).

———. *The Soul of Hip Hop: Rims, Timbs, and a Cultural Theology*. Downers Grove, IL: InterVarsity Press, 2010.

Hodge, Daniel White, and Pablo Otaola. "Reconciling the Divide: The Need for Contextual and Just Models of Fundraising in Vocational Youth Ministry." *Journal of Youth Ministry* 15, no. 1 (2016).

hooks, bell. *Yearning: Race, Gender, and Cultural Politics*. Boston: South End Press, 1990.

Howell, Brian, and Rachel Dorr. "Evangelical Pilgrimage: The Language of Short-Term Missions." *Journal of Communication & Religion* 30, no. 2 (2007).

Howell, Brian M. "Mission to Nowhere: Putting Short-Term Missions into Context." *International Bulletin of Missionary Research* 33, no. 4 (2009).

———. *Short-Term Mission: An Ethnography of Christian Travel Narrative and Experience*. Downers Grove, IL: IVP Academic, 2012.

Hughes, Richard T. *Myths Americans Live By*. Champaign: University of Illinois Press, 2003.

Hurt, Byron. *Hip Hop: Beyond Beats and Rhymes*. DVD. Northampton, MA: Media Education Foundation, 2006.

Iannaccone, Laurence R. "Religious Practice: A Human Capital Approach." *Journal for the Scientific Study of Religion* 29, no. 3 (1990).

Iverem, Esther. "The Politics of 'Fuck It' and the Passion to Be a Free Black." In *Tough Love: The Life and Death of Tupac Shakur*, edited by Michael Datcher and Kwame Alexander. Alexandria, VA: Black Words Books, 1997.

Jeffry, Paul. "Beyond Good Intentions: Short-Term Mission Trips." *Christian Century* 118, no. 34 (2001).

Jenkins, Philip. *The Next Christendom: The Coming of Global Christianity*. New York: Oxford University Press, 2011. Kindle ed.

Jennings, Willie James. *The Christian Imagination: Theology and the Origins of Race*. New Haven: Yale University Press, 2010.

Johnson, Andre E., ed. *Urban God Talk: Constructing a Hip Hop Spirituality*. Lanham, MA: Lexington Books, 2013.

Jones, Kenneth, and Tema Okun. *Dismantling Racism: A Workbook for Social Change Groups*. Amherst, MA: Peace Development Fund, 2001.

Jones, Robert P. *The End of White Christian America*. New York: Simon & Schuster, 2016. Kindle ed.

Jones, Robert P., Daniel Cox, Betsy Cooper, and Rachel Lienesch. "Anxiety, Nostalgia, and Mistrust: Findings from the 2015 American Values Survey." Washington, DC: Public Religion Research Institute, 2015.

———. "The Divide Over America's Future: 1950 or 2050?" Washington, DC: Public Religion Research Institute, 2016.

Jones, William R. *Is God a White Racist? A Preamble to Black Theology*. C. Eric Lincoln Series on Black Religion. Garden City, NY: Anchor, 1973.

Jordan, Winthrop D. *The White Man's Burden: Historical Origins of Racism in the United States*. London: Oxford University Press, 1980.

———. *White Over Black: American Attitudes Toward the Negro, 1550–1812*. Chapel Hill: University of North Carolina Press, 2012.

Joseph, Jamal. *Tupac Shakur: Legacy*. New York: Atria Books, 2006.

Kain & Abel, with Master P. "Black Jesus." *The 7 Sins*. Priority Records, 1996.

Kant, Immanuel. "Physical Geography." In *Race and Enlightenment: A Reader*, edited by Emmanuel Chukwudi Eze. Malden, MA: Blackwell, 1997.

Kärkkäinen, Veli-Matti. *Christology: A Global Introduction*. Grand Rapids: Baker Academic, 2003.

Kelley, Robin D. G. *Race Rebels: Culture, Politics, and the Black Working Class*. New York: Free Press, 1994.

Kim, Rebecca Y. "Made in the U.S.A.: Second-Generation Korean American Campus Evangelicals." In *Asian American Youth: Culture, Identity, and Ethnicity*, edited by Jennifer Lee and Min Zhou. New York: Routledge, 2004.

Kinnaman, David, and Aly Hawkins. *You Lost Me: Why Young Christians Are Leaving Church—and Rethinking Faith*. Grand Rapids: Baker, 2011.

Kirk-Duggan, Cheryl A. "The Theo-Poetic Theological Ethics of Lauryn Hill and Tupac Shakur." In *Creating Ourselves: African Americans and Hispanic*

Americans on Popular Culture and Religious Expression, edited by Anthony B. Pinn and Benjamín Valentín. Durham, NC: Duke University Press, 2009.

Kirk-Duggan, Cheryl, and Marlon Hall. *Wake Up! Hip-Hop, Christianity, and the Black Church*. Nashville: Abingdon Press, 2011.

Kirk, J. Andrew. "Following Modernity and Postmodernity: A Missiological Investigation." *Mission Studies* 17, no. 1 (2000).

Kitwana, Bakari. *Why White Kids Love Hip-Hop: Wankstas, Wiggers, Wannabes, and the New Reality of Race in America*. New York: Basic Civitas Books, 2005.

Kraft, Charles H. *Communication Theory for Christian Witness*. Maryknoll, NY: Orbis Books, 1991.

Kreitzer, L. Joseph. *The New Testament in Fiction and Film: On Reversing the Hermeneutical Flow*. Biblical Seminar 17. Sheffield, UK: JSOT Press, 1993.

———. *The Old Testament in Fiction and Film: On Reversing the Hermeneutical Flow*. Biblical Seminar 24. Sheffield, UK: Sheffield Academic Press, 1994.

Kyle, Richard G. *Evangelicalism: An Americanized Christianity*. New Brunswick, NJ: Transaction, 2006.

Lamar, Kendrick. "The Heart Pt. 2." *Overly Dedicated*. Top Dawg Entertainment, 2010.

Lash, Scott. "Postmodernism as Humanism? Urban Space and Social Theory." In *Theories of Modernity and Postmodernity*, edited by Bryan S. Turner. Thousand Oaks, CA: Sage, 1990.

———. *Sociology of Postmodernism*. New York: Routledge, 1990.

Leonard, Neil. *Jazz: Myth and Religion*. New York: Oxford University Press, 1987.

Lincoln, Eric C., and Lawrence H. Mamiya. *The Black Church in the African American Experience*. Durham, NC: Duke University Press, 1990.

Lindsay, Michael D., and Robert Wuthnow. "Financing Faith: Religion and Strategic Philanthropy." *Journal for the Scientific Study of Religion* 49, no. 1 (2010).

Logo, Luis, Alan Cooperman, Cary Funk, Gregory A. Smith, Erin O'Connell, and Sandra Stencel. "'Nones' on the Rise." Pew Research Center, October 9, 2012. www.pewforum.org/2012/10/09/nones-on-the-rise.

Lupton, Robert D. *Toxic Charity: How Churches and Charities Hurt Those They Help (and How to Reverse It)*. New York: HarperOne, 2011.

Lynch, Gordon. *Understanding Theology and Popular Culture*. Malden, MA: Blackwell, 2005.

Lynskey, Dorian. "Kendrick Lamar: 'I Am Trayvon Martin. I'm All of These Kids.'" *The Guardian*, June 21, 2015.

Lyotard, Jean-François. *The Postmodern Condition: A Report on Knowledge*. Minneapolis: University of Minnesota Press, 1984.

Major, Brenda, Alison Blodorn, and Gregory Major Blascovich. "The Threat of Increasing Diversity: Why Many White Americans Support Trump in the 2016 Presidential Election." *Group Processes & Intergroup Relations*, October 20, 2016. http://journals.sagepub.com/doi/pdf/10.1177/1368430216677304.

Malone, E. F. "Kerygmatic Theology." In *New Catholic Encyclopedia*. Detroit: Gale, 2003.

Marks, Jonathan. "Racism: Scientific." In *Encyclopedia of Race and Racism*, edited by Patrick L. Mason. Detroit: Macmillan Reference, 2013.

Maslow, Abraham H. "A Theory of Human Motivation." *Psychological Review* 50 (1943).

———. *Toward a Psychology of Being*. New York: Van Nostrand, 1968.

Matusitz, Jonathan. *Terrorism and Communication: A Critical Introduction*. Thousand Oaks, CA: Sage, 2013.

McClatchy, Rick. "Building a Multi-Cultural Organization in Texas." *Review & Expositor* 109, no. 1 (2012).

McCrisken, Trevor B. "Exceptionalism." In *Encyclopedia of American Foreign Policy*, edited by Richard Dean Burns, Alexander DeConde, and Fredrik Logevall. New York: Charles Scribner's, 2002.

McFarland, Daniel A., and Reuben J. Thomas. "Bowling Young: How Youth Voluntary Associations Influence Adult Political Participation." *American Sociological Review* 71, no. 3 (2006).

McGavran, Donald A. *Effective Evangelism: A Theological Mandate*. Phillipsburg, NJ: P&R, 1988.

McGlathery, Marla Frederick, and Traci Griffin. "'Becoming Conservative, Becoming White?' Black Evangelicals and the Para-Church Movement." In *This Side of Heaven: Race, Ethnicity, and Christian Faith*, edited by Robert J. Priest and Alvaro L. Nieves. New York: Oxford University Press, 2007.

McIntosh, Peggy. "White Privilege: Unpacking the Invisible Knapsack." *Independent School* 49, no. 2 (1990).

McRobbie, Angela. "Recent Rhythms of Sex and Race in Popular Music." *Media, Culture & Society* 17, no. 2 (1995).

"Meritocracy." In *International Encyclopedia of the Social Sciences*, edited by William A. Darity Jr. Detroit: Macmillan Reference, 2008.

Miles, Jack. *Christ: A Crisis in the Life of God*. New York: Vintage eBooks, 2011.

———. *Christ: A Crisis in the Life of God*. New York: Alfred A. Knopf, 2001.

Miller, Monica R. *Religion and Hip Hop*. New York: Routledge, 2013.

Moltmann, Jürgen. *The Way of Jesus Christ: Christology in Messianic Dimensions*. San Francisco: HarperSanFrancisco, 1990.

Morgan, Joan. *When Chickenheads Come Home to Roost: My Life as a Hip-Hop Feminist*. New York: Simon & Schuster, 1999.

Moss, Otis. "Real Big: The Hip Hop Pastor as Postmodern Prophet." In *The Gospel Remix: Reaching the Hip Hop Generation*, edited by Ralph Watkins. Valley Forge, PA: Judson Press, 2007.

Neal, Mark Anthony. *New Black Man*. New York: Routledge, 2005.

———. "Sold Out on Soul: The Corporate Annexation of Black Popular Music." *Popular Music and Society* 21, no. 3 (1997).

———. *Soul Babies: Black Popular Culture and the Post-Soul Aesthetic*. New York: Routledge, 2002.

———. *What the Music Said: Black Popular Music and Black Public Culture*. New York: Routledge, 1999.

Nelson, Angela S. "Theology in the Hip-Hop of Public Enemy and Kool Moe Dee." In *The Emergency of Black and the Emergence of Rap*, edited by Jon Michael Spencer. Durham, NC: Duke University Press, 1991.

Nelson, George. *Where Did Our Love Go? The Rise and Fall of the Motown Sound*. Music in the American Life. 2nd ed. Chicago: University of Illinois Press, 2007.

Nieves, Alvaro L. "An Applied Research Strategy for Christian Organizations." In *This Side of Heaven: Race, Ethnicity, and Christian Faith*, edited by Robert J. Priest and Alvaro L. Nieves. New York: Oxford University Press, 2007.

Nouwen, Henri J. M. *In the Name of Jesus: Reflections on Christian Leadership*. New York: Crossroad, 1989.

Ogunnaike, Lola. "The Passion of Kayne West." *Rolling Stone*, February 9, 2006.

One, K. R. S. *The Gospel of Hip Hop: First Instrument*. Brooklyn, NY: power-House: I Am Hip Hop, 2009.

Otto, Rudolph. *The Idea of the Holy*. 2nd ed. London: Oxford University Press, 1950.

Paris, Peter J. *The Social Teaching of the Black Churches*. Philadelphia: Fortress Press, 1985.

Paton, David MacDonald. *Christian Missions and the Judgement of God*. London: SCM Press, 1953.

Peralta, Stacy. *Crips and Bloods: Made in America*. Verso Entertainment, 2009.

Perkins, John. *With Justice for All*. Ventura, CA: Regal Books, 1982.

Perry, Samuel. "Diversity, Donations, and Disadvantage: The Implications of Personal Fundraising for Racial Diversity in Evangelical Outreach Ministries." *Review of Religious Research* 53, no. 4 (2012).

———. "Racial Habitus, Moral Conflict, and White Moral Hegemony Within Interracial Evangelical Organizations." *Qualitative Sociology* 35, no. 1 (2012).

———. "Social Capital, Race, and Personal Fundraising in Evangelical Outreach Ministries." *Journal for the Scientific Study of Religion* 52, no. 1 (2013).

Peters, Ken. "Tupac Vs." DVD. Dennon Entertainment, 2001.

Pineda-Madrid, Nancy. "In Search of a Theology of Suffering, Latinamente." In *The Ties That Bind: African American and Hispanic American/Latino/a Theologies in Dialogue*, edited by Anthony B. Pinn and Benjamin Valentin. New York: Continuum, 2001.

Pinkney, Alphonso. *Black Americans*. 5th ed. Upper Saddle River, NJ: Prentice Hall, 2000.

Pinn, Anthony B. *The Black Church in the Post–Civil Rights Era*. Maryknoll, NY: Orbis Books, 2002.

———. "Black Theology in Historical Perspective: Articulating the Quest for Subjectivity." In *The Ties That Bind: African American and Hispanic American/Latino/a Theologies in Dialogue*, edited by Anthony B. Pinn and Benjamin Valentin. New York: Continuum, 2001.

———. *Embodiment and the New Shape of Black Theology*. Religion, Race, and Ethnicity. New York: New York University Press, 2010.

———. *The End of God-Talk: An African American Humanist Theology*. New York: Oxford University Press, 2012.

———. *Terror and Triumph: The Nature of Black Religion*. Minneapolis: Fortress Press, 2003.

———. *Why Lord? Suffering and Evil in Black Theology*. New York: Continuum, 1995.

Potter, Russell A. *Spectacular Vernaculars: Hip-Hop and the Politics of Postmodernism*. New York: State University of New York Press, 1995.

Powell, Kara E., and Chap Clark. *Sticky Faith: Everyday Ideas to Build Lasting Faith in Your Kids*. Grand Rapids: Zondervan, 2011.

Powery, Luke A. *Spirit Speech: Lament and Celebration in Preaching*. Nashville: Abingdon Press, 2009.

Price, Emmett G., III, ed. *The Black Church and Hip Hop Culture: Toward Bridging the Generational Divide*. New York: Scarecrow, 2011.

Priest, Robert J., and Joseph Paul Priest. "'They See Everything, and Understand Nothing': Short-Term Mission and Service Learning." *Missiology: An International Review* 36, no. 1 (2008).

Priest, Robert J., Terry Dischinger, Steve Rasmussen, and C. M. Brown. "Researching the Short-Term Mission Movement." *Missiology: An International Review* 34, no. 4 (2006).

Putnam, Robert D. *Bowling Alone: The Collapse and Revival of American Community.* New York: Simon & Schuster, 2000.

Putnam, Robert. "As Social Issues Drive Young from Church, Leaders Try to Keep Them." Interview by David Green. NPR, Losing Our Religion series, January 18, 2013. www.npr.org/series/169065270/losing-our-religion.

Rah, Soong-Chan. *The Next Evangelicalism: Freeing the Church from Western Cultural Captivity.* Downers Grove, IL: InterVarsity Press, 2009.

———. *Prophetic Lament: A Call for Justice in Troubled Times.* Downers Grove, IL: IVP Academic, 2015.

Reed, Stephen A. Review of *Exodus* by Terence E. Fretheim. *Theology Today* 48, no. 3 (1991).

Reed, Teresa L. *The Holy Profane: Religion in Black Popular Music.* Lexington: University Press of Kentucky, 2003.

Renaud, Myriam. "Myths Debunked: Why Did White Evangelical Christians Vote for Trump?" University of Chicago, January 19, 2017. https://divinity.uchicago.edu/sightings/myths-debunked-why-did-white-evangelical-christians-vote-trump.

Richards, Sally. *Futurenet: The Past, Present, and Future of the Internet as Told by Its Creators and Visionaries.* New York: Wiley, 2002.

Ritzer, George. *The McDonaldization of Society.* Thousand Oaks, CA: Pine Forge Press, 2004.

Rogers, Glenn. *A Basic Introduction to Missions and Missiology.* Bedford, TX: Mission and Ministry Resources, 2003.

Roof, Wade Clark. "American Presidential Rhetoric from Ronald Reagan to George W. Bush: Another Look at Civil Religion." *Social Compass* 56, no. 2 (2009).

Root, Andrew, and Kenda Creasy Dean. *The Theological Turn in Youth Ministry.* Downers Grove, IL: InterVarsity Press, 2011.

Rose, Tricia. *The Hip Hop Wars: What We Talk About When We Talk About Hip Hop—and Why It Matters.* New York: Basic Civitas, 2008.

Said, Edward W. *Orientalism.* 25th anniv. ed. New York: Vintage Books, 2003.

Seay, Davin Neely Mary. *Stairway to Heaven: The Spiritual Roots of Rock 'N' Roll, from the King and Little Richard to Prince and Amy Grant.* New York: Ballantine Books, 1986.

Sekou, Osagyefo Uhuru. *Gods, Gays, and Guns: Essays on Religion and the Future of Democracy.* Cambridge, MA: Campbell & Cannon Press, 2011.

Shakur, Tupac, and The Outlawz. "Black Jesuz." *Still I Rise.* Interscope Records, 1999.

Sharpley-Whiting, T. Denean. *Pimps Up, Ho's Down: Hip Hop's Hold on Young Black Women*. New York: New York University Press, 2007.

Shenk, Wilbert R. *Changing Frontiers of Mission*. Maryknoll, NY: Orbis Books, 1999.

————. *Enlarging the Story: Perspectives on Writing World Christian History*. Maryknoll, NY: Orbis Books, 2002.

————. *The Transfiguration of Mission: Biblical, Theological & Historical Foundations*. Missionary Studies 12. Scottdale, PA: Herald Press, 1993.

Sides, Josh. *L.A. City Limits: African American Los Angeles from the Great Depression to the Present*. Los Angeles, CA: University of California Press, 2003.

Sills, David M. "Missiology in a Changing World Since World War II." *American Society of Missiology* 21 (2012).

Singleton, Harry H. *White Religion and Black Humanity*. Lanham, MD: University Press of America, 2012.

Singleton, Micah. "To Pimp a Butterfly: Kendrick Lamar's New Album Is Perfect." Vox Media, March 19, 2015. www.theverge.com/2015/3/19/8257319/kendrick -lamar-album-review-to-pimp-a-butterfly.

Smith, Christian, David Sikkink, and Jason Bailey. "Devotion in Dixie and Beyond: A Test of the 'Shibley Thesis' on the Effects of Regional Origin and Migration on Individual Religiosity." *Journal for the Scientific Study of Religion* 37 (1998).

Smith, Christian, Kari Christoffersen, Marie Davidson, Hilary Herzog, and Patricia Snell. *Lost in Transition: The Dark Side of Emerging Adulthood*. New York: Oxford University Press, 2011.

Smith, Christian, with Patricia Snell. *Souls in Transition: The Religious and Spiritual Lives of Emerging Adults*. New York: Oxford University Press, 2009.

Smith, Donald K. *Creating Understanding: A Handbook for Christian Communication Across Cultural Landscapes*. Grand Rapids: Zondervan, 1992.

Smith, Efrem, and Phil Jackson. *The Hip Hop Church: Connecting with the Movement Shaping Our Culture*. Downers Grove, IL: InterVarsity Press, 2005.

Smith, Gregory A. "America's Changing Religious Landscape." *Pew Research Center*. May 12, 2015. www.pewforum.org/files/2015/05/RLS-08-26-full-report.pdf.

Smith, Gregory A., and Jessica Martínez. "How the Faithful Voted: A Preliminary 2016 Analysis." *Pew Research Center*. November 9, 2016. www.pewresearch .org/fact-tank/2016/11/09/how-the-faithful-voted-a-preliminary-2016-analysis.

Smith, Rogers M. "Religious Rhetoric and the Ethics of Public Discourse." *Political Theory* 36, no. 2 (2008).

Soja, Edward W. *Postmetropolis: Critical Studies of Cities and Regions*. New York: Blackwell, 2000.

Spencer, Jon Michael. "Book Notes Rhapsody in Black: Utopian Aspirations." *Theology Today* 49, no. 2 (1992).

———, ed. *The Emergency of Black and the Emergence of Rap*. Black Sacred Music 5. Durham, NC: Duke University Press, 1991.

———. *The New Negroes and Their Music: The Success of the Harlem Renaissance*. Knoxville: University of Tennessee Press, 1997.

———. *Protest and Praise: Sacred Music of Black Religion*. Minneapolis: Fortress Press, 1990.

———, ed. *Sacred Music of the Secular City: From Blues to Rap*. Vol. 6. Durham, NC: Duke University Press, 1992.

———. *Sing a New Song: Liberating Black Hymnody*. Minneapolis: Fortress Press, 1995.

———. *Theological Music: An Introduction to Theomusicology*. Contributions to the Study of Music and Dance. New York: Greenwood Press, 1991.

Stapert, Calvin. *My Only Comfort: Death, Deliverance, and Discipleship in the Music of Bach*. Calvin Institute of Christian Worship Liturgical Studies Series. Grand Rapids: Eerdmans, 2000.

Stump, Roger W. "Regional Migration and Religious Commitment in the United States." *Journal for the Scientific Study of Religion* 23, no. 3 (1984).

Sullivan, Lawrence Eugene. *Enchanting Powers: Music in the World's Religions*. Religions of the World. Cambridge, MA: Harvard University Press, 1997.

Sunquist, Scott W. *The Unexpected Christian Century: The Reversal and Transformation of Global Christianity, 1900–2000*. Grand Rapids: Baker Academic, 2015.

Sylvan, Robin. *Traces of the Spirit: The Religious Dimensions of Popular Music*. New York: New York University Press, 2002.

Taylor, Keeanga-Yamahtta. *From #BlackLivesMatter to Black Liberation*. Chicago: Haymarket Books, 2016.

Taylor, Paul C. "Post-Black, Old Black." *African American Review* 41, no. 4 (2007).

Thompson, William E., and Joseph V. Hickey. *Society in Focus*. 7th ed. New York: Pearson Books, 2011.

Thurman, Howard. *Jesus and the Disinherited*. Boston: Beacon Press, 1976.

Tillich, Paul. *Theology of Culture*. New York: Oxford University Press, 1959.

Tocqueville, Alexis de. *Democracy in America*. Edited by Tom Griffith Ware. Wordsworth Classics of World Literature. Hertfordshire, UK: Wordsworth, 1998.

Trinitapoli, Jenny, and Stephen Vaisey. "The Transformative Role of Religious Experience: The Case of Short-Term Missions." *Social Forces* 88, no. 1 (2009).

Tuman, Joseph S. *Communicating Terror: The Rhetorical Dimensions of Terrorism.* 2nd ed. Thousand Oaks, CA: Sage, 2010.

Twiss, Richard. *Rescuing the Gospel from the Cowboys: A Native American Expression of the Jesus Way.* Downers Grove, IL: InterVarsity Press, 2015.

US Census Bureau. "Los Angeles County Quick Facts." www.census.gov/quickfacts/fact/map/losangelescountycalifornia/IPE120216.

Utley, Ebony. "Kanye West's Yeezus May Be Sexist but Is Not Blasphemous." *Huffington Post.* June 20, 2013. www.rapandreligion.com/yeezus.

———. *Rap and Religion: Understanding the Gangsta's God.* Santa Barbara, CA: Praeger, 2012.

Valentín, Benjamín. "Tracings: Sketching the Cultural Geographies of Latino/a Theology." In *Creating Ourselves: African Americans and Hispanic Americans on Popular Culture and Religious Expression,* edited by Anthony B. Pinn and Benjamín Valentín. Durham, NC: Duke University Press, 2009.

Ver Beek, Kurt Alan. "The Impact of Short-Term Missions: A Case Study of House Construction in Honduras After Hurricane Mitch." *An International Review* 34, no. 4 (2006).

Walls, Andrew F. *The Cross-Cultural Process in Christian History: Studies in the Transmission and Appropriation of Faith.* Maryknoll, NY: Orbis Books, 2002.

———. *The Missionary Movement in Christian History: Studies in the Transmission of Faith.* Maryknoll, NY: Orbis Books, 1996.

Watkins, Ralph Basui. *Hip-Hop Redemption: Finding God in the Rhythm and the Rhyme.* Engaging Culture. Grand Rapids: Baker Academic, 2011.

Watkins, S. Craig. *Hip Hop Matters: Politics, Pop Culture, and the Struggle for the Soul of a Movement.* Boston: Beacon Press, 2005.

Webber, Melvin M. "The Post-City Age." In *The City Reader,* edited by Richard T. Le Gates and Frederic Stout. New York: Routledge, 1996.

Weigle, Lauren. "Whitney Alford, Kendrick Lamar's Fiancee: 5 Fast Facts You Need to Know." *Heavy.* February 15, 2016. http://heavy.com/entertainment/2016/02/whitney-alford-kendrick-lamar-fiancee-girlfriend-wife-dating-who-is-net-worth-ring.

Weisinger, Judith Y., and Paul F. Salipante. "A Grounded Theory for Building Ethnically Bridging Social Capital in Voluntary Organizations." *Nonprofit and Voluntary Sector Quarterly* 34, no. 1 (2005).

Wells-Barnett, Ida B. *On Lynchings: Southern Horrors, a Red Record, Mob Rule in New Orleans.* The American Negro, His History and Literature. New York: Arno Press, 1969.

West, Cornel. *Prophetic Thought in Postmodern Times: Beyond Eurocentrism and Multiculturalism.* Vol. 1. Monroe, ME: Common Courage Press, 1993.

———. *Race Matters*. Boston: Beacon Press, 1993.

West, Traci C. "When a White Man-God Is the Truth and the Way for Black Christians." In *Christology and Whiteness: What Would Jesus Do?*, edited by George Yancy. New York: Routledge 2012.

"Whiteness." In *International Encyclopedia of the Social Sciences*, edited by William A. Darity Jr. Detroit: Macmillan Reference, 2008.

Whyte, William H. "The Design of Spaces." In *The City Reader*, edited by Richard T. Le Gates and Frederic Stout. New York: Routledge, 1996.

Wiese, Andrew. *Places of Their Own: African American Suburbanization in the Twentieth Century*. Historical Studies of Urban America. Chicago: University of Chicago Press, 2004.

Wilder, Amos N. *Early Christian Rhetoric: The Language of the Gospel*. Peabody, MA: Hendrickson, 1999.

Williams, Jeffrey R. "Racial Uplift." In *American History Through Literature 1870–1920*, edited by Tom Quirk and Gary Scharnhorst. Detroit: Charles Scribner's Sons, 2006.

Wilsey, John D. *American Exceptionalism and Civil Religion: Reassessing the History of an Idea*. Downers Grove, IL: IVP Academic, 2015.

Winters, Joseph. "Unstrange Bedfellows: Hip Hop and Religion." *Religion Compass* 5, no. 6 (2011).

Wise, Tim J. *Between Barack and a Hard Place: Racism and White Denial in the Age of Obama*. Open Media Series. San Francisco: City Lights Books, 2009.

———. *Colorblind: The Rise of Post-Racial Politics and the Retreat from Racial Equity*. Open Media Series. San Francisco: City Lights Books, 2010.

———. *White Like Me: Reflections on Race from a Privileged Son*. Rev. ed. Berkeley, CA: Soft Skull Press, 2008.

———. *Little White Lies: The Truth About Affirmative Action and "Reverse Discrimination."* Blueprint for Social Justice. New Orleans: Twomey Center for Peace Through Justice, Loyola University, 1995.

Wuthnow, Robert. *The Religious Dimension: New Directions in Quantitative Research*. New York: Academic Press, 1979.

Yinger, J. Milton. *Religion, Society, and the Individual: An Introduction to the Sociology of Religion*. New York: Macmillan, 1957.

Yong, Amos. "Race and Racialization in a Post-Racist Evangelicalism: A View from Asian America." In *Aliens in the Promised Land: Why Minority Leadership Is Overlooked in White Christian Churches and Institutions*, edited by Anthony B. Bradley. Philipsburg, NJ: P&R, 2013.

Zanfagna, Christina. "Under the Blasphemous W(RAP): Locating the 'Spirit' in Hip-Hop." *Pacific Review of Ethnomusicology* 12 (2006).

Žižek, Slavoj. *In Defense of Lost Causes*. New York: Verso, 2008.

Zulu Nation. "Zulu Beliefs." Universal Zulu Nation. http://new.zulunation.com /zulu-beliefs/.

SCRIPTURE INDEX

ALSO BY
DANIEL WHITE HODGE

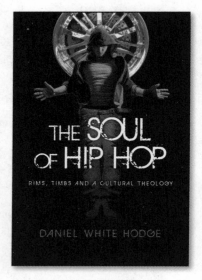

The Soul of Hip Hop
978-0-8308-3732-8